REVISITING THE
TRANSATLANTIC TRIANGLE

REVISITING THE TRANSATLANTIC TRIANGLE:
The Constitutional Decolonization of the Eastern Caribbean

RAFAEL COX ALOMAR

Ian Randle Publishers
Kingston • Miami

First published in Jamaica, 2009 by
Ian Randle Publishers
11 Cunningham Avenue
P.O. Box 686
Kingston 6.
www.ianrandlepublishers.com

ISBN 978-976-637- 298-9

A catalogue record for this book is available from the National Library of Jamaica.

NATIONAL LIBRARY OF JAMAICA CATALOGUING-IN-PUBLICATION DATA

Cox Alomar, Rafael
    Revisiting the Transatlantic Triangle : the
constitutional decolonization of
the Eastern Caribbean / Rafael Cox Alomar

    p. : ill., maps; cm.

    Bibliography : p. - Includes index.

    ISBN 978-976-637-298-9 (pbk)

1. Decolonization - West Indies, British - Historiography
 2. Postcolonialism - West Indies
3. Great Britain - Colonies - Administration   4. Great
Britain - Relations - West Indies
5. West Indies - History - 20th century 6. West Indies -
Politics and government - 20th century
I. Title

325.309729 - dc 22

Cover image © Federico Farrington. All rights reserved.
Cover and book design by Ian Randle Publishers
Printed and bound in the United States

*To Rafael Cox Rosario and Noemí Alomar Suárez,
my parents, who to my eyes have always been paradigms of
culture, dignity and integrity.*

Table of Contents

List of Illustrations

List of Figures

List of Tables

List of Maps

The Caribbean Basin

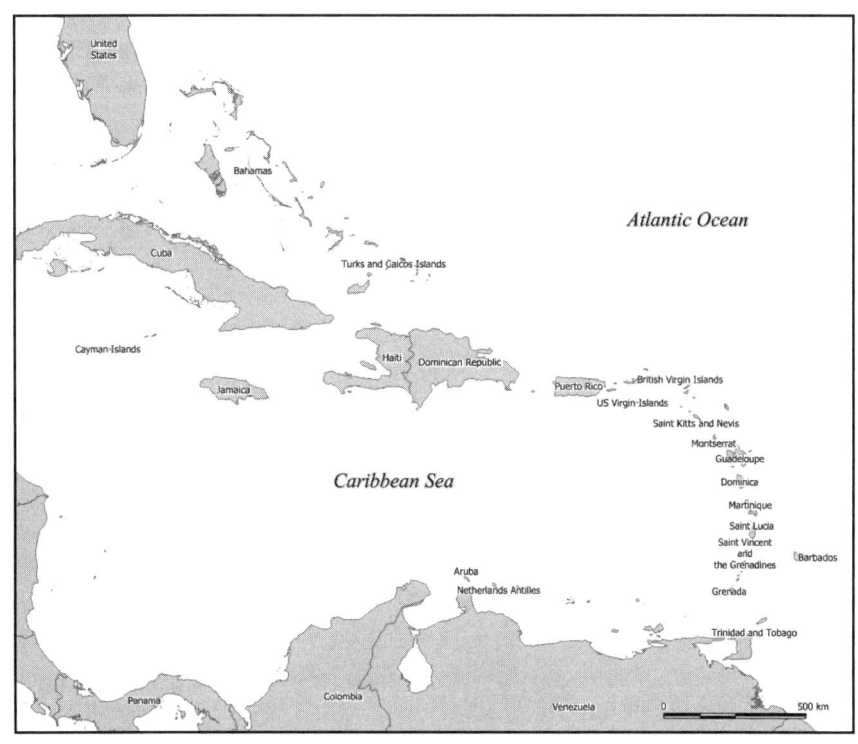

The British Leeward Islands

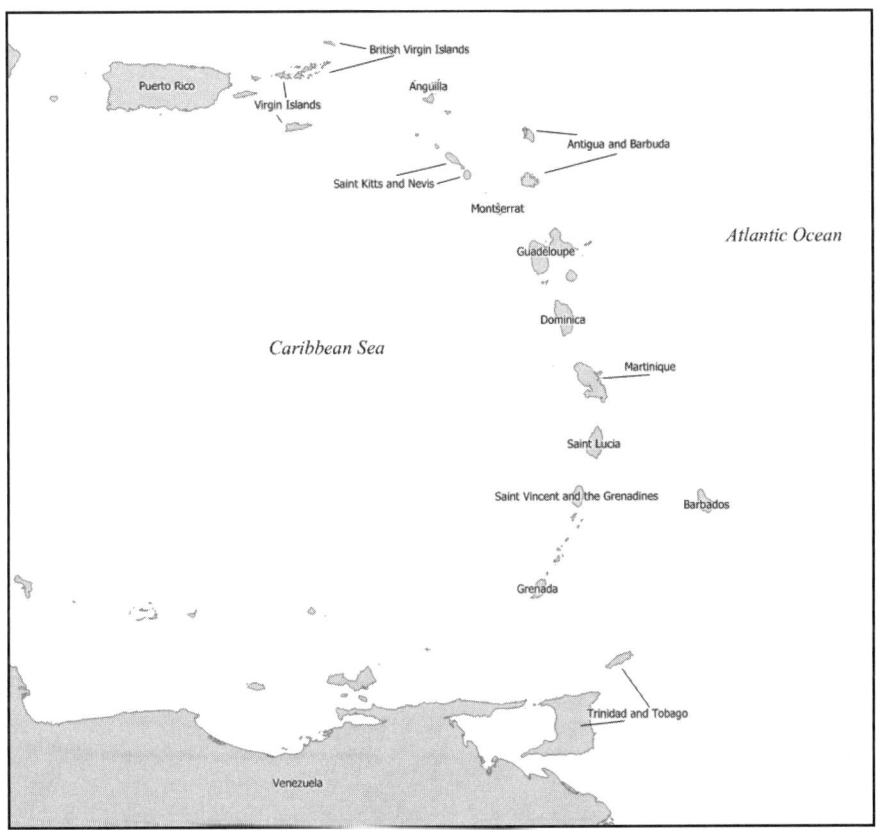

© 2007 Antonio González Toro

The British Windward Islands

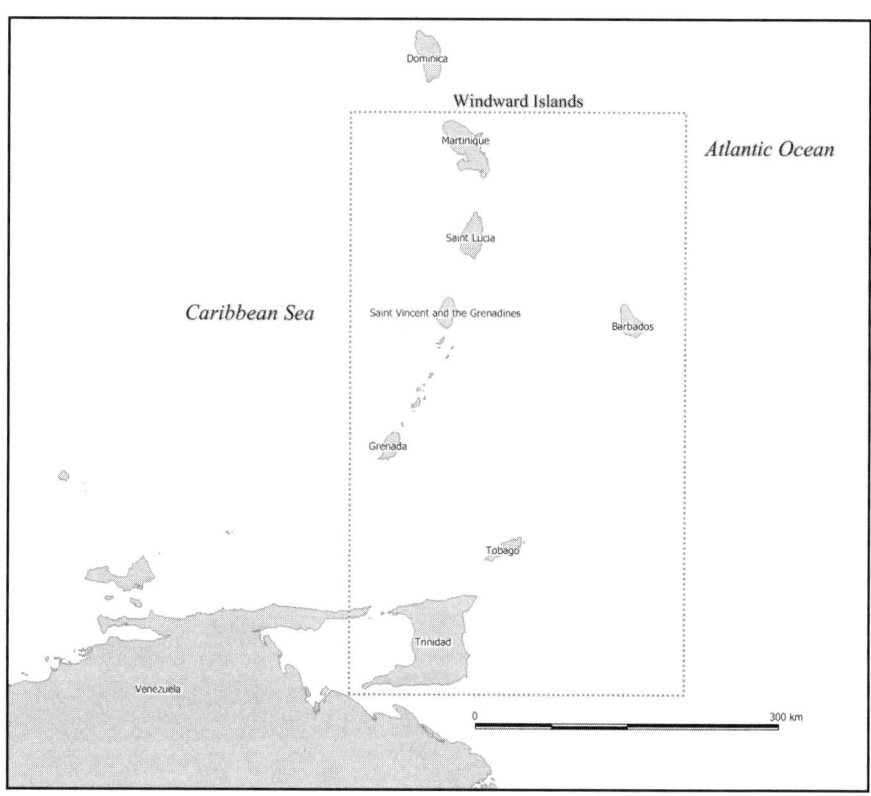

© 2007 Antonio González Toro

Barbados

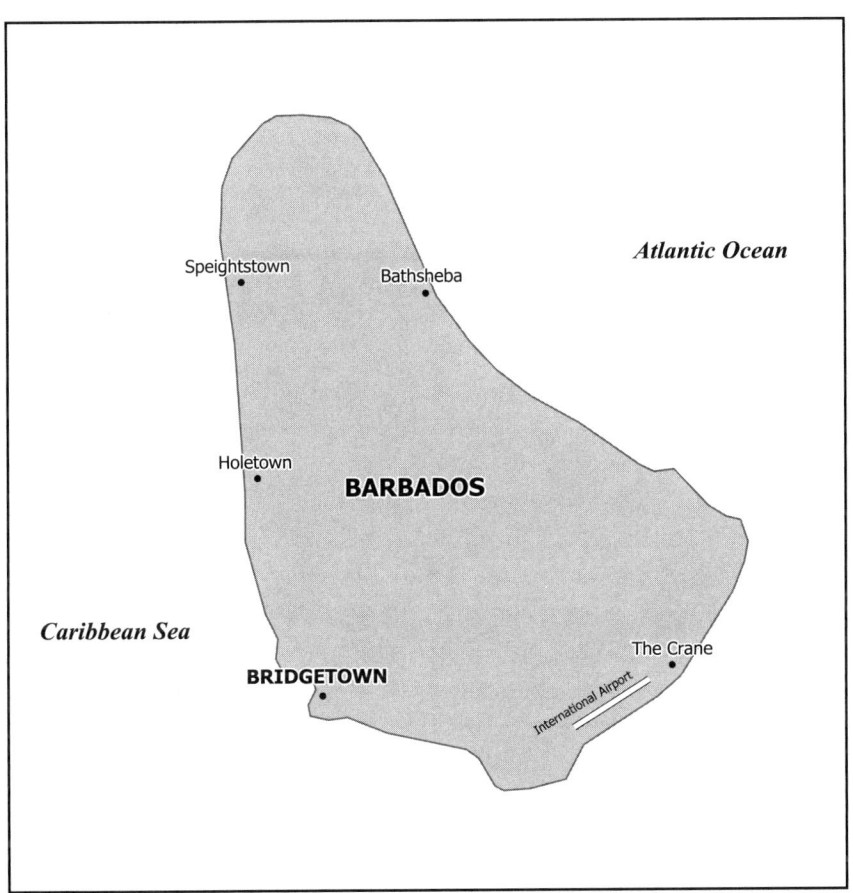

Foreword

Existing conceptual frameworks of the decolonizing agenda and subsequent nation-building project in the English-speaking Caribbean sub-region have long been considered inadequate. The field, as a result, has awaited a detailed comparative study rooted in historical research and informed by a political science sensibility. The uneven pace of the process across the region, and the spatial distribution of efforts, have forcefully indicated the inability of binary colonial-metropolitan conflict resolution models of decolonization to satisfactorily explain the extreme variation of experiences. As a conceptual approach, it has been evident that it could not withstand the scrutiny of robust empirical research. The attractiveness of Cox Alomar's analysis is that it moves us away from the generalities of the relationship between individual colonies and imperial power, and focuses our attention on the incessant internal logic of anti-colonial politics in each jurisdiction and engagement with wider international geo-political forces, particularly those emanating from Washington. In each of the eight colonies that sought political union after the 1962 debacle that was the Federation of the British West Indies, the resonance of radical rhetoric determined the temperature that drove the reaction in Washington and London as the Cold War laid ground rules for a postcolonial Caribbean policy.

The release for public consumption of 1960s official colonial documents by the British government now enables scholars to have a closer look at political patterns and ideological variation within and throughout the region, and to examine the public posturing and private interaction of politicians across the old and emerging imperial boundaries. This text brings us to the edge of innovative thinking about new imperialism in the Caribbean that is rooted in fresh research. The case of Barbados between1961 and 1966 is more clearly illuminated and the unwillingness of the Colonial Office to treat the neighbouring Windward Islands with the same even hand and open mind tells the story of how the ideological leanings of internal politics served to set the timetable of the decolonizing agenda in ways hitherto misunderstood. This is a fine, long overdue study of a settled and neglected subjected. The peace is now disturbed and the historiography troubled.

Hilary McD. Beckles
General Editor, Forgotten Histories of the Caribbean Series

Acknowledgements

The inspiration to produce this book emerged from my long-standing desire to explore and understand the complexities embedded in the decolonizing dialogue. As member of a national community that for the past five centuries has lived along the puzzling and often vague borderline separating the colonial from the postcolonial, I have always found the intimate interplay between metropolitan centres and their colonial peripheries fascinating.

In the process of thinking, researching and writing this book I have been fortunate to receive advice and encouragement from numerous friends and scholars. My first words of gratitude must go to Dr John G. Darwin, who was my academic supervisor while pursuing my doctoral studies at Oxford. Without a doubt, his thorough guidance and unwavering support have been invaluable to me. I am also grateful to Dr Peter Carey who was my moral tutor while at Trinity College, Oxford.

The long hours of archival work in Britain, Barbados and the US yielded a fascinating array of very relevant documents — thanks to the support I received from many indefatigable archivists. I would like to acknowledge the immense help I received from Jacqueline Shepherd, Production Manager at the National Archives, in Kew Gardens, London. Peter Allmond, from the Bodleian Library, and Allan Lodge, from the Rhodes House Library, were also of great assistance. A special acknowledgment must also go to the executors of Lord Duncan Sandys' Trust for granting me access to the late colonial secretary's private papers, housed at the Churchill Archive Centre in Cambridge. At the same time, I would like to recognize the enormous hospitality of Churchill College, Cambridge, where I stayed for over a month, while looking at the Sandys and Hailes Papers.

In Barbados, Velma Newton, the Law Librarian of the University of the West Indies in Cave Hill, was of enormous assistance. In addition, Ephraim Norville, archivist at the Public Archives in Black Rock, was very generous with his time. Special thanks must go to Former Prime Minister Erskine Sandiford, the late Prime Minister Sir Harold St. John, the late

Senator John Wickham, Senator Philip Greaves, Professor George Bell, Dr Richard Cheltenham and Robert Best, for agreeing to discuss with me seminal aspects of Barbados's transition to independence.

Regina Greenwell from the Lyndon Johnson Presidential Library in Austin, Texas, provided invaluable material, which so far had remained untouched, both from the White House Central Files and the National Security Files. I am also indebted to the staff at the National Archives and Records Administration in College Park, Maryland, for granting me access to all the consular correspondence between the US consuls general in Bridgetown and their superiors in Washington.

The process of articulating an argument as well as of exploring concepts was immensely enriched by the opportunity to deliver two papers in the course of the writing process. Thanks to the invitations of Professor Jid Kamoche, from the University of Oklahoma, and Professor Andrew Porter, from the University of London, I was able to interact with other students of decolonization. Others such as Professor Richard Chapman, from the University of Durham, Professor Raymond Cohen, from the Hebrew University of Jerusalem, and William J. Holmes, have been mentors, proof-readers and, above all, friends.

Both the artistic talent of my friend Federico Farrington and the generosity of Antonio González Toro have endowed this book with an eloquent front cover and with a set of well-designed maps of the Caribbean Basin.

But without the financial support from the Marshall Aid Commemoration Commission, which in 1997 awarded me a Marshall Scholarship, and the University of Oxford, which awarded me consecutive scholarships with which to finance my third and fourth years of doctoral studies, this work would not have been completed. Moreover, I want to acknowledge the decisive financial support I received from the Board of Managers of the Beit Fund, the Cyril Foster Fund and the Governing Body of Trinity College, Oxford, under the leadership of the Honourable Michael J. Beloff.

At a more personal level, I would like to express my gratitude to those who made it all happen: my loving parents, my sister, María de Lourdes, and younger brother, Pedro Rafael. There are no words that can truly describe how indebted I am to them.

Introduction:
Britain's Colonial Disengagement from the Eastern Caribbean

This study focuses on Britain's colonial disengagement from the Eastern Caribbean. The term Eastern Caribbean,[1] as used in this work, refers to Barbados, Antigua–Barbuda, St. Kitts–Nevis–Anguilla, Montserrat, Dominica, St. Lucia, St. Vincent and Grenada. The intention behind this study is to evaluate, in the light of newly available archival sources, the negotiating processes leading to the independence of Barbados in November 1966 and to free association with Britain for Antigua–Barbuda, St. Kitts–Nevis–Anguilla, Dominica, St. Lucia, St. Vincent and Grenada between February 1967 and October 1969.[2] This book illustrates the complex set of challenges, discontinuities and puzzles that the British Government faced as it attempted to withdraw from the Eastern Caribbean archipelago at the height of the Cold War. This work intends to dispute some of the basic misinterpretations perpetuated in Commonwealth historiography as to the nature and scope of these negotiations. Essentially, what Lloyd George called with derision 'slums of empire' and Charles de Gaulle disparagingly dismissed as 'specks of dust,'[3] did pose a formidable challenge to London's policy of colonial disengagement throughout most of the Macmillan and Wilson years.

Commonwealth historiography,[4] all too often, conveys the impression that due to their small size, economic underdevelopment and, hence, dubious viability, these eight territories attracted hardly any attention from the metropolis. Some have simply limited their scholarship to reiterating what the available records already suggest; that this was an area of low priority from which successive British Governments were anxious to withdraw. There can be no doubt that by late 1961, immediately after the collapse of the West Indies Federation, the consensus in London was that no significant British commercial or defence interest lay in these islands any longer. The ties between Britain and these territories were seen as largely cultural, moral and sentimental.[5] Thus, it should not come as a surprise that, when under scrutiny, these islands tend to be viewed as insignificant footnotes of a far more elaborate historical narrative. Yet, it is precisely their peripheral status that makes them such a fascinating case study. In taking to task their alleged irrelevance, this volume also shows how the transfer of political authority in this archipelago tested the very meaning of decolonization.

During the period under scrutiny the British Government and the colonial leadership in the Eastern Caribbean embarked on an intense reappraisal of their constitutional relationship. The dual outcome that finally emerged from such a prolonged negotiating process — namely Barbados's independence, and associated statehood for the rest — stood as a prominent illustration of the arbitrariness and unpredictability of decolonization. Authority, in this area of the British colonial world, was not devolved to the subaltern periphery at once. Rather, the undoing of the colonial relationship was achieved gradually. The surrender of political sovereignty, which many still see as the hallmark of decolonization, came in instalments. Even the more superficial constitutional modifications seem to have obeyed the maxim of 'evolution not revolution'. But if these islands were so unimportant, why not transfer authority at once? Why did Whitehall find it so difficult to withdraw altogether?

These are the seminal questions that begin to arise once the apparent contradiction has become ever more evident. Yet, more importantly, that discrepancy opens up a very useful window through which to study decolonization as a socio-political phenomenon. In the final analysis, as this book argues, the decolonizing experience is not a monologue but a multifaceted dialogue. As this case study illustrates beyond doubt, any comprehensive transfer of political authority from the metropolitan centre to the colonial polity usually rests on the intimate interplay of wider imperatives. These elements are not exclusively domestic and insular in scope but all too often tend to be extraterritorial and international. For instance, the constant conflict between contending colonial politicians as well as the unending tension between them and their local constituencies swayed, at crucial times, the process of devolution in these latitudes. By the same token, that problematic alliance between the political and labour wings of the colonial progressive movements did play, in some instances, a destabilizing role as well. However, in the particular case of these islands, the complex interplay between those wider forces or catalysts, coexisted with an even more problematic and volatile imperative.

In no other area under Britain's jurisdiction did the US have as many defence and security interests as in the Caribbean Basin. This element in itself, particularly at the height of the Cold War, added yet another dimension to an already tense decolonizing dialogue. Geography had conspired to make this archipelago an uneasy buffer zone between the British and American empires. After the sobering experience of Suez and the debacle of the old Federation, a further constitutional miscarriage or a hasty departure on Britain's part could have very well lacerated the so-called special relationship, with unforeseen consequences for the British. As the succeeding chapters illustrate, the triangle joining London and Washington to these eight islands was not merely rhetorical, emotional or philanthropic; it was, instead, real, far-reaching and geopolitical. In the sombre words of President Eisenhower, the US Government was 'vitally interested'[6] in the political future of these British dependencies. It was no secret, as Lord Home eventually conceded in a letter to British Prime Minister Harold Macmillan, that the Americans saw Britain's presence in this area as a 'stabilising force'.[7] The tragic schism with Cuba, the vexatious resilience of Guiana's Cheddi Jagan, and the new anxieties which the Vietnamese conundrum was now producing, obliterated the US's anti-colonial beliefs. This largely explains why Iain Sutherland, from the British Foreign Office, scribbled in a note to his opposite number in the Colonial Office, 'the Americans do not want us to follow policies which would result in any British withdrawal from the area'.[8]

The intention behind this book is not to argue that this is a unique case study. While these eight islands, Britain's oldest colonies, did exhibit some peculiarities such as the absence of real indigenous populations with customary institutions, their wider colonial experience was not necessarily atypical. The intellectual aim here is to relocate these territories within the wider Commonwealth historiography. Far from being a removed scholastic abstraction, the purpose behind this, at its most basic level, is to explore anew Britain's retreat from empire as the winds of change blew through the Caribbean Basin. As the following chapters will contend, the journey these islands embarked upon in 1962 illustrates rather vividly some of the precipices Britain itself faced during the so-called 'crisis of decolonization'.[9]

This is precisely why this book has avoided focusing on the dual outcome alone. This analytical exercise would be patently incomplete if, in the first place, the process leading to such result, together with the intricately woven set of forces shaping it, were not looked at rigorously.

Figure 1
Conceptual Map of the Eastern Caribbean's Decolonizing Process

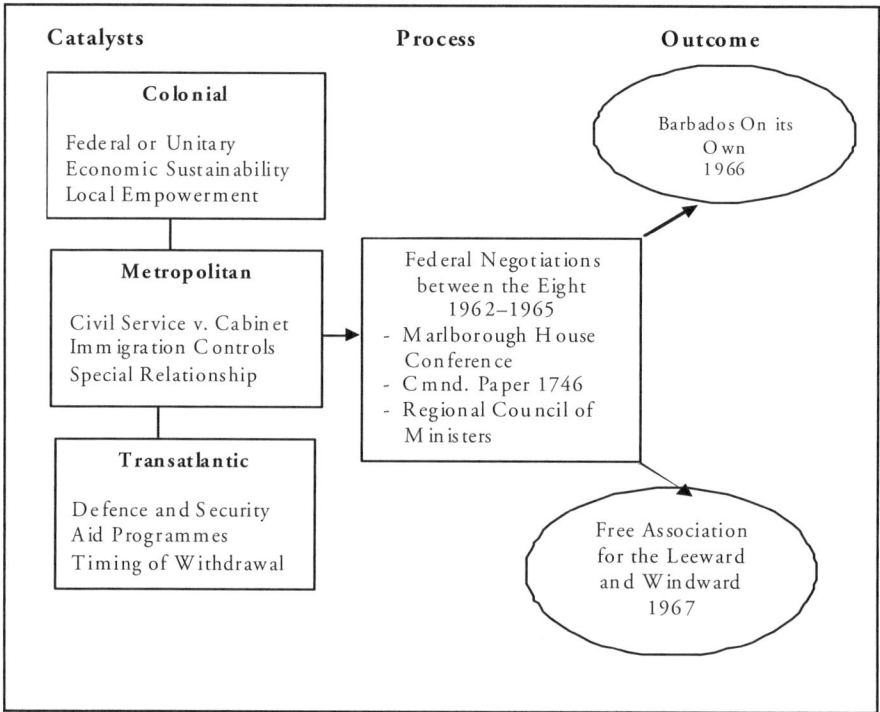

Hardly any of the available studies on the recent politico-constitutional history of these territories pays any attention to the five-year period scrutinized here. And the few which do, more often than not, merely report that,

> Following the dissolution of the Federation of the West Indies in 1962, when Jamaica and Trinidad proceeded to separate independence, discussions began between the remaining Federal territories with a view to their forming a new federation. In August 1965, the Barbados Government issued a White Paper announcing that, since there seemed little prospect of the discussions leading to the territories concerned being able to achieve early independence in a federation, it was their intention to seek separate independence for Barbados.[10]

The existence of such an immense vacuum in the historiography has led some voices to dismiss this period of the Eastern Caribbean's history as highly inconsequential. And, ironically, most students of the Caribbean seem to have accepted such a superficial contention as axiomatic. Notwithstanding its apparent insignificance, newly released records reveal a completely different picture. Far from dull, this was a period of intense political effervescence at the colonial level and constant rearrangement at the heart of that complex Anglo–American–Caribbean triangle. This is why this book, anchored as it is to this periodization, is able to address a wide array of relevant themes that go a long way in re-evaluating the more conventional interpretations of decolonization.

In so doing, the following chapters pay unwavering attention to the way in which catalysts at the colonial, metropolitan and transatlantic levels derailed a process which had been proposed and designed by the so-called 'small island politicians' in close collaboration with London. The intense and protracted federal discussions, spanning from 1962 to 1965, between these eight territories and the British Government, instead of laying the groundwork for yet another federation in the area led, paradoxically, to an unexpected denouement. In the light of this, the obvious questions that seem to arise are, firstly, why the turnaround occured and, secondly, what this volte-face says about decolonization in general and this process in particular. And, yet, while at first glance answering these might appear fairly simple, arriving at a balanced and accurate explanation, as this study demonstrates, constitutes a far more complex task — not least because this exercise demands total immersion in a dense entanglement of tensions, imperatives and rearrangements, that surpass the narrowness of the colonial relationship. Nevertheless, the few interpretations available have altogether missed the richness of such a colourful tapestry. Most voices, for instance, have agreed with Sir Arthur Lewis's contention that the greatest obstacle in the way of a federation of the eight was 'the continued silence of the British Treasury'.[11] Others such as Sir John Mordecai and Eric Williams have vehemently blamed island jealousies, poor leadership and the constant clash of personalities as the chief culprits for the collapse of these federal discussions.[12] After all, as Reginald Maudling put it, 'they [colonial politicians] were always having rows, those chaps'.[13] And hence, as most have seen it, the British Government had no alternative but to allow

Barbados to go it alone while maintaining some sort of association with the remaining units. Against this background the outcome emerging from the federal process tends to be seen as totally inevitable. Most of the time, the whole experience is simply reduced to a laissez-faire operation, as if predetermined by the invisible hand of fate.

The most salient problem with these conventional accounts is their marked tendency to draw conclusions, rather unabashedly, from a relatively shallow pool of variables. Most of these studies, moreover, have had a propensity for oversimplifying the scope of this process and in some instances even overstating the importance of tangential elements. While this book concurs, in principle, that the Treasury's silence on the future of British aid to the archipelago considerably heightened the level of tension and suspicion between London and the colonial leadership, it argues that this was not the sole catalyst. At the same time, it would prove impossible to deny that inter-island animosities and clashes of colonial personalities certainly thickened the plot, but these were bound to happen in most communities attempting to organize themselves as 'federal societies', [14] particularly in territories with such small populations.

This book not only takes to task the factual misinterpretations perpetuated in previous works, but, at a more basic level, challenges the way in which this subject has been approached earlier. The central argument of this study is that there was no such inevitability. The independence of Barbados and the establishment of associated statehood in the British Leeward and Windward Islands, as the constitutional package coming out from this decolonizing dialogue, was not a given. As the next chapters contend, such an outcome evolved, not from an indolent process of random elimination, but from the complex, intimate and dynamic interaction of ever-changing variables. For instance, why free association and not protectorate status as in the Maldives and Tonga? Why not confer upon them full internal self-government as in Mauritius and Basutoland? These are just some of the highly relevant questions that go to the heart of what decolonization really means and cannot be answered by applying the somewhat linear or one-dimensional reasoning that most conventional accounts exhibit.

At the colonial level this book pays special attention to how by January 1962, immediately after the demise of the old Federation, the politicians in the remaining federal units re-articulated a federal project for the eight. Why were they asking for yet another federation? Why not annexation to a larger territory such as Jamaica or Trinidad and Tobago? The start of the federal negotiations between the Colonial Office and the so-called Little Eight coincided with an unparalleled rearrangement in the wider relationship between the colonial politicians and their constituencies. With only ten years of universal adult suffrage, the people of these islands had hardly been exposed to the political process with all that it entailed. Even more importantly, by this period the constitutional position of the Leeward and Windward Islands had been considerably enhanced. With the introduction, late in 1960, of responsible government, locally elected politicians now commanded more authority and as such much more was expected from them. Hence, it would also become more difficult for politicians to delegate some of that power to a federal centre. The relevant element here is to observe how the colonial leadership approached that difficult disjunctive between competing centres of power. Yet, more importantly, the essential conundrum was how best to reconcile the electorate's expectations of economic development and economic sustainability with constitutional advancement. What should take precedence: procuring the economic viability of these territories or achieving a meaningful degree of further self-government?

This book also pays considerable attention to the type of pressure stemming, not only from the local constituencies, but also from the condition of these territories' respective economies. In the end, was there a stark choice between economic sustainability and constitutional evolution? Was this tension a prevalent component of the decolonizing dialogue taking place at this time in the archipelago? Which catalysts were setting the agenda in the Little Eight?

This work also addresses the question of whether, at the colonial level, the new federal project enjoyed any grassroots support, or whether it was merely an elitist construct, adhered to exclusively by the traditional political and labour elites. On a purely empirical basis, as this study contends, it would be very difficult to demonstrate or disprove claims as to whether the common man or woman in the archipelago was or was not a staunch federalist. While the following chapters do not address this subject directly, mostly due to methodological constraints, this book argues that little attention has been paid to the fact that the so-called masses did entertain opinions, feelings and ideas of importance to this process. The fact that by April 1965 the federal consensus amongst the colonial leadership, namely that federation 'was not a way of life but the only way', had finally crumbled cannot be divorced from the public mood. This is why the intimate connection between the small-island politicians and their constituents cannot possibly be dismissed; since, as the following chapters reveal, the colonial electorate was one of the most prominent interlocutors in this decolonizing dialogue.

Meanwhile in London competing imperatives were also colliding with one another. This work explores in depth the question of whether there were divergences of opinion between senior civil servants in the Colonial Office and members of the Cabinet regarding the future of these islands. In fact, as the following chapters show, the British civil service and the British politicians were not always on the same wavelength. That dissonance did sway the process in the Eastern Caribbean, not just procedurally but substantively as well. The burden on London was how to strike a balance between Britain's overall interests, such as strengthening the Anglo-American special relationship, applying for entry to the European Economic Community, and controlling immigration, without alienating the colonial leadership. More specifically, this book looks in depth at the crucial debate over the future of British aid to the area that effectively split the Treasury, the Colonial Office and the newly established Ministry of Overseas Development. It is precisely here that the transatlantic catalysts begin to figure prominently in the picture since the debate on the two most crucial variables, namely aid and the timing of withdrawal, were mostly dealt with at that level. Was there any quid pro quo between London and the Johnson Administration? In other words, did the timing of Britain's withdrawal respond to US pressure? And, equally importantly, was the US's participation in the Tripartite Survey, between 1964 and 1966, a precondition for London's gradual transfer of political authority in the archipelago? Moreover, did the US's status as one of the major colonial powers in the Caribbean play any part in Britain's policy-making process? Was the US's colonial role in the Caribbean one of the principal considerations behind Britain's intention not to embarrass its transatlantic allies?

Once the federal negotiations finally collapsed and Britain and these eight dependencies started plodding along new roads, in an attempt to achieve their initial aim of transferring political authority, a new set of complex considerations immediately came to the fore. As the following chapters contend, associated statehood, as implemented in the Leeward and Windward Islands, represented a *sui generis* constitutional model. Unprecedented as it was, this new status was never to be used again. Then, why engage at this particular stage in this new relationship? And, conversely, why did the colonial leadership settle for something less than full independence? The independence of Barbados raises difficult questions as well. With the sharp ideological divide that followed the publication of the independence White Paper, in August 1965, was the right to self-determination upheld? The independence of Barbados, like the proclamation of associated statehood in the remaining islands, also opens the door for a deeper analysis of the evolutionary nature of decolonization. While Britain retained considerable reserve powers in regard to the associated states, Barbados even after independence retained most of the colonial trappings, such as the constitutional monarchy and the appeal as of right to the Judicial Committee of the Queen's Privy Council. There was no radical or dramatic departure from the *ancien régime*. The colonial superstructure remained relatively unchanged. It is at this juncture that this study begins to test more fully the boundaries of decolonization. To what extent, in the light of what took place in the Eastern Caribbean during the period under scrutiny here, is decolonization an arbitrary or inflexible process? Is there only one modality of decolonization? Or should decolonization be envisioned as a flexible evolutionary process which colonizer and colonized must tailor to the particular conditions and demands of their wider interests?

Those are just some of the themes raised throughout the course of this book. The intention behind this academic exercise is to arrive at a fuller explanation, which can only emerge if all colonial, metropolitan and transatlantic catalysts are scrutinized both individually and collectively. Doing otherwise would lead to the missing of potentially significant pieces of a very elaborate jigsaw puzzle. As elsewhere in Britain's ever contracting colonial world, the process of politico-constitutional devolution in the Eastern Caribbean rested on the intimate interplay of a multitude of variables. And the type of answers this study seeks to uncover lies precisely at the epicentre of that avalanche of catalysts.

In terms of methodology, this study challenges the traditional approach of excluding competing focal points. B.W. Higman and others, for instance, have argued that one of the basic problems facing the students of the Caribbean is deciding whether to circumscribe their academic focus to a Commonwealth, a British Caribbean or a purely insular perspective.[15] Yet, the entrenchment of this methodological practice explains, for the most part, why the local historiography in the Caribbean all too often omits the essential contacts and exchanges between the outer world and these islands that so distinctly shaped and swayed their decolonizing experience.[16] Not surprisingly, most studies produced in the colonial periphery tend to draw strict boundaries between the islands, leaving out the richness of their common connection to the metropolitan centre.[17]

This study, moreover, acknowledges the enormous gaps existing in most colonial archives. A considerable number of progressive movements, trade unions, and local politicians and labour leaders in the area hardly preserved any records. While, undoubtedly, this constitutes a major obstacle in the way of academic historians, such an absence means that the scope for further study remains wide open. This book, owing to temporal and methodological constraints, has relied almost exclusively on recently declassified records preserved in Britain and the US. Yet, the corpus of sources was greatly enriched by a series of visits to the Public Archives of Barbados and by a wide array of interviews with some of the most prominent political actors involved in this drama. This book does not intend to be an area study. In fact it would prove highly difficult to box-in or typecast this work as colonial or regional, metropolitan or international. In the final analysis, its intellectual purpose is to reconstruct, not only the historical context, but the richness and complexity of a decolonizing dialogue that surpassed the neat boundaries of conventional geography and historiography.

Abbreviations and Acronyms

AACC	Anglo-American Caribbean Commission
ACJ	Arthur Creech Jones Papers
BGA	Banana Growers Association
BLP	Barbados Labour Party
BNP	Barbados National Party
BWU	Barbados Workers Union
CAB	Cabinet Papers
CD&W	Colonial Development and Welfare Funds
CLC	Caribbean Labour Congress
CO	Colonial Office Papers
CPA	Commonwealth Parliamentary Association
CPC	Colonial Policy Committee
DFS	Draft Federal Scheme
DLP	Democratic Labour Party, Barbados
DLP	Dominica Labour Party
DO	Commonwealth Development Office Papers
DSND	Duncan Sandys's Papers
EEC	European Economic Community
FO	Foreign Office Papers
GAWU	Guyana Industrial and Agricultural Workers' Union
GNP	Grenada National Party
GULP	Grenada United Labour Party
HAIS	Lord Hailes' Papers
HMG	Her Majesty's Government
JLP	Jamaica Labour Party
LBJ	Lyndon Johnson Presidential Library
MOD	Ministry of Overseas Development
MPCA	Man Power Citizen's Association, British Guiana
MSWWU	Montserrat Seamen and Waterfront Workers Union
NARA	National Archives and Records Administration
NASA	National Aeronautics and Space Administration

NLM	National Labour Movement, St. Lucia
OAS	Organization of American States
OPD	Defence and Overseas Policy Committee
PNM	People's National Movement, Trinidad and Tobago
PNP	People's National Party, Jamaica
PPP	People's Progressive Party, St Lucia
PREM	Prime Minister's Office Papers
RCM	Regional Council of Ministers
SVLP	St. Vincent Labour Party
UWI	University of the West Indies
UWM	United Workers Movement, Montserrat
UWP	United Workers Party, St. Lucia

PART ONE

THE FEDERAL PROJECT

What are the Antilles? A natural geographic midpoint between one part and the other of the continent, producer also of a transcendental fusion of the races, the Antilles are politically the faithful balance, the true federal bond of the gigantic federation of the future; humanely social, the natural centre of the fusions, the definite crucible of the races … therefore they will be some day the home of the pilgrims of humanity. Therefore, also, it is treason against God to try to separate them from their destiny.

Eugenio María de Hostos, 1870

Introduction

The main argument put forward in the first part of this work is that any analysis of the Caribbean's constitutional evolution must go beyond the context of the region itself. There was nothing wholly inevitable about the decolonizing process that began to unfold with decisive intensity in the aftermath of the Second World War.

The rise of political movements, the contact between colonial leaders and metropolitan policy-makers and, most importantly, the explosion of urban riots, were not phenomena exclusive to the inter-war period. While during the latter part of the nineteenth century such outbursts had led to the imposition of crown colony rule across most of the region,[1] by the mid 1940s, confronted with a comparable constellation of circumstances, the British Government reacted completely different.[2] Instead of taking away powers, these were transferred, albeit slowly, to the local political and labour leadership. This is illustrative of the shifts, discontinuities and rearrangements of London's colonial policy in the Caribbean.

Although the riots and the labour movement did spring from the distressing conditions endured by these islands throughout most of the 1930s and early 1940s, it does not follow that these elements were the sole catalysts provoking a metropolitan reaction of constitutional magnitude. Any attempt to understand this process of colonial disengagement must incorporate, as the following chapters show, the geopolitical imperatives of the Anglo-American transatlantic alliance, together with the impact that internal tensions between the different actors in London, such as the Colonial Office and the Treasury, had in these negotiations. The constitutional and political implications of the 1961 Jamaican Referendum, as these next chapters suggest, should be seen within this context. Once the West Indies Federation failed, the British Government found itself in a most difficult position. From then on, its priority would be, in the words of Colonial Secretary Reginald Maudling, to disentangle a sturdy constitutional knot.

1

The Federal Concept

> We carry on the same fight, we fight for the same ideal, over us hang
> the same threats, can we refrain from living the same life? We will
> become intimately related, we shall form a nation of true builders.
>
> Ramón Emeterio Betances, 1870

Any serious study of an aspect of the Caribbean's history, while acknowledging its diversity must, as C.L.R. James and others have clearly observed, pay close attention to the parallel experiences of the different communities inhabiting the region.[1] Although undoubtedly a discontinuous mass of land characterised by 'its fragmentation, instability, reciprocal isolation, cultural heterogeneity and syncretism,'[2] the so-called British, Danish, French, Spanish and Dutch Caribbean all share a common heritage. European colonization and evangelization, the systematic genocide of native populations, the cruel whip of slavery, the patronizing hand of emancipation and the illness of economic dependency are all indivisible components of that collective denominator. For the most part, colonial officials in London, Paris, Madrid, Copenhagen and The Hague never saw the area against the background of a pan-Caribbean context. After all, these powers during most of the seventeenth, eighteenth and nineteenth centuries had fought one another either to defend or annex each other's possessions in the area. In many ways, the available literature reproduces the conventional arrangement whereby the experiences of these Caribbean communities tend to be viewed as appendages of a wider metropolitan narrative. It is not that little attention has been paid to the study of the archipelago's history, but that most have merely chosen to circumscribe their scholarship to outdated colonial boundaries.

It should not come as a surprise that most scholars, who have studied and written on the concept of closer union in the Anglophone Caribbean, have failed to trace the origins of that ideal on a pan-Caribbean basis. The notion of union did not emerge from the shy experiment of the Leeward Islands Federation, which the British Government established in 1871, or from the loose association that until 1884 bound British Honduras to Jamaica.[3] Those arrangements were but metropolitan designs for administrative convenience. The project for closer union, which influential leaders in the Anglophone Caribbean put forward during the inter-war period, echoed much of what influential voices in the so-called Spanish Caribbean had been espousing since the nineteenth century. As early as 1869 Ramón Emeterio Betances had advocated the establishment of a politically independent confederation of the Caribbean.[4] Betances, inspired by Bolívar's *La Gran Colombia*, articulated a project that included Puerto Rico, Cuba, Santo Domingo and Haiti. His political conception went beyond any linguistic or colonial boundary. Some scholars, such as Paul Estrade and Carlos M. Rama, have suggested that as early as 1882 Betances met the then British Prime Minister William Gladstone with the intention of petitioning the inclusion of Jamaica, then a crown colony, in such a project.[5] Betances's main biographer, Luis Bonafoux, has contended that the meeting took place and that, more importantly, Gladstone had shown considerable interest in the initiative.[6] Eugenio María de Hostos, together with Betances, was also a fervent advocate of closer union. In one of his most celebrated speeches, before a highly distinguished audience in the Ateneo of Madrid in 1868, Hostos contended,

> Because I am an American, because I am a colonial, because I am Puerto Rican, I therefore am a federalist. From my island I see Santo Domingo, I see Cuba, I see Jamaica, and I think of Confederation... I prophesy a providential Confederation.[7]

While in the Hispanic Caribbean the proponents of a closer union faded away, particularly after the successive deaths of José Martí, Antonio Maceo, Gregorio Luperón, Anténor Firmin, Betances and Hostos, their ideas did not perish.[8]

Although all the projects for closer union which historically have sprung up in the region, to a large extent, have shared the same inducements and predisposing factors, their philosophical underpinnings have not always been consistent. While metropolitan inducements for closer association, at least prior to the post-war period, rested on the assumption that the colonial relationship would remain unaltered, the projects for closer association originating in the Caribbean archipelago itself always responded to the twin aspirations of political empowerment and economic sustainability.

It is essential to note, however, that federalism, in the classical usage of the term, has been defined as a particular kind of government 'in which central and regional governments, none subordinate to the other, exist within a single country'.[9] Conversely, in a confederal form of government the centre is subordinate to the regional governments, being the antithesis of unitary statehood. While Betances, Hostos and others fervently advocated a closer union between the islands, their project does not necessarily fall within the bounds of federalism as defined above. Although in their writings the terms federal and confederal were used interchangeably, the archival evidence suggests that there was no clear consensus on whether the islands should become a bona fide federation or just a confederation. Indeed, the English-speaking Caribbean represents the only community, within the region as a whole, where the metropolitan and colonial elites did engage in an ongoing process of constitutional experimentation on a federal basis. This might explain why most students of the Anglophone Caribbean have overlooked the obvious influences stemming from the neighbouring Spanish-speaking islands.

Since the beginning of Britain's colonial experience in the area, the idea of uniting two or more of these units had enjoyed some popularity in London. The underlying hypothesis was that any such union would yield administrative and economic advantages. Yet, in practice, there had not been much unification.

The real push for federation in the English-speaking Caribbean gained special momentum after the Great War, although mostly confined to the Leeward and Windward Islands.[10] As the First World War broke out in Europe, a considerable number of West Indians, among them Arthur Cipriani of Trinidad and Tobago, Clennel Wickham of Barbados and Norman Manley of Jamaica, volunteered to fight for Britain's cause in the British West Indies Regiment.[11] For the most part stationed in Egypt, their experiences abroad shaped their character and refined their ideas about the world. Close interaction with other West Indian soldiers, from neighbouring territories, increased their awareness of the plight of the black masses across the region; providing these young West Indians with a new kind of shared identity.[12] The militant advance of socialism in Britain and the spread of Marcus Garvey's pan African movement shaped in a decisive manner the thought and future political discourse of many of these men. As early as 1919, for instance, Wickham[13] had already written that 'liberalism was a spent force' and that the ultimate contest would be between conservatism and socialism, which he saw as 'the only evidence of progressive thought which twentieth century civilisation can offer'.[14] Almost a year after the end of the hostilities, most of these colonial soldiers returned to their respective territories with a strong sense of mission. The correlation between a set of refreshing and invigorating experiences and the articulation of a novel political project was quite apparent. Before this period all proposals and schemes for closer association had come 'from above',[15] now the initiatives were to come from within the colonies themselves; and amongst the most important figures behind this project were Arthur Andrew Cipriani[16] and Theophilus Albert Marryshow.[17]

In essence, the idea of federation was brought forth by a cadre of emerging colonial politicians, pertaining almost exclusively to the middle classes, who were simultaneously driven by a strong desire for self-government and notions of socio-economic improvement. Some voices, such as Sir Hugh Springer, have suggested that this generation shared 'a distinct sense of West Indian nationalism'.[18] This latter observation is very relevant, as it throws some light on the nature of the movement emerging during the inter-war period. The question of whether there was a truly 'West Indian' national sentiment has always been disputed and there is strong evidence to suggest it never existed.[19] However, what is even more interesting is the hypothesis, contended for instance by R.L. Watts, that so-called Westernized elites have the propensity of embracing a 'wider nationalism'.[20] In that sense the behaviour of the archipelago's colonial elite was consistent with this observation; meaning that since its inception the idea of forging a federation out of these discontinuous territories was not so much a popular but rather an elitist construct. In some ways the idea of federation, at this particular juncture, represented an attempt by the black middle classes to assert their ascendancy before the colonial authorities.[21] Interestingly, some of the most outspoken defenders of federation, at least during this period, did not see universal adult suffrage as a prudent goal to pursue. The lack of a clear consensus on this crucial issue should not come as a surprise particularly at a time when the electorate in these territories, as contended below, ranged between 2 and 10 per cent of the adult population.[22] This impasse eventually led Cipriani, by then already known as the 'champion of the barefooted man', who adhered to the more radical wing of the colonial labour movement, to coin his most acclaimed corollary, 'no federation without self-government and no self-government without the franchise'.[23]

The effervescence of this federal feeling led the British Government to revisit the possibility of fostering some kind of constitutional union between its dependencies in the Caribbean. In 1922, with Winston Churchill as colonial secretary, Major Wood included in his official report on the conditions of the archipelago an evaluation of the plausibility of fostering some type of regional unity.[24] The Wood Report concluded that according to public opinion, which within that study's constrained context meant the views of the region's mostly white oligarchy,[25] it would be 'both inopportune and impracticable'[26] to effect any immediate changes. However, that preliminary judgment, as Sir John Mordecai and others have clearly observed, was highly questionable because the views of the indigenous black middle classes 'were not taken seriously in the Report'.[27] While Major Wood did recommend several important constitutional reforms for individual colonial units, especially for the Windward Islands, his recommendations fell short of what the black middle classes had expected.[28] It seems as if the basic lesson learned from this experience was quite simple: progressive movements could not achieve much if acting separately. The success or failure of any bid for regional unity would depend on extra-territorial collaboration.

While the idea of federation was gaining pre-eminence in the eastern rim of the Anglophone Caribbean,[29] in London the attitudes towards that project were far from monolithic. Here there was no consensus, at least during the inter-war period, regarding this matter. Yet, a few politicians in Westminster did show an interest in the idea. Arguably the nature of some of these metropolitan opinions could have been called into question since most of their proponents had obvious links with the powerful entrenched economic interests that, for all practical purposes, were governing the region. Others, such as the influential Lord Olivier, opposed the establishment of any federal arrangement. Colonel Wedgwood, as late as 1938, contended that federating all British possessions in the area would amount to a 'deplorable step backward'.[30] In that same debate the then colonial secretary, Sir William Ormsby-Gore, forcefully asserted that 'there was no question of federation in the West Indies'.[31] However, less than a decade later the initiative for self-government within a federal structure would come from London itself. This metropolitan turnaround would coincide not only with a rearrangement of the colonial leadership but, more importantly, with the re-articulation of its political discourse. By then such discourse would not revolve exclusively around the aspirations of the middle classes, but would also address working class demands. The interests of the working classes would be forced to the foreground. Thus, the fundamental question is what process or set of processes had taken place, between the late 1930's and mid 1940's, which so significantly altered the Caribbean's socio-political scenario.

The answer to that question lies, not in the narrow confines of the region itself, but within the context of an international environment fraught with increasing geopolitical tension. As contended in the next chapters, the imminent explosion of yet another global conflagration, particularly as seen from Washington, brought to light the appalling socio-economic and constitutional conditions in an area of the utmost importance for the US's overall military strategy. Both the abject state of affairs in these territories and the imperatives of war led to a comprehensive reassessment of London's policy in the archipelago. The coalescence of these elements, with their subsequent impact in the constitutional evolution of these territories, would have far-reaching consequences. The decolonizing dialogue between the metropolitan and colonial elites beginning with the Montego Bay Conference would, to a considerable extent, reflect them.

2

Slums of Empire

Educate, agitate but do not violate.

Clement Payne, 1937

The international collapse in the price of sugar, together with increasing immigration restrictions in the late 1920s and 1930s, had produced great pressure on wages and employment throughout the archipelago. The price paid for Barbadian sugar in the London market fell, for example, from 26 shillings per hundredweight in 1923 to 9s in 1929, then diminishing to less than 5s in 1934 and remaining at that level for the next three years.[1] In the smaller islands, with few uncultivated areas and an unsustainable excess of population, even under favourable circumstances, migration had always been an effective way of searching for jobs that were hard to find at home.[2] Tens of thousands of British West Indians had successfully migrated, earlier in the century, to the US, Brazil, Canada, Cuba, the Dominican Republic and especially to Panama. Many, for instance, had worked in the construction of the Panama Canal, which by 1904 had already begun.[3]

Unfavourable economic conditions throughout the area, aggravated by a global depression, severely curtailed the availability of any such opportunities. The 1930s were to an extent what Hoyos, Lewis and Williams have described as turbulent years, marking the road to revolution.[4] The underlying tensions throughout the region reached boiling point in the years between 1935 and 1938. The chronology proved fateful and can speak for itself; the spectre of violent confrontation spread 'like a fire along a tinder track'[5]: a sugar strike in St. Kitts, 1935; a revolt against an increase of custom duties in St. Vincent, 1935; a coal strike in St. Lucia, 1935; labour disputes in the sugar plantations of British Guiana, 1935; an oil strike, which became a general strike, in Trinidad, 1937; urban riots in

Barbados, 1937; renewed revolt on the sugar plantations of British Guiana, 1937; a sugar strike in St. Lucia, 1937; acute disturbances in Jamaica, 1938.[6] In the course of these three years every colonial governor called for warships, marines and airplanes; the total number of casualties amounted to 29 dead and over 115 wounded.[7]

While the Caribbean was the oldest colonial region of the Empire, the British public seldom heard of it. For more than two centuries these territories, especially the Leeward Islands, Jamaica and Barbados[8], had been the scene of great prosperity; however by the nineteenth century that buoyancy had vanished. Some voices have contended that the region's relative economic decline stemmed partly from Britain's free trade policies.[9] The diversification of the imperial project into richer and more diverse areas of the world, namely the Asian sub-continent, Africa and the Middle East, meant that these colonies ceased to be of 'turbulent concern'.[10] Consequently, these territories faded into obscurity, lending credence to Lloyd George's infamous aphorism referring to these islands as 'slums of empire'. Professor Macmillan's stark contention that any 'social and economic study of the West Indies is necessarily a study of poverty',[11] summed up the grim picture. Others, such as Havinden and Meredith, have suggested that during this period the archipelago represented 'the depressed area' of the British Empire.[12]

Over 80 per cent of the population in these territories was of African descent and mostly engaged in agriculture.[13] The remaining portion worked in urban areas, mainly in commerce, transport, light industry and domestic service. This group personifies the recurrent term of 'the masses' to which the political and labour leadership would refer incessantly in the following decades. A considerable proportion of these men, women and children contended with an infra-human existence; 'living in barracks, relics of the not so distant age of slavery'.[14] Many had no more shelter than a minute hut made either from mud or unpainted wood or even coconut branches. The typical case was to find whole families living in a single hovel.

Historically these colonies had always been governed to suit the economic interests of the mostly white merchant and planter classes. In essence, these two socioeconomic groupings represented the same values and interests and, by most standards, pertained to the same social class. Constant intermarriage had led, particularly in Barbados, to the consolidation of commercial and agricultural interests in the same oligarchic hands. The Barbadian case clearly illustrated the skewed picture; by 1937, for instance, 98.1 per cent of the island's exports depended on the sugar industry, exclusively controlled and owned by a white plantocracy that amounted to no more than 3 per cent of the population.[15] The most disastrous element in this equation was not the excessive emphasis on sugar as such, but rather the Colonial Office's apparent reluctance to denounce, condemn and dismantle this monopoly. In Trinidad, where oil had supplanted sugar as the most prominent industry, a cartel of five refining companies alone accounted for 88 per cent of the total output.[16] Rexford Tugwell, shortly before his appointment as Governor of Puerto Rico, toured the British colonies in 1937 and wrote 'it is sheer economic monopoly that exists, long established and ruthlessly maintained, coming directly from the days of slavery.'[17] The obviously acute inequality between the races then constituted an explosive ingredient, if combined with the already disturbing centralization of the means of production.

By the 1930s the demographics in the English-speaking Caribbean suggested an interestingly diverse landscape; 2.5 million people mostly of African, European, East Indian and Chinese descent. Although, as mentioned earlier, the outright majority of the population was of African ancestry, the politico-constitutional and economic power resided with the minute white population. While the white element was relatively small, averaging about 3 per cent of the total, it dominated almost every aspect of 'West Indian life'.[18] It owned the most profitable plantations, stores and banks. Only its members sat in the legislative councils, thus entrenching through legislation their individual and collective interests. A robust sugar economy, in colonies such as Barbados and St. Kitts, had led to the rise of a very powerful white plantocracy, characterized by its 'reactionary conceit'.[19] In the particular case of Barbados, that white presence had led to the establishment of a rigid social hierarchy mostly based on racial distinctions.[20] The white oligarchy was at the top, while the black masses remained at the bottom. The following extract from the impressions of a Barbadian religious minister who returned to the island for a holiday in 1938 sheds some light on this aspect of Barbadian society:

> Sixteen years ago when I last visited my native Barbados, it was still a rare thing to see men of colour occupying positions in the Civil Service. There were only

two gentlemen of colour in the House of Assembly. One coloured clergyman in our Anglican Church, just a very few before the Legal Bar, and none on the Bench; one or two physicians.[21]

The black middle classes were positioned just beneath the small white community, in the colonial social scale. These were the people, of mostly African and mixed descent, also referred to as the indigenous petite bourgeoisie.[22] Among them were professionals, namely physicians, lawyers, secondary school teachers, other university graduates and a few successful businessmen. In spite of their achievements, most members of the black middle classes, although politically enfranchised, were relegated to de facto second class citizenship as an outgrowth of their ancestry. There is strong evidence to suggest the Colonial Office was not completely oblivious to the existence of a colour bar in these territories. In his first report as governor, addressed to Viscount Cranborne, Sir Henry Grattan Bushe expressed sharp disagreement with the disturbing racial attitudes of Barbados's white plantocracy. In reference to the strict colour line, he stated, 'I fear I never bothered my ear much about it, but now that I have seen it I find it hateful'.[23] Sir Henry added,

> I asked [Grantley] Adams and his wife to a private dinner. He came in next day to say that I would never find what it had meant for him, since it was the first time he had been asked to Government House. And, of course, he is barred from every club in the island.[24]

The Colonial Office itself published in 1938 that wages for sugar workers ranged from 1s 3d to 2s per day.[25] In that same publication the price of a 4-lb loaf of bread is given as 1s 4d, 'almost double the English figure'.[26] Consequently, the Colonial Office reached the tragically obvious conclusion that in fact 'the negroes eat little bread'.[27] For instance, 44 per cent of Jamaican children were classified as undernourished. Besieged, not only by hunger, but also by diseases such as malaria, yaws and hookworm, the children of the black working-classes vanished in large numbers before their first birthday. By 1937 the infant mortality rate in Jamaica illustrated the morbid picture: 130 out of every 1,000 newly-born babies would not survive infancy. Not only were the masses confined to squalor and sustained economic exploitation, but also to political disenfranchisement.

The political machinery, as with the economic means of production, was also in the hands of a few. These territories (with the exception of Bermuda, the Bahamas and Barbados) were, as mentioned earlier, crown colonies. Although a handful of seats in the legislative councils of these units were open for election, less than 10 per cent of the population held the right to vote. Income, ownership of property and educational qualifications were the major requirements for the franchise as well as for eligibility to stand as a candidate.

Table 2.1
Number of Electors in the Eastern Caribbean, c.1938

Colony	Number of Electors	Percentage of Population
Antigua	1,048	3.06
Montserrat	260	1.90
Dominica	1,248	2.46
St. Lucia	1,509	2.18
St. Vincent	1,598	2.78
Barbados	6,359	3.30

Source: CO 318/436/6

In Barbados, for example, eligibility to stand as a candidate for the House of Assembly was defined by income. A salary of £200 per annum was the bare minimum required, meaning that only a select few could hold elected office. Even though in Barbados there were two legislative chambers, namely an all-appointed legislative council and an elected assembly, both were controlled by the white oligarchy. While on theoretical grounds Barbados's representative government was more advanced than that of her neighbours, in reality this system offered even more scope for oppression. The levels of accountability and responsibility were minimal as the masses had no voice in the legislative process. As Wickham eloquently suggested,

> A wealthy little parish magnate might elect himself a member of the House of Assembly and continue there year after year until perhaps mercifully removed by Providence, without ever performing one single action or giving utterance to one single sentiment which showed anything of an intention to be honest.[28]

Ownership of land at an annual value of not less than £5 or the occupation of property assessed at an annual £15 or higher were prerequisites for the franchise. Income of no less than £50 per annum or an annual minimum dividend of £15 from investments in the island could substitute the previous requirement. Alternatively, the payment of at least £15 annual rent for lodgings could also replace the aforementioned condition. Clearly, this was a very restricted and highly expensive franchise. In effect two of the main requirements, an annual income of £50 and ownership of freehold land of equivalent value, were far beyond the reach of the vast majority of the population. The income qualification alone meant a daily wage of at least 77 cents (approximately 3 shillings and 2 pence half-penny) throughout the 52 weeks of the year, working six days a week. However, not only were the wages of most people far below this level, as suggested above, but year-round employment was limited to only a few skilled and white-collar occupations. Additionally, any occupation in agriculture, particularly in the sugar industry, was by its very nature seasonal and assured an income for only part of the calendar year.

This, in sum, was the scenario upon which the violent drama of the riots unfolded itself. The writing was clearly on the wall for policy makers in the Colonial Office and in the Cabinet; indifference to these ills would inevitably lead to further unrest and renewed violence. W.J. Makin, a reporter from the *Daily Herald* dispatched to Kingston, summed up the needs and aspirations of British colonial subjects across the Caribbean,

> What the people in the West Indies want is simple. They want wages a sight better than the 9s. a week earned now by the average unskilled man. They want better social services particularly health and housing services. They want some peaceful means of expressing their grievances and securing attention to them. To secure better wages they need their own strong trade unions to argue for them with the rich and powerful oil and sugar companies. To secure better social services and a chance to put their case where it will be listened to, they need direct representation in the legislatures on a broad franchise. They have not got these things. A British Colonial Secretary worth his salt would see that they got them.[29]

Arthur Creech Jones, in the preface to a short volume published by the Fabian Society on the Caribbean (1939), echoed that message and added,

The workers in the West Indies want not only proper protection in employment, a sound labour code and free trade unionism. Not only a colonial service, which will implement and operate the instructions of Downing Street, but also drastic constitutional and political reform … together with imaginative economic planning.[30]

Clearly, pressure was mounting on the British Government from all quarters to alleviate conditions in the archipelago. In the House of Lords, shortly after the explosion of violence in Jamaica, Lord Olivier condemned in a forthright manner the lack of attention these territories received from the government.[31] During the course of the following months, Creech Jones and other members of parliament constantly put questions to the colonial secretary on a variety of issues regarding the sour state of affairs in the region. More importantly, there is enough evidence to suggest that during this period the link between the emerging labour leadership in the colonies and the British Labour Party was strengthened. The archives have preserved a copious exchange of letters, for instance, between Manley (Jamaica), Bradshaw (St. Kitts–Nevis–Anguilla), Adams (Barbados), Bird (Antigua) and Creech Jones, during this period. This intimate connection, although by no means unprecedented, between the politically more liberal voices in London and the more progressive elements of the colonial leadership would exert even more pressure on the Cabinet and the Colonial Office. In spite of all these efforts, the Colonial Office reacted as it had during previous critical moments: it appointed a commission of enquiry, namely the Moyne Commission and sanctioned the curtailment of civil liberties.

There is not enough evidence to demonstrate that the riots themselves, together with the unrelenting pressure on the metropolis, significantly influenced the way in which the British Government approached this crisis. While there can be no doubt that the riots did radicalize the discourse of the colonial political movements, these fierce disturbances represent but a piece of a wider and more complex jigsaw puzzle. La Guerra and other students of this period, for example, have contended that previous outbursts had been no more than 'isolated, sporadic and blind reactions to social and economic grievances'.[32] This position echoes the spirit of the Moyne Commission Report, which suggested that in comparison to previous outbursts these were 'of a different character'.[33] The conventional characterization has been that this explosion was atypical in that it had been regional in scope; being 'one of the few West Indian responses to common problems'.[34] More importantly, this hypothesis is closely intertwined with the assumption that somehow these disturbances were the sole catalytic element propelling the Caribbean into a process of political evolution during the post-war period and, thus, leading to the misguided experiments in federalism.

While the riots and the radicalization of the colonial leadership facilitated that constitutional metamorphosis, it would constitute an immense leap of faith to attribute all the succeeding social, economic and especially politico-constitutional reforms to the disturbances alone. A careful analysis of the chronology, let alone a detailed study of the archival records, suggests a robust correlation between the British Government's response and the impending preparations for the Second World War. Less than two months after President Roosevelt had given instructions for the expansion of the American naval squadron in the region, the Colonial Office finally decided to dispatch the much-awaited Moyne Commission to the Caribbean. Additionally, the deliberations and negotiations within the British Government leading to the enactment of the 1940 Colonial Welfare and Development Act coincided with the fall of Holland and France. The German threat compelled London to re-articulate its policy of colonial development, placing special emphasis on these islands. The strategic importance of the erstwhile slums of empire had dramatically come to light once the theatre of war became apparent. From a neglected peripheral area of the British Empire, the Caribbean became in a matter of months the 'show window'[35] where British and American interests intersected each other. In the coming years, external forces — mostly transatlantic — would sway the delicate relationship between an assailed colonizer and an ever eager colonized.

3

The Anglo-American Caribbean Commission[1]

> Something must be done without delay to pull things together in the Caribbean.
>
> *Franklin D. Roosevelt, 1941*

Even before the negotiations leading to the 1901 Hay-Pauncefote Treaty had taken place,[2] the British Government had long since acknowledged the US's vital interest in the Caribbean Basin. By 1904–05, the strategic rethinking that preceded the Great War led to the withdrawal of the British naval squadron from Caribbean waters.[3] Since that time, the US had become the de facto guardian of all British possessions in the region. The solidification of the Anglo-American alliance, once the theater of the Second World War extended to the North Atlantic seaboard and the Pacific, brought the Caribbean even closer to the US. Indeed, the archipelago 'lay like a fleet of great stationary plane-carriers'[4] in the path of any would-be attacker of the Panama Canal or the oriental coast of the US. The Second World War, as Donald Yerxa has suggested, illustrated the area's critical importance as a strategic pivot for the American Navy. For the first time in its history the US faced an authentic security threat from the Atlantic and the Pacific simultaneously.

In his political memoirs, Rexford Tugwell recalled that in 1937, almost two years before the formal hostilities began, President Roosevelt had dispatched an unofficial American commission to tour the British, French, and Dutch possessions in the Caribbean Basin.[5] This party, made up of Tugwell and Charles Taussig,[6] had 'seen and heard much that was disquieting'.[7] While the US acknowledged their military significance, the islands' potential for instability was seen as disturbing. Although under the formal tutelage of their European colonial masters, conditions in the archipelago were clearly ripe for chaos and insurgency. This, in itself, was cause for concern. Not only were these islands strategically positioned between North and South America, but some of them had even limited quantities of copper, gold, silver, bauxite,[8] long staple cotton,[9] and oil.[10]

By January 1939, influential voices in the US Navy were convinced that establishing naval bases throughout the Caribbean, without limiting the effort to those areas under the American flag,[11] was vital for safeguarding the national interest. By then, persistent rumours were circulating about secret Axis airfields being built in Central America for raids on the Panama Canal. The strategic value of the region, as a major naval operation centre, was not lost on President Roosevelt. In a letter to the influential Senator David I. Walsh,[12] amidst the negotiations leading to the 1941 Anglo-American Destroyers-Bases Agreement, the president wrote, 'honestly Dave these islands are of the utmost importance to our national defence as naval and air operating bases'.[13] The level of pre-war anxiety ran so high and the position of the archipelago was so critical to the overall military strategy that the president was confronted with the option of actually annexing most of it.[14] While entertained in closed presidential circles, this idea was not made public and simply faded away.

By this time the recommendations of Britain's Moyne Commission were but a vague rumor in Washington.[15] Few had seen them and none had studied them.[16] Their exposure of grave ills and injured morale, however, led the US to pay closer attention to these far-flung 'specks of dust'.[17] From a neglected peripheral area of the British Empire, in a matter of months the Caribbean became the 'show window'[18] where Anglo-American interests coincided.

The British Government, for its part, saw in the imperatives of war the need for closer Anglo-American collaboration. This urgency led to an overall colonial reassessment. Lord Moyne's recollection is consistent with this premise: 'when I took office the prime minister told me that in his opinion the close connection with the Americans made it even more important than it was before to press on with the rehabilitation of social conditions in the West Indies'.[19] In the same letter, addressed to Major Sir Hubert Young, the colonial governor of Trinidad and Tobago, and forwarded to all other colonial administrators, Lord Moyne enclosed a Note on the Future of Anglo-American Relations.[20] Whitehead's publication advocated a closer relationship with the US. In London's diplomatic circles the overall consensus was that closer ties should be fostered while old prejudices should be discarded.[21]

If there had been any doubts as to the strategic importance of the Caribbean and of the need for a closer Anglo-American alliance in matters of colonial administration, these were dissipated after the tragic fall of Holland and France.[22] This now meant that Germany could occupy both the Dutch and French colonies in the area, disrupting the transportation of essential goods sustaining the allied effort in Europe, especially oil. The other fundamental issue that emerged was the power of Nazi propaganda. During this period an internal memorandum, circulated in the US State Department, concluded that if the British Isles fell, German foreign policy, in relation to Latin America and the Caribbean, would assume a highly positive character, 'constituting therefore a threat to the peace and security of the entire continent'.[23] Captain Alan Kirk, US naval attaché in London, saw in the preservation of the British Empire the most effective tool for containing the German threat. In August 1940 he wrote to his superiors in the Pentagon, 'the safety of the US would be definitely in jeopardy should the British Empire fall'.[24] The morale of the people in the Caribbean now became of the utmost concern for both London and Washington.[25]

President Roosevelt's contention, in April 1941, that 'something had to be done without delay to pull things together in the Caribbean',[26] should be seen within this context. There is enough evidence, stemming mainly from American archives, suggesting that policy-makers in the Roosevelt Administration saw great advantages in encouraging the different powers in the region to cooperate in matters of colonial development and administration.[27]

On July 15, 1941, Lord Moyne informed all colonial administrators of Whitehall's inclination to set up a joint consultative committee with the US.[28] The unfolding of this proposal was no coincidence and should be seen in the light of President Roosevelt's statement. It is important to note that, for the British Government, regional cooperation, as a concept, was no superimposition from Washington; the Moyne Commission itself had already argued that closer regional union was 'an ideal to which, in our opinion, policy should be directed'.[29] The timing of the announcement, however, was highly influenced by the US's acute geopolitical worries.

The month of October 1941 saw the establishment of a Caribbean Division within the US State Department.[30] This development undoubtedly represented a decisive step. It conveyed, in no uncertain terms, that the Caribbean was indeed a national security priority.[31] It is essential to note that the military chronology sped up the policy-making process. By March 1942, barely four months after Pearl Harbor and at the start of the German campaign in Caribbean waters,[32] the intention of setting up a joint consultative committee finally came to fruition with the establishment of the Anglo-American Caribbean Commission.[33] It functioned as a bilateral body with two separate wings, namely a British and an American section.[34] While the British division worked closely with the Colonial Office in London and the British Colonies Supply Mission in Washington, its American counterpart enjoyed unobstructed access to President Roosevelt, reporting directly to him.[35]

The fact that the Anglo-American Caribbean Commission, in its official despatches, usually referred to and discussed socioeconomic issues did not mean that politico-constitutional matters went unnoticed.[36] Some voices clearly understood that 'the trouble in these parts is really going to be political as much as social'.[37] Sir Henry Grattan Bushe, colonial governor of Barbados, saw this quite plainly when in a letter to Sir George Gater, permanent under-secretary of state for the colonies, he suggested that 'the real hope for the islands' political and constitutional difficulties is the development of progressive political parties'.[38] Sir Henry's statement conveyed an unequivocal acknowledgement that socioeconomic development could not be divorced from constitutional evolution. As perceived in influential quarters, for the British Government to miss this point would be tantamount to capitulating in its effort to thwart the Axis threat.

The chronology of constitutional development in the archipelago during the war years was quite remarkable. The timetable itself, as shown below, suggests an indivisible correlation between immediate security concerns, as seen from London and Washington, and the obvious needs of the area. Without a doubt, the region's constitutional evolution, albeit initially sluggish, served as an efficient weapon for counteracting German propaganda. A glance, for instance, at the first report published in 1943 by the Anglo-American Caribbean Commission is enough to support this suggestion. With an opening salvo such as 'while the guns are booming and men dying in the war for human freedom, several concrete moves have been taken in advancing the Caribbean towards the goal of world-wide democracy',[39] the constitutional agenda becomes self-evident. Interestingly, that flowery rhetoric was intimately connected to the 1941 Atlantic Charter adopted both by the British and American Governments. While conveying an impression that London and Washington shared an unambiguous anti-colonial policy, these proclamations, in encouraging high morale amongst the colonial subjects, distorted what essentially amounted to no real commitment to a swift decolonizing process.[40] Without defining the extent to which colonial trusteeship would develop in the post-war scenario, the Anglo-American Caribbean Commission opened the door for the region's slow political evolution.[41] The archives also show that the remaining European colonizers with stakes in the area, in particular France and Holland, plodded along the same path as their British and American counterparts, although at a faster pace.

Jamaica, for instance, soon enjoyed universal adult suffrage. Only two months prior to the inauguration of the Anglo-American Caribbean Commission, Lord Moyne suggested: 'the introduction of universal adult suffrage represents the essential foundation of any scheme of constitutional reform in Jamaica'.[42] Almost a year later, Colonel Oliver Stanley offered Jamaica a new constitutional instrument, which enshrined universal adult suffrage as one of its basic tenets. In Barbados, moreover, immediately after the 1942 local elections, Sir Henry Bushe nominated for the first time a black labour leader, namely Grantley Adams, to the governor-sitting-in executive committee.[43] At the same time, Governor Bushe introduced before the local house of assembly a bill for the extension of the electoral franchise, which reduced the annual income qualification for voters from £50 to £20 and granted women the suffrage.[44] The thought-process leading Sir Henry to introduce this bill illustrated, to a considerable degree, the Anglo-American sine qua non: slow evolution rather than swift revolution. In reference to the imminent increase in the number of eligible voters, Sir Henry confided in Sir George Gater that 'to talk, for example, about universal suffrage is to show an inability to face up the facts'.[45] While justifying a gradual expansion of the franchise, he warned 'to go too far would be simply to substitute mob rule for the present liberally infused oligarchy, and turn what might be a peaceful revolution into a bitter and possibly bloody conflict'.[46] Thus the ongoing dilemma for both Britain and the US — one that shaped their more often than not uneasy partnership in the Caribbean — was how to strike a fine balance between reaction and revolution, 'without inducing in progressive leaders a feeling of frustration, which could only drive them to excesses as the only method of getting their views considered'.[47]

The legitimate governments of Holland and France, while in exile, also felt the need to articulate a vision for the future of their colonies in the Caribbean. Their responses should also be seen in the light of what they considered to be yet another threat, namely the possibility of seeing the US annex their far-flung possessions. This might explain why, early in December, 1942, Queen Wihelmina of Holland declared that a Netherlands Commonwealth would be established after the war, on 'a solid foundation of complete partnership'.[48] The Dutch vowed that in this partnership there would be 'no room for discrimination according to race or nationality'.[49] Queen Wihelmina's proclamation, furthermore, stated that Holland, Indonesia, Surinam and the Netherlands Antilles would 'participate with complete self-reliance and freedom of conduct for each part regarding its internal affairs but with readiness to render mutual assistance'.[50] At the same time de Gaulle, who understood this conundrum very clearly, and his colleagues from the Free French Movement all threw their support behind the idea that Guadeloupe, Martinique and French Guiana should no longer be colonies but departments of France.[51]

It should not come as a surprise that all these measures coincided with Herr Dönitz's devastating raids in the Caribbean. Even more importantly, there was an intimate connection between the intelligence reports coming in from Martinique, Guadeloupe, Aruba and Curaçao, and the initiation of the process of constitutional devolution. By no means reassuring, those despatches revealed that prominent members of the neighbouring communities were already collaborating rather actively with the enemy. Clearly, the time was ripe for further constitutional progress. That was, after all, one of the most eloquent ways of deterring any potential form of cooperation between the colonial elites and the Germans.

It would be very difficult to understate the seminal role the Anglo-American Caribbean Commission played in the archipelago's constitutional evolution. While its inception responded more to the needs of the metropolitan powers than to the aspirations of the colonial subjects, the existence of a joint commission legitimized the concept of regional cooperation, which many voices in the area had espoused for so long.[52] In many ways the Anglo-American Caribbean Commission represents that missing link, sometimes absent from Anglo-Caribbean historiography, between the economic crisis and labour disturbances that took place in the 1930s and the islands' slow constitutional evolution. Considered by Lord Hailey and Colonel Stanley as the best example of regional cooperation, the Anglo-American Caribbean Commission set the stage for what eventually became an ongoing debate on post-war colonial administration.[53] Moreover, it left the door open for the transfer of political authority to the colonial leadership.

It is no secret that influential voices in London and Washington, emboldened by the effectiveness of the Anglo-American Caribbean Commission, saw in the archipelago an ideal area of the world where to test the notion of regional cooperation. Coupled with the long-standing appeal that concept had enjoyed amongst the colonial elites, it was but a matter of time before the British Government officially addressed the issue. Less than two months prior to VE Day, Colonel Stanley, now the colonial secretary, sent a despatch to all colonial governments in the area. In it he explicitly stated that 'the aim of British policy should be the development of a federation in the Caribbean',[54] enjoying 'internal self-government within the British Commonwealth'.[55] Undoubtedly the geopolitical imperatives of the war, the impact of the Anglo-American entente and the uncertainties of the post-war scenario, without overlooking the radicalization of the political discourse in most islands, led Whitehall to re-evaluate its policy towards these territories.

4

From the Montego Bay Conference to the Jamaican Referendum

> After 200 years of British rule England still wants to have us here as subjects, instead of giving us our freedom, instead of giving us self-government.
>
> *Alexander Bustamante, 1947*

In the aftermath of the war, the British Government did not envision an immediate withdrawal from the Caribbean archipelago. While there was no consensus as to the future of imperial trusteeship, there was an understanding that if Britain was to play her part in the post-war world, she could only do so 'as part of the British Empire and British Commonwealth and not in isolation'.[1] There is enough evidence suggesting that by this early stage, the tendency prevailing in London envisaged a gradual substitution of 'control for counsel'.[2] The initial stages of the Eastern Caribbean's post-war constitutional development, namely the period that goes from 1947 to 1961, should be seen against this context.

The end of the war brought to light the extent to which the colonial scenario had evolved since the disturbances of the late 1930s. Close to a decade later a new set of colonial movements had positioned themselves at the forefront of the region's constitutional debate; their chieftains, mostly British-educated and members of the black middle classes, assumed the role of intermediaries between the rural and urban masses and the Colonial Office. Commonly characterized as 'new' the area's post-war leadership, with some notable exceptions, was made up of the usual black middle-class elements.[3] However, contrary to what had happened during the inter-war period, a sizeable proportion of these leaders were no longer outsiders but full members of most legislatures and executive councils.[4] Arguably these movements, unlike most of their predecessors, enjoyed the benefit of institutional legitimacy as their official recognition in London and in the colonies themselves attested. Hence, in some ways, as Mordecai outspokenly suggested, 'the initiative had already passed from the spokesmen of planters and merchants to the spokesmen of the electorates'.[5] In spite of this, the discussions that ensued, soon after Colonel Stanley's memorandum, between the Colonial Office and the colonial leadership demonstrated yet again how much influence the metropolis, together with the new set of forces operating in the post-war international scenario, still exerted over the region's political process. An unpublished letter from Vere Bird, future chief minister of Antigua, to Richard Hart, by then an influential member of Jamaica's People's National Party, summed up the mood of the archipelago's political and labour leadership,[6]

> I notice that we are thinking alike with respect to Dominion status for the West Indies. After Burma, Ceylon and India I fail to see West Indians demanding less than Dominion status. If we were to do so we would be telling the world that we admit we are less advanced than a lot of other people.
>
> We have not yet decided our stand on Closer Association in a formal manner, but I guess by now you are fully aware of the wishes of our people and that you will at least assist in seeing we start off the W.I. Nation with general satisfaction.[7]

The assertion that Bird advanced in this letter, namely self-government within the context of dominion status, symbolised the guiding principle in the agenda of the colonial leaders.[8] As a matter of fact, this aspiration had been considerably solidified since the first post-war conference of the Caribbean Labour Congress held in Barbados in September 1945.[9] While the policy adopted then stressed that 'federation should be sought with or without dominion status',[10] by 1947 the position had consolidated to 'federation with self-government, a Caribbean dominion'.[11] For Norman Manley,[12] as his fiery speech at the 1947 Conference of the Caribbean Labour Congress, held in Kingston, clearly demonstrated, this aspiration was non-negotiable. On that occasion, the founder of Jamaica's People's National Party and soon-to-be premier of the island argued,

> I reject totally any sort of mismarriage between colonial rule and federation. I would predict for such a marriage an abortion, as politics has never seen. I say that a federated West Indies cannot aim at any smaller immediate objective than dominion status.[13]

Although their position, as conveyed through these uncompromising statements, seemed immovable; it did not last for long. By the end of what some voices already described as an all-important and historic meeting with the colonial secretary in Montego Bay, the rank and file of the colonial leadership had committed itself to a process of politico-constitutional devolution that did not envision such a large degree of local empowerment. This begs the following question — what effected such a blatantly obvious change of heart? Unearthing a coherent explanation in itself constitutes a challenge to the way Commonwealth historiography has attempted to describe and evaluate the process leading to the only federal experiment ever seen in the area. Most studies on the origins of the West Indies Federation have chosen to evaluate that experience from the point of view of the colonial political elites. However, their unwavering attention to this angle has perpetuated an obviously narrow explanation for why events unfolded as they did. It is just not enough to suggest an apparent correlation between the rhetoric of self-determination espoused during the war, namely in the Atlantic Charter and in the reports of the Anglo-American Caribbean Commission, and the articulation in London of a federal project for the area. A fuller and far more serious analysis comes to life once the proceedings of the aforementioned Montego Bay Conference are closely scrutinized against an array of confidential documents, pertaining almost exclusively to the Colonial Office and the Foreign Office's erstwhile American Department.

The deliberations that took place at this conference, which the colonial secretary had convened for discussing proposals for closer association, must be evaluated paying special attention to the positions adopted both by Creech Jones and Alexander Bustamante.[14] The lines, even before the official inauguration of the drafting process, had already been drawn between those who believed in the British Government's sincerity and those who looked at the latter's federal proposal with unease and suspicion. From a chronological perspective, this conference opened up a lengthy set of discussions between London and the colonial politicians leading up to the inauguration, in January 1958, of the West Indies Federation.[15] Before going any further, a careful examination should be given to Creech Jones's opening speech at the conference. From the outset the colonial secretary drew the attention of the audience to what he described as a 'very difficult time in the affairs'[16] of Britain. Clearly, and in no uncertain terms, Creech Jones conceded that post-war metropolitan constraints would impinge on the constitutional process about to start. Along these lines the colonial secretary suggested,

> Our economic problems are acute, but we are determined to work our way through our present difficulties and to emerge with a greater sense of our international responsibilities and a deeper consciousness of the obligations to our Colonial peoples which history, by its legacy, has given to us. We have, in Britain, a very difficult road to walk, but I am sure that the experience will forge closer links between Great Britain and the far-flung Colonies inside the Commonwealth.[17]

On the substantive issue of the British Government's imminent policy towards the Caribbean, the colonial secretary's expressions conveyed what by then had become London's post-war position regarding its overseas responsibilities. Creech Jones emphatically contended,

> We have moved as a nation from a conception of Colonies as provinces for material exploitation for the benefit of alien interest to a conception of Commonwealth in which that Commonwealth shall include free nations living out their own lives and all co-operating for the good, the stability, the peace and the happiness of the world. It is our task as a British Government to create, so far as we can, the conditions which are essential for good nationhood in all the territories under our control, and we have therefore, latterly, at a very great pace been trying to apply these liberal principles in all the territories inside the Empire. It is not only to make modifications so that representative government shall be achieved, but also to see that responsibility pass increasingly from London to the peoples of the territories themselves. That is demanded of the modern world: if we delay then disaster overtakes us.[18]

Although somewhat concealed in his highly deferential speech, the position the British Government had adopted on the most delicate aspects of the project became quite apparent: the upcoming federation would remain a colonial entity and federation would be a pre-requisite for full self-government.[19] On the desirability of a federation as the only viable and thus sensible alternative for the region's political future the colonial secretary argued,

I submit that this problem has now to be considered in the light of our experience in this post-war world. In the light of modern conditions, whatever be those difficulties, if we were to go forward at this speed and meet the social pressures of our people, if we were to satisfy their legitimate clamour for change, for reform, for material needs, then some conception of federation must be realised at the present time.[20]

Creech Jones then added,

Some surrender of ultimate authority in certain major issues does become necessary if the small units of the West Indies are in the future to maintain any true measure of responsibility and independence in all aspects of their government.[21]

I regard these movements as running together, not only that I would personally, and as Secretary of State, desire to see a widening responsibility in the individual territories there should also be an increasing sense of relationship between the territories in the region.[22]

Undoubtedly, there was no intention of granting dominion status to any of the British territories in the Caribbean. Arguably the colonial politicians had no other alternative but to get on board a project already articulated in London. Admittedly at this stage the initiative stemmed from the metropolis, as the project had been consistently designed in the first place to suit the interests of the British Government. As will be suggested in the succeeding chapters, these conditions would in subsequent years exacerbate the natural tensions which usually engulf colonized and colonizers, while engaged in this type of negotiations. The aims of the metropolis and the aspirations of the anxious colonials would soon resemble competing centripetal and centrifugal forces. However, almost all the delegations, with the notable exception of the ones coming from the continental territories, namely British Honduras and British Guiana, left Montego Bay endorsing Creech Jones's design.[23]

Without any doubt an analysis of why most colonial leaders acquiesced to the Colonial Office's intentions, hence modifying their discourse, still deserves further scholarly attention. Such a study must incorporate and attempt to reconcile Bustamante's stridently dissident voice, since the views he voiced at Montego Bay constituted the antithesis to mainstream opinion at the conference. In addition, Bustamante's premonitions seem, if observed in hindsight, prophetic. Even the simple fact that here was a Jamaican adopting rather uncompromising views makes this incident even more relevant. After all Jamaica, as the anti-climactic denouement of the West Indies Federation eventually demonstrated, would inflict the *coup de grâce* on that constitutional experiment. Thus, for more than one reason, Bustamante's distinct position cannot go unheeded.[24] The reaction espoused by the then chief minister of Jamaica set the stage for what, years later, became an environment tainted with distrust. In his opening statement, after suggesting that he was 'a matter-of-fact speaker coming from the gutter',[25] Bustamante argued,

> I am sorry to say that the opinion that I have formed is that he [the colonial secretary] has come here with his mind absolutely made up to push something down our throats…. He said that unless we accept federation for the Colonies there will be calamity and disaster. I do not share the Chairman's prophecy… I am more than suspicious of the motive behind this federation, and I will tell you why…. The reason why I have become suspicious about the motive relative to the formation of this federation is that, whilst most of us West Indians have been asking for self-government, we are told that self-government for the time being is really not good for us and the thing we deserve is federation. That is not good enough reason for me nor for Jamaica and I speak for the majority of the people in this country.... Why is it that instead of offering us that which we are entitled to, that which is our heritage and right — freedom — you strongly suggest, not alone suggest, but recommend, federation, with almost a threat that unless we accept it there will be calamity and disaster in the Colonies?[26]

Bustamante went even further,

> It makes me angry, and really angry, that after 200 years of British rule England still wants to have us here as subjects instead of giving us our freedom, instead of giving us self-government. Why does England want to keep us? Is it to keep us in the same filth, mud, squalor? … What am I asking for the present? I have already said we as Jamaicans are adults, we are quite ready to throw our burden on our shoulders and face the danger of independence.[27]

Last but not least the Jamaican chief minister raised two legitimate issues, which years later would inevitably come back to haunt the federal venture: first, Britain's appraisal that constitutional uniformity between the various colonies should not be a prerequisite for federation; and secondly the inaccuracy of the rumour, circulated by both British and moderate colonial voices, that federation would bring about an instant financial panacea. Using highly picturesque similes and metaphors Bustamante asserted,

> Jamaica is walking politically, Trinidad is creeping, Barbados is right behind Trinidad or almost the same, St. Kitts and St. Vincent are attempting to creep and only attempting and Antigua is creeping, and for all the other small islands, some can barely creep on the palm of their hands, and others on hands and feet, and others not at all, yet you say to us "we want you to federate".[28]

> Some people think federation is like trees in Panama where the gold used to grow and that gold is coming from St. Kitts, St. Vincent and St. Lucia. The people in the country have no idea or knowledge of the true meaning of federation and when you say that by federating the British West Indies will become prosperous you do not have in mind to deceive the people, I can tell you it is deception. It is deception of the worst type. If you know that most of the British West Indies are almost bankrupt and pauperised how is this prosperity to come overnight?[29]

Bustamante's *casus belli* centred on the colonial secretary's inflexibility and uncompromising attitude on handling the region's constitutional evolution. Bustamante's impassioned expressions did not intend to answer but rather to raise very tough questions; the explanations of which lie, at least partly, in the realm of Anglo-American relations. No discussion of this episode can be complete without referring to the US's role and interest in the process about to commence. The transcripts of the Montego Bay Conference proceedings demonstrate that some colonial leaders were not completely oblivious to this fact. There was a feeling in some quarters that should the British Government refuse to transfer further instalments of local authority, then some type of territorial annexation to the US would be far more desirable. Along these lines the Barbadian Wynter A. Crawford suggested,[30]

> So far as the Colony from which I come is concerned, the people desire self-government for the West Indies… If they were to remain as a Colony, for purely practical considerations, they might make it clear that they would prefer to be under American control rather than British control.[31]

Beyond any trace of reasonable doubt, the Caribbean witnessed during the post-war period the perpetuation of its condition as an uneasy meeting place where the strategic interests of the US coincided with London's intention of maintaining an imperishable and ever stronger Anglo-American alliance.[32] President Eisenhower's contention in 1957 that 'the US Government and its people are vitally interested' in the region, together with Harold Macmillan's private reassurance to the president that 'all this liquidation of colonialism is going so well that I would be sorry if there was any hitch, especially one in the Caribbean!' eloquently illustrate this position.[33] The documents currently available, particularly those pertaining to the US State Department, portray the Americans as keen supporters of the West Indies Federation; from this picture emerges the hypothesis that had the Federation survived, both the Kennedy and Johnson Administrations, as well as the US Congress would have been ready to develop a very close relationship with it.[34] But why such an enthusiastic and unrelenting support? A closer look at the historical record yields a far more complex picture. The archives invariably reveal how successive American administrations saw in the federal experiment a quasi colonial construct, embodying the role of a regional stabilizing force. This rationale lay behind the principle that, by preventing territorial fragmentation, the West Indies Federation would inexorably contain communist 'intrigue and infiltration'.[35] Such a maxim was, nevertheless, premised on the expectation that the British Government would not transfer all political authority at once.

In the meantime there was a strong feeling, particularly amongst the members of the Cabinet's Colonial Policy Committee, that every opportunity should be seized to show the Americans that the processes of devolution taking place in most British possessions had no relation with out-of-date conceptions of colonialism, but were a 'constructive job of nation-building' which they had 'a duty as well as an interest to support'.[36] The documents also reveal that for the British Government, at least up until Iain Macleod's tenure as colonial secretary, 'hasty withdrawals did not constitute good advertisements of past British rule',[37] particularly in colonies of high strategic value such as those in the Caribbean. For instance, on Duncan Sandys appointment as minister for commonwealth relations, in August 1960, Macmillan clearly warned him of the importance of maintaining the 'right balance between going too fast and going too slowly'.[38] The policy pursued in the Caribbean, from the Montego Bay Conference to the inauguration of the Federation, undoubtedly ran parallel to this tenet. Alan Lennox-Boyd summed it up in a confidential despatch to Macmillan, when he admitted 'there can be no question of independence for the West Indies until they are viable both financially and in other respects'.[39]

Unmistakably the polyhedric set of forces swaying the federal experiment superseded the unidimensional colonized *vis-à-vis* colonizer relationship. In some ways this condition accelerated the inevitable superimposition of a Cold War scenario on the Caribbean archipelago. Even before Castro's rise to power in January 1959 the British Government had granted the US almost unlimited access on matters of an ideological and military nature. This had far-reaching politico-constitutional consequences for the region. The systematic purges, especially after the Montego Bay Conference, of the so-called extremist elements within the Caribbean Labour Congress and the initiation of American military exercises off the coast of Antigua as part of the Pentagon's guided missile range programme, would complement the US's ideological campaign.[40] As becomes apparent in the following chapters, this multifaceted interplay of regional, metropolitan and international aims gathered special momentum with the dismantling of the West Indies Federation.

There is no need to reproduce here a detailed analysis of the immediate catalysts leading to the disintegration of the Federation, as this subject is perhaps one of the best documented episodes in the region's modern history.[41] Nevertheless, before going any further, some important observations must be made. First, most conventional post mortems point to the continuous personal disagreements between the colonial leaders as the cause behind the collapse.[42] A brief prepared in the Colonial Office for the British prime minister, for instance, consistent with this position, blamed the 'West Indian temperament with its side of childish vanity and readiness to petulance'[43] for most of the failure. That type of observation tends to perpetuate the misguided perception that the British Government had no responsibility for the federal miscarriage, although, in essence, some of the most acute difficulties came from London's hasty decisions and misjudgments. As the next chapters suggest, Commonwealth historiography reproduces this same arrangement in its evaluation of what happened between 1962 and 1967. And secondly, the constitutional position of the Caribbean had evolved considerably since the Montego Bay Conference. By the time of the dissolution, all federal units had been enjoying universal adult suffrage since 1951; and by 1960 even the Leeward and Windward Islands had nearly achieved full responsible government.[44] Consequently, the debate in the following years would revolve more around the issues of economic viability and modernization than constitutional development per se.

The outcome of the Jamaican referendum, held on September 19, 1961, namely a majority vote in favour of that island's withdrawal from the Federation, created a peculiarly complex and somewhat unexpected scenario for both London and the nine remaining federal units. The fact that Jamaica alone accounted for more than half of all the wealth and population of the Federation complicated the scenario even further.[45] As the majority of the Jamaican people voting, 54.11 per cent to 45.89 per cent, decided their country should move to independence within the Commonwealth, the remaining federal units, namely Barbados, Antigua, St. Kitts-Nevis-Anguilla, Montserrat, Dominica, St. Lucia, St. Vincent and Grenada, with the exception of Trinidad and Tobago,[46] faced a highly uncertain future. A closer look at the archival records reveals how both the British and the Americans had not been expecting such an outcome. A confidential telegram, produced in the US Embassy in London and addressed to US Secretary of State Dean Rusk, throws some light on how the Americans saw the referendum a few days before it was held:

> For obvious reasons, [the] British would regard it most delicate at this point for them to give any indication their being behind Manley's effort to win [the] referendum in favour of Federation in Jamaica and, accordingly [the] Colonial Office will treat [the] referendum as a purely internal matter on which no UK public statement would be appropriate. We would think it might be at least as delicate for [the] US to indicate in any public way our interest in [the] outcome of referendum. We anticipate, of course, [the] Consul [General] will express his congratulations to Manley orally, and at [the] same time express any other thoughts [the] Department considers desirable.[47]

Jamaica's secession brought the federal experiment full circle. The consensus which since Montego Bay had existed between the British Government and most of the colonial leadership had come to an abrupt end. Even the tacit Anglo-American understanding on how to facilitate the region's politico-constitutional evolution had also come to a halt. At around this time the British Government had produced the often-cited memorandum stressing that the Caribbean was an area of the world where no vital British interests and few strategic considerations were at stake and thus the fundamental aim should be 'political disengagement'.[48] At the same time the US Government, still assessing the landscape, saw things differently. A secret despatch, produced in the Pentagon a few months after the Jamaican referendum, illustrated the sharp divergence of opinion between the transatlantic allies in respect of the Caribbean,

> We concur with the [US] Consul General that the future of the West Indies, including Jamaica, is a UK problem. For the present we should not permit ourselves to be lured into a position where the US would be vulnerable to pressure to assume responsibilities which quite properly fall within HMG's sphere of responsibility.[49]

Many complex questions were raised once Jamaica decided on independence. The triumvirate made up of the colonial politicians, the British Government and Washington faced a variety of formidable challenges. On the one hand, for the US the main challenges consisted in containing further fragmentation in the region while ensuring that the British did not walk away from their responsibilities. On the other, for the British Government the set of issues was somewhat more complex: the timing of the withdrawal would undoubtedly constitute the most trying decision. A hurried departure had the potential of ending up in embarrassment before the US, let alone before an international community in which a militant Afro-Asian bloc had already gained considerable influence at the UN. And, of course, the economic aspects of this conundrum would play an even more significant role as Britain desperately attempted to enlist American and Canadian financial aid for the former federal territories. Barbados, Antigua, St. Kitts–Nevis–Anguilla, Montserrat, Dominica, St. Lucia, St. Vincent and Grenada were for the most part caught up in this crossfire.

The period spanning from 1962 to 1967, although commonly overlooked by Commonwealth historiography, was to be one of unprecedented effervescence in the archipelago. For the colonial leadership the challenge would be two-fold. While attempting to articulate a new constitutional project for the region, the colonial politicians also had to meet the expectations of modernization and further local empowerment entertained by the newly enfranchised masses. A new chapter was about to start in the delicate relationship between London and the Eastern Caribbean. Perhaps an unpublished letter Norman Manley sent to Creech Jones, immediately after the Jamaican referendum, underlines better than most official documents the understanding that indeed an era had finished and a new one was about to begin:

> I can well understand how you must have felt to know that fourteen years after the Montego Bay Conference Federation had come to the point where Jamaica withdrew and where it was doubtful whether the rest of the Federation would survive.
>
> We put up a tremendous fight and everybody thought the fight was won (and that includes the Opposition) but the fact of the matter was that we just could not overcome the natural fear of the country people about what might happen under Federation.
>
> I am concerned for the future of the Federation but no one will know till the Trinidad elections are over. My guess is that Trinidad will try for its survival. As for us there is only one course — to go ahead on the road decided on by the people as fast and as hard as we can.[50]

Part One: Conclusion

There was nothing wholly inevitable throughout the historical narrative that goes from the late 1930s up until the inauguration of the West Indies Federation. The riots and the rise of the labour movement sprang up as a direct consequence of the archipelago's appalling socio-economic and political backwardness. However, it does not necessarily follow that these conditions alone led to the region's constitutional evolution during the post-war period. The only credible explanation is that both metropolitan and international considerations considerably shaped the process. The war had accentuated the need to re-articulate London's colonial policy not only in the Caribbean but also throughout the waning British Empire.

Yet, unlike what was occurring in most of its African colonies, particularly in British West Africa, the transfer of political authority in the Caribbean had, so far, been considerably more gradual. The reason for this did not lie in the complacency or obedient patience of the area's leadership, but in the perception in the Colonial Office and in the Cabinet that the size, population and economic base of these territories were far too small to sustain independence. Different from other British possessions, such as Sierra Leone or the Gold Coast, the proximity to the US added to the complexity of this scenario. The superimposition of the Cold War scenario onto Caribbean latitudes would be far more dramatic than in many other parts of the British Empire. The withdrawal of Jamaica came unexpectedly, throwing all major players off balance. The apparent stability, which since the war had existed in the area, was shattered. The only alternative now available to the colonial leadership and the metropolitan policy-makers in London was to disentangle such a disturbing colonial knot as swiftly and effectively as possible.

PART TWO

THE DISENTANGLEMENT OF A
COLONIAL KNOT

We are not here to sit as a coroner's jury to discover the cause of failure of the past attempts at union, but rather, in the light of such past failures, to determine the conditions of lasting survival of the structure which the leaders of the eight countries here represented fully determined a month ago to establish. The desire for unity, the wish for peace, the longing for accord deeply implanted in the human heart have stirred the most powerful emotions of the race and have been responsible for some of its nobler actions. These desires and longings, we the people of the Eastern Caribbean share with the rest of mankind.

Errol Barrow, 1962

Introduction

This second part of the book reveals colonial policy-making at the highest levels of the British Cabinet. It disputes the notion that for the British Government these small territories were wholly insignificant. On the contrary, the Eastern Caribbean territories were closely monitored from London, particularly within the context of their geopolitical significance and financial uncertainties. Encouraging them either to unify with Trinidad and Tobago or to forge a new federation amongst themselves, became the two competing policy options before the Cabinet and the Colonial Office. What seemed inevitable or perhaps insignificant on the surface was seen from above in a different light. For instance, while at the beginning of 1962 the Colonial Office with the concurrence of the islands' chief ministers had almost completely agreed to the establishment of a federation of the Little Eight, the Cabinet grandees in London still did not see it that way. Although accepting in principle the federal option, the members of the Cabinet's Colonial Policy Committee never completely abandoned their intention of unifying these territories with Trinidad and Tobago. Such divergence of views, amongst Cabinet ministers and senior civil servants in the Colonial Office, exemplifies some of the most fascinating metropolitan discontinuities shaping this process. The next chapters penetrate this scenario, as they throw invaluable light on some of the questions this study seeks to answer. These chapters also bring the Little Eight to the fore, where the various options and assumptions espoused by the political elites in the archipelago are scrutenized.

In terms of structure, this part of the study begins with Colonial Secretary Reginald Maudling in the Eastern Caribbean attempting to disentangle what he had termed the 'muddle.' As this section of the book progresses, it reveals how the possibility of establishing a new federal arrangement in the area slowly begins to evaporate. The next chapters suggest that there was, from the outset, an inconsistency between the intentions of the British Government and the aspirations of the colonial leadership.

5

The Colonial Office and the Eastern Caribbean Crisis

Ten minus one leaves nought, not nine.

Eric Williams, 1961

The outcome of the Jamaican referendum had caught by surprise, not only the British and American authorities as contended in the previous chapter,[1] but most chief ministers and members of the Federal Cabinet. Barely a day after the Jamaican vote Iain Macleod, in a secret despatch to Harold Macmillan, outspokenly suggested 'we expected and hoped for a narrow but clear affirmative, the result is a narrow but clear negative'.[2] For Harold Macmillan, as months later he confided to Sir Anthony Eden (Lord Avon), 'it was a great disappointment that the Federation broke down and it is not easy to see the way forward'.[3] The immediate reaction from the Colonial Office acknowledged that, in spite of the regret in London and Washington, halting the independence of Jamaica was not politically or legally sustainable. In that first submission to the prime minister, the colonial secretary cited the recent cases of Cyprus (1960) and Sierra Leone (1961) as precedents for Jamaica's unavoidable admission as a separate member of the Commonwealth.[4] Additionally, there was an obvious desire to avoid any action that could embitter relations with the leadership of the Jamaica Labour Party, which had led the movement for that island's secession from the West Indies Federation.

Now, the fundamental question before the British Government was whether the nine remaining territories would stay federated despite Jamaica's defection. By this time there was a clear consensus, in the Colonial Office as well as amongst the political leadership in the region, that the answer depended heavily on the attitude of Trinidad and Tobago. Macleod, however, already entertained a strong suspicion that the leadership of the People's National Movement,[5] then the ruling party in Port-of-Spain, might not be prepared to take on the responsibility of carrying what remained of the Federation.[6] Indeed Eric Williams,[7] the Trinidadian premier, had already warned both the British Government and his colleagues at the last Inter-Governmental Conference held in Lancaster House between May and June 1961 that 'ten minus one leaves nought, not nine'.[8]

The archival record suggests that, immediately after the referendum, the consensus in the Colonial Office was that if the local authorities in Trinidad and Tobago demanded independence nothing could be done to prevent them from going it alone.[9] Certainly, denying such a claim while openly negotiating independence with the Jamaican leadership would have proven highly embarrassing. Yet, there was widespread concern that Trinidad and Tobago's potential withdrawal could seriously jeopardize London's position in the area. A closer look at a myriad of newly available documents shows that at the highest echelons it was still difficult to see how a rump federation of the smaller islands could survive without Trinidad and Tobago.[10] Moreover, there were real and serious doubts on whether further fragmentation could be contained at all. At least by this stage, the Colonial Office had reasonable misgivings about whether the colonial leadership of Antigua and Barbados would want to remain as units of the ailing Federation. For one thing, Antigua, and in particular its Chief Minister Vere Bird,[11] had historically shown a distinct pro-Jamaican attitude. This in itself lent credence to a misguided assumption that if confronted with the spectre of remaining in the Federation without Jamaica versus forging some sort of quasi-colonial association with Jamaica, the Antiguan Government would prefer the latter option.

In addition, senior civil servants in the Colonial Office had reason to believe that Barbados, pending the results of the upcoming local elections, might decide to revert to separate self-governing status. These prospects would have left London saddled with six minute islands, all but one of which were in the red,[12] supported financially by the British Treasury and incapable of sustaining independence. The plausible imminence of such a dismal possibility led Macleod to consider whether to encourage these territories, including Antigua and Barbados, to join Trinidad and Tobago either through unitary statehood or a new federal arrangement. At least for the next few months, until the beginning of January 1962, the Colonial Office openly hoped that Jamaica's withdrawal would induce Eric Williams to lead in his own terms what remained of the Federation. The departure of Jamaica, at least as Macleod saw it, had provided Eric Williams with the opportunity of pressing for the tighter form of federation he had always advocated, namely with strong central powers over sensitive matters such as taxation and development policy.[13] Equally important for Macleod was the fact that if Williams claimed the federal helm then the British Government could see its financial responsibilities for the smaller territories dramatically diminished.

As the Colonial Office scrutinized these potential scenarios, other regional considerations did not go unnoticed. For instance, the first paper Macleod put forward for the consideration of the Cabinet's Colonial Policy Committee, in the wake of the referendum, advocated the establishment of a new federation in the Eastern Caribbean comprising the remaining territories, including Trinidad and Tobago. This suggestion garnered considerable support because, as various ministers argued, its implementation might have increased the 'likelihood of bringing in British Guiana, which has always been one of our aims'.[14] Alec Douglas Home and even Sir Norman Brooke, head of the civil service, considered that the East Indian majority in British Guiana would be more agreeable to joining the Federation when the 'predominantly negro population of Jamaica were removed from it'.[15] There was even mention of attracting British Honduras, with her traditional antipathy towards Jamaica, to embrace the federal experiment. Some believed that, with Jamaica out of the way, it would prove far easier than before to entice British Guiana and British Honduras. As becomes apparent below, the attempt to include these continental territories owed more to the particular interests of London and Washington, than to the aspirations of the people in any of these two colonies.

Nonetheless, in merely considering these possible angles, London acknowledged that the re-articulation of its colonial policy could not be confined to the Little Eight alone but had to encompass the region as a whole. This explains, at least initially, why at the highest levels references to how British Guiana and British Honduras could fit into the picture were made on an almost constant basis. While the suggestion that the British Cabinet had by then made a conscious decision to withdraw from the area is quite accurate, the fundamental questions before it still remained unaltered. Deciding on the right timing, assessing what an affordable financial settlement should be and, of course, determining the constitutional framework upon which any such transfer of power should rest were still in the air.

Before analyzing the reaction in the colonies themselves, particularly amongst the colonial politicians, attention should be paid to the arrival of the newest actor in the cast. Very early in October 1961, the British prime minister had announced publicly that Reginald Maudling would replace Iain Macleod as colonial secretary.[16] Although in essence those two men, as Macmillan years later acknowledged,[17] shared relatively similar views towards colonial issues, the transition was nonetheless of importance for these territories. What makes Maudling's tenure so momentous — at least his initial months at the Colonial Office while he was acquainting himself with the area — was that it began against the backdrop of the impending Bermuda talks held on December 21–22, 1961 between Macmillan and Kennedy.[18] In a series of pre-summit briefings addressed to the prime minister and to the foreign secretary, Maudling strongly urged Macmillan to discuss the situation of the Eastern Caribbean with Kennedy. There is enough evidence suggesting that the new colonial secretary considered that ever since the Jamaican referendum the US Government was 'either re-appraising or uncertain about future policy towards the West Indies'.[19] In these highly sensitive briefs Maudling touched on a string of critical issues. In the first one he sternly warned that,

> Small though they are, our Caribbean colonies have been growing steadily more expensive in recent years. At the same time our future commitments elsewhere will not make it possible for the UK alone to provide sufficient development assistance to satisfy West Indian expectations, (which are not modest), or even, in some cases, simply cope with their disastrous population explosions.[20]

The picture was further complicated, as the colonial secretary admitted, since 'we have not, frankly, decided what, in these circumstances, the ultimate political future of these territories would be'.[21] While there was a consensus within the Cabinet that the Little Eight could not remain as colonies in perpetuity, there was also an understanding that without Canadian and, most importantly, American economic assistance the transfer of political authority could turn rather sour. With competing demands from her African colonies, which Macleod before him had often described as the 'cauldron of the Colonial Office',[22] the colonial secretary saw no way the British Government on its own could address the region's long-term financial demands. The immediate objective, as Maudling put it to Macmillan, should be to persuade President Kennedy, so that he '[does] not feel that current political uncertainties make the fundamental problems of the area less pressing'.[23] Amongst the panoply of threats facing the Caribbean as a whole, the colonial secretary identified 'population pressures, the gradual closing of doors to migration, the European Common Market,[24] the nearness of Cuba (with the unsettling influence of *Fidelismo*) and a re-emergence of racial tensions (particularly in Jamaica)'.[25] In a passage from another brief, written a few days later and fully reproduced below, Maudling expounded on what he saw as the sombre background which could soon engulf the Caribbean.

> There events are moving fast and not always to our advantage. Whilst American defensive interest in the area is alarmed and quickening, British capacity and interest in maintaining stability diminishes. In the Colonial Office we can no more look after the American flank in the Caribbean than the British Navy the Monroe Doctrine. It must therefore be recognised that in her own interests America must play a larger role in the British area.
>
> Nevertheless, not only is it important to both Governments to maintain political stability in the area, but probably neither Government could do it at this time without the help of the other. We can continue to offer our Commonwealth and colonial connection, some aid [as well as] some minor defence arrangements for internal security purposes.[26]

Maudling's cardinal thesis, as he stated at the end of this statement to the prime minister, was that 'in view of the changing circumstances and of our own special problems the need for a change in US policy is urgent'.[27] Suggesting that the Macmillan–Kennedy exchange, that winter in Bermuda, had a tangible or discernible instant impact on the relationship between the Little Eight and the British Government would constitute a misrepresentation of the historical record. The importance of the Bermuda talks, however, resides in the fact that for the first time since the war the uncertainties and challenges confronting the Caribbean constituted summit material. Clearly the demise of the original Federation and, most traumatically, the unwrapping of this Pandora's box, led to the understanding that this state of affairs required discussions at the highest levels. While there was no immediate re-articulation of US policy, as Maudling was expecting, the re-emergence of the Caribbean in the transatlantic agenda would in time influence the expectations entertained both by colonizers and colonized.[28]

During this exchange Maudling openly disclosed his intention of visiting the archipelago in January 1962, in the first place, to acquaint himself with the region and, secondly, to see if he could engage in a constructive dialogue with those in a position to influence events there. This aspect of the drama brings to centrestage the internal political condition in the colonies. There, as Sir John Mordecai, deputy governor-general of the moribund Federation, suggested to Ambler Thomas,[29] the immediate timing of the process raised the most pressing uncertainties.[30] Questions such as when to introduce legislation in the British Parliament for Jamaica's independence, together with the issue of how to reshape the Federation, if at all, raised a series of key challenges. In a legal opinion of importance, the constitutional advisers to the Federal Cabinet concluded early on that 'although the legal instruments may remain substantially unchanged after Jamaica's secession, the agreement between the territories will have come to an end'.[31] Thus, the political institution that they had originally created, namely the West Indies Federation, 'will have been transformed and an entirely new Federation established'.[32] This meant that the withdrawal of the Jamaican members from the Federal House of Representatives would clearly affect the capacity of the existing Government to continue in office without new elections, as it dramatically disrupted the constitutional balance of power.

In the judgment of the Federation's legal team, if steps were taken 'under the authority of an Act of Parliament to allow Jamaica to withdraw before agreement was reached on the future relationship of the remaining territories'[33] Trinidad and Tobago could then claim the original compact existed no more; thus providing its insular leadership with enough legitimacy to declare independence unilaterally. This partly explains why the Federal Prime Minister Sir Grantley Adams,[34] during his last meeting with Macmillan, asked the British prime minister not to introduce an independence bill for Jamaica 'too soon'.[35] Such a delay, according to

Adams, would give the 'federalists an opportunity to get to work'[36] as well as time to encourage the Trinidadian leadership to stay on board. Whether Adams really favoured a new federation with or without Trinidad and Tobago still needs further clarification,[37] but what emerges quite clearly from the historical record is that, by December 1961, Maudling had already decided that legislation for Jamaica's independence should be enacted no later than March 1962.[38] This decision poses the question: if a new federation without Trinidad and Tobago was not deemed to be desirable, did the ministers not realize that granting early independence to Jamaica would in essence encourage the Trinidadian leadership to follow suit — in effect, leaving the British Government stuck with the remaining eight territories? Why did Macmillan and Maudling contravene the advice received from the Federation's legal advisers, particularly when months later Maudling confided to Viscount Kilmuir that 'this recent precedent on the secession issue will no doubt be brought to the [Rhodesia and Nyasaland constitutional] discussions'?[39] This was a clear sign of his concern with the potentially disruptive influence the Caribbean conundrum might exert on the Central African scenario. However, an overriding desire to deter any accusation of colonial highhandedness, which if necessary the Jamaicans could have aired at any minute, did have an impact; particularly at a time when members of the Cabinet were quite fond of characterizing Britain as 'an enlightened colonial power'.[40] Already during this period several voices in the Colonial Office had adopted the notion that 'it would be irritating, but not disastrous if Barbados and the small islands are left on our hands'.[41] Consistent with this premise, in the event of Trinidad and Tobago's withdrawal, the British Government could always claim that no really vital British interest was at stake and that it did its 'best to give them independence within the Federation, the break-up of which was not our fault'.[42]

A few years later, in a retrospective interview on his tenure as colonial secretary, Maudling revealed that he 'felt early on that Eric Williams was not prepared to carry on the Federation, he was taking Trinidad out and that was that'.[43] This means that Maudling had travelled to the Eastern Caribbean convinced that Trinidad and Tobago's participation in a new federal experiment was highly unlikely and that in the future he might have to deal with the Little Eight on their own. It made no sense then to delay Jamaica's independence when most indications suggested Trinidad and Tobago would eventually leave the existing Federation; hence, the British Government did not have much to gain from dilatory tactics. Maudling's recommendation to the Colonial Policy Committee, advocating the enactment of an enabling bill 'to deal with the West Indies Federation',[44] acknowledged that reality. In a submission to the Lord Chancellor, a few days before his trip, Maudling expounded on the need to approve that legislation as it would confer on the Colonial Office authority to 'make changes in territorial constitutions in consequence of the withdrawal of [units] from the Federation'.[45] The intention behind the soon-to-be-drafted 1962 West Indies Act,[46] as the colonial secretary suggested, was 'to put the various West Indian houses in order'[47] and thus to 'disentangle the present muddle in the Caribbean'.[48] Essentially, the passing of this bill not only signalled the passing away of the old Federation of the West Indies but also Britain's subtle acceptance that Trinidad and Tobago would inevitably go it alone. The future of the Little Eight was now hanging in the balance.

6

The Little Eight Scenario

> We have been educated for the past three hundred years for self-government. All we in the Windward, Leeward and Barbados want to know is when is the examination.
>
> *Errol Barrow, 1962*

The colonial secretary's visit to the Eastern Caribbean, although limited to Port-of-Spain and Bridgetown, began in earnest on January 14, 1962. In hindsight, Maudling would contend that he had embarked on this trip with the specific purpose of advising the Federal Cabinet that 'that was the end' and seeing 'what best could be salvaged from the wreckage'.[1] One of the most useful pieces of advice tendered to Maudling during this brief but intense period came from the St. Lucian economist Sir Arthur Lewis.[2] Although promoting the inclusion of Trinidad and Tobago in any federal arrangement, Professor Lewis confirmed what numerous confidential despatches streaming from the archipelago were already suggesting, namely that the likelihood of Trinidad and Tobago joining in another federation was very slim.[3] Lewis, however, raised with Hugh Fraser the concept of unitary statehood, as he believed Maudling was to be confronted with that option at his upcoming meeting with Eric Williams. After a close study of the premier's private demeanour and public speeches following the Jamaican referendum,[4] Lewis concluded that,

[Williams] would prefer 'association' with other territories to going it alone, but will go alone if he does not get his terms. 'Association' does not mean federation. It means a unitary state, with the other territories having the status of Tobago. He knows this will not be acceptable to all the other territories. He would be content to have Grenada and St. Vincent come in alone; St. Lucia and Dominica too if they so desire. He will probably ask for a dowry as the price of taking any of the smaller islands into association; and will probably refuse if there is no dowry.[5]

Undoubtedly, the meeting between Maudling and Williams attracted overwhelming attention.[6] Yet it proved rather anti-climactic, as merely a few hours earlier, the General Council of the People's National Movement (PNM) proclaimed that Trinidad and Tobago would 'proceed forthwith to national independence, along with any island which wished to join her in a unitary state'.[7] Some voices immediately characterized that development as another ploy by the 'little doctor,' as Macleod had often referred to Williams privately,[8] to undermine the visit of the colonial secretary and to show 'who is boss around here'.[9] Maudling took it in his stride. The minutes from their private discussions show a confident Williams, emboldened by his recent electoral victory,[10] firmly advocating the unification of the Little Eight with Trinidad and Tobago.

During the course of their conversation Williams described in glowing terms the advantages he saw in a unitary state. The premier suggested to the colonial secretary in no uncertain terms that under unitary statehood there would be a 'taut civil service' in contrast to what he perceived as a 'wasteful number of jobs,' under the outgoing Federation, and a 'rational financial and development policy'.[11] Referring to the case of Tobago, Williams illustrated the full extent of his proposition. His prolonged delineation of Tobago's local authority, which had no power over fiscal matters and in effect functioned as an agency of the Central Government in Port-of-Spain, left no ambiguities as to what the neighbouring islands could expect. At the same time, the archival record reveals another side to these proposals. Williams denounced his serious concern that 'under federation his political enemies, having lost Trinidad, might engineer to take control of the federal government'[12] and that, he added, 'would be intolerable'.[13] The premier agreed that 'under a unitary state this could not happen, as the PNM would have a better chance of organisation in the other islands'.[14] Following their meeting Maudling scribbled in his diary 'this all sounded rather sinister!'[15] Although the colonial secretary privately conceded that Williams was 'a man of great brilliance' with whom he 'enjoyed very much dealing',[16] the latter's apparent paranoia was not particularly encouraging. It most certainly clouded the prospects of his plan ever garnering serious regional support. Yet, as becomes apparent below, the possibility of adopting this set of proposals and thus fostering a union would not be dismissed altogether by the British Cabinet, in particular by the members of the Colonial Policy Committee.

In the light of the testimony from Professor Lewis it was highly unlikely that the chief ministers would have accepted Williams's invitation, which essentially amounted to an asphyxiating administrative straightjacket. As recently as the preceding day Lewis, who by then had met privately with each chief minister, had already revealed to the colonial secretary that 'no government would enter [into] unitary statehood with Trinidad; Bird and Barrow[17] would sooner be dead'.[18] If, as Professor Lewis had suggested a fortnight earlier, 'Barrow, Bird and Williams are the only three who matter'[19] the unitary proposition was in trouble. Clearly, with a majority of that triumvirate firmly against it, the idea of union with Trinidad and Tobago was really a non-starter.

The archival evidence now available suggests the advice the colonial secretary was by then receiving from his senior civil servants was also unfavourable towards the unitary option. Ambler Thomas, Douglas Williams and Sir John Stow,[20] for instance, all agreed that Trinidad and Tobago's annexation of some or all her neighbouring territories would not necessarily prove the best option either for the British Government or for the Little Eight themselves, the main argument being that even if unitary statehood, on Williams's terms, became acceptable to various territories there was bound to be dissension. What would happen to the disaffected islands? The threat of possible fragmentation did have a clear and decisive impact on this preliminary assessment. Additionally, the prospect of having to offer Eric Williams a hefty dowry while coercing as many as possible of the small territories into unitary statehood would, almost certainly, create friction between the Colonial Office and the Treasury. Another important reality confronting Maudling was that, with the Federal Cabinet in shambles[21] and the Trinidadian premier set on independence, the chief ministers of the remaining islands were now beginning to wield more influence than ever before. If the constitutional knot was to be disentangled, their active participation and advice had to be sought and, more importantly, their views understood. Consequently, the first official exchange between them and the colonial secretary merits close consideration.

In preparation for their meeting with Maudling the chief ministers, in close consultation with Professor Lewis, drafted an outline of a federal constitution for the eight territories. Their project rested on two fundamental premises, namely the establishment of a customs union area with freedom of movement for the inhabitants of the archipelago. At least by this stage, they reached a broad consensus on critical matters such as federalizing the judiciary, the magistrates, the police and the prisons; while at the same time pre-selecting Bridgetown as the federal capital. Although most of these issues were to be revisited in the coming months, this early congeniality confirmed that federation as a concept, even after the defections of Jamaica and Trinidad and Tobago, still enjoyed considerable support within the colonial political leadership. Some voices have gone as far as suggesting that their initial agreement had more to do with collective shock and utter uneasiness over an uncertain future than with a principled vote of confidence in the federal idea itself. While intellectually provocative, this contention implicitly oversimplifies the robust hold that for so many decades the federal ideal had exercised over the archipelago's intellectual and political elites. While baffled by the recent failure, the archival evidence shows that by this stage the political leadership throughout the remaining eight territories saw federation as an ideal worth fighting for. The position expressed by the colonial administrator of Antigua, during the opening session of the local Legislative Council lucidly encapsulated this feeling,

> A year ago I referred to the historic events then taking place in the West Indies. Alas, during the past year those hopes have been shaken by events outside our control. Now the future is uncertain but this Government is still convinced that Federation of these territories offers the best means by which West Indians can achieve independent nationhood and the only opportunity open to the people of this territory to advance to sovereign citizenship.[22]

If a federation of the Little Eight was to blossom, by sheer force of political gravity the centre of the solar system had to shift to Barbados. Whether her most prominent leadership was willing to assume the responsibility that such a role entailed represented one of the most crucial questions. Unlike the premier of Antigua, who from the outset had pledged his help in 'refashioning the Federation',[23] Errol Barrow's initial reaction had been slow. Scholarly reappraisals of Barbados recent history cite a few reasons of relevance behind his cautious response.[24] Having won the recent 1961 election on a minority vote Barrow and his colleagues were walking a very thin tightrope.[25] Clearly his adversaries had enough power to thwart the implementation of his legislative programme, which had been at the heart of his party's narrow electoral success. A stagnant economy together with high unemployment complicated the picture even further. This explains why the initial priorities of the leadership of the Barbados Democratic Labour Party (DLP) were solidifying its political base, reconciling itself with the powerful sugar and mercantile interests, abating unemployment and reactivating the local economy. Barrow's first days in power hardly allowed him any time to consider extraterritorial affairs. Arthur Lewis, in his aforementioned letter to Hugh Fraser confirmed this impression,

> When I first met him (on December 9–10, 1961) he had not yet read any of the documents or given serious thoughts to the problems.[26]

Ironically it had been Barrow's own party that in 1960 had unanimously approved and delivered a resolution to Iain Macleod stating an unwavering commitment to the 'maintenance and strengthening of the Federation of the West Indies'.[27] Nonetheless, in spite of his early sluggishness, by the time the colonial secretary finally visited the region, Barrow had given his conditional acceptance to the idea of establishing a new federation made up exclusively of the Little Eight. Most certainly unrelenting pressure from other chief ministers, especially from his long-time friend Vere Bird and the proven federationist fibre of the DLP's top brass, allayed his original misgivings.

The archival record suggests that Maudling returned to London, late in January, eager to brief his colleagues in the Colonial Policy Committee.[28] A few days after arriving, he met them at Admiralty House. The only subjects on their agenda were Kenya and the Eastern Caribbean, two of the most critical colonial issues then confronting the British Government. Present at this meeting were Prime Minister Harold Macmillan, the Lord Chancellor Viscount Kilmuir, the Secretary of State for Commonwealth Relations Duncan Sandys, the Joint Parliamentary Secretary of State for Foreign Affairs the Marquise of Lansdowne, the Paymaster General Henry Brooke, a representative from the Treasury and, of course, Colonial Secretary Maudling.[29] In what amounted to a de facto recognition of Trinidad and Tobago's right to independence, Maudling immediately recommended the approval of an Order in Council, officially dissolving the West Indies

Federation.[30] On the future constitutional status of the remaining eight territories, Maudling offered a conservative assessment of the proposals put forward by the chief ministers in conjunction with Professor Lewis. The following exposition represented the first comprehensive indication of what his thoughts were after returning from Port-of-Spain,

> I regard the proposed new Federation of the Eight as a promising initiative and a preferable alternative to disintegration of the smaller islands into separate units; but it requires much more study. The project was hastily prepared and it is necessary to be assured that it holds the prospect of stability.… . It is essential that there should be some real prospect of the new Federation attaining some degree of economic and financial viability. There must be in particular a strong central government with overriding powers of financial control and economic development… . It is clear to me that it will not be possible to agree to the recommendation of the chief ministers that the new Federation of the Eight should come into existence during this summer on the basis of it being an independent state.[31]

The intense discussion that followed this opening statement deserves careful analysis. The essential substance of that dialogue is contained in the succeeding extracts from the meeting's confidential minutes.

> It would not be practical to withhold the grant of independence to Trinidad, but it should be our object to ensure that as many as possible of the smaller islands were grouped with Trinidad in a unitary state. The advantages to Trinidad are that the accession of other islands would help counteract the rapid growth of the Indian population in Trinidad itself. The advantages to Britain would be that such a unitary state might be financially viable and would reduce to some extent the subsidy required to keep the smaller islands going. A separate federation of the smaller islands should not be ruled out but would need careful examination in the light of the scheme that they are now understood to be preparing.[32]

> There would be no question of automatic Commonwealth membership for West Indian territories attaining independence, although we had already entered into an understanding with Jamaica to support her application. There would be particular difficulty about Commonwealth membership for British Guiana. No formal procedure for Commonwealth membership had ever been laid down; this had advantages and disadvantages, but at least it makes it possible to look at each case on merit.[33]

It could be argued that it would be justifiable for HMG, in spite of the dissolution of the Federation, to grant independence to all the smaller islands of the West Indies as well as to Trinidad and leave them to work out their future. As against this, the Government could not altogether avoid a moral obligation to avert the chaos and bankruptcy in the smaller islands that might well ensue. In the particular case of Trinidad it would be difficult to make conditions about independence in the form of requiring her to accept responsibility for her smaller neighbours in view of the fact that for all practical purposes she was independent already.[34]

Before adjourning the proceedings, the Colonial Policy Committee endorsed the following course of action,

Agreed that the West Indies Federation should be dissolved.

Took note that the colonial secretary would arrange for legislation that would enable HMG, by Order in Council, to provide for the dissolution of the Federation, and to create at the same time an organisation under a commissioner to maintain existing federal services.

Agreed that independence should be conferred on Trinidad and that a conference to discuss the details should be arranged in the near future.

Invited the colonial secretary to urge upon Trinidad the advantage to her of associating as many as possible of the smaller islands with her in an independent state.

Invited the colonial secretary to circulate a memorandum to the Cabinet to be taken on Tuesday, February 6, 1962, outlining proposals for constitutional development in the West Indies in the light of this discussion.

Invited the colonial secretary and the chief secretary to the Treasury to arrange for an examination of the economic problems involved in the constitutional development of the West Indies.[35]

These recommendations and the points raised during the discussion conflicted with the advice given by the senior civil servants in the Colonial Office. This apparent hiatus raises an unavoidable question, why had the annexation project raised far more effervescence and interest at Cabinet level than at the Colonial Office? Attempting to answer it goes to the heart of the colonial policy-making process. This instance is a remarkable illustration of the kind of discontinuities influencing that process. Far from homogeneous or monolithic, the variety of aims before London brought forth a plethora of competing views and ideas clashing against each other. At first glance, the ministers' enthusiastic response to the annexation project hardly makes any sense. Indeed, the case against it seems quite compelling. If examined against the aspirations of the colonial leadership and, equally important, from financial and administrative perspectives, then annexation to Trinidad and Tobago would lead to a perilous course. The contention that it would have proven less of a financial burden than a federation of the remaining territories was highly misleading. Unitary statehood would have meant a uniform salary scale all through the archipelago. Civil servants in the neighbouring islands would be entitled to Trinidad salaries at an extra cost, which *circa* 1962, would have elevated the yearly expense in salaries to about $13 million British West Indian dollars (some £2,204,733).[36] The minute savings derived from an absence of federal ministers, roughly 2 per cent of the estimated annual budget, would be inconsequential if compared to the upkeep of the civil service alone. Yet, essential public services in critical areas such as health care, education and overall infrastructure would also require extraterritorial uniformity. Was all this to be financed by local taxes levied from Port-of-Spain or, to a large extent, by foreign aid mostly coming from the British, American and Canadian Treasuries?

The ministers' assertion that unitary statehood would reduce British subsidies in the region rested on rather faulty or insufficient evidence. The fundamental premise behind it was that, as Maudling himself suggested in his paper to the Colonial Policy Committee, Trinidad was 'financially self-supporting and has substantial economic resources and potential, particularly in oil'.[37] However, in spite of this over-optimistic forecast, the evidence now emerging suggests that Trinidad and Tobago's economy *circa* 1962 was somewhat unstable, with unemployment on the rise and clear signs of recession.[38] Even more alarming was the atmosphere of heightened racial tension which was beginning to aggravate the already uncertain picture. Under these circumstances unitary statehood, without substantial allowances from London, might have led to bankruptcy and as such fostered regional instability. This self-evident conflict, between the economic realities of Trinidad and Tobago and how the British Government understood them to be, resurfaced in November 1962 during the financial settlement negotiations between London and Port-of-Spain preceding Trinidad and Tobago's independence.[39]

Running parallel to these matters was the issue of administrative micro-management. The intelligence reports openly confirmed what Professor Lewis had already suggested, namely that the leadership of the neighbouring islands deplored the intense degree of centralization which by definition a unitary state entailed. The reasons behind such an aversion were quite obvious. Most of the chief ministers, particularly Bird and Barrow, felt very strongly that their territories would be overlooked if local leaders were deprived of the initiative in social, economic and other matters. Their aspiration was to retain that responsibility. They had seen and heard much that was disquieting about unitary arrangements: not far away were Anguilla, Nevis, Redonda, Barbuda, the Grenadines and even Tobago, and, without exception, the history of these far-flung units had been one of neglect.[40] Another powerful element distancing the chief ministers from the concept of unitary statehood was, in a sense, the electoral process. Constituencies throughout the archipelago were pressing, rather vigorously, for modernization. By effectively compelling their local representatives to exercise their newly gained authority, the prospects of unification, on Williams's terms, considerably dwindled. And, of course, the unwillingness of the colonial politicians to surrender that power made union with Trinidad and Tobago even less likely. But why were the British ministers endorsing such an idea?

The answer to this question lies, for the most part, in a *mélange* of Cold War considerations. Only if seen against London's legitimate geopolitical concerns did the unitary project make some sense. Clearly, those positioned higher up in the ministerial pecking order did not lose sight of these particulars. The archival evidence now accessible reveals that, at least during this period, the East Indian communities both in Trinidad and Tobago and in British Guiana were perceived in London, although more so in Washington, as a potential focus for subversive or so-called anti-Western activities. This explains, albeit partly, the apparent inclination to neutralize the clout of the East Indian community in Trinidad and Tobago by means of unitary statehood. And even more pressing, as the historical record shows, was the eagerness to contain the impact that events in British Guiana might have had on the political attitudes of the East Indian community in Trinidad and Tobago itself.[41] A vast corpus of newly declassified documents shows that the British Government was delaying the independence of British Guiana in a deliberate attempt to comply with the wishes of the Kennedy Administration. This angle must be looked at in some detail in order to appreciate more fully the appeal that unitary statehood was enjoying amongst influential members of the Colonial Policy Committee.

As suggested earlier, London's chief concern was how to withdraw from its political and financial responsibilities in the area both swiftly and effectively, without any major embarrassment. However, for that type of political disengagement to succeed, the British Government could not afford to brush aside Washington's concerns. After evaluating a wide array of documents pertaining to the Colonial Policy Committee and to the Office of the British Prime Minister, it becomes evident that during this period the British Government was struggling to reconcile contrasting transatlantic expectations.[42] The historical record demonstrates that British Guiana, for example, represented one of the most sensitive points of contention in the so-called Anglo-American special relationship. The issue of how and when to withdraw from British Guiana proved to be one of astounding difficulty for the British Government and, not surprisingly, played a role in London's articulation of a new policy towards the Little Eight. The constant uneasiness and clashes with Cheddi Jagan and the incisive American intrusion exacerbated the nature of the challenge. It was indeed the prospect of British Guiana developing on the same lines as Cuba that was causing most concern to the US Government. The pressure was so intense that late in March 1962, Hugh Fraser, on his way back from Georgetown, would be asked by the American State Department to stop in Washington. There Fraser met President Kennedy for over two hours to discuss in detail the political future of that colony. The records available from that discussion, at least those preserved in the National Archives in London, suggest the president and his national security team were adamant in their request to postpone any British withdrawal at least until after the removal of Jagan from power.[43] Less than six weeks after these thorough discussions, Macmillan, along with Alec Douglas Home, also visited Washington and met with President Kennedy in an attempt to improve the mechanisms for Anglo-American consultation in addressing the Caribbean's colonial conundrum.[44]

Before superimposing these transatlantic considerations on the Little Eight scenario, another matter, closely intertwined although often overlooked, must be addressed and that is the acute tension that lay beneath the seemingly close Anglo-American partnership. Missing this element would lead to a gross oversimplification of the complexities embedded in this process of colonial disengagement. Fresh archival records have unearthed evidence suggesting that during this period both the British and the American Governments sharply disagreed over crucial issues such as the British Independent Nuclear Deterrent, Berlin, and the transfer of political authority in allegedly troublesome spots like the Far East and the Caribbean.[45] This quiet animosity was further aggravated, to some extent, by the attitude the Kennedy Administration had adopted since taking office. Ever so wary of the 'hour of maximum danger' the president, especially after the embarrassing mishandling of the Bay of Pigs crisis in Cuba the previous spring, both in his rhetoric and foreign policy usually expressed himself resolutely embattled for the all-out nuclear showdown he and his advisers clearly expected.[46] It is no secret that the British Cabinet itself was deeply divided on how to accommodate, if at all, the views entertained in Washington. In the case of Cuba itself, for example, even after the missile crisis of October 1962 the position in London was to resist any pressure from the US Government to break off diplomatic relations with Havana.[47] The historical record has also uncovered a fascinating side to this Anglo-American contention, in the guise of a rather resentful Macmillan, barely a fortnight after the meeting of the Colonial Policy Committee, accusing the Americans 'not of colonialism but Machiavellianism' and 'cynicism'.[48]

Certainly these considerations, some of which were unbeknown to most civil servants in the Colonial Office, did exert enormous influence at the Cabinet level. Indeed the substance of what the members of the Colonial Policy Committee discussed and preliminarily concluded, reflected these pressures. Essentially unitary statehood, if seen against this background, represented a reasonable quid pro quo by which Washington could preserve the stability of the area on its own terms while London oversaw the details of a complete withdrawal. More pressingly, this new and predominantly

Afro-Caribbean nation would effectively isolate British Guiana while neutralizing the allegedly extreme elements of the East Indian community in Trinidad and Tobago. Accommodating or adjusting to American imperatives, at least for the British Government, meant that the US Government would be expected to more than fill the gap between what the unitary state required economically and what the British Government, with all its African exertions, was able to supply in development capital. Yet, in spite of all this, could the British Cabinet blatantly ignore the demands raised by the political and for the most part trade union leadership of the Little Eight? The historical record tends to convey that it was not possible. Even if these geopolitical considerations did play a seminal role, the British Government was facing a strong surge of colonial pressure that simply could not be overlooked. As the next chapters illustrate, while the concept of unitary statehood did attract considerable support from the British ministers, competing forces were already taking on a momentum of their own. Less than a week after the meeting of the Colonial Policy Committee, Sir John Stow warned the Colonial Office that the tide of events in the area was moving quite rapidly and that the pressure on Barrow was mounting.

> Barrow is under pressure here to get a move on with the establishment of a Federation of the Eight. I have tried to convince him that it is very difficult, if not impossible, for the Secretary of State to give his support to such a Federation now. He appears, nonetheless, to be convinced that the Secretary of State is more inclined to back an association of the smaller islands with Trinidad rather than a Federation of the Eight. I understand privately, he has sent off a telegram to the Chief Ministers of the other islands asking them if it would be a good idea for him to approach Gaitskell, with a view of sending a delegation of Opposition MP's to attend the conference he proposes to convene in the week that starts on the 26th February. The reason for this move is apparently that Barrow feels that the present British Government is unable emotionally and ideologically to comprehend the attitude of the Eight towards federation and eventual independence … he is under pressure and may do anything.[49]

Similar tension can be appreciated in the telegram Ebenezer Joshua, chief minister of St. Vincent, sent to the Colonial Office, 'we join in protest against the quietude or slight at the proposals of eight territories desiring to continue [in a] federation'.[50] The chief minister of St. Kitts-Nevis-

Anguilla, Charles Southwell, echoed this feeling:

> The Government and people [of] this territory most concerned [about the] impending state [of the] Federation. Overwhelming public support for immediate and independent new Federation of [the] eight units. Therefore [we] propose [that it is] essential [that] we meet urgently this month, with firm constitutional and economic proposals, for an early inauguration of the new Federation, so that HMG can be quickly asked to arrange [a] conference for putting our wishes into effect.[51]

The chief ministers also had their strategies. Clearly their plan was to push as hard as possible for the federal arrangement they were then envisioning. Maudling's first statement to the House of Commons on the future of the archipelago suggested that this pressure did not go totally unheeded. Maudling asserted that, 'the [proposed] federation of Barbados, the Leeward and Windward Islands represents a promising development'.[52] The Earl of Perth, replying to a question posed by Lord Watson, concurred with Maudling.

> My Lords, the position is that the Premier of Barbados and the Chief Ministers of the other seven territories have themselves suggested that they should form a federation. In the view of HMG this suggestion is a promising one. I understand they are meeting together this week to consider this suggestion further. HMG welcomes this move. Clearly a plan with a reasonable chance of success must be worked out before HMG can be committed to encouraging its formation.[53]

This first public reaction from London should be seen, for the most part, in the light of that vigorous colonial undercurrent. Although privately leaning towards unitary statehood, the British Cabinet attempted to reconcile all its conflicting aims. Any inflexible position at this stage might have derailed any possibility of achieving the fundamental objective, which was withdrawing from the area. The upcoming Eastern Caribbean Conference, staged in Marlborough House (London), would be an outgrowth of this conciliatory policy. But, as became evident soon thereafter, tensions between the Colonial Office and the Treasury as well as discrepancies between the colonial politicians themselves acutely swayed the process.

7

The Marlborough House Conference

Indeed it would in all but name be a unitary state.

Reginald Maulding, 1962

The colonial effervescence triggered by Trinidad's departure led to the first formal meeting between the chief ministers of the Little Eight, held in Bridgetown between February 26 and March 3, 1962. It is essential to analyze the decisions made by the regional leadership there and how the British Cabinet reacted to them. Missing the richness of this interplay would obscure the wider picture. Although some voices have suggested that Barrow still by then was 'playing by ear',[1] the archival record reveals that he took the initiative of inviting his fellow chief ministers and even the leaders of the two opposition parties in Barbados to this conference. The presence of the regionally acclaimed trades union leader Frank Walcott[2] (by then president of the Barbados Workers Union), together with a dignified public inauguration, added to this environment of congeniality. This all generated a sense of optimism and enthusiasm. For the most part, conventional accounts suggest that this gathering 'made a firm beginning,' that 'it achieved much' and thus 'provided a firm basis' for subsequent negotiations.[3] The bulk of the decisions reached rather hurriedly in Port-of-Spain, barely a month earlier, were confirmed here. For instance, the chief ministers agreed to hand over the audit, customs and excise departments to a federal centre. They endorsed once again the idea of maintaining company law, external affairs, internal movement of persons, judicial services, postal services, police, prisons, regulation of trade between federal units and telecommunications (other than broadcasting, television and territorial phone services) under federal control.[4] They agreed, on a preliminary basis, that the federal government should derive its revenues from import duties, postal services, court fees, currency profit and income tax.[5] Even more importantly, the conference acknowledged that the new federation should be, from its inception, an independent state within the Commonwealth.[6] Without a doubt the dynamo behind this seemingly harmonious meeting was the chief ministers' strong sense of urgency. Although not overtly apparent in the documents, they did share an implicit desire to avoid being commandeered by London. Taking the initiative of convening this gathering seemed the safest way of preventing that from happening. Furthermore, the chief ministers were under the impression that Maudling's hesitant performance at their previous meeting in Port-of-Spain meant that the British Government was both uninformed and unprepared to deal with this crisis and that the sooner they came up with a project the easier it would be to garner London's favour. The specific wording of the only resolution approved during this conference reflected the decisive demeanour of the chief ministers:

> The Conference of [the] Premier of Barbados, Chief Ministers [of the] Leeward and Windward [Islands] with [their] Advisers in plenary session desires to convey to you [the Colonial Secretary] our unanimous decision to enter into a Federation of Eight without any hiatus.[7]

The chief ministers added to their statement,

> That the Secretary of State for the Colonies should be asked to summon a Conference of the eight unit territories concerned, to meet in London before the dissolution of the existing Federation, to make arrangements for the establishment of the new Federation.[8]

Throughout the following weeks the colonial leadership kept pressing relentlessly for the convening of a constitutional conference in London. Some of the most salient illustrations of the Little Eight's offensive are revealed, for example, in a moving letter from the political leader of the St. Vincent Labour Party (SVLP) and in a memorandum the chief minister of St. Kitts-Nevis-Anguilla sent to his colleagues late in March 1962. In his message to H. Burrowes, colonial administrator of St. Vincent, Milton Cato asked, on behalf of the people of the territory, for inclusion in any forthcoming constitutional negotiation. His letter made direct reference to a mass gathering held at Market Square in Kingstown, in which over a thousand Vincentians demanded participation in any such discussion.[9] Charles Southwell, on the other hand, kept insisting that,

> Now that the Conference report has been issued and received I am anxious that we should make a joint and adamant call on the Rt. Hon. Secretary of State for the Colonies to convene a Conference of the Eight to discuss the proposals without delay. We should insist, by all means in our power, on immediate Federation leading to Independence.[10]

These requests were sustained by a widely held expectation that some type of talks with the Colonial Office would before long ensue. The historical record conveys that the British Cabinet was feeling pressure not only from the Eastern Caribbean to act along federal lines, but also from influential civil servants and even from a former British prime minister. Sir John Stow was expressing, far more emphatically than before, his confidence in a federal project for the eight territories. In a telegram to Maudling, almost a fortnight after the Bridgetown Conference, Stow touched upon the advantages he saw in advocating the establishment of a federation similar to the one envisioned by the area's political leadership.[11] Only a few days later Lord Hailes, still the nominal head of the apoplectic West Indies Federation, adopted a similar line in a letter to Ambler Thomas. Therein the outgoing governor general concluded,

> I strongly feel that the chances of achieving a satisfactory union of Trinidad and all the Leeward and Windward Islands are slight and that a partial grouping would be unsatisfactory. We should do nothing to encourage efforts in that direction so long as there is a chance of forming a viable Federation of the Eight. It seems to me now to offer the best chance of avoiding indefinite fragmentation in the Eastern Caribbean and of achieving political and economic stability.[12]

What especially matters about these observations is that, presumably, any opinion entertained by Lord Hailes had the potential of exerting special influence at the highest echelons of the British Government. Lord Hailes was no ordinary civil servant. His private papers and, in particular, his personal correspondence reveal a close and enduring relation with the likes of former British Prime Minister Sir Anthony Eden, the Chancellor of the Exchequer R. A. Butler and, although to a lesser extent, with Harold Macmillan. Indeed the evidence now available suggests that even after his appointment, Lord Hailes remained intimately associated with that circle, tendering more often than not political advice and counsel.[13] Another angle now emerging, not only from the Hailes archival collection but also from the records of the Colonial Office and the Cabinet, is Sir Anthony Eden's palpable interest in the Eastern Caribbean's constitutional crisis. The immediate explanation for his curiosity lies in the fact that, immediately after his resignation in the aftermath of the Suez crisis, Eden had decided to spend most of his retirement in the minute island of Bequia, off the southern coast of St. Vincent.[14] His future biographers must elucidate, in the light of all the newly available documentation, whether Eden commanded any serious influence in Whitehall during the Macmillan years. Nonetheless, what clearly falls within the scope of this study is an evaluation of the recommendations the former prime minister was by then making. As early as February 11, 1962, barely a week after the Colonial Policy Committee met for the first time to discuss the status of the Little Eight, Eden confided in Macmillan:

> Having been down to Trinidad for a few days and seen several politicians from the defunct Federal Government as well as those with present powers, I thought that you might like a few comments. Williams, probably the most intelligent among them, is convinced of troubled times ahead for the islands. Even allowing for some wishful thinking, I think he is right. For the Little Eight, some form of federation is probably the only course, though it may be expensive. But, and this is important, these little island governments must not be given any more powers until they are in federation and have made some show of it. Otherwise you will have a number of little dictators and endless trouble with them. Jagan has his imitators. These would like more powers to impose the control they would otherwise lose at the next electoral opportunity. Ours in St. Vincent are not exceptional. They have already voted themselves salaries free of income tax and muddled the sugar position. This does not matter much, provided they do not get enough power to enable them to ignore the people's will as they would like.[15]

By April 13, only two days after the Colonial Policy Committee had resumed its deliberations on the crisis in the Caribbean archipelago (the sole item in the agenda), Eden once again made known his impressions of what the region should look like. While there is still no conclusive answer on whether this concomitance was coincidental or not, it is difficult to believe that a man of Eden's experience, stature and connections was completely unaware of the Cabinet's inner timetables and processes. On that occasion, in a letter to Maudling, the former Tory leader openly suggested a course of action:

> With some hesitation I write to you on the subject of the Little Eight. I do not pretend to be any kind of expert on West Indian affairs, but it does seem that this is an instance where we ought to do everything we properly can to encourage the Little Eight to hold together. Admittedly they will be feeble then, but they are very likely to become chaotic if they drift apart. Moreover, may it not be salutary for both Trinidad and Jamaica, if the Little Eight could make a good show together? Admittedly, the chances of this might not be very great, but any alternative seems to be worse. Patrick Hailes' (Lord Hailes) opinion would obviously carry the most weight on this question. I think myself that if encouragement is given to a Federation of the Little Eight, it should be quite clear that the rewards must only accompany the completion of the exercise and not its opening. I am sure that these small islands should not be given any more power at the present time.[16]

As shall be seen, Eden's recurrent theme of encouraging a federation with a strong centre, together with his explicit lack of confidence in the colonial leadership did strike a chord with several ministers in the British Cabinet. The archival record reveals that after the Bridgetown Conference, the Colonial Office was monitoring even more closely the events unfolding in the area. By the end of March, senior civil servants, under the chairmanship of Douglas Williams, had already discussed the proposals put forward by the colonial politicians.[17] The intention behind this preliminary evaluation was to suggest possible modifications along the lines of what some already referred to as the 'criteria of the Colonial Office'.[18] The substance behind these principles came to light, rather vividly, in a paper Maudling put forward for the consideration of the Colonial Policy Committee.[19] After two months of frantic deliberations both in the archipelago and in the Colonial Office, the discussions reverted back to the Cabinet.[20] Although on this occasion Macmillan did not participate, the Colonial Policy Committee met once again to evaluate the latest developments in the Eastern Caribbean. Present were the Lord Chancellor, who hosted the meeting, Duncan Sandys, the Marquise of Lansdowne, Anthony Barber on behalf of the Treasury, and Maudling in his capacity as colonial secretary. And contrary to what happened during their previous exchange, Maudling was now in full control. His submission constituted the sole basis for discussion and the Committee unanimously stood behind him. His initial statement spelled out what British policy should be following the Bridgetown Conference.[21] In no uncertain terms Maudling argued as follows:

> I should say that my general conclusion is that some kind of association between the eight territories would be preferable to their continuing to exist as eight separate administrations… . The only alternative possibility would be that individually they should accept the offer of the premier of Trinidad to join him in a unitary state. This was the course [that] seemed to find most favour when the matter was discussed by the C.P.C. [Colonial Policy Committee] on the 2nd February and it clearly has many attractions … I am now very doubtful whether there is much prospect of its happening at any rate within any period ahead we can foresee … I am therefore in favour of some kind of closer association among the Eight in preference to the other possible courses immediately open to us … I would not rule out the possibility that if we can devise such an association and make it work, it might be possible within the not too distant future for it to enter into some kind of union with Trinidad.[22]

In the light of this initial suggestion Maudling literally dissected the chief ministers' enhanced proposals, expounding on what he considered their 'serious weaknesses'.[23] His concern stemmed from a sharp distrust of the scheme's economic and political structures.[24] These misgivings went to the heart of the proposals. Maudling identified the following constitutional failings:

> Although they envisage the new Federal Government having greater powers than the present one, particularly in finance and economic development, they still leave very considerable powers in the hands of the units. In form, the new Federation is a replica of the old, with all the paraphernalia of nine Queen Representatives and about thirty five ministers to handle the affairs of less than 700,000 people. This is, altogether, too much harness for so small a horse. Indeed, it is clear to me that the unit ministers, although claiming to support the idea of a stronger federation, have in fact been at pains to keep a good deal of power in the hands of the units. This is serious.[25]

Only a federation with a robust centre, according to him, could place these territories in a position to attract foreign investment. That would make the islands potentially viable, while averting further fragmentation. However, as becomes apparent below, considerations of a more immediate nature were also swaying Maudling's thoughts. Fresh allegations of misappropriation of public funds by local politicians in, for example, Antigua, Montserrat and Grenada, strengthened his resolve of pressing for that tighter federal centre which could keep the units on a tight leash.[26]

> Information, which has come to light in the past few months, has shown a grave situation developing in the administration of most of the Leeward and Windward Islands. The constitutional changes introduced in 1959, although they fall short of internal self-government, give unit ministers a very considerable degree of control over their own affairs, especially over their own finances .... In practice, however, in most cases the results have been unfortunate. The small island ministers have shown themselves financially irresponsible and administratively incompetent. Antigua is virtually bankrupt. In Montserrat it would seem that most British assistance funds have been utterly misspent. In Grenada the new chief minister — a ruthless demagogic gangster — appears to have incurred considerable sums of unauthorised expenditure and is using all the means, which the courts provide, to resist any proper inquiry. In most cases the unit chief ministers regard any form of political opposition as downright subversion. They take the same view of any advice submitted by civil servants which runs contrary to their views; and most of them have been guilty of interfering improperly with the Civil Service and of making threats against any civil servant who did not appear thoroughly loyal to their party. If the proposals embodied in this report are accepted, they will perpetuate this state of affairs beyond remedy and these small islands will degenerate into little paradises for political boss rule.[27]

Although this paragraph clearly illustrated Maudling's genuine concern, its tone reveals an often forgotten side of these proceedings. This passage, consistent with Eden's position, depicts an overt feeling of complete distrust in the colonial leadership. It seems as if there was an inclination to characterize, somewhat indiscriminately, the colonial leadership as monolithically rotten and incapable. Even though the accusations leveled against some of the local politicians were fully substantiated, Maudling's disdainful tone brings to the fore London's condescending attitude towards the other side. It permeates most of the archival records. Ironically, that patronizing attitude ran counter to what both colonized and colonizers were attempting to achieve: a transfer of constitutional authority and, as such, an open recognition of political maturity. Only a meticulous sociological investigation into the relations between the metropolitan policy-makers and the colonial politicians could possibly attempt to uncover the real nature of that interaction. Although that analytical exercise does not fall within the purview of this study, its relevance lies in the fact that the existence of such tension at a relatively early stage did not bode well for the smooth running of the subsequent negotiations.

In the meantime, Maudling's uneasiness also responded to his dissatisfaction with the proposed economic model. His appreciation was that the chief ministers' financial projections were fundamentally flawed. However, before moving any further, their economic plan deserves a closer look. The scheme before the consideration of the Colonial Policy Committee, as years later Professor Lewis wrote, rested on the principle that political independence had to carry an assurance of financial independence.[28] Therefore, the fundamental aspiration behind it consisted in reducing the islands' dependency on external aid, particularly on the grants-in-aid from the British Treasury, then subsidizing most of these territories' recurrent budgets.[29] The transfer of direct allowances from London was to be tapered down by 15 per cent per annum until 1968, with the expectation that by then the territories would be able to balance their recurrent budgets.[30] In terms of figures, this meant (according to Professor Lewis) that grants-in-aid would decrease from BWI$9 million (approximately £1,520,064) to BWI $2 million (approximately £557,728) over the next five years and then be stabilized at that level.[31] Yet, this overture came with a caveat. The chief ministers were also asking that a similar sum be paid into a capital fund, guaranteed for the next five years at a rate of BWI $7 million per annum (approximately £ 1,182,272), with the purpose of stimulating the economies of the Leeward and Windward Islands.[32] The colonial secretary, refusing to concur with this programme at its face value, considered that,

> In view of the exorbitant demands for aid put forward by the West Indies in the past, it is surprising that they now appear to be contemplating independence in a Federation, with assistance from us of only £1.76 million per annum as compared with the present level of aid which is running at something like £3

million per annum. There is a temptation to accept such an offer at such a bargain price. Appearances here, however, are likely to be deceptive; and it is probable that, having first persuaded us to accept their Federation in principle, the Governments of the Little Eight will then conduct a detailed exercise to prove that £1.76 million is so far from inadequate to their needs. We should also consider whether we have any interest or responsibility in ensuring that Professor Lewis' proposals are based upon reasonable and realistic assumptions.[33]

Maudling was disputing the accuracy of the three basic presumptions ingrained in the chief ministers' model: firstly, that the output of commodities (mostly sugar and bananas) over the next decade would increase by 30 per cent in the Leeward Islands, 35 per cent in the Windward Islands and 36 per cent in Barbados; secondly that there would roughly be a threefold increase in the value of receipts from tourism; and thirdly that the civil service salaries would remain at their present level and would not be allowed to rise with any increases that might occur in other incomes and prices.

In a lengthy exposition on what he saw as the shortcomings of these economic proposals Maudling conclusively suggested to the Colonial Policy Committee,

It is in my view extremely doubtful whether these assumptions are realistic. To be certain on the point would require an examination, which would probably take an expert a month or six weeks to perform. I am advised that the increase in the output of the commodities envisaged by Professor Lewis does in fact appear to be considerably higher than has been achieved over the past decade. Of all the major commodities produced in the area, only bananas have shown a substantial increase, and the output of most other commodities is not only not rising but has, in some cases, fallen substantially. Secondly, there is in Professor Lewis' projections a hidden assumption that any increase in the volume of production will not be counteracted by a fall in price. In fact, however, the principal commodities on which the area is dependent — sugar and bananas — are facing highly uncertain market conditions and prices may well fall over the next few years. Thirdly, Professor Lewis maintains that Civil Service salaries will have to be kept at their present level even though other prices rise. In the smaller islands it is already difficult enough to get civil servants of decent calibre and, as a result, much of the assistance we have given to them has been misspent. In my view, if Professor Lewis' recommendation is implemented, the Civil Service, in their higher levels at any rate, would be in danger of running down completely. On the other hand, his assumption that there might be a threefold increase in incomes derived from tourism may not be out of the question.[34]

In the light of the pressure from the colonial politicians, the members of the Colonial Policy Committee understood that there were three different courses of action available to the British Cabinet. The most fascinating aspect, by far, of this analytical exercise is evaluating the thought process leading the Cabinet to embrace one of these options. This begs the question of what alternatives were open to it. Its choices were in essence quite simple: either rejecting the federal project produced in Bridgetown; unconditionally adopting its recommendations; or producing counter-proposals containing a discernible federal subtext. The possibility of discarding a new federal arrangement altogether was immediately rejected. Conveying the reasoning behind that decision, Maudling argued,

> This course I do not recommend. The idea of some kind of a federation among these units has caught on and for us not to give it some serious consideration will be regarded as a sharp rebuff by the governments concerned.... The result would most probably be that we should have these eight separate units on our hands for an indefinite period. They would have to continue to be heavily grant-in-aided and, in view of the way in which most of them have been mismanaging their affairs, I should under these circumstances have to assume a greater control over their affairs than any which we have had in the past three years. This, although it might be good for the islands, would be a serious reversal of policy and one which would expose us in some quarters to a good deal of criticism. It might also face us with a good deal of unrest in the territories concerned and prove expensive.[35]

An unconditional vote of confidence in this project was never entertained either in the Colonial Office or in the Policy Committee. However, if glanced at superficially, this alternative was somewhat attractive. It should have proven less contentious and, by default, far easier to secure an agreement with the eight territories on the basis of the programme their leaders had already concurred. This would have meant that both parties could have moved ahead with its implementation fairly rapidly. Last, but certainly not least, in following this course of action the British Government would have settled its part of the bargain for external assistance on a scale no higher than that advanced in Bridgetown. Yet, this road was not entirely freed from abysmal difficulties. Setting a precedent for granting bilateral budgetary aid to an independent country with little hope of long-term economic viability was seen by many in the Cabinet as unsatisfactory. But bearing full responsibility for a constitutional project it disapproved of became London's major concern. This road offered no legal recourse, short of the ultimate power to suspend the constitutional arrangements, to intervene in the event of a crisis. The problematic dichotomy of responsibility without power had to be avoided at all costs. However, the theme of nominal accountability without de facto authority did not wither away but resurfaced during the establishment of the arrangement of free association between Britain and the smaller islands. Thus, the only viable alternative open to the British Government was articulating counter-proposals of its own.

Meanwhile, the burning question before the consideration of the Colonial Policy Committee was the extent to which the Bridgetown draft should be amended. On this count Maudling suggested measures which considerably increased the powers of the federal centre, while reducing what he used to call the 'trappings of the units.' Consistent with the advice from Douglas Williams, Maudling argued that the main aim should be to reduce as far as possible the size, functions and power of the local governments. Both he and the senior civil servants in the Colonial Office argued, for example, that eight elected councils should replace the ministerial system envisaged for each unit; and that the legislative and executive functions should be fused therein, with elected commissioners, not premiers, acting as heads of the unit governments.[36] The colonial leadership ultimately endorsed these constitutional measures and allowed for their inclusion in subsequent federal drafts. But what merits close attention at this stage is the clear discrepancy that arose over the economic aspects of the project.

While Maudling kept pressing for further studies on the economic needs of the area, Douglas Williams and his team hailed Bridgetown's economic proposals as 'astoundingly modest' and a 'bargain settlement'.[37] They went as far as contending that 'the alternative to [this] scheme would be eight bankrupt islands'.[38] Douglas Williams, in particular, exclaimed, 'I cannot see that we could do it any cheaper on any other basis, whether within a federation or dealing with individual units'.[39] The fundamental question here is why the colonial secretary and his Cabinet colleagues refused to follow the advice from the senior civil servants on this particular aspect of the project. A superficial glance at the archival record now available brings to the surface two peripheral explanations. First, the ministerial rule that if papers involved financial commitments they should not be put before the Colonial Policy Committee without prior consultation with the Treasury must have accounted for Maudling's caution on the financial question. And secondly, the presence of a high-ranking member of the Treasury in all major meetings may have stiffened his prudence. However, a clearer picture begins to emerge once the documents start revealing that within the Cabinet, more so than in the Colonial Office, there was a strong consensus around the dogmatic view that the economic structure of the federation should be inextricably bound up with its constitutional form. This does not mean that in the Colonial Office these subtleties went unnoticed, but suggests how at the Cabinet level the future of the archipelago was seen from a variety of different angles. New evidence reveals what may have been the most fundamental difference in the way the Colonial Office and the Cabinet saw this conundrum and, not surprisingly, it leads to the theme of unitary statehood. While the chief ministers in Bridgetown and the senior civil servants in the Colonial Office envisioned a federation as the ultimate goal, the ministers in the Cabinet's Colonial Policy Committee still saw unitary statehood as the ultimate policy objective. This aim sprang to life when Maudling admitted that, 'indeed it would in all but name be a unitary state'.[40] He insisted that,

> In fact, though we would not admit as much, they [the counter-proposals] would be designed to make the Federation much more like a unitary state. If we could publish these counter-proposals in advance of a conference, I believe we should find considerable support for them not only in the West Indies but also in this country on both sides of the House.[41]

If combined with the two conditions described above this state of affairs elucidates, for the most part, why there was uneasiness with regard to Professor Lewis's financial projections. There was profound uncertainty on whether that model could hold the islands together and, more importantly, groom them for a potential unitary state, with all the economic demands this entailed. The members of the Colonial Policy Committee agreed with Maudling's ulterior aims and unanimously ratified his counter-proposals.[42] The Committee finally, authorized the colonial secretary to put forward a reply to the memorandum submitted to him by the chief ministers. The counter-proposals would be based on a robust federal centre along with a corresponding diminution of the powers and size of the eight different local administrations.

In following this course of action the British Cabinet made a conscious departure from the precedent Iain Macleod had set during the 1960 talks leading to the Jamaican referendum.[43] The colonial secretary emphatically underlined that,

> [This] course would be a considerable departure from the line we have taken in recent years in dealing with the West Indies, when we have adopted the attitude that it was for them to come forward to us with proposals showing what they wished to achieve…. In view of the parochialism of these small islands, however, it will not be an easy course to carry through successfully and we shall probably have to exert considerable pressure on the Little Eight to get them to accept.[44]

These deliberations, in the short run, cleared the way for convening the Marlborough House Conference, also known as the Eastern Caribbean Federation Conference, held in London between May 9 and 24, 1962. In the long run, however, the policy embraced by the Colonial Policy Committee would in no small measure contribute to the definitive failure of the federal negotiations. Barely two days after the meeting of the Colonial Policy Committee, Sir John Stow, in a confidential despatch to Ambler Thomas, saw clearer than most the potential pitfalls contained in the counter-propositions,

> The application of a brake on further constitutional reform coupled with the application of firm external control of grant-in-aid and Colonial Development and Welfare Funds will certainly lead to considerable frustration and possibly political unrest…. It is not that control is not desirable, it is the way in which that control is applied that is all important.[45]

It was generally felt, both in the Colonial Office and in the eight territories, that more progress could be achieved along these lines if a summit took place in London where binding decisions could be made. Some, such as Ian Turbott, colonial administrator of Antigua, considered that a conference in London would provide a better opportunity 'for bringing some of the more volatile politicians of the Eight down to earth'.[46] Without a doubt, the success or failure of the Marlborough House Conference would depend on how smoothly the Bridgetown propositions were, if at all, reconciled with the British Cabinet's expectations in respect to financial control and power at the federal centre. For the most part, conventional accounts of this Conference have tended to view it as the 'high water mark'[47] of the federal negotiations. Several voices have gone as far as suggesting that the preliminary constitution drafted at Marlborough House, and delineated in Command Paper (Cmnd.) 1746, provided an 'excellent foundation for a new federation'.[48] However this appreciation, if seen in the light of all the newly released documentation, is utterly deceiving.

Possibly the most effective metaphor for describing the metropolitan and colonial parties, at the outset of this Conference, is that of two tectonic plates joined by a thin fault on the verge of implosion. While most bargaining processes usually begin with contrasting claims about what is and what should be, whatever the parties disagree about they usually start out by agreeing on the meanings of the issues at stake.[49] The archival record reveals that this new set of federal negotiations ran counter to that principle. It was clear from the beginning of the proceedings at Marlborough House that the metropolitan and colonial parties hardly understood each other's goals. The transcripts of the various sessions convey that the environment all through this Conference was one of heightened suspicion and acute recrimination for previous failures and disappointments. At the most basic level London's counter-proposals were anathema to what the chief ministers had envisioned in Bridgetown. Surrendering constitutional power at unit level, for example, would certainly have imperilled the political position of the colonial leadership in the insular arena.

The approaching impasse and subsequent failure of the negotiations had more to do with this type of substantive issue than with other aggravating elements. The best way of illustrating where the most critical tension lay is by superimposing on the spirit of the colonial secretary's counter-proposals — namely, that overriding desire to woo the territories into a de facto unitary state — the chief ministers' opening remarks at Marlborough House. For the purpose of this exercise, looking at the Colonial Office's intelligence reports on each chief minister is essential. These intelligence reports, recently declassified, shed considerable light on one of the most disruptive elements throughout this process, which was London's remarkably low opinion of the so-called island politicians.

Table 7.1
Intelligence Reports on the Colonial Leadership *c.*1962

Colonial Politicians	Intelligence Reports	Colonial Politicians' Opening Remarks at the 1962 Marlborough House Conference
Vere C. Bird[50] (Antigua-Barbuda)	One of the mellower small island politicians. He is vulnerable within his own party. In difficulties he is governed by emotion rather than by argument. He is slowly learning, against the odds of a trade union background and limited intellectual abilities, the difficult process of government.	As far as we are concerned, we are prepared to contribute by surrendering the services that seem best for regional and national administration. But we are not here merely to transfer Colonial Office control from London to another place, even if it is to one of the territories amongst the Eight.
Charles Southwell (St. Kitts-Nevis-Anguilla)	Possibly the ablest small island politician. He speaks in a studied and rather learned academic manner, in which he takes some pride. He has a ready turn of cynical but cheerful humour. He is more rewarding company than most of his fellow chief ministers... . He looks like a black version of Emperor Maximillian. He has Falstaffian girth and habits.[51]	We come, therefore, with a determination to tackle these difficulties and these problems very quickly. To prevent a deterioration of the sentiments in favour of closer association, which are at the peak in these eight units. We ask you at least not to put any obstacles in the way of that success. I think the challenge to us on this problem that has arisen in the [Eastern] Caribbean is a greater challenge than to you in the Colonial Office, because, with due respect, it is not your country, it is ours.
William Bramble (Montserrat)	A care-taker of donkeys before joining the trade union movement, his record has been one of mischief maker. He is a demagogue and has severely hindered past efforts to improve conditions in Montserrat.	There are conflicting views about the reasons for the failure of the West Indian Federation. However, it is beyond doubt that the main cause of the collapse of the Federation was the great gulf that existed

	He was elected to the Federal House of Representatives in 1958, where he had an undistinguished record. As chief minister he has had a depressing effect on Montserrat. Perhaps the most dole minded, least intellectually gifted and most simian featured[52] of the small island politicians.	between the economic viability of the larger islands and the under developed condition of the smaller ones. The parsimonious pattern set by Mr. Creech Jones was followed by Viscount Boyd and Mr. Iain Macleod; it is my earnest hope that the present Secretary of State will succeed where his predecessors failed.
Edward Le Blanc (Dominica)	Quiet mannered, he is by occupation a small planter. Between 1958 and 1960 he was a member of the Federal House of Representatives, where he seldom spoke and made little impression. Became chief minister of Dominica in January 1961. He seems basically moderate and sensible. At meetings with his fellow chief ministers he has shown himself to be too easily led and liable to fall in with the political demands of his neighbours.	Who should bear the blame for the disastrous situation is still a moot point that I do not propose to go into at this stage. When an English newspaper [Daily Express, May 7, 1962] tells us that we are no longer wanted by Great Britain as her colonies, we face the bitter truth that the period of our usefulness has come to its end. But, whatever happens, we will not become colonies of any independent state in the archipelago of the Caribbean.
George Charles (St. Lucia)	President of the St. Lucia Labour Party, he was the main instigator of the 1950 sugar strike. Charles has been the chief minister since 1960. He is a man of very little intelligence and a weak character. His work suffers from his strong addiction to alcohol. Charles is quiet-mannered and seldom adopts provocative attitudes in meetings. He is always asking for money. Unfortunately, his slowness of intellect and lack of	I believe that a speedy development of these islands would be more easily pursued with an independent West Indies, as it would have the right to enter into agreements with other nations and be able to carve out its own future, with the promotion of foreign investment, to create employment at home and raise the standard of living of our people.

	concentration outweigh his positive qualities.	
Ebenezer Joshua (St. Vincent)	He has only primary education. A minister since 1957, Joshua became chief minister in 1960. He owes his political career to his trade union activities. In the early days he was considered wild and is still emotionally unstable and unpredictable. He is said to have remarkable powers of political recovery and shrewd common sense. He is usually unnaturally subdued and incoherent at any discussion with ministers. This makes it easy to underestimate his very real political powers and potentially dangerous propensities.	We are still knocking at the door of the Colonial Office for a Federation that should have now been an accomplished fact.
Eric Gairy (Grenada)	A man of very little depth of intelligence, he cuts little ice at the conference table or in any serious discussion. However, he is a shrewd politician and cunning rabble-rouser. He has an extraordinary hold over the masses, they regarding him as some kind of messiah. He poses as a saviour of the people and claims to possess divine powers. His behaviour in and out of office has shown that he is a thug and a gangster.	Please allow me Mr. Secretary to rest the failure for the passing of the West Indies Federation firmly, squarely and immovably on the shoulders of the Colonial Office. I give this out as a warning ... I might be considered a little insignificant leader from one of the West Indian islands ... but I am giving this out as a premonition: unless the Colonial Office should change its attitude towards the people's elected representatives and should stop condoning and supporting a local administration for disrespecting and embarrassing the people's elected representatives,

		people in the West Indies might have to look for another doctrine (as opposed as what he termed 'Britishism').
Errol Barrow[53] (Barbados)	Has brains and drive, he is a very popular leader.	All we in the Windward and Leeward Islands and Barbados want to know at this Conference is when is the examination. The normal period of tutelage at a higher education level spreads for fourteen years … I think it would be an indictment, not only of the metropolitan country, but also of our powers of assimilation, if after three hundred years we have not imbibed at the fountain of democracy and learned the lessons so as to be in a position to pass the examination whenever it is set.

Source: CAB 133/ 202

At first glance, the outcome of what many already called the Eastern Caribbean Federation Conference was misleadingly perceived as 'quite promising',[54] in the words of the colonial secretary. Whereas on the politico-constitutional front the British Government did not succeed in securing 'any radical reshaping of the unit constitutions',[55] on the economic side it did achieve its objective of bypassing Professor Lewis's model.[56] More specifically, the British Government obtained an agreement from the chief ministers that all external aid should be made available through the federal centre and not directly to the units;[57] also that the representative of the Crown, following an adverse report by a commission of enquiry, could dissolve a local legislature and arrange for fresh elections.[58] And equally important for the Colonial Office, the eight territories saw fit to introduce a unified public service that would staff posts in both the units and federal governments.[59] Yet what Maudling usually described as 'top heavy bureaucracies', namely the ministerial system at the local level, remained intact even after the Marlborough House Conference.[60]

The crux of the matter, however, revolved around the economic understandings arrived at during the Conference. Therein lay the missing pieces of the puzzle. The archival record shows that, although recognizing that the area was in need of external assistance, the British Government undertook to set 'in train a survey of these requirements', [61] bearing in mind, but without committing itself to implement, the recommendations made by Professor Lewis.

The decision to produce an updated survey of the economic potential and capital needs of the archipelago, which in turn led to the establishment of both a Fiscal and a Civil Service Commission, amounted to a moratorium on the economic discussions between the chief ministers, the Colonial Office and the Treasury. [62] The rendering of the reports of the newly appointed commissions and their acceptance by the colonial leadership now became prerequisites for the resumption of the economic negotiations between London and its Caribbean outposts. As Maudling saw it, moreover, the question of independence for these islands would only be addressed if and when the new federation was finally established. [63]

Since a federation of the Little Eight would not be valid or properly established until the economic uncertainties were cleared, everything would essentially be on hold until the commissions rendered their financial and fiscal appraisals. And although the chief ministers would, in the meantime, convene periodically under the auspices of what became known as the Regional Council of Ministers (RCM), [64] this indefinite delay would open the lid on powerful insular and metropolitan forces for undermining the markedly fragile agreement reached at Marlborough House. Prior even to the adjournment of the Conference, Douglas Williams, in a letter to F.G. Burrett from the Treasury, hinted at the unnerving effect this hiatus could have on the overall process. It was 'hardly to be expected', according to Williams, that 'they will be willing to consider them [the proposals put forward by the Colonial Office] without having any idea of their financial prospects'. [65] The chief minister of Grenada, for instance, expressed on behalf of his colleagues deep uneasiness with London's delay in disclosing a definite amount of financial aid for the territories. Gairy's argument focused on the uneasiness such uncertainty would certainly create amongst the inhabitants of Grenada and the neighbouring islands,

The people in the West Indies are vitally interested in what aid is forthcoming and it will be essential for the delegates to be able to indicate this when they explain what Federation will mean.[66]

In the end, the British Treasury's 'refusal to play',[67] as some have contended, did not trigger on its own the federal project's erosion, but a rather more basic and perhaps tragic inconsistency. While ministers in London were attempting (albeit behind the scenes) to bind the islands in a unitary state, the colonial leadership, accountable to eight different constituencies, was still embroiled in a frantic effort to cement the political empowerment of these territories through a more decentralized or loose form of federation. Hence, the odds of arriving at a mutually suitable or convenient compromise, when all the other aggravating elements are considered, were very slim indeed.

8

The Suspension of the Grenada Constitution

> We have a difficult problem in deciding what to do with the remaining islands.
>
> *Duncan Sandys, 1962*

A whirlwind of competing tensions were now enveloping both the metropolitan and colonial scenarios. Although, as previously suggested, the role played by the Treasury was not the sole cardinal element leading to the miscarriage of the federal negotiations, its interaction with the Colonial Office following the Marlborough House Conference would nevertheless be inextricably bound to this hyper-charged environment. The establishment of the Regional Council of Ministers, for instance, gave rise to a lively exchange between the Colonial Office and the Treasury which, to a large extent, illustrates the contradictions embedded in their uneasy partnership. Almost a week before adjourning the Conference, the Colonial Office on behalf of Sir John Stow, had petitioned the Treasury to disburse £40,000 in order to meet part of the expense of setting up the Council of Ministers.[1] The reply coming from the Treasury illustrated in an unambiguous way why its relationship with the Colonial Office was far from harmonious,[2] and, even more relevant to this study, how that inherent dissonance clouded the prospects of establishing a new federal government in the archipelago. On Williams's petition for funding, F.G. Burrett swiftly concluded that,

> While we [in the Treasury] see that such a gesture might be helpful politically, we think that it would set an unfortunate precedent if we were to offer a substantial contribution towards the cost of the first federal overhead. In any case, the Eight will cease to pay contributions towards the costs of the present Federation and it would not be difficult for them to find the necessary finance. I am afraid, therefore, that we cannot agree with your proposal.[3]

Less than a month later, and far from deterred by such a stern rebuff, Sir John Stow and Douglas Williams appealed once again to the Treasury for a financial contribution. This time, however, the Regional Council of Ministers was asking for a £10,000 grant in order to finance, albeit partially, the upkeep of its staff. Acknowledging the Treasury's misgivings, this subsequent proposition came along with an explicit set of terms and conditions: only the Chairman of the Council (Sir John Stow) would be allowed to send applications for staff within the block grant as and when required. By this method, as Stow confided in Williams, the Treasury would be able 'to scrutinise the staff taken on'.[4] Obviously, the intention behind this more detailed proposition was to allay any opposition that might arise in the Treasury. By June 19, 1962, a few days before the second meeting of the Regional Council of Ministers, Douglas Williams wrote once again to F.G. Burrett arguing that the case for a grant should be reconsidered along the lines proposed by Sir John Stow.[5] The reply from the Treasury arrived over a week later. Burrett, in one of his traditional one pagers and with his usual caustic tone, once again rejected the Colonial Office's overture on the grounds that,

> Although the costs of your proposal have been substantially reduced, we are still opposed to the idea of making a UK contribution. It seems to us that the Eight should be left to help themselves and that this is essential if there is to be a successful Federation.... Obviously we are more likely to look at their major needs with a sympathetic eye if they show willingness to shoulder their responsibilities in the smaller things ... it ought to be possible for them to find £10K.[6]

If seen in the light of the wider context, the hard line adopted by the senior civil servants in the Treasury, commonly referred as 'the most important institution of the British Government',[7] was for the most part ill advised and somewhat myopic. Burrett's reply implicitly suggested that the eight territories were responsible for the slowing down of the negotiations and as such had to sustain the Regional Council of Ministers on their own, when, on the contrary, it had been the unfaltering appeal unitary statehood still enjoyed in Cabinet circles which had led to the rejection of the economic proposals put forward in Bridgetown and, consequently, to the establishment of the Council of Ministers.[8] But perhaps the most problematic element present in Burrett's brief exposition was his apparent lack of concern for political subtleties. While the archival record clearly shows (as illustrated above) that the Treasury had had full participation in the deliberations of the Colonial Policy Committee, there is no correlation between the ministers' willingness to modify (albeit moderately) their positions for the sake of maintaining the negotiations with the islands alive and the Treasury's non-malleable stands. Unmistakably, and particularly if seen against the background of the chief ministers' opening statements in Marlborough House, such inflexible posturing would no doubt heighten the already tense environment between the metropolitan and the colonial parties. In the end, it was the unwillingness of the senior civil servants in the Treasury to play the political game that, ironically, led to the intervention of the political wings of both the Treasury and the Colonial Office to salvage the wreckage left from this exchange. The correspondence between Hugh Fraser and Edward Boyle, (his counterpart in the Treasury), while putting an end to this impasse, conveyed in no uncertain terms their contrasting priorities. In his letter to Boyle, Fraser argued as follows:

> Nevertheless, politically it is very important that we should make some small but concrete gesture to them well in this venture. You will recall that prior to the Marlborough House Conference the Ministers of the Little Eight were deeply suspicious of our attitude towards them. They had interpreted our insistence on a strong form of federation as a reluctance to see any kind of federation brought into being at all ... fearing that instead we wished to keep them perpetually in a dependent status. We must do all we can to restore confidence in our good intentions and to remove this impression. Nothing in our view would achieve this end so successfully as making a contribution towards the costs of the Secretariat. Your Department suggests that the Little Eight should expect more sympathetic treatment over major needs if they shoulder lesser ones themselves. My own view is that an act of generosity on this lesser matter will have a disproportionate value to us, in inducing them to be sensible over major problems.[9]

While overruling his subordinates in the Treasury, Boyle finally agreed to the disbursement of the funds, not without including a very relevant proviso:

> If you really think that it is essential to give this money and that it can be represented at once and for all as a gesture of goodwill to set them on the way

to federation, I am ready to agree. I must ask you, however, to ensure that from now on we stick to the formula that was agreed at the time of the Eastern Caribbean Federation Conference in May, regarding possible UK aid, and that there will be no additional call upon the Exchequer as a result of the progress towards federation.[10]

During this period, however, no other event exacerbated the uneasy relationship between the British Government and the Little Eight as much as the suspension of the Grenada Constitution on June 19, 1962. While tipping the balance against Gairy's Grenada United Labour Party (GULP), this constitutional injunction in turn led to Grenada's permanent withdrawal from the federal negotiations. The catalysts behind this disquieting episode were the alarming findings of the Field Commission.[11] On January 22, 1962, J.M. Lloyd, Grenada's colonial administrator, had appointed a three-member panel 'to enquire into the control of public expenditure in the territory of Grenada during the financial year commencing on January 1, 1961'.[12] Maudling, in a confidential letter to Harold Macmillan, expounded on how the Commission's conclusions led him to suspend Grenada's constitutional status:

> I thought I should just let you know that I am publishing on Monday an Order in Council, made last week, that temporarily suspends the Constitution of Grenada. New elections will be held shortly. In the meantime, the Administrator will use his special powers of legislation to tighten up his financial controls in the Constitution. This action will not be unexpected. I appointed a Committee of Enquiry under a Judge [Mr. Justice Frank E. Field] to investigate certain financial scandals in the island. I recently published the report. It contained a scathing indictment of the Chief Minister and disclosed a wholly deplorable lack of financial control. They [the members of the Field Commission] also made it clear that the civil servants in the island had been demoralised as a result of the bullying tactics from the Chief Minister. I have asked the Chief Minister for his answer. His explanations are wholly unsatisfactory and consist mainly of hurling abuse at everyone. The action I have taken, therefore, is essential in the interests of good government and the safeguarding of moneys voted by the Parliament.[13]

Whereas the prime minister plainly scribbled on the margin of Maudling's despatch 'I am sure you're right',[14] in the House of Commons the reaction was, for the most part, one of concern for the stability of

British colonial policy in the Eastern Caribbean. There was a clear perception in parliamentary circles that suspending the Grenada Constitution, albeit justified, might imperil the ongoing negotiations in the area.[15] The archival record openly demonstrates that that was, indeed, a fair assessment.

While destabilizing the internal balance of political power within Grenada, this action clearly affected the relationship between the territories and London. The appointment of the Field Commission and, subsequently, the suspension of the statutory instrument (pending new insular elections) provided fertile terrain for the consolidation of a politically-viable anti-Gairy opposition. The foundation of the Grenada National Party (GNP), under the leadership of Herbert Blaize, should be seen as the most obvious expression of that sentiment. This constitutional injunction accentuated the divide that for some time had existed within Grenada's political and labour leadership on the question of the island's future. Should the territory continue, alongside its neighbours, designing a federal government for the region or, conversely, embark on a unitary venture with Trinidad and Tobago? This question had surfaced in Grenada on a continuous basis following the Jamaican referendum but, so far, without any discernible answer. This explains why, while attending the Eastern Caribbean Federation Conference, Gairy and his team had already held talks with Eric Williams on the possibility of facilitating Trinidad and Tobago's annexation of Grenada.[16] Whether Gairy's overtures to Port-of-Spain were merely a political facade intended to woo the island's pro-annexation element or, simply, an outgrowth of his genuine desire to consider what for many in Grenada was a natural option, is not altogether clear. Yet, both of these considerations must have played a crucial role in shaping Gairy's thoughts. Additionally, and apart from the purely partisan aspects, in Grenada, more so than in any other island, there were deeply rooted emotional links to Trinidad and Tobago. The evidently close relationship between these two territories was such that, at least until then, numerous voices often contended that no family in Grenada could boast of not having any relative either working or living in Trinidad and Tobago.[17]

In spite of that, the discussions between Gairy and Williams led nowhere. While the reaction from the Trinidadian delegation had been largely favourable, on meeting his fellow chief ministers in Bridgetown,

Gairy had notoriously announced, 'I am definitely for a federation of the Eight'.[18] Even more emphatically, he openly proclaimed, 'Grenada is not joining in any unitary government with Trinidad'.[19] The archival record reveals that what Grenada had sought amounted more to an association than to de facto unitary statehood. Having no other alternative, Eric Williams was compelled to make it clear, much to Gairy's chagrin, that there would be no degree of autonomy for the components of any such union. Blaize's rise to power in September 1962,[20] following the defeat of Gairy's GULP, brought these discussions back to centre stage — as the tenet that held the GNP together, apart from an intense dislike for Gairy, was the concept of union with Trinidad and Tobago. The archival record reveals how, close to a fortnight after the local elections, Grenada's colonial administrator offered the Colonial Office a post-electoral analysis consistent with this observation. In his telegram to Duncan Sandys, the new colonial secretary,[21] J.M. Lloyd contended that,

> The join Trinidad issue was the decisive factor in the election result. I consider that [the] GNP is committed to carry out its pledge to seek association with Trinidad, on [the] basis of unitary statehood. Blaize proposes to seek your approval [to] commence discussions at an early date and for you to indicate this to the Trinidad Government. He also seeks your assistance in the negotiating process.[22]

The opinion of the British High Commissioner in Port-of-Spain, N.E. Costar, coincided with Lloyd's assessment and, in a confidential despatch to his superiors in London, argued that,

> The defeat of the Grenada United Labour Party, headed by Gairy, by the Grenada National Party, headed by Blaize — whose slogan is 'Join Trinidad Now' — has a substantial political significance for Trinidad.[23]

The newly elected Government of Grenada had a clear mandate to steer the island's course away from federation and into unitary statehood with Trinidad and Tobago. Thus, for all practical purposes, the ongoing federal negotiations were then circumscribed to the British Government and the remaining territories, now the 'Little Seven'. The events in Grenada constituted a turning point in the relationship between the British Government and the islands. The documents clearly show that these developments were being closely observed from London. An impromptu meeting between Duncan Sandys and Eric Williams made things clearer. Sandys understood that if the overall transfer of political authority in the area was to run smoothly, a thorough understanding of Trinidad and Tobago's intentions towards Grenada was highly relevant. The minutes from that exchange show how Williams's position hardly varied from the one he had adopted at his first meeting with Maudling.[24] From a constitutional perspective, nonetheless, a potential union between Grenada and Trinidad and Tobago faced some formidable challenges. Williams's advisers concluded, early on, that the incorporation of Grenada or, for that matter, any other territory, would involve amending various entrenched provisions of the new Trinidadian Constitution.[25] The support of at least three quarters of the local House of Representatives would be needed for amending these clauses. This meant that the present opposition, made up of a vigorous East Indian element, could veto the move, even if all other obstacles were overcome, as it held ten out of the thirty available seats in the House.[26] While the remaining chapters address the question of whether Blaize and his followers in Grenada successfully cleared these hurdles, what now acquires far more importance is assessing how the civil servants in the Colonial Office and the political leadership in the region reacted to developments in Grenada. The attitude exhibited by the Colonial Office merits close consideration as it, undoubtedly affected its relationship with the colonial leadership. The correspondence between N.E. Costar and Walsh Atkins throws some light on how senior civil servants perceived this sensitive subject. In a letter to his colleague at the Commonwealth Relations Office, Costar argued:

> I had the impression before I left London that the Colonial Office's attitude was that if there was a clear express demand for union it would be impossible to oppose it. While a union between Trinidad and the Little Eight would be welcomed, there was far less enthusiasm in London for union between Trinidad and Grenada, followed possibly by St. Vincent and perhaps another Little Eight. The chances of a Little Seven, or a Little Six, coming into being and, when in being, becoming viable would be less the smaller the number. On the basis of these impressions my provisional attitude here [in Port-of-Spain] will be one of displaying interest in developments on an entirely non-committal basis. However, I will not go out of my way to either encourage or discourage Trinidad. Encouragement would only lead to raising the economic issue; discouragement would, of course, be atavistic colonialism.[27]

It seems clear that from London's perspective, any untimely show of either support or condemnation could very well precipitate further fragmentation and, in turn, imperil the prospects for economic viability. That possibility was wholly incompatible with a sound withdrawal which, as stated earlier, was the prime policy objective. Under these circumstances, the solomonic position adopted by Sandys was hardly surprising. In a confidential telegram to Lloyd, Sandys advised him as follows:

> I have no objection to your Government having talks direct with the Government of Trinidad on this subject; on the understanding that they are purely exploratory at this stage ... without commitment to you or the British Government. The question of HMG joining in any such negotiations can be considered later in the light of the results of the initial talks.[28]

But already by April 1962, with the Field Commission having barely initiated its inquiry, the reaction throughout most of the archipelago was highly unfavourable. For instance, during a common services conference in St. John's (Antigua) Eric Gairy, Vere Bird and William Bramble continually emphasized that in as much as the people had put them in office they were, hence, responsible only to the people. They went on arguing that criticisms of over-expenditure and extravagance were meaningless since they came from local civil servants and 'stooges such as colonial administrators'.[29] This sharp-tongued and strident response is consistent with how most chief ministers reacted to Grenada's constitutional suspension. In a confidential letter, also containing a detailed transcript of the Regional Council of Ministers' second meeting (held between July 5 and 7), Stow described in depth the reaction from the area's leadership,

> The second point of irritation has been the suspension of the Grenada Constitution. The Conference opened up with speeches all around (taking 1.75 hours) condemning the action of the Secretary of State. At one stage four out of seven Ministers (Bird, Bramble, Joshua and Charles) were in favour of absenting themselves from the Common Services Conference as a gesture of protest. Alternatively they suggested the Conference to be postponed until after the Grenada elections. Eventually it was agreed that a sub-committee of Ministers draft a telegram of protest. However, when the draft came up for agreement in [the] plenary session, Barrow, Southwell and Le Blanc insisted that the telegram should contain a passage to the effect that the Council did not condone Gairy's actions in any way. Bird and Joshua opposed the insertion

of any such passage on the ground that it would prejudice Gairy's chances in the next elections and would alienate his sympathies for the Seven. After a monumental waste of time, it was decided that no telegram of protest be sent as no agreement on the text could be reached.[30]

It seems that there was no coherent consensus on the impact Grenada's overtures to Trinidad and Tobago would have, if any, on the Little Eight's negotiations with the British Government. As the archival record demonstrates, this divergence accentuated the cleavages which for some time had existed amongst the remaining seven territories. It would be very difficult to dismiss the suggestion that, albeit to varying degrees, the chief ministers were highly suspicious of the British Government's role in these most recent developments. London's apparent complicity in the dialogue between Grenada and Trinidad and Tobago, without a doubt exacerbated the environment. Various voices, entertaining similar levels of skepticism, did not hesitate in denouncing what they perceived as the British Government's subtle way of pushing them further into the hands of Eric Williams. While the ever-deepening divisions within the archipelago's political and labour leaders are closely examined in the following chapter, their initial misgivings should not go unheeded, especially as the Grenadian episode had made these disagreements all the more apparent. What makes this analytical exercise yet more interesting is that during this period the insular local legislatures were also evaluating the report produced at Marlborough House.[31] Such a coincidence opens up an opportunity to assess the prevailing mood in the islands. Almost a month prior to the local elections in Grenada, the Legislative Council of St. Kitts–Nevis–Anguilla had approved in principle the federal proposals as described in the report from the Marlborough House Conference. While consistent with the attitudes of St. Lucia and St. Vincent, the wording of that resolution deserves careful consideration as it stood in sharp contrast to the mood in Montserrat, Dominica, Barbados and Antigua.

> Be it resolved that this Legislative Council approve the proposals contained in the Report of the Eastern Caribbean Federation Conference as a basis for a Federation of the territories concerned and for their independence at the earliest practicable time after the establishment of the Federation.[32]

In a meeting held by the Executive Committee of the ruling St. Lucia Labour Party similar views were unanimously upheld,[33]

St. Lucia will intensify her efforts to effect a union of Barbados, the Leeward and Windward Islands … or as many as may decide to join;

The Party would never support any idea of joining the unitary state of Trinidad and Tobago;

Any Federation of the Eastern Caribbean that may eventually be formed should proceed immediately to independence and membership of the Commonwealth and the United Nations;

Any attempt by HMG to debase the constitution of this territory will be resisted to the utmost and with all the power at our command;

The St. Lucia Labour Party recognises that only a political union with the remaining territories of the Eastern Caribbean will satisfy the hopes and aspirations to economic viability, political dignity and social respect of the people of St. Lucia.[34]

A few days later, Joshua outspokenly confirmed the resolve of his People's Political Party (PPP) to bring about a federation of the Seven. Along these lines, the *Vincentian* quoted the chief minister as suggesting that,

The Government of St. Vincent reaffirms its faith in the proposed Federation of Barbados, the Leeward and Windward Islands. It is determined to work to bring such Federation into being, for it to attain independent status and membership to the Commonwealth. It objects strongly to any interference by Trinidad or any other territory on the affairs of the proposed new nation.[35]

By then William Bramble, described by many in the Colonial Office as 'the West Indian Caliban', had sent a circular letter to various influential sectors of the Montserrat community, most notably to the island's Teachers Union, arguing as follows:

Recent events appear to indicate … that the proposed Federation of the remaining territories is not as feasible as heretofore envisaged. In the existing circumstances any person who is interested in the welfare of Montserrat is bound to give deep consideration as to its future. I should therefore be grateful to have your views as to whether unitary statehood with Trinidad would best serve the interests of the people of our island.[36]

While no reasonable solution was reached at these meetings, their participants raised perhaps one of the most intriguing options before the islands, which was annexation to Canada.[37] Although this possibility had been sporadically entertained since 1884 both in Ottawa and in the archipelago,[38] revisiting it at this particular juncture conveyed a diminishing rate of confidence in the federal project's ultimate success. The machinations that Edward Le Blanc and his closest associates in Dominica were by then engineering behind the scenes were startling. The archival record vividly portrays Douglas Williams's uneasy surprise when early in November 1962 he received a highly confidential note signed by E.L. Sykes from the Commonwealth Relations Office. In his secret communication Sykes felt compelled to disclose the following:

> I enclose a copy of a note received from the High Commission in Ottawa. It reports a further attempt to run away from the Little Eight — this time by Dominica. You will see that we are asked specially to limit the distribution of this information to avoid embarrassment with the Canadians.[39]

In addition, the note from the Commonwealth Relations Office contained an abridged transcript of the discussions between E.O. Laird, British High Commissioner in Ottawa, and L.A.D. Stephens, Head of the Commonwealth Division in the Department of External Affairs of Canada, at which the Canadians revealed to the British Government Le Blanc's overtures. The substance of that exchange is both fascinating and somewhat relevant to the subsequent unfolding of the federal negotiations; thus it deserves full consideration here. Laird's recollection seems quite accurate and the newly available documents have preserved it as follows:

> I called on Mr. L.A.D. Stephens by appointment on the 30th October to talk about the Sino–Indian conflict and the West Indies. At the outset Mr. Stephens said that he had asked to and had been given authority to let me have the following information for transmission to London. He said that about the middle of September, Mr. Le Blanc had written to Mr. [John] Diefenbaker [the Canadian Prime Minister] proposing that Dominica should become a province of Canada. Mr. Le Blanc had said that this was entirely his idea and that he had discussed it only with his closest colleagues. Mr. Stephens showed me Mr. Diefenbaker's reply, but he could not let me have a copy. Although friendly in tone, it quite firmly turned down the idea. It said, in effect, that the possibility of some or all the West Indian islands becoming part of Canada had come up frequently since the establishment of the [Canadian] Confederation. The British North America Act[40] did not, however, provide for the accession to the

Confederation of territory outside the area bounded by the Atlantic and Pacific Oceans and the Canada–US border and the Artic. Canada had no desire to extend its territory. Public opinion would not accept such a proposal. The Canadian Government would, however, be only too glad to work closely with the Government of Dominica in other ways giving the island all possible help. Mr. Stephens said that Le Blanc's proposal had not been dismissed out of hand; on the contrary, it had been carefully considered. He also said that if the Canadian Government had been interested it would have consulted HMG.[41]

Close to a fortnight after Sykes had sent his note to the Colonial Office, Alec Lovelace, then Dominica's colonial administrator, confronted with this surprising turnaround, confessed that,

> I had no idea that any such suggestion as that to which you refer was made; nor could anyone who had heard Le Blanc speak on Federation and Independence ever conceive of him putting it forward.[42]

Lovelace's initial reaction is very telling and, more importantly, Le Blanc's manoeuvrings lead this aspect of the study back to Errol Barrow and the Barbadian scenario. From the outset the British Government had identified Barbados and, in particular, Barrow as 'the real hope for the future of this area'.[43] Copious references, throughout the archival record, to Barrow as 'a man of strength and a fixer'[44] or as being 'head and shoulders above all the Little Eight leaders'[45] seem to confirm that impression. However, a closer look at the documents conveys a less promising picture. Not only were Barrow's relations with most of his colleagues already under considerable strain, but his misgivings about the federal project itself had increased dramatically. Almost a month prior to the Marlborough House Conference, the Barbadian premier had already confided in Sir John Stow that he was doubtful whether 'to go along with the total lack of responsibility'[46] shown at the various meetings by Gairy, Bramble and Bird. Behind the scenes, Barrow had openly accused them of 'deliberately flouting democratic procedures, which they know very well'.[47] Barrow's confession, close to a week after the third gathering of the Regional Council of Ministers, that he was not 'temperamentally suited' to deal with the chief ministers of the neighbouring islands stood as an eloquent remainder of the challenges which lay ahead.[48] Not surprisingly, after witnessing a shouting match at that meeting between Barrow and Robert Bradshaw, adviser to the chief minister of St. Kitts–Nevis–Anguilla, Stow finally conceded that 'the prospects of the Federation succeeding do not look very bright'.[49] In particular, as he saw it, in Barbados there was 'no real enthusiasm for the proposals at all'.[50]

This apparent lack of fervour, however, could not have sprung exclusively from these clashes of personalities. As contended briefly in the first chapter, while an aggravating element, that type of tension cannot possibly account for the wider picture. A careful analysis of Stow's assertion reveals how, by the autumn of 1962, there was no clear consensus within Barbados's political and labour leadership on whether to go ahead at full steam with the federal project. Indeed, the attempts at stalling went in crescendo. Gone were days when an eager Barrow had passionately argued that the Eight would 'pass the examination whenever it is set'.[51] The historical record demonstrates that even before receiving Stow's warning, the Colonial Office had already gotten a dire indication of where Barrow's thoughts were heading. On September 13, 1962, coincidentally the day when Grenada's local elections were held, Douglas Williams met with Barrow in London. His recollection of their meeting, preserved in a note to Ambler Thomas, merits serious consideration.

> I have just had an extremely interesting conversation with Mr. Barrow. He stressed that the information he was giving me was, under no circumstances, to be allowed to leak to anybody in the West Indies. He wished me to know, however, that with regard to federation the longer it could be delayed the happier he would be. He hopes indeed that we will be able to make a radically different approach to the whole problem from anything we had been contemplating until now. What Mr. Barrow wants is that before any political federation is set up we should first create a series of common services. He would like us to start with a customs union, proceeding afterwards to the setting up of other common services, viz., the audit and the courts. At all costs, he said, we must avoid any federal elections within the next twelve months. He personally would not participate in any such elections if they were held within that time. He was not going to be diverted from dealing with what he regarded as the more urgent problems of Barbados.... He would do his best to delay things by tactics such as being dilatory in replying to our correspondence and by prolonging the discussion of items affecting the federation in the RCM. If the worst came to worst he would be prepared to come out in public and say that Barbados was not going to be rushed.[52]

This did not sound like the same Barrow who two months earlier, while introducing a resolution in the local legislature to approve the report of the Eastern Caribbean Federation Conference, had publicly suggested that 'once we put our hands to the plough there cannot be any turning back';[53] the one who had openly advocated 'ploughing a very straight furrow, which will have no bends or crookedness'.[54] By the time of his meeting with Douglas Williams, Barrow had already concluded that failing to contain the pace of the negotiations would have almost certainly relegated him to isolation. The winds of political expediency were blowing far too vigorously for Barrow to ignore them. Although the Barbados Workers Union was still throwing its weight behind the federal project, the evidence now available illustrates an increasingly fragmented landscape. A thorough appraisal of the positions espoused by the major opposition parties, while the House of Assembly debated the Marlborough House Conference Report (Cmnd. 1746),[55] sheds abundant light on this matter. The de facto leader of the conservative Barbados National Party (BNP), Ernest D. Mottley, mayor of Bridgetown, speaking on behalf of his party's delegation in the House of Assembly, declared that,

> [If] federation means more taxation with Barbados carrying the heaviest load, we would have to face up with it. From the economic viewpoint can we bear it?[56]

Furthermore, Freddie L. Miller, interim leader of the Barbados Labour Party (BLP), voiced a similar concern:

> We are in full agreement with the Government's attitude on this matter of federation, although there are a lot of things we are not quite happy about.[57]

Without a doubt the cloud of uncertainty which still hung over the archipelago's economic prospects was at the heart of their collective misgiving. The island's powerful business community, under the auspices of the widely respected Chamber of Commerce, had echoed, early on, a similar apprehension towards Cmnd. 1746. While arguing that the powers granted to the federal centre were not strong enough, it identified the ambiguity over the financial contribution from the British Exchequer as a major cause for concern.[58] It seems as if the conventional wisdom adopted by a significant proportion of the merchant classes was that as long as the costs of federation remained unknown, Barbados should not commit itself wholeheartedly. This pattern appears to have been reproduced in other places, most notably in St. Lucia, where late in October 1962 the front page of a major newspaper read 'Businessmen say no to White Paper'.[59] In the case of Barbados, however, an expeditious glance at the archival record would be enough to conclude that, to a considerable degree, the sustained pressure from the business lobby had swayed Barrow's attitude. Within that context, what lay behind the premier's petition for an early customs union becomes much clearer. Facing an onslaught of skepticism from such influential quarters Barrow's only way of remaining politically afloat was by systematically dissipating their doubts. The safest way of achieving that end was by setting up the customs union, together with key common services, much earlier than expected. After all, most economists agreed that Barbados was likely to be at an advantage over the neighbouring territories in attracting industries producing for the customs union area. Clearly, the presence in Bridgetown of the proposed federal government and other federal institutions, such as the federal Supreme Court, would stimulate investment and attract capital.[60]

Yet, the widespread perception that Britain's entry into the European Economic Community was imminent, and an unforeseen decision by the local authorities in Antigua (in November 1962) to grant a foreign oil company concessions to set up a refinery, complicated the equation even further.[61] If the British Government no longer based its trade policy on the Commonwealth preferences of the Ottawa Agreement,[62] as would be the case on becoming a full member of the EEC, the Barbadian economy and in particular the still dominant sugar industry would reach a disturbing crossroad. The news stemming from St. John's, on the other hand, hinted at an even more immediate and conflicting challenge. Not only was the prospect of direct competition with Barbados's own oil refinery alarming, but from all angles this was not an auspicious foreshadowing in respect to the federal negotiations. Beyond merely encouraging unregulated competition amongst the economies of the islands, Antigua's decision openly contravened the spirit upheld at Marlborough House, where it had been unanimously agreed that a regional planning board should prevent at all costs these types of clashes from ever transpiring.[63] And obviously, it would have been considerably harder for Barrow to persuade the merchant classes to endorse the federal project if it could very well yield unchecked competition from within. However, the minutes of a highly confidential meeting between Barrow and Eric Williams, held in Port-of-Spain as early as July 1962, reveal how by then Barrow was entertaining, *sotto voce*, a whole new set of possibilities, of which the Leeward and Windward Islands were not a part. Agreeing that the federal experiment might very well fail and that the demise of the Ottawa Agreement could soon materialize, these two men reached a preliminary understanding that some kind of economic association between Trinidad and Tobago and Barbados would soon be needed. Williams went as far as outlining, rather prematurely, the details of a transoceanic trade alliance between what he termed the 'southern Caribbean', meaning Trinidad and Tobago, Barbados and British Guiana, and Nkrumah's Ghana, as well as Nehru's India.[64] Whether that *tête-à-tête* had a direct impact on Barrow's thoughts would be difficult to evaluate, particularly in the absence of his private papers, but the difficulties he was already facing were so acute that by the beginning of December 1962 the premier felt compelled to make an astonishing revelation. At a political rally in Bridgetown, for the first time, he openly argued that,

> No one can stop Barbados from getting independence. The constitution is already drafted and when the Colonial Secretary comes to Barbados later this month, he will see it.[65]

This was the unsettling environment that Duncan Sandys faced as he embarked on a 'rapid tour of these islands'.[66] While in his public statements, particularly before the Commons, the new colonial secretary seemed highly assured and confident of the developments in the area,[67] in private his concern was all but concealed. Sandys was fully acquainted with the Eastern Caribbean, not only in his capacity as former secretary of defense (in 1957), but as an outgrowth of his current position at the helm of the Commonwealth Relations Office. He was also a prominent member of the Colonial Policy Committee. This is why the observation he shared with Macmillan, contained in a confidential letter written in October 1962, that 'we have a difficult problem in deciding what to do with the remaining islands',[68] should be looked at closely. Obviously, Sandys's decision to travel to the region, at the most sensitive stage of the European Common Market negotiations, demonstrates how critical the situation had become. In more than one way, his was a delicate diplomatic mission. While taking the region's temperature, Sandys had to put to rest the conflicting tensions and misgivings, which were already eroding British policy. During the course of his sojourn in the archipelago (from December 22 to 28, 1962), Sandys held incessant discussions with Sir John Stow, the colonial administrators of St. Lucia, St. Vincent and St. Kitts–Nevis–Anguilla and, more importantly, with the colonial leadership.

All through these exchanges the most salient subject raised, especially by the politicians representing the Leeward and Windward Islands, was the bleak prospects for sustained socioeconomic development in most of their territories. This whole negotiating process became for them, more than merely a constitutional affair, an opportunity to make the case for modernity. Constant petitions, during their talks with Sandys, for financial help with the construction of roads, airfields, water supplies and electrical facilities, illustrate vividly the nature of their priorities.[69] An unvarying concern with the negative impact any gap in external aid could have, together with a pervasive distrust of central planning and the 'accompanying concentration in Barbados',[70] increased their preoccupation. Equally importantly, hypothetical questions such as 'Shall we be taxed more?' or 'Will Barbados take over our key posts?' had by now led a few voices to raise with Sandys the constitutional model of Western Samoa as a potential option for the smaller territories.[71] It seemed as if the devolution of constitutional authority per se was not as urgent as correcting the dire conditions, still prevalent in most of the islands. Thus, the momentous test before the parties to the federal negotiations was whether they could bring about a constitutional project capable of improving the quality of life of the people or, to put it less mildly, of the almighty electorate.

The minutes from the fourth meeting of the RCM, held on the final day of the colonial secretary's visit (December 28, 1962), illustrate that the negotiating process had turned out to be more complex than most in London had initially envisioned. Duncan Sandys, with Ambler Thomas by his side, opened the proceedings, stating that the immediate goal should be 'to determine the next step towards the attainment of a federation'.[72] Immediately, Vere Bird interjected, 'When are the reports of the Fiscal, Civil Service and Economic Survey Commissions to be ready?'[73] Although a reply came rather swiftly from Thomas,[74] the truth of the matter was that anxieties were running high. Indeed, the environment was quite tense from beginning to end. Following that exchange, Sandys suggested that each local government 'should seek the approval of its Legislature for the White Paper as a basis for the creation of a federation'.[75] Yet he added that the insular authorities should 'leave themselves free to express their views at the [final London] conference'.[76] Sandys argued that 'if the delegates arrived in London for the final conference with their hands tied up it would be a most unfortunate and tragic thing'.[77] Clearly, the strategy behind such an appeal was attempting to strike a fine balance between tying them up to the federal bandwagon, hence preventing further defections, and maintaining a degree of flexibility if the need for substantial amendments arose.

But once again Bird, by far the most outspoken, interrupted the colonial secretary's train of thought, arguing that his government already entertained a few seminal reservations to the report produced at the Marlborough House Conference. The leader of the Antiguan delegation stressed that industrial development should be left with the units and, additionally, made it clear that he did not intend to surrender any of these reservations at the final Conference.[78] Barrow, whose closest aides privately referred to the smaller islands as 'awkward customers',[79] followed suit. In direct reference to the Grenada conundrum, the Barbadian premier contended that the other territories viewed this issue with anxiety. He asserted, rather forcefully, that 'the silent acquiescence of the British Government to the talks now being held between Grenada and Trinidad did nothing to improve matters'.[80] Although reiterating the official line, namely that it was up to Grenada and Trinidad and Tobago to negotiate and that he was not represented at those talks, the colonial secretary failed to diffuse the prevailing mood of suspicion. After all, as suggested earlier, this had always been a sensitive issue for London. Sandys understood very well that a successful union between Trinidad and Tobago and Grenada could lead the smaller islands in that direction. But he knew as well that such a course might precipitate further fragmentation. Barrow's intervention, nonetheless, triggered a highly relevant crossfire between his delegation and the Antiguans. As Barrow went on to advocate an early customs union, Bird cut him short stating that 'without federation, we cannot agree to customs union'.[81]

By this stage, even a casual observer could have concluded that the lines of battle between the islands and the British Government, but even more dramatically, amongst the territories themselves, were out in the open. The colonial secretary's announcement, close to the adjournment, that Nigel Fisher (under-secretary of state) would be sent to the region in May 1963 to hold a 'preparatory conference' appears to confirm that impression. There was an obvious urgency, especially from the Colonial Office's perspective, to flatten out the rugged terrain before hosting the final conference in London. In the light of that, Sandys' subsequent observation in a personal letter to Sir John Stow that 'our meeting with the Chief Ministers was helpful and strengthened their confidence in the prospects of federation'[82] seemed like an exercise in wishful thinking. Rather than levelling the playing field, the so-called 'preparatory conference' inevitably led to the re-opening of other issues that had already been settled. Almost a year after the first meeting between Maudling and the colonial leadership, the set of local, metropolitan and international forces swaying this process were still engaged in combat. The horizon was not yet visible. Indeed, as the historical record shows, the negotiating process between the British Government and the territories of the Eastern Caribbean was about to come full circle.

Part Two: Conclusion

Since January 1962 the unspoken theme underlying these negotiations, resurfacing all too often, was that of incompatibility in both priorities and purposes. For the British Government the main policy objective was withdrawing as smoothly, tidily and swiftly as possible from the archipelago. Clearly, the transfer of political authority, and especially the timing, responded to wider imperatives. The British Cabinet, for instance, had identified unitary statehood with Trinidad and Tobago or, at least, a highly centralized federation, as the safest way of guaranteeing such an outcome. Conversely, the colonial leadership saw the question of the territories' constitutional future in the light of the area's pressing needs. For the so-called small island politician, institutionalizing modernity, on the basis of sustained socioeconomic development and industrial growth, preceded any other consideration. Such a clear inconsistency between colonized and colonizer, within the context of such a complex and sensitive decolonizing process, was bound to produce an impasse.

PART THREE

THE EPILOGUE OF
THE FEDERAL AGENDA

Why are we federating? Is it to federate our politicians or to federate our economy? Is it to provide those people in our backward villages motorable roads to their homes or is it to read in the papers the eloquent speeches that the honourable member for so-and-so made in the Federal House? The Government of St. Lucia holds that if we are federating we are doing so in order that we should have some advancement in the living standard of the people of this island. Without that, federation to us is completely and absolutely meaningless.

John Compton, 1965

Introduction

This section prepares the groundwork for the concluding chapters of the book, which evaluate in detail the opening of new roads for the transference of political authority in these territories. Consistent with the arguments raised earlier, the next chapters illustrate how the interests of the British Government and the colonial leadership were, for the most part, incompatible. In them I dispute the interpretation that the subsequent impasse between both parties resulted exclusively from the inaction of the British Treasury. At its most basic level, the stalemate arose from a conspicuous conflict between contending constitutional views, interests and aspirations.

This part of the book identifies a variety of new pressures and strains swaying these negotiations. Intense discussions between the Foreign Office and the US State Department, as to the best way of shaping the area's constitutional future, meant that Anglo-American relations would impact the process even further. Numerous intelligence reports stemming from these islands also reveal tremendous colonial anxiety, especially in Antigua, Barbados and St. Lucia, between opposing politico-labour movements — some of which, by 1964, had already dismissed the validity of the federal project itself. The cracks, in what had been a consensus on the desirability of the federal project, were all too obvious. This third part of the book concludes with Sir Stephen Luke recommending to Anthony Greenwood, Labour's new colonial secretary, that the British Government had no other option but to put the federal project in 'cold storage'.[1] Indeed, by then, federation, as Frank Walcott suggested, had become an 'intellectual exercise, impossible at [that] time to get it across to the man in the street'.[2] By the spring of 1965 the possibility of transferring political authority in the Eastern Caribbean by means of a federation was non-existent.

9

Dissension within the Ranks

> The Federation of Seven Islands of the Eastern Caribbean has been set back, for how long no one knows.
>
> *William Bramble, 1963*

Nigel Fisher's intervention must be evaluated in the light of the imminent publication of the findings of the Fiscal and Civil Service Commissions.[1] Sir John Stow, in a confidential communication to Ambler Thomas, made a few interesting observations on the prevailing mood just a few weeks prior to their release.

> It must generally be admitted that there is really no emotional desire to federate. Paradoxically, the steps towards the establishment of a new federation seem to be proceeding with the inevitability of a Greek tragedy, though the publication of the Reports will naturally give rise to renewed interest and debate.[2]

As soon as the final reports were circulated the debate between the colonial politicians and the British Government intensified, reaching new heights of stridency.[3] In no other territory was the reaction as strongly negative as in Antigua. This was no surprise to the British. The archival record reveals that close to a fortnight prior to their publication, Ian Turbott, the colonial administrator of Antigua had reported to the Colonial Office that Bird was seeing the coming 'preparatory conference' with Fisher as a case of Antigua versus the others. The colonial administrator's impression was that Bird felt that the remaining islands wanted to 'cash in on Antigua's assets'.[4] The regional press, most notably in Barbados, amply reported Bird's contention that the report of the Fiscal Commission (also referred to as the Hicks Report) was both 'colonial and unrealistic'.[5] Although Bird's reservations had become quite apparent at the RCM meeting held late in December 1962, which the colonial secretary had chaired, they were sharpened after the publication of this report. By this stage, it was quite clear that the overall financial design of the federation, and, in particular, the proposed fiscal arrangements, constituted Bird's 'main headache'.[6] Bird and his political associates were, for instance, staunchly opposed to the concept of transferring Antigua's import revenues to the federal government, which would then re-allocate them.[7] But, why were the Antiguans retreating from their initial stance? If the recommendations of the Hicks Report were anchored on principles already ratified in Bridgetown and in Marlborough House, what could have possibly accounted for Bird's uneasiness? The answers to these questions merit close consideration, as Antigua's qualms significantly influenced the negotiating process.

The archival record reveals an intimate correlation between the state of Antigua's economy, during this period, and the position now espoused by its most influential political and labour leaders. Although historically considered by many as 'the poor relation of the Leeward Islands',[8] since early 1962 its macroeconomic indicators were already showing a remarkably different picture. In just ten years, namely between 1953 and 1962, Antigua's gross domestic product (GDP) had increased from BWI $12.1 million to $22.5 million.[9] And, in one year alone, the rate of growth of its GDP had gone from 2.0 per cent in 1962 to 7.2 per cent in 1963.[10] The island's per capita GDP also added to this perception of buoyancy. By 1962 it stood at BWI $368, second only to Barbados's $421.[11] Without a doubt, at least at this stage, Antigua had the fastest growing economy in the archipelago. Interestingly, this economic boom had very little to do with the agricultural sector.[12] On the contrary, as both the historical and economic records illustrate, it rested on an aggressive development policy coupled with a pro-active use of the island's fiscal autonomy. The fact that Antigua's customs revenues, between 1962 and 1963, had increased by almost 30 per cent (more than in any other territory) attested to the effectiveness of that strategy.[13] The most salient dynamo behind this relative prosperity was an expanding tourist and entertainment industry. The opening of twelve hotels and a casino since 1961 had brightened the island's economic prospects by increasing its revenues from custom duties and property taxes, as well as by opening new outlets for employment.[14]

The impact of Ursula Hicks's recommendations on Antigua must be evaluated against this background. The underlying principle behind her report was that the federal centre, right from its inception, had to be financially independent from the units. Acknowledging the preliminary agreements reached at Marlborough House,[15] she recommended the immediate federalization of the basic fiscal departments.[16] Hicks made it abundantly clear that all revenue accruing from import duties, rather than remaining in the local treasuries, would have to go to the federal coffers.[17] Additionally, company law (including incentive legislation) and external borrowing would be transferred to the centre.[18] The implementation of these measures, for all practical purposes, would have deprived Antigua of its most important source of revenue. The only discernible way of offsetting that loss would have been by increasing the local rate of property taxes, but that could have made the island less attractive to foreign investors, potentially stalling the expansion of its incipient hotel industry. Local politicians in Antigua would now have less room to manoeuvre and, thus, to deliver. The recommendation to substitute the traditional grants-in-aid for the so-called 'general grants', to be awarded (as were grants for the British local authorities) without regard to the local budgets, aggravated the picture even further.[19] Many failed to understand, for instance, why St. Lucia and St. Vincent, where most of the total revenue also came from import duties, would receive a 'general grant' over three times that of Antigua's.[20] While the technical reason was fairly simple, namely the smaller the GDP per capita the bigger the grant, its economic and, more importantly, political implications proved to be a burden on Bird and his political associates.[21] On the one hand, the local authorities would now have less funds available with which to tackle the 'terrible backlog of neglect' (soon to be revealed in O'Loughlin's Economic Survey) of such utilities as roads, water supplies, electricity and communications.[22] On the other, earnest support for these recommendations would certainly have imperilled the chief minister's political position. Fresh evidence shows that, by the time of the publication of the Fiscal Report, Bird was under unusually intense pressure. This challenge came from within as well as from without Antigua's Trade and Labour Union.

In an intelligence report to the Colonial Office, corresponding to the month of April, 1963, Ian Turbott hinted that Bird was 'not entirely satisfied with the way other groups are developing on the island in opposition to his party'.[23] The colonial administrator went even further, suggesting that 'the Junior Chamber of Commerce and some of the lawyers may form a party'.[24] More interestingly, in this document Bird was described as 'allowing himself to be pressurised by the more unpleasant and less desirable elements in his party into extreme action'.[25] Turbott was under the impression that the 'anti-federation' McChesney George (minister without portfolio) had 'emerged as the main adviser to the Chief Minister, who says very little without George's approval'.[26] A superficial glance at Antigua's modern political history would have been enough to conclude that Bird was not accustomed to this level of opposition. Since 1951 his Antigua Labour Party, the political wing of Antigua's Trades and Labour Union, had ruled unobstructed, controlling the island's seven constituencies and holding all ten elected seats in the local Legislative Council. Thus, his virile opposition to Hicks's recommendations was closely related to deep-seated instincts of political self-preservation. If, as the archival record demonstrates, the Colonial Office was completely aware of the new complexities embedded in Antigua's economic and political scenario, why did the colonial secretary's instructions to Nigel Fisher, in anticipation of the preparatory conference, not reflect this? That particular exchange between Sandys and Fisher also deserves a closer look as, for the most part, it sealed the fate of the forthcoming gathering.

Sandys's private papers reveal that the day before Fisher's arrival in Bridgetown, the Colonial Office had finally decided on what attitude to adopt towards Antigua's recalcitrant position. Without acknowledging or even alluding to the peculiarities of the island's internal situation, Sandys, in the company of Hilton Poynton, Douglas Williams and Ambler Thomas, asked Fisher to take 'a tough line' with Bird.[27] The Colonial Office's strategy was based on threatening Bird with going ahead and forming the Federation without Antigua. Sandys thought that if the remaining six units, once within the federal arrangement, were to establish a customs union area discriminating against Antigua, it would not be long before the island's leadership would want to join it. Newly released evidence demonstrates that by the time of this mini-caucus the Colonial Office had already received a series of confidential despatches from Antigua suggesting that Bird and most of his colleagues, if forced to comply with the Fiscal Report, might withdraw from the federal negotiations altogether. The archival record also reveals that the Antiguans understood that even outside the federal area, they would nonetheless retain a 'greatly advanced constitution'.[28] Under these circumstances and, of course, without losing sight of Antigua's newly found riches, it must have looked highly improbable that such a threat might have seriously swayed their resolve. If seen in hindsight, it is remarkable that Sandys and the senior civil servants in the Colonial Office did not realize that their inflexible stratagem could very well alienate not only Antigua, but also the other major actor in this drama, namely Barbados. Although brief, these deliberations, held at the highest echelons of the Colonial Office, as the coming days showed, revealed how far removed the British were from the political mood in the archipelago. Not surprisingly, several voices, most notably Sir Arthur Lewis, commented that the atmosphere at the so-called preparatory conference was terrible.[29] The fact that Nigel Fisher was hardly acquainted with the region did not facilitate matters.[30] Most students of the process of devolution in the archipelago tend to describe this conference in harsh terms, as shattering the possibility of forging a federal arrangement in the area. Whether this pivotal episode was the defining catalyst of the subsequent impasse or simply the clearest indication, so far, of what was to come, its overall impact must still be looked at in some detail.

Interestingly, by the time the meeting with Fisher got under way influential elements within the colonial leadership were bent on broaching a highly sensitive subject — which since the secessions of Jamaica and Trinidad and Tobago had been kept relatively under wraps — namely the timing of independence. By this stage the question of independence had become entangled, even more so than before, with the still unresolved issue of British aid. On the one hand, independence meant eligibility to receive financial aid from abroad, particularly from places such as Canada and the US. The chief ministers of the smaller islands, but especially the premier of Barbados,[31] had learned much to their disappointment that political limbo did not lead to external aid. Not even a fortnight before Fisher's arrival, President Kennedy and the Canadian prime minister had expressed their 'readiness to explore the possibility of a further cooperative effort to provide economic and technical aid to the countries of the Caribbean area which have recently become independent or which are approaching independence'.[32] On the other hand, imminent developments in the outer Caribbean, such as the initiative by the Governments of Trinidad and Tobago and Puerto Rico of establishing (*c.* 1964) an all-encompassing Caribbean Economic Community, meant that these matters needed prompt resolution if the islands were to stand any chance of inclusion and future competitiveness.[33] But the British Government, saddled with complex geopolitical considerations, showed some ambivalence towards the desirability of facilitating the immediate independence of these islands. Thus, Barrow and Fisher were heading towards a major collision. Before evaluating the set of forces influencing the colonial and metropolitan scenarios, the minutes of this sixth meeting of the RCM, commonly referred to as the 'preparatory conference,' must be examined.

Although the British delegation had arrived on Tuesday May 21, 1963, the deliberations began three days later in Sherbourne House, on the outskirts of Bridgetown.[34] While Fisher came along with only Douglas Williams, a financial officer from the Colonial Office and his private secretary, the chief ministers brought numerous advisers. All in all, including Sir John Stow and his personal secretary, thirty-one people attended these sessions. Acknowledging the pitfalls lying ahead, Fisher's opening remarks began on a rather suggestive note, 'given goodwill, co-operation, a spirit of compromise and a real and united belief in the concept of federation, [our] aim could be achieved'.[35] In what amounted to a regurgitation of Creech Jones's statement at Montego Bay,[36] Fisher went on to assert that 'independence could only be achieved through federation',[37] warning that 'the new federation must avoid the mistakes of the past one'.[38] But after this initial exchange of pleasantries, the colonial leadership took over the initiative. Openly disregarding Fisher's invitation to go through the Fiscal and Civil Service Reports together, the chief ministers immediately focused their attention on a document that had been put together by the Government of Barbados in conjunction with most of the other delegations and hastily entitled 'the Areas of Agreement'.[39] The archival record shows that Barrow himself had been the driving force behind the drafting of this document. With the internal situation in Barbados remaining much the same since Sandys's visit, Barrow felt politically compelled to reach a compromise with Antigua. As George Charles would argue in the coming days, putting forward the Areas of Agreement was an effort 'at securing general unanimity'.[40]

It becomes quite obvious by this stage that Barrow had decided to modify the position he had advocated the previous December 1962. He now understood that the chances of creating a customs union area as well as a series of common services, before establishing the federation, were very slim indeed.[41] Barrow, always wary of the political climate at home, realized that immediate independence within a federation would not only bring about these arrangements but with it an unlimited potential for external aid. However, his counter-proposal was totally inconsistent with the major principles already agreed to. More than merely watering down the initial compromise, the Areas of Agreement at its core nullified the Marlborough House Conference Report (Cmnd. 1746) and rejected both the Fiscal and Civil Service Reports. This colonial volte-face, as shown below, signalled the demise of Maudling's hard-fought quasi-unitary arrangement.[42] Fisher saw this clearly and a few days later would tell the colonial leadership, 'I must be quite frank and say that in your Areas of Agreement paper you have gone back on Cmnd. 1746'.[43]

Table 9.1
Comparison of Marlborough House Conference Report and Areas of Agreement

Marlborough House Conference[44]	Areas of Agreement[45]
Procedure for the Establishment of the Federation: The 1962 West Indies Act did not provide authority to create a quasi-legislative authority like that envisioned in the "Areas Agreement". This subsection contained a clear proviso to the effect that legislative or judicial authority could not be conferred by the existing West Indies Act. Only a new Act of Parliament could provide the Regional Council of Ministers with this type of power.[46]	**Procedure for the Establishment of the Federation:** The establishment of the Federation by Order in Council and the appointment of a Governor General under the provisions of the 1962 West Indies Act. The creation of a Federal Council as a corporate body with executive and advisory powers. Legislation during the period before full federation to be exercised by the Governor General on the advice of the Federal Council.
On Income Tax: In consequence of the foregoing, the following services at present provided by Unit Governments would be transferred to the Federal Government … Income Tax.[47] Administration of income tax would be a federal responsibility.[48]	**On Income Tax:** The administration of the income tax should remain a unit responsibility. The units would legislate with respect to the rates of personal income tax allowances.

On the Judiciary:	On the Judiciary:
In consequence of the foregoing the following services at present provided by Unit Governments would be transferred to the Federal Government … Judiciary, including not only Judges but also Magistrates and the administration of Courts.[49]	While the administration of justice should be federal, it was also proposed that the administration of Magistrate Courts should remain the responsibility of the units.
On the Police:	**On the Police:**
In consequence of the foregoing the following services at present provided by Unit Governments would be transferred to the Federal Government … the Police.[50]	While the Federal Government should be responsible for the Police Training School and for the creation of a special security force, each unit should remain under control of its police force.
On the Postal Services:	**On the Postal Services:**
In consequence of the foregoing the following services at present provided by Unit Governments would be transferred to the Federal Government … the Postal Services.[51]	It was agreed that the unit governments should administer their postal services, but the postal legislation should be on the exclusive list.
On the Unification of the Civil Service:	**On the Unification of the Civil Service:**
The Conference attached the greatest importance to the general question of the public services of the Federal and Unit Governments … . The Conference felt that there would be great advantages for the Federation as a whole in having a unified civil service for the Unit and Federal Governments … . Finally, the Conference considered that a unified civil service would help in fostering the federal spirit.[52]	It was further considered that the unification of the public services, as proposed in the Manktelow Report,[53] could not be undertaken at the present time.

Attempting to show Fisher that there was unanimous support behind the Areas of Agreement, Barrow suggested that its main departure from the Marlborough House Conference Report was 'one of timing'.[54] But Southwell's immediate interjection, 'my territory is not the only one not to agree' stained the glossy picture.[55] He voiced not only one, but several misgivings about the Areas of Agreement. First, St. Kitts could not agree to a governor general acting on the advice of the Regional Council of Ministers for an indefinite period of time.[56] Although prepared to grant limited legislative authority to the Council for the specific purpose of easing the transition process to federal status, Southwell said it would be dangerous to confer that type of power on any body unless duly elected for that purpose.[57] Second, referring to the issue of the postal services, soon to take considerable pre-eminence, he suggested that the unit territories 'could not enter into a federation without making some sacrifice of their fiscal and legislative way of life'. In other words, the Antiguans should budge. Third, his delegation could not subscribe to the idea, as some of his colleagues were now suggesting, that the unification of the public or civil service was not a sine qua non for establishing the federation. Contradicting Barrow, who had just contended that the 'delegates did not think that a unified public service was desirable at this stage',[58] Southwell argued rather forcefully that 'a government cannot function properly without an efficient civil service'.[59] The subliminal message was more than evident, the success or failure of the envisioned federation, at least as seen by the delegates from St. Kitts, would depend on the professionalism and independence which only a unified public service could provide. At this juncture Le Blanc, fragmenting the colonial landscape even further, asserted with unusual clarity that 'the proposal put forward by the Premier of Barbados was a complete departure from the terms of Cmnd. 1746'.[60] Conveying more self-confidence than he used to, Edward Le Blanc, the chief minister of Dominica, admonished his colleagues that immediate 'independence has wide implications'.[61] In particular, as he contended, his delegation felt 'unsure' as to 'the wider implications of independence on grant-in-aided territories'.[62] Bramble swiftly echoed Dominica's concern, describing early independence as a matter about which his people in Montserrat 'knew nothing and which had assumed prominence only since his arrival in Barbados'.[63] But, in particular, Le Blanc's uneasiness about early independence could not have been a surprise for Fisher or Douglas Williams, coming from the same man who just a few months earlier had secretly petitioned annexation to Canada.[64]

Interestingly, the intervention from the delegation of Dominica prompted a reaction from Bird, who so far had remained silent throughout the discussions. Implying that Le Blanc's and Bramble's misgivings were reconcilable with the Areas of Agreement, the Antiguan chief minister rather skilfully returned to the issue of unanimity. He told Fisher that there was 'broad agreement with the proposals put forward by the Premier of Barbados, except by the delegation of St. Kitts'.[65] Pre-empting any attempt at coercion by Fisher, Bird went on the offensive. In an impassioned statement he argued that his delegation had compromised on a number of matters but 'if the areas on which agreement had been won were to be re-opened and revised, it would be difficult for Antigua to make further compromises'.[66] Bird had just thrown down the gauntlet. The message was quite clear. If the Kittitian delegation and, more importantly, the British delegation did not subscribe to the Areas of Agreement, Antigua would be forced to reassess its position on whether to participate any further in these negotiations. Barrow immediately reinforced this onslaught, reiterating that the issue of timing was the sole defining element of his paper.

In the midst of this ardent session, Fisher made an extraordinarily revealing announcement: that he had just been asked to visit British Guiana and would remain in Georgetown for almost a week, returning to the chair as late as Thursday May 30, 1963.[67] That same evening (on May 24), before flying to the Guianese capital, Fisher wrote to the colonial secretary. In his letter, preserved in Sandys's papers, Fisher revealed what his impressions were after having adjourned the initial session of the preparatory conference.

> The situation here so far is roughly this: Barrow is the self-appointed mediator between Bird and the others. To some extent he has succeeded in getting Bird off his perch — but in the process he has — of course — had to compromise on some issues and in so doing has gone way to weakening the federal structure agreed by them all in London, last summer. Charles of St. Lucia, Joshua of St. Vincent and the extraordinary Bramble of Montserrat say nothing but go along with Barrow. Only St. Kitts and Dominica still stand completely firm on the London Conference White Paper. There is a good deal of acrimonious cross-talk, but I have so far managed to prevent any major row. I am not at present very optimistic about getting agreement and if I could do so it would be at the cost of weakening the federation which I am loath to do. I go to British Guiana tomorrow morning (Sat) and hope it won't be necessary to stay there more than 2 or 3 days. I think it would be unfortunate for the atmosphere and prospects here if I could not be back by Tuesday.[68]

Before resuming the narration of these proceedings, a few matters deserve further attention. For instance, the rapprochement between Barrow and Bird, as the archival record demonstrates, predated the preparatory conference. Already in March, following the fifth meeting of the RCM, Sir John Stow had warned the Colonial Office of their 'close understanding'.[69] He could not help but notice that 'Southwell, Bramble and Le Blanc seemed to form a separate bloc [while] Charles and Joshua [remained] indeterminate'.[70] Stow finished his observations with a potentially ominous foreshadowing: 'this [factionalism] made the reaching of any conclusions extremely difficult'.[71] Nonetheless, the essential questions remained unanswered. First, why was Barrow now colluding with Antigua? Second, why were St. Kitts and Dominica less inclined to abide by the Areas of Agreement than their neighbours? And third, was there any connection between Fisher's sudden assignment to British Guiana and the transfer of political authority in the archipelago?

Barrow understood that without Antigua inside the federal area further defections might ensue, in which case federation would not be either desirable or politically feasible for Barbados. The local Chamber of Commerce, together with the powerful Barbados Workers Union as well as influential elements of the political leadership, would not be satisfied with just a federation between Barbados and barely a handful of highly underdeveloped Windward territories.[72] With its national and per capita incomes being one-and-a-half times as much as that of Dominica, St. Lucia and St. Vincent combined, Barbados's economic superiority was far too obvious.[73] Not surprisingly, some in Bridgetown were dreading the mere mention of such an uneven union. At a time when, as the archival record reveals, 'the honeymoon period of the new government [was] drawing to a close',[74] the premier was acknowledging the importance of acting with caution. Additionally, and as suggested earlier, informed public opinion in Bridgetown did not regard federation as the only constitutional avenue open to the island. Barrow himself had already hinted, only days before Sandys's visit, at the possibility of Barbados 'going it alone'.[75] Since making that pronouncement Barrow's international engagements had gained more prominence. His most recent schedule, before the meeting with Fisher in May 1963, included travelling to the UN headquarters in January,[76] meeting with Eric Williams and Cheddi Jagan in March,[77] and spending almost two weeks in Ottawa for discussions with Canadian officials.[78] These exchanges clearly went beyond the archipelago's context. It seems that even as the preparatory conference got under way Barrow was still determined to keep all avenues open.

In the meantime, the scenario in Basseterre and Roseau was considerably different. Far from the political effervescence seen in St. John's or Bridgetown, here the leadership of Southwell and Le Blanc, respectively, was relatively uncontested. Their grasp of the local political landscape, at least during this period, was far-reaching.[79] This meant that the delegations from Dominica and St. Kitts were under less domestic scrutiny than the ones coming from Barbados and Antigua. They could compromise more freely with the Colonial Office. Both Southwell and Le Blanc had enough political capital to follow through with Cmnd.1746. They saw no need to dismantle the compromises already brokered at Marlborough House. The Areas of Agreement could scarcely have meant anything to them. Yet, the substantive reason why these territories did not see the need for a local turnaround had more to do with their economic and financial uncertainties.

For instance, at the last budget sitting of the Kittitian Legislative Council (March 18 and 19, 1963) Southwell had characterized what he was about to deliver as a 'crisis budget'.[80] Warning that 1964 might be a 'decisive year for the territory's finances',[81] all through his address the chief minister placed most of his hopes on the imminence of federation as well as on the grants the British Treasury was then extending the island.[82] Southwell realized that the economy of his territory had been caught, since the late 1950s, in a period of acute stagnation. Not surprisingly, he had pinned most of his hopes for recovery on the federal project. This practice of standing wholeheartedly behind the federal ideal in times of economic malaise was not uncommon. Jamaica had also plodded along that road in the early 1950s, only to make an about-face at the time of the bauxite boom.[83]

That hypothesis also sheds some light on why, as Barrow travelled abroad, Southwell dedicated most of his time to federal matters closely related to the forthcoming preparatory conference. In February he had visited both Jamaica and Trinidad and Tobago for discussions concerning the future of the University of the West Indies and the regional shipping services, respectively.[84] And, while both Barrow and Bird had allocated hardly any time to read, let alone study, the Fiscal and Civil Service Reports,[85] Southwell, along with his official advisers, had been evaluating this set of documents since publication in April 1963.[86]

However, a discussion of why St. Kitts and Barbados strongly disagreed would remain incomplete if the more human elements were not factored in. The promotion of Robert Bradshaw to the Executive Council of St.

Kitts, albeit without portfolio, late in January 1963, had strengthened the resolve of the local leadership in Basseterre to press for a federation with a strong centre.[87] Bradshaw, the former finance minister of the late West Indies Federation, had already gained a reputation for being a staunch supporter of highly centralized federal structures. The position adopted by St. Kitts at the first session of the preparatory conference undoubtedly reflected it. Yet, Bradshaw's strong and, more often than not, dogmatic views did not endear him to many of his regional colleagues. More interestingly, by this stage his personal relationship with Barrow had reached its nadir, especially after their slanging match in October 1962.[88] Whether the obvious animosity between them swayed Southwell's opinions is not clear. However, the archival record reveals that the chief minister, just prior to the conference with Fisher, was entertaining a remarkably low opinion of Barrow as a leader. In a secret report to the Colonial Office, produced in early May, Henry Howard, colonial administrator of St. Kitts–Nevis–Anguilla, touched upon this sensitive subject.

> The Chief Minister has expressed himself with some severity on the subject of the Premier of Barbados, of whom he has little opinion as a negotiator or chairman of a conference. He clearly resents Barrow's handling of many problems confronting the RCM. Additionally, he has little confidence in Barrow's ability to lead the delegates of the Seven towards overcoming the many difficulties that are likely to arise at the May Conference in Barbados and subsequently in London.[89]

This also accounts, albeit partially, for St. Kitts' opposition to the conferment of legislative authority upon the Council of Ministers.[90] There was absolutely no intention, either from the chief minister or from his new colleague in the Kittian Executive Council, of guaranteeing Barrow's premature investiture as the leader of the emerging federal area. The mood in Basseterre was against granting Barrow, or for that matter Bird, any degree of unchecked or far-reaching authority. Such an aversion, on Southwell's and Bradshaw's part, did not necessarily spring from political greed. These men saw an overriding need to defend their philosophical conception of federation. While Barrow and Bird had shown themselves to be pragmatists, these Kittitians belonged to the same school of thought as Marryshow and Cipriani.[91] Only a strongly centralized arrangement, so they argued, could flourish where the original federal experiment had failed. In their eyes any deviation from that type of structure could very well lead to a replay of the previous hecatomb, with terrible consequences for St. Kitts. Therefore, anything that went against the agreements already reached at Marlborough House, especially if piloted by Barrow and Bird, was bound to meet considerable suspicion and resistance.

The situation in Dominica followed a similar pattern, although with some slight differences. While the economy of St. Kitts was based, for the most part, on the production of sugar, in Dominica bananas were reigning supreme. Whereas the price as well as the output of sugar had remained stagnant for the last five years,[92] the acreage under banana production in Dominica and its value in the European markets had more than trebled since the mid 1950s.[93] But, like St. Kitts, Dominica was still afflicted by widespread poverty and deplorable public utilities.[94] And although the macroeconomic cycle did not look as bleak as in St. Kitts, Le Blanc was now attaching considerable importance to the federal project. More specifically, after Canada's Prime Minister Diefenbaker's flat refusal even to consider annexing the island to Canada, the chief minister and other prominent members of his Dominica Labour Party had been compelled to re-evaluate their options. After that sobering exercise, pressing for a strong federal area once again seemed like the most sensible course of action.

On the whole, the political leadership in Basseterre and Roseau was far more concerned with the structural or constitutional matters raised in the Areas of Agreement than with the timing of independence. Although difficult to substantiate, a point could be made to the effect that had London agreed to accelerate that process Bramble, Le Blanc and even Southwell would have gone along with it. So, to a large extent, the major obstacle in the way of the timing for independence proposed in the Areas of Agreement paper was the British Government itself. Not surprisingly, some have failed to understand London's unwillingness to embrace Barrow's abridged timetable. Sir Fred Phillips, for instance, in his most celebrated constitutional study of the area, has argued that,

> [I]n 1963 when the United Kingdom's Under-Secretary of State came to the West Indies to finalise arrangements for the federation he was approached with a demand, initiated by the governments of Barbados and Antigua, that the projected federation be granted full independence at the very inception. Why

this request was rejected is difficult to understand, especially when one considers that only four years later, in the case of the Associated States, the level of constitutional advance granted them went in some respects far beyond what was asked for.[95]

Attempting to elucidate the unanswered question raised in that passage is highly relevant for understanding this particular stage of the process; and, as shown below, reveals an intimate connection between Fisher's trip to Georgetown and London's refusal to speed up its withdrawal from the archipelago. Even if the colonial leadership had stood unanimously behind the Fiscal and Civil Service Reports, the British Government would still have adhered to the original timetable. At first glance, the British position seemed quite predictable. The issue of timing had already been settled at the Marlborough House Conference and, therefore, there was no need to re-open it.

Table 9.2
Preparatory Steps for the Setting Up of the Federation

Marlborough House Timetable[96]	Areas of Agreement Timetable[97]
Step 1: During the June Conference, precise instructions would be given to the legal draftsmen for producing the constitution of a dependent (or colonial) federation.[98] Additionally, the Regional Council of Ministers would become an interim corporate body with no legislative or executive powers.	**Step 1:** Immediately after the preparatory conference, precise instructions would be given for the establishment of an interim organisation with legislative and executive powers. This body would operate until the full federal constitution and first federal elections were brought into force.
Step 2: Following the drafting process, affirmative resolutions from both Houses of Parliament would be required for bringing it into force and, thus, for establishing the dependent federation. The provisions of the new constitution would also enable the first federal elections to take place.	**Step 2:** Following the June Conference, a draft containing precise instructions should be given to the (Colonial Office's) legal draftsmen for preparing the federal constitution. Simultaneously, the process of clearance with other Commonwealth governments would be carried out and a fresh Act of Parliament would be prepared. As soon as the federal constitution is brought into force, the federation would proceed towards full independence.

Step 3:	Step 3:
After the new dependent Federation had been established and a new elected Federal Government was in office, the Secretary of State for the Colonies would be prepared to enter into discussions concerning independence for the Federation. These discussions would include a review of the provisions contained in the existing federal constitution.[99]	Step 2 of the 'Areas of Agreement' paper condensed steps 2 and 3 of Cmnd. 1746. It offered no buffer zone between the enactment of the federal constitution and the declaration of independence.

As is evident from Table 9.2, there was no profound discrepancy between the timetable already agreed to the previous May and the one advanced in the Areas of Agreement. Why then was London clinging on to the slower track version, at a time when key colonial actors such as Barrow and (although to a lesser degree) Bird wanted to speed up the withdrawal? And if, as Phillips observed, 'only four years later' the British Government would transfer almost total authority to the units, what forces were preventing all that from crystallizing at the time of Fisher's visit? Once again, the process in the archipelago was being swayed by wider geo-political imperatives. After all, as Fisher himself would suggest to the colonial leadership, 'here you are at the centre of things'.[100] The final excerpt from his letter to Sandys throws some light on that broader picture.

> I have just received a long office telegram giving me Grey's [Sir Ralph Grey, colonial governor of British Guiana] reactions to our new policy. Despite them, I believe we should stick to our decision, particularly if the US will pump in some money. It is probably not a long-term solution, but the alternatives of the present drift to disaster or giving British Guiana independence and, in so doing, handing it over to chaos and civil war are even less attractive.[101]

Ironically, Barrow's petition for a swifter transition to independence came at a time when the political crisis in neighbouring British Guiana was finally reaching its climax. Since late March 1963 the fiercely contested struggle between the Guyana Industrial and Agricultural Workers' Union (GAWU), run by Jagan, and the labour unions controlled by the Anglo-American oriented Man Power Citizen's Association (MPCA) had brought about an overwhelming general strike. Led by the civil service and allegedly financed by the American CIA, this impasse, which lasted almost eighty days, was accompanied by widespread arson, racial violence and murders. The prospects were so dire that barely a fortnight prior to Fisher's arrival in Bridgetown, Sir Ralph Grey had declared on May 9, 1963, a state of emergency in the territory. Without a doubt Fisher's presence in British Guiana coincided with the most neuralgic point in this whole episode. Although their private papers are in need of thorough examination, it is not difficult to imagine the discussions between Fisher and Grey being circumscribed to the implementation of London's newly articulated policy for British Guiana.[102] The widening prospects of a covert Cuban-Soviet intervention and the collateral damage this crisis could inflict on Britain's policy for the neighbouring archipelago and on its special relationship with the US loomed very large in the background. It was becoming evident that there would be no British withdrawal from this colony until the ruling People's Progressive Party (PPP) met Sandys' demand for proportional representation, which in the end triggered Jagan's downfall from political power. Not surprisingly, amidst this convoluted and tense scenario, committing to an earlier-than-expected timetable for complete disengagement from the archipelago was not tenable, particularly by late May and early June 1963. Moreover, as Fisher himself argued, there were 'serious Commonwealth and parliamentary difficulties' in meeting such an abridged timetable. Once the preparatory conference resumed, following his return from Georgetown, the under-secretary of state suggested to Barrow that for the upcoming June Conference in London to be an 'independence conference' decisions would have to be taken on a much wider range of issues.

> [These] are issues, in many cases, to which you have as yet given very little thought, and on which you have reached no agreement. Indeed, you are still divided among yourselves about what kind of federation you want.[103]

Fisher was alluding to, among other things, the status of the independent Federation in relation to the Commonwealth,[104] and the applicability of the UK Nationality Acts[105] (if at all) to the citizens of the new state. And, clearly, with the final constitutional, financial, defence and diplomatic arrangements still in the air, the possibility of agreeing to the islands' almost immediate independence was very remote indeed. During that morning session, which was taking place on Thursday May

30, Fisher said that having listened to their views, it was his duty to outline the position of the British Government. He was prepared to recommend to the colonial secretary that the June Conference in London, to draft the constitution of a dependent federation, should take place, from June 24 to July 7, 1963, provided that all chief ministers and the premier of Barbados were prepared to accept,

That the establishment of the Federation shall be by the three-phase process, accompanied by the assurances concerning independence;

That the Federation should not be precluded by the constitution from having executive powers over matters in the Legislative Lists. There will, however, be arrangements for delegation and we will examine further with you how these arrangements can be applied to Income Tax, the Postal Services and the Police;

That the arrangements about loans laid down in Cmnd. 1746 should stand;

That a Unified Public Service for administrative, technical and professional grades be accepted, although exactly which posts this would apply to has to be worked out;

That the Federal Government shall have its own independent source of finance and that there will be nothing in the constitution to prevent the provision of funds adequate for the Federal Government's responsibilities.[106]

Vere Bird was the first colonial politician to react to Fisher's paper. Adhering to his initial position, he insisted that the Antiguan delegation wanted a federation with legislative and supervisory powers only, with severe restrictions put on the Federal Government's loan-raising powers and without a unified public service. Bird remained resolute. He argued that the Areas of Agreement paper should be adopted and its terms written in the future federal Constitution. Otherwise, his delegation would prefer to see the RCM operating indefinitely as a corporate body 'in the hope that nationhood and independence be finally achieved'.[107] Bird was also the first local politician to recognize that, in view of this inevitable stalemate, the London Conference should be called off.

As the British delegation expected, Barrow also reacted quite strongly to Fisher's five points. He described them as 'too dogmatic and inflexible'. As Barrow put it, the under-secretary's paper did not meet with his government's approval. The premier expounded on the reasons behind his opposition. He argued that his delegation could not be told to negotiate for independence some time in the future because, as he claimed, that question had already been settled when the people of Barbados elected his party to power.[108] He felt that Barbados had to strive for independence either within or without a federation. Pledging that his Government would not accept anything less than an independent federation, Barrow denounced the fact that for the first time in the island's history its local constitution was in danger of being affected by an Order in Council.[109] However, Barrow's most acerbic criticism went to what he described as the British Treasury's 'attempt to evade its proper financial obligations'.[110] Reiterating that the obstacles put forward for independence were 'shibboleths', the premier kept pounding rather strongly that the British Government should not walk away from its pecuniary responsibilities. Barrow's tone hardly concealed a feeling of recrimination. The following statement conveys it rather clearly:

> Mr. Maudling, a former Secretary of State for the Colonies, had said that the islands must federate so that they could seek financial aid from Canada and the US. The position is that those Governments have told the units that aid would not come unless they become independent. It is a matter for regret that application for financial aid has remained in the Colonial Office unanswered for years.[111]

In the meantime, and while agreeing in principle with Fisher's paper, Southwell and Le Blanc coincided with Bird, Barrow, Charles, Bramble and Joshua that without unanimity there was no need to go to London. Confronted with such a blatant collapse in the discussions, Fisher felt compelled to adjourn the preparatory conference and to cable the colonial secretary, asking for the indefinite postponement of the June Conference. As Sandys would confide in Sir Anthony Eden, over a fortnight later, the political future of these islands was 'very much in the melting pot'.[112] Interestingly, the mood in the archipelago, at least as described in the local intelligence reports for the months of May and June 1963, does not convey any such sense of urgency, collective disquiet or even disappointment at the latest impasse. The following observation, written by Alec Lovelace, becomes emblematic of the popular feeling across most of the area,

The failure of the Barbados Conference on the Eastern Caribbean Federation passed almost without comment. Having been brain-washed by 5,000 copies of the White Paper the public could have been expected to react to the complete volte-face of the political leaders, but neither political party has been able to raise any enthusiasm.[113]

A closer look at the archival record, however, reveals that while the public hardly showed any interest in the more abstract constitutional discussions, the unsettled issue of British aid was now attracting considerable attention. And, not surprisingly, after over a year of ambiguity the colonial politicians were about to face intense pressures from their local constituencies. The time of reckoning had finally arrived. The onus of confronting the British Government and, thus, defining the exact quantum of metropolitan assistance, as far as the public was concerned, lay squarely on the politicians' doorstep. This explains why, after their return from Bridgetown, the chief ministers' public statements dealt with the question of aid. Bramble, for instance, in a radio broadcast following the conference with Fisher made it abundantly clear that,

> To talk of independence from the start raises the question of obtaining more money, when the question how we are going to obtain less money was not even settled.[114]

Southwell seemed, on the one hand, to be on the same wavelength. In a press release, amounting to a progress report on the federal negotiations, the Kittitian chief minister was now urging the Colonial Office to produce 'the details of the financial assistance from HMG'.[115] Moreover, he was arguing that such a matter should be decided 'at the earliest possible date, before the initiation of any action towards the formation of the Federation'.[116] On the other, as Lovelace soon reported to his superiors in the Colonial Office, Le Blanc agreed with Southwell and was intending to press the Colonial Office 'for an assurance of financial aid for a period of five years before immediate independence is agreed to'.[117] The archival record also reveals that in neighbouring St. Lucia the unanswered question of British assistance was about to take special prominence in Charles's agenda. While embroiled in a very tense pre-election season, the passing of Hurricane Edith produced damages of over BWI $1.4 million to the island's banana industry.[118] Elucidating the aid conundrum could not wait much longer.

Meanwhile in Antigua, Bird had not made any gesture to explain to the local press or the public the outcome of his discussions with Nigel Fisher. However, the intelligence reports from Ian Turbott tend to indicate that with the chief minister in the midst of a thorough political re-assessment, the more vociferous elements of his Antigua Trades and Labour Union were very busy indeed. To no one's astonishment, their continuous observations conveyed an overriding distrust of the British Government. In a series of detailed articles, published in the summer of 1963 in the *Workers Voice* (main organ of the ruling party's labour wing), London's elusiveness came under heavy attack. Openly indicting the British Government, McChesney George and his allies kept reminding their readers that,

> Dr. Williams, much to his remorse, has learned what British promises of assistance are like after one has achieved independence; are we to find ourselves in a similar predicament?[119]

In Barbados, where Barrow's favour with the electorate was plummeting after bringing in new taxation in two successive budgets and with the legendary Grantley Adams having just made his political comeback as leader of the opposition,[120] the internal situation was becoming more complicated than in the neighbouring islands. Here, for example, the timing of independence was raising far more public interest and overall political effervescence. Within this particular context, the uncertainty over aid was causing special anxieties; not least because it was widening a rather problematic divide in the local Cabinet, between those ministers in favour of independence within a federation and the ones pressing for independence without it.

Over a month after Fisher's visit and during the course of an impromptu meeting between Sir John Stow and Duncan Sandys,[121] Barbados's colonial governor confessed that he had been told that apart from Barrow, Wynter Crawford, Cameron Tudor and Erskine Ward no other minister 'was in favour of it'.[122] The minutes from this discussion also reveal that when Sandys asked whether Barbados would demand immediate independence, if the proposal for a federation came to nothing, Stow had showed himself 'confident that she would'.[123] Equally importantly, just before the end of their brief conversation, Sandys urged Stow to, in his capacity as Chairman of the RCM, 'keep the participants off the question of British aid as much as possible'.[124] The colonial secretary himself, only a few days later, stood his ground when Barrow exhorted him 'to settle the financial provisions'.[125] As he put it to the premier, 'HMG wanted to know first what sort of a federation they were being invited to contribute to'.[126] Early in August, in an official despatch to the colonial leadership, Sandys asserted that,

> As stated in paragraph 32 of Cmnd. 1746, Her Majesty's Government recognises that a Federation would stand in need of external assistance for a period after it was established, both in capital and budgetary account.... I see, however, no possibility of considering at the next conference the levels of aid for as long a period as ten years ahead.[127]

With the British still unprepared to give more assurances about the scale of British aid than were given at the Marlborough House Conference, the publication of the Economic Survey began to attract singular attention. Although concluded in April 1963, Carleen O'Loughlin's report was finally published in August, thus coinciding with the release of Sandys's despatch. The Survey came down strongly in favour of what connoisseurs of colonial development used to call the 'big push approach'.[128] This meant injecting large amounts of capital in a short time into all relevant sectors of the economy, with the object of breaking the vicious cycle of low incomes/low investment/low incomes.[129] Therefore, O'Loughlin was recommending that the British Government pour around £59.5 million pounds sterling into these territories over a period of ten years, of which some £28.5 million should be spent in the first three years. The report concluded that with such a degree of investment all the islands, with the exception of Montserrat, could become economically viable by 1973. Not surprisingly, as Sir Arthur Lewis wrote some years later, Carleen O'Loughlin had become the 'heroine of the Seven'.[130] And, much to Sandys's chagrin, the premier and the chief ministers now demanded that, before convening a further conference, the British Government should agree to provide the full cost of the development programme envisioned in O'Loughlin's Economic Survey. Their joint reply to Sandys's despatch was categorical,

> Ministers strongly felt that the statement contained in paragraph 20 of your despatch, that no possibility was seen at the next conference of considering the levels of aid for a period as long as ten years, could seriously jeopardise the

success of the Federation as a whole. The Conference [held at the seventh meeting of the RCM] unanimously endorsed a request that financial assistance on the scale envisaged in Dr. O'Loughlin's Economic Survey be made available… and that no conference to settle the details of a constitution for an independent Federation would be held until satisfactory assurances about the quantum and duration of assistance from HMG had been obtained.[131]

In the amusing words of Eric Williams, the overwhelming perception in the area was that having 'sucked the orange dry' the British were now desperately trying to 'avoid slipping on the peel'. But what forces, tensions or pressures were influencing the Colonial Office's own attitude towards aid? Was the Treasury keeping Sandys on a tight leash? Or were the Americans and the Canadians unwilling to contribute? These critical questions, as the next chapters demonstrate, deserve the fullest analysis and evaluation before moving any further.

10

Aid within a Transatlantic Triangle

> If the response continues to be negative, the US and Canada, from a
> point of view of self-interest rather than of Christian charity, will probably
> be forced into the act. We should be prepared.
>
> *Eileen R. Donovan, US Consul General in Bridgetown, 1964*

The uncertainty over aid had not only led to a stalemate between the
Colonial Office and the Eastern Caribbean dependencies but, even more
importantly, had exacerbated the already tense relationship between the
Colonial Office and the Treasury. The following letter, authored by Duncan
Sandys, addressed to John Boyd-Carpenter, chief secretary to the Treasury,
and written on November 26, 1963, throws abundant light on the
enormous complexities surrounding the question of aid.

> There has been correspondence between our officials about my wish to give an
> assurance to the dependent Governments of the Eastern Caribbean that, if
> Federation can be brought about in satisfactory terms, more British aid will be
> made available to the area than it is at present receiving.

> I understand that your officials are reluctant to agree to this proposal. In Sharp's
> letter to [Douglas] Williams of 7th November several points have been raised, to
> which I consider that convincing answers can be given and these are set out in
> a note which I enclose.

> But the case for Federation rests on a broader basis than financial and economic
> considerations alone. I am most anxious, now that all our major dependencies
> have achieved or are achieving independence, to find permanent solutions for
> our smaller territories, defensible at the UN.

> Many of these territories present special problems, which make it difficult to
> apply the conception of early independence to them. It is questionable whether

any of these islands — apart from Barbados — could properly achieve independence on its own.

If they were to, they would quickly degenerate under the corrupt and incompetent administration of island bosses and enter into an economic decline, which would lead to political unrest and offer scope for Castro-style intrigue and infiltration. They would not be a good advertisement for past English-rule.

The alternative of letting them continue indefinitely as British dependencies is equally unattractive, for different reasons. There would be an atmosphere of continuous frustration and we should be open to all the usual anti-colonial attacks.

At the same time we should be expected to go on paying for them in circumstances which would provide no hope of ultimate viability.

I do not pretend that the proposed Federation is ideal. But at least it offers the prospect of independence on a reasonably satisfactory basis. With a population of 700,000 and some pooling of resources, it could cut a respectable figure internationally. The central Government, as strong as we could make it, would impose some control over island bosses and through a unified public service would control a number of essential services. The economic climate would be much more favourable for attracting outside aid and for making the best use of any aid so attracted.

It may be asked why, if the case for Federation is so good, it is necessary for us to offer a financial inducement to bring it about. The answer is mainly to be found in the attitude of Barbados. She is being asked to federate with territories with a lower standard of living and, unless as an inducement we can promise more aid to the Federation, they will see on our part a device to off-load on to them responsibility for the poorer islands. They will not agree to join a federation on that basis and without Barbados it has no future.[1]

In an addendum to this letter, the colonial secretary carried on arguing that,

[T]he question whether the Federation can become viable within the foreseeable future depends principally on the amount of investment which can be attracted.

If we can induce the islands to federalise and can give a lead to other donors of aid by increasing our own aid, it is possible that the level of public investment postulated by this Report can be achieved. In offering £15 million over three years, we should have to make it clear that this level would not be maintained indefinitely, but was our contribution towards the £28 million in three years recommended by the O'Loughlin Report. Thereafter we could hope to taper off our development assistance.

If the islands do not federate there is no prospect of their ever ceasing to need British aid on the present scale. We know that the US Government is more likely to give aid to these islands if they federate. The proposition that if through Federation these islands can attract more aid from other sources they should then receive less British aid cannot be accepted.

These territories already have a lower *per capita* income than any other territory in the Caribbean (including the French and Dutch units) with the possible exception of Haiti.

Unless we get them (units) federated (for which it is necessary to offer increased aid) they will not attract aid from other sources. British aid will be more worthwhile within a framework likely to produce a viable economic unit than in circumstances where aid will go on indefinitely without raising the islands from a care and maintenance basis. To give more aid now may save aid later.[2]

After reading this long extract, some of the first questions that must be addressed are these, of what had British aid to the archipelago historically consisted, and what was the exact scale of the Treasury's assistance just then?

For the most part, British assistance to these territories had come from 'grants-in-aid'[3] and from the funds administered by the Colonial Development and Welfare Acts,[4] commonly referred to as 'CD&W.' And although London was facilitating further aid through the limited commercial investments of the Commonwealth Development Corporation (CDC)[5] and trade preferences, most notably the Ottawa Agreement,[6] the aforementioned sources bore the brunt of it.

By the end of 1963, the British Exchequer's aid to the now called Little Seven was estimated at £4,235,000 per annum. However, this level of spending represented just 45 per cent of what O'Loughlin had already recommended, which amounted to £9,500,000 per annum for each of the first three years of federation.

Table 10.1:
Allocations of British Aid to the Seven, 1963–66

Territory	Grants-in-aid (£000) 1964	CD&W grants (£000) 1963–66	CD&W loans (£000) 1963–66
Barbados	Nil	592	3,070
Antigua - Barbuda	Nil	666	Nil
Dominica	230	738	Nil
Montserrat	220	271	Nil
St. Kitts-Nevis-Anguilla	270	678	500
St. Lucia	75	681	Nil
St. Vincent	290	664	Nil
Regional	nil	1172	420
Total	1,085	5,462 (approx. 1,820 p.a.)	3,990 (approx. 1,330 p.a.)

Source: FO 371/173580.

The archival record reveals that there was a prevailing perception, not only in the Treasury but also in certain quarters of the Colonial Office, that these islands were 'nearly all shameless mendicants', always complaining 'loudly about the past' and trying 'to make exorbitant demands for the future'.[7] Even further, influential voices in both ministries believed these seven territories had been receiving more than their fair share of British assistance. It would not be very difficult to conclude that such viewpoints constituted major stumbling blocks in the way of any attempt by Sandys to increase the aid assigned to them. But were these opinions justified?

The available evidence, pertaining almost exclusively to the CD&W allocations, suggests that the Seven had indeed fared considerably better than most other British dependencies. While the percentage of their allowance in relation to the totality of the funds available, ever since the days of the Colonial Development Fund,[8] had remained basically unaltered, oscillating between a 7.08 per cent and 7.25 per cent of the whole,[9] the breakdown of their actual share was nonetheless fairly significant. In total 22 per cent of all CD&W grants and loans, since 1946,[10] had gone to the 16 units comprising the so-called British Caribbean.[11] More interestingly, if compared to the CD&W allocations to most of the remaining African or even Pacific dependencies, for instance, the funding level earmarked for the Caribbean was considerable. At first sight, the evidence supporting this observation is staggering. While the Caribbean, with a total area of 105,231 square miles and a population (c.1964) of 4,569,300,[12] had received £15.62 per capita (in CD&W funds),[13] British Africa, with 2,180,138 square miles and 68,403,529 inhabitants had only got £2.13 per capita.[14] In comparing, for example, the expenditure in essential areas such as roads and health-care, a more accurate picture begins to emerge. Evaluating the expenditure in these sectors, to which most money had gone,[15] facilitates useful points of comparison.

Table 10.2
Total CD&W Allocations to Other Colonies for Roads and Health since 1946

Territory	Allocations for Roads (£000)	Allocations for Health (£000)
Uganda (1962)[16] Area: 93,981mi² Population: 6,536,616[17]	2,597	1,958
Kenya (1963) Area: 220,000mi² Population: 8,636,263	1,435	961
Zanzibar (1963) Area: 637mi² Population: 299,111	156	172
Northern Rhodesia (1964) Area: 290,000mi² Population: 3,408,500	900	25
Gambia (1964) Area: 4,000mi² Population: 315,999	1,162	399
Nyasaland (1966) Area: 37,000mi² Population: 156,257	2,289	178
Basutoland (1966) Area: 12,000mi² Population: 641,674	752	909
Bechuanaland (1966) Area: 275,000mi² Population: 320,675	634	603
Aden and the Protectorate of South Arabia (1967/68) Area: 111,000mi² Population: 138,441	1,613	1,733
Swaziland (1968) Area: 6,700mi² Population: 237,041	1,738	628
Mauritius (1968) Area: 720mi² Population: 681,619	674	1,392
Fiji (1970) Area: 7,000mi² Population: 345,737	3,201	971
Seychelles (1976) Area: 160mi² Population: 41,425	709	206

Source: Cmnd. 4677, Table 1.

Table 10.3
Total CD&W Allocations to the Seven for Roads and Health since 1946

Little Seven	Allocations for Roads (£000)	Allocations for Health (£000)
Barbados Area: 166mi² Population: 242,000[18]	103	1,259
Antigua-Barbuda Area: 108mi² Population: 60,000	197	327
St. Kitts-Nevis-Anguilla Area: 136mi² Population: 62,000	187	252
Dominica Area: 290mi² Population: 64,000	2,176	253
St. Lucia Area: 238mi² Population: 94,000	1,269	471
St. Vincent Area: 150mi² Population: 85,000	1,223	227
Montserrat Area: 39mi² Population: 13,500	237	66

Source: Cmnd. 4677, Table 1.

For instance, the combined CD&W allocation for roads in Dominica, St. Lucia and St. Vincent had been, by far, amongst the most generous. On the one hand, these three Windward territories obtained a joint total of £4,688,000 or approximately £6,885 per square mile. While on the other, Gambia (6 times their combined area) received close to £290 per square mile, Nyasaland (55 times their area) obtained £61.86 per square mile and Bechuanaland (400 times their area) was awarded £2.31 per square mile. On the health front, whereas Barbados received £5.20 per capita, Bechuanaland and Gambia, with nearly one-and-a-half times more people, obtained £1.88 and £1.26 per capita, respectively. More interestingly, Mauritius, with almost three times the inhabitants of Barbados, and entitled to two more years of CD&W funding than the latter,[19] only got £2.04 per capita.

Even if analyzed within the context of the British Caribbean area itself, the Seven had fared relatively well. Out of the £71,366,460 in CD&W funds allocated to the region as a whole, the Seven received very close to a third (32.97 per cent) or £23,530,000. This was a very significant portion. After all, the Seven represented nothing but 1.07 per cent of the region's entire area (including the continential territories) and were inhabited by only 13.51 per cent of the region's total population. And even if Jamaica and Trinidad and Tobago (where the flow of CD&W grants stopped with independence in 1962) were taken out of the equation, the Seven would only amount to 1.14 per cent of the archipelago's size and 27.71 per cent of its population.

This type of empirical evidence, coupled with the constant allegations of misappropriation of public funds surrounding the archipelago's political leadership,[20] were fuelling Boyd-Carpenter's inflexible position and that of his team in the Treasury. However, the wider picture would be blurred if the CD&W allocations to the Mediterranean dependencies,[21] in particular to Malta, as well as those to British Guiana and British Honduras were not looked at more closely. Those three units, along with Nigeria, Kenya and Tanganyika, had received the most funding;[22] even though Kenya, the smaller of these African dependencies, was almost two-and-a-half times their combined size and had eight times as many inhabitants.[23] But why was Malta given a larger share than, for instance, Tanganyika, which had nearly 30 times more people and close to 30,000 times that island's area? Or, why did the CD&W allocations in British Honduras and British Guiana amount to, on average, £72.36 per capita and in Nigeria and Kenya to £1.99?

To the naked eye these apparent discrepancies may very well seem shocking; nevertheless, they open an important window from which to appreciate even better the debate over aid. While the six dependencies mentioned above fitted very closely the classical description of under-developed communities, Malta,[24] British Honduras and British Guiana, because of their strategic value, small size and low viability prospects, had always stood a better chance of getting far more assistance than Nigeria, Tanganyika or even Kenya.[25] This also explains why the Seven had done relatively better than most other colonies in attracting British aid. And, as Sandys himself had just pointed out to Boyd-Carpenter, the case for increasing their allocation rested on similar grounds.

If viability was defined by the extent to which a community could function or even survive 'as an autonomous entity',[26] then the Seven fell short. These islands, with an average of 88,000 inhabitants and 161 square miles per unit, suffered from the typical hardships afflicting minute, isolated and highly fragmented units.[27] The high costs of extraterritorial communications and transportation (with the accompanying impact on prices),[28] the absence of raw materials, the acute shortages of water supplies and electricity, together with unrelenting soil erosion,[29] among many others, severely curtailed their viability potential.[30] Not surprisingly, the overall condition of most of the Seven (with the notable exception of Barbados) remained stagnant and far from satisfactory. And, under such trying circumstances, the difficulties in articulating a coherent development policy were tremendous. Sandys, who had not forgotten their geopolitical significance, was now seeing this quite clearly and, therefore, insisted that the Treasury disburse more money to the area.

Over eighteen months later, in an unusual intervention, Prince Philip, the Duke of Edinburgh, would echo Sandys's position. Although so far the Seven's share of aid had been relatively higher than in most places, geography and size continued to conspire in their favour. In a letter to Lord Longford, Prince Philip openly argued that,

> On the whole these islands are not in a very good state.... The basic necessities for health, education, transport, public utilities and communications have been neglected. Government Houses, almost without exception, are disintegrating and badly equipped owing to the unfortunate system of making them a charge on the islands' resources.

> The hospitals are not much better in spite of some activity in recent years. Roads, which are after all the basis of economic development, are primitive and often totally inadequate. Public health, in the form of sewerage, water supply, town planning, slum control and electric power, is not much better.

> I suspect that much of this is due to the system of grant-in-aid which is merely subsidising inadequate government machinery and results in hand-to-mouth existence instead of any form of planned development.

> The offer of so-called constitutional advance is merely the cheapest and easiest way of trying to restrict general dissatisfaction in the islands. It is not the constitutional position which worries the inhabitants, it is the efficient

administration and their economic future.

The whole situation on the eve of constitutional discussions is rather discouraging. If these islands had been as conveniently remote as the Pacific islands or the Seychelles all this might have passed unnoticed. Unfortunately the West Indian islands are being discovered at a great rate by a tourist traffic which is likely to become a flood in a short time. Not only are the islands totally unprepared for this, but the tourists, who come from all over the world, can see only too clearly for themselves the results of stagnation and neglect.

Whatever the outcome of the constitutional discussions, we cannot avoid responsibility for the state of these islands. They have been associated with the British Crown for up to three hundred years and I believe we are morally bound to make a real effort to put them on their feet or at least bring them into line with their French and Dutch neighbours.[31]

Now, as suggested both in Prince Philip's letter and in Sandys's discussions with the Treasury, the Seven's relative backwardness with respect to the neighbouring French, Dutch and American dependencies could not be altogether ignored. This apparent disparity in incomes and overall resources, as the colonial secretary saw it, could very well precipitate 'Castro-style intrigue and infiltration'.[32] In his opinion, owing to geopolitical and development concerns, aid to the Seven should be apportioned in relation to what their neighbours were then receiving. It was essential, as the Duke of Edinburgh was to suggest, 'to bring them into line' with these other islands. But were the French, Dutch and American territories genuinely better off than the Seven? What do the figures reveal?

Table 10.4
National Income in French, Dutch and US Dependencies 1963–64

French, American and Dutch Caribbean	National Income[33] ($US 000,000) 1963–64	National Income per capita ($US) 1963–64
Martinique Area: 425mi² Population: 275,000	96	349.09
Guadeloupe Area: 583mi² Population: 270,000	95	351.85
Puerto Rico Area: 3,500mi² Population: 2,353,297	1,600	679.90
US Virgin Islands Area: 133mi² Population: 32,099	24.2	753.92
St. Croix St. John St. Thomas		
Netherlands Antilles Area: 380mi² Population: 194,371	175	900.34
Aruba Bonaire Curaçao St. Maarten St. Eustatius Saba		

Source: Caribbean General, Volume 1, National Security File, Box 1, LBJ Presidential Library.

Table 10.5
National Income in the Seven, 1963–64

Little Seven[34]	National Income ($US 000,000) 1963–64	National Income per capita ($US) 1963–64
Barbados	59.6	246.28
Antigua-Barbuda	11.5	191.67
St. Kitts–Nevis–Anguilla	9.6	154.84
Dominica	10.0	156.25
St. Lucia	12.7	135.11
St. Vincent	12.5	147.06
Montserrat	1.8	133.33

Source: Caribbean General, Volume 1, National Security File, Box 1, LBJ Presidential Library.

Although all these islands, with the obvious exception of Puerto Rico, were about the same in area and population, the Seven were, nonetheless, at a clear disadvantage both economically and politically. Both the constitutional position of the non-British islands and their financial relationships with Paris, The Hague, Washington and even Brussels deserve further attention.

Martinique and Guadeloupe, separated from one another by 120 miles, were *Départements d'Outre Mer* of France.[35] Each island sent three deputies to the National Assembly in Paris, two senators to the French Senate and a representative before the Economic and Social Council. And, as French citizens, their inhabitants also had the right to elect the president of the French Republic.[36] Hence, several voices have suggested that this level of participation in the affairs of the metropolis gave their interests a political weight which the British islands lacked in Westminster. More importantly, since the early 1950s, Martinique and Guadeloupe had achieved special fiscal, tariff and investments concessions from Paris. For instance, special legislation in 1952 and 1960 had allowed the French Antilles to offer a number of fiscal incentives to attract new industry, particularly tourism, and to encourage profit re-investment.[37] Company and personal taxes in the French Antilles, under the new fiscal provisions, were close to 30 per cent less than in metropolitan France.[38] Additionally, the erstwhile *vieilles colonies* were receiving more aid per capita than the average *Département* in the mainland.[39] Much the same as in the Seven, the assistance accruing from the *metropole* for infrastructure, social welfare and the civil service, most of it through the *fonds d'investissement des Départements d'Outre Mer*, amounted to over half of their GDP.[40] But unlike their British neighbours, Martinique and Guadeloupe were also associate members of the European Economic Community and, therefore, entitled to further assistance from the EEC's Development Fund.[41] This explains why both islands had received so far two grants of £10.75 million each,[42] over a ten-year period (1959–69), to build roads, ports, hospitals and schools. While, by 1963–64, the Seven were receiving yearly close to £6.86 per capita, both in grants-in-aid and CD&W funds, the French Antilles were getting over half of this (£3.95 per capita) in aid from Brussels alone. By the mid 1960's their overall economic position, with respect to the British islands, was to improve even further, once their sugar and canned pineapples gained full access to the EEC, subject to the latter's price subsidy and tariff protection.[43]

The Netherlands Antilles, on the other hand, had enjoyed since 1954 a higher degree of internal self-government than the Seven. They were, together with Holland and Surinam, equal members of the Kingdom of the Netherlands.[44] They also benefited from direct financial subsidies from The Hague and access on preferential terms to private and public Dutch capital. For instance, during the early 1960s, almost 70 per cent of all bilateral Dutch aid went to these islands and Surinam.[45] But, different from the British or French islands, the Netherlands Antilles were constitutionally entitled to financial assistance from The Hague. The Kingdom Statute (*Staatsblad* no. 503) clearly stipulated that all three units would 'accord each other aid and assistance'.[46] Not surprisingly, the tiny Sint Maarten (only 20 miles long), Sint Eustatius and Saba were exempted from all import duties and excise taxes, thus becoming free ports, which was an extraordinary advantage for the attraction of tourists.[47] Aruba, Bonaire and Curaçao, for their part, had been taking full advantage from their proximity to the Venezuelan oilfields and recent access to the EEC (since 1964)[48] to attract foreign investment.[49] Moreover, like Martinique and Guadeloupe, all the Dutch islands were soon to receive allocations from the European Development Fund. The first instalment, about to be disbursed, would amount to a yearly sum of £11.01 per capita and thus position them at an even more advantageous position than their French neighbours.

Similar to the French and Dutch islands, Puerto Rico and the US Virgin Islands were linked constitutionally to the metropolitan centre.[50] Although unincorporated territories of the United States,[51] goods and capital from either dependency entered the mainland duty-free. Much the same as Martinique and Guadeloupe, though different from the Seven and the Netherlands Antilles,[52] they were fully within the American monetary union, based on the US dollar. However, despite being US citizens,[53] their inhabitants, unlike their French neighbours, could not vote to elect the US president or send a meaningful representation to the Congress.[54] Notwithstanding this, the level of aid coming from Washington was fairly substantial. For instance, by 1960, the funds earmarked for the Puerto Rican local government were $US46.2 million (£16.56 million).[55] Even further, the direct financial transfers to individuals, in the form of social security, pensions for war veterans, nutritional assistance and other payments, during the same year, were $US79.6 million (£28.53 million).[56] Moreover, by 1969 these figures would climb up to $US234.10 million (£83.90 million) and $US 283.60 million (£101.65 million), respectively.[57] Hence, by the mid-1960s, Puerto Rico was receiving over two-and-a-half times more aid per capita than the Seven.

However, no comparative discussion would be complete without a brief mention of these territories' capacity or incapacity to export labour. Whereas *circa* 1963–64 the inhabitants of the French, Dutch and American dependencies, as nationals of their respective metropolitan centres, were enjoying open access to the labour markets of metropolitan France, Holland the US, the Seven's capacity to encourage migration to Britain was being severely impaired. In the case of Martinique and Guadeloupe, spontaneous migration to France was totally unrestricted, although it only occurred on a limited scale. Interestingly, the passing of the 1962 Commonwealth Immigrants Act coincided with the establishment in France of the *Bureau pour le Développement des Migrations Intéressant les Départements d'Outre Mer*, which sponsored migration to the *metropole*. The evidence available reveals that by the late 1960s the numbers of Martiniquans and Guadeloupeans migrating to metropolitan France was close to 8,000 per annum.[58] The figures stemming from the Netherlands Antilles were strikingly similar. While by the early 1960s between 1,000 and 2,000 people per annum were migrating to Holland, by the end of the decade the figure would be close to 10,000 per annum.[59] The numbers in the American dependencies, particularly in Puerto Rico, were far more dramatic. Since 1945 over 600,000 Puerto Ricans had left for the United States, making it easier for the local government to cope with the severe effects of unemployment and underemployment.[60]

It was fairly obvious that the Seven were at a clear disadvantage, on all fronts, if compared to their neighbours. At a time when politicians in Westminster, from most persuasions, were in favour of regulating, controlling and reducing black immigration from the Commonwealth, the case for further assistance to the Seven seemed reasonable.[61] This explains, to an extent, why the chief ministers and the premier were demanding more aid, but equally important it explains why Sandys was now asking the Treasury to increase the aid available to these islands.

Unfortunately for them, the question of whether or not to increase the Seven's allocation was entangled within a much wider and more complicated debate. While the major players within the Treasury were attempting to elucidate their policy differences on the impact external aid was having on Britain's relative macroeconomic stagnation, time was running out for the Colonial Office.

The evidence now emerging from the Cabinet's records suggests that by the turn of 1963 there was, in the words of Thomas Balogh,[62] a 'current balance of payments problem'.[63] Most observers at the time agreed that it had partly arisen out of over-extended obligations abroad as well as from the insufficient competitiveness of British exports and substitute imports. As a matter of fact, from 1964 until 1967, Britain was to lose between 15 per cent and 18 per cent of its total foreign assets.[64] Not surprisingly, there was a wide consensus, both in and outside the Treasury, that the only way of balancing the visible and invisible current accounts was by increasing exports, decreasing imports and cutting expenditure. But whether or not to include overseas aid in the category of expenditure to be trimmed was far from settled. In particular, this question would cause acute acrimony between senior civil servants in the newly created Ministry of Overseas Development[65] and their counterparts in the Treasury. The following observation by Professor Robin Marris, soon to be in charge of the World Economy Division of the Ministry of Overseas Development, conveyed rather vividly the intensity of the debate.

> You will recall that those chaps in the Treasury have expressed the view that 50 per cent of our overseas payment is a foreign-exchange cost. For reasons explained below this is by no means true even in the short run.[66]

And while the Ministry of Overseas Development and the Treasury were engaged in combat, new political developments in Westminster were also beginning to influence, albeit indirectly, the interaction between Sandys and Boyd-Carpenter with respect to the question of aid to the Seven. Macmillan's unexpected resignation on October 18, 1963,[67] had brought the pre-electoral season closer and along with it had opened up a period for reassessing colonial policy so far. Before leaving Downing Street the outgoing prime minister had asked all ministers to send him detailed progress reports, with special reference to pending matters. The Seven figured prominently in Sandys's last submission to Macmillan. The uncertain future of the federal negotiations was among the first items registered in the 'list of problems' the Colonial Office had yet to resolve.[68] After more than a decade in power and with their electoral appeal considerably eroded, many Tories felt any such unsettled commonwealth or colonial question was, in itself, a political liability. This perception comes out clearly in the following exchange between the new prime minister, Alec Douglas-Home, and the colonial secretary.

> I have been reviewing Government policy with the Election in mind and have come to the conclusion that we are very vulnerable on our Commonwealth policies. I have therefore brought together the various ideas, which have been sent to me by yourself, the Lord Privy Seal and by various members of our Party inside and outside the House. They may not find universal favour in the Commonwealth; that remains to be seen. But they look reasonably imaginative and sensible and I think would have a considerable appeal here. Many of them have the virtue of being cheap. I could be grateful if you could give the proposals your urgent attention. I am sending a copy of this minute to the Chancellor, the Chief Secretary, the Secretary of State for Industry and the Foreign Secretary.[69]

Sandys' replied, over a week later, that,

> [T]he main point which we should continue to stress is the way in which we have continued the policy of converting an Empire into a Commonwealth. The list of territories that have become independent since 1959 fully demonstrates how sincere we have been in pursuing this policy. I am, at the moment, considering the possibility of making a statement in Parliament in the near future about what we have done so far and how we hope to discharge our remaining colonial responsibilities. The continuing and increasing flow of capital aid and technical assistance which we have given to Commonwealth countries deserves a mention.[70]

Clearly, time was of the essence not only for the so-called island politicians but for the Tories as well. Within this context, it was highly desirable to reach a decision as soon as possible, one way or another, on the scale of assistance to be made available to the Seven. Against this convoluted background, Sandys and Boyd-Carpenter finally met on February 17, 1964, along with Sir Hilton Poynton and three members of the chief secretary's staff. The minutes from that gathering reveal that Sandys opened the discussion by arguing that the real question before them was 'whether it would not be worthwhile to spend some money in bringing about a semi-viable federation of the Eastern Caribbean territories'.[71] Otherwise, he contended, these islands could very well 'go forward to independence as permanent pensioners of HMG'.[72] Sandys was essentially in search of clearance from the Treasury before officially notifying the chief ministers and the premier that they would be financially better off under federation than separate. More specifically, Poynton suggested that the Colonial Office was in need of a formula or general statement which could be used as 'a bait to bring the island governments to the Conference table' as well as a precise figure to be disclosed 'at the appropriate time'.[73] Poynton went even further, reiterating what Sandys had already suggested in his initial letter to Boyd-Carpenter, saying that his team in the Colonial Office was leaning towards £5 million per annum for the first three years of the federation. Following this statement, and in an attempt to appease any misgivings the Treasury's chief secretary might have entertained, Poynton stressed that there was no intention of disclosing any figures to the colonial leadership, unless and until a satisfactory federal constitution had been worked out.

By now, Boyd-Carpenter had broken his silence and readily stated that the Colonial Office's proposal raised certain critical questions. For example, if the British Exchequer disbursed £5 million per annum in development aid for three years, what would happen thereafter? Poynton immediately replied that the British Government would not be committed to maintaining its assistance to the Seven at that same level after the expiration of the initial federal period. He also reminded the chief secretary that an injection of more development aid would, no doubt, help reduce their grant-in-aid commitment in the area, which was still substantial. Boyd-Carpenter felt, nonetheless, that such an amount of aid was out of all proportion to the population involved. Moreover, he feared that if a specific figure were given it was bound to be pushed up towards the level of aid which O'Loughlin had only recently recommended.

Thus, the chief secretary made it plain clear that at least for the moment any statement on the future of aid should lack specificity. He suggested, for instance, something along the lines of 'over the three years following the establishment of the federation, the territories would not be worse off and might even be better off'.[74] At this stage Sandys intervened saying that he would rather declare that the aid allocated to the future federation 'over the next five years would be at least as great as the sum total of development aid they were at present receiving'.[75] Interestingly, Boyd-Carpenter showed himself quite receptive to Sandys's revised formula and on that note the conference was adjourned.

Barely a week after his meeting with the chief secretary to the Treasury, Sandys finally answered the despatch which the Regional Council of Ministers had sent the previous September 1963.[76] In his reply, addressed to Sir John Stow, the colonial secretary acknowledged that,

> The Council has requested further information about the prospects of British aid. The Council is already aware of the statement about aid in paragraph 32 of Cmnd. 1746. You can now give them the further assurance that if Federation can be brought about on satisfactory terms, British aid will continue and that over the first five years of Federation, the amount will not be less than these territories are together receiving from Britain at present.[77]

But what was lying behind this vague statement? What had really been decided in the seemingly harmonious exchange between Sandys, Poynton and Boyd-Carpenter? In sum, what would the Treasury's financial commitment finally be, if any, with respect to the Seven?

The first element to bear in mind is that, as mentioned earlier, the Seven were by then receiving £4,235,000 per annum, namely £3,150,000 from CD&W funds and £1,085,000 from grant-in-aid. Now, Sandys's only assurance was that the level of overall aid over the first five years of federation would not be of less than £3,150,000 per annum. And, of course, this offer was conditional on the chief ministers and the premier subscribing to a satisfactory federal constitution. More specifically, the archival record tends to confirm that for each of the first three years Sandys was intending to recommend an allocation of at least £5 million in development aid.[78] If compared to what they were then receiving in CD&W funds, this represented an increase of, more or less, £1,850,000 per annum. But whether such a boost would have had a real impact on the livelihood of these territories was far from clear. After all, both Sandys and Poynton had gone to great lengths to reassure the chief secretary that further development assistance would necessarily lead to a drastic reduction in grant-in-aid. A credible case could have been made, to the effect that the additional funds for development would come, for the most part, from the £1,085,000 originally allocated for grant-in-aid.

The gap between what O'Loughlin had recommended and what Sandys now offered was significant indeed. For instance, for each of the first three years the difference could very well amount to almost £4.5 million.[79] Hence, the total quantum of aid for that triennium would barely reach half of what had been proposed in the Economic Survey.[80] And although during the fourth and fifth years the gap would shrink to almost £1.28 million per annum,[81] Sandys's statement gave no assurance whatsoever of assistance for the succeeding five years. Unlike O'Loughlin's plan, based on a ten-year period,[82] the offer coming from London was limited to only five years. In the final analysis, the disparity between what the Seven expected and what the British Government seemed willing to give was becoming insurmountable. Clearly, the only available course open to the Colonial Office for reconciling these differences was procuring further assistance both from Canada and the US, which leads us to the last stage of this discussion.

Both the Canadians and the Americans were not totally oblivious to the negotiating process between the British and the Seven. Intelligence had been reaching Ottawa and Washington not only from their local consulates but also from their respective missions to the UN. And as they were soon to find out, developments at that forum were about to take a difficult turn for the British Government. As a matter of fact, barely a month after sending Sandys' vague financial assurance to the RCM, the Colonial Office received a very interesting memorandum from the British Mission to the UN.

> As the Caribbean territories may well come up for discussion in the Committee of the Twenty-Four, or its newly established Caribbean Subcommittee, in the near future, it would be useful for us to have any of the working papers or briefs ... particularly [those] dealing with the political-constitutional situation.[83]

A few weeks later the much dreaded debate would indeed take place. The following extract from the speech of the Trinidadian Ambassador at the UN set the tone for what was to become a gruelling session for the British delegation. Sir Ellis Clarke vigorously argued before the Committee of the Twenty-Four[84] that,

These islands, once a string of pearls in which the administering power took great pride and from which it derived great profit, now seem like a leaden chain fit only to be cast off … . But the people of these countries are sophisticated enough to realise that what's being offered to them is not the genuine article. That is why they refuse to take it. That is why one abortive conference follows another. If freedom means freedom to starve, freedom to be unemployed, freedom to see chaos replace law and order, above all freedom to become the satellite of the highest bidder, then these countries are being offered freedom.

But if freedom implies the right to an infrastructure which gives reasonable possibility of standing on one's own feet and seeking to solve one's problems with self-respect … then freedom is certainly being denied to our neighbours and relatives. To put it bluntly, an administering power is not entitled to extract for centuries all that can be got out of a colony and when that has been done, to relieve itself out of its obligations by the conferment of a formal but meaningless political independence.[85]

It was becoming increasingly clear to the Canadian and US Governments that the British position was weakening and that it would not be long before London solicited their assistance. Hence, it could not have come as a surprise that while the British delegation endured such an onslaught at the UN, the colonial secretary embarked on an official trip to Ottawa. In particular, his discussions with Paul Martin, Canada's minister of external relations, warrant special attention. Although they had originally intended to hold a comprehensive discussion on Commonwealth affairs, the Seven consumed a considerable portion of their meeting. The evidence available suggests that Martin saw the prolonging of political uncertainty, coupled with poverty and overcrowding, as a potential catalyst which could stir civil unrest along the lines of what was taking place in British Guiana.[86] As they went into further detail, the minister of external relations said that Canada would be increasing its aid to the Caribbean, including Jamaica and Trinidad and Tobago, from £2 million to £10 million per annum. And even though he made it clear that any relaxation in immigration restrictions was out of the question, Martin, nonetheless, gave further assurances that his colleagues were looking carefully at the overall question of getting closer to the British Caribbean.[87]

If looked at on its own merits, the Canadians' intention of increasing their allocation to the region did not amount to much. On the one hand, there was no clear indication of what each territory would receive or even what type of aid was being offered. On the other, the tendency in Ottawa had always been to tie up overseas aid to Canadian exports and only in exceptional circumstances had assistance been allocated to meet local costs.[88] Sandys knew this very well and also understood that only fresh Canadian legislation could change such an inflexible policy. However, Martin's offer proved a very useful leverage in pressing the US Government into action. The mere supposition of an Anglo-Canadian joint effort went a long way in impressing on the Americans that assistance was needed and, more importantly, that the metropolitan power in question had not rescinded from its primary responsibility. Notwithstanding this, the position of the US Government remained, as noted below, far from clear.

While the Americans had stopped assisting the Seven after the collapse of the West Indies Federation,[89] they were now beginning to reappraise their policy with respect to these territories. The first meaningful exchange of views between British and American officials on this subject, since the aforementioned debacle, had taken place in mid-December 1963. The minutes from that initial conversation, produced by Iain Sutherland from the British Embassy in Washington, throw some light on the attitudes entertained by some in the US State Department. Although during that month attention in Washington was mostly focused on the Anglo-Guatemalan talks, Sutherland and Ambler Thomas, from the Colonial Office, were also questioned, rather unexpectedly, on the future of the Seven. It is important to point out that William Burdett from the US State Department's Bureau of European Affairs was leading the discussion, aided to a lesser degree by Gordon Knox, from the State Department's Office of British Commonwealth Affairs and Robert Tepper, from the Bureau of Inter-American Affairs. The composition of the American delegation was of significance, especially at a time in which an intra-departmental battle was raging at the heart of the State Department. By the turn of 1963, and increasingly in 1964, the Inter-American and European Affairs Bureaus were fighting each other for responsibility over all the British dependent territories in the Caribbean.[90] Whether this bureaucratic struggle had a direct impact on the more substantive aspects of the US Government's policy would be difficult to ascertain. Nonetheless, it did slow down the State Department's policy-making process.

Following Ambler Thomas's general account of events up until Fisher's visit, Burdett made it quite clear that while the US Government had not taken any position on the subject, he could not welcome the creation of a new economically and politically weak state. Indeed Burdett went so far as to say that he did not like the idea of independence per se and that it was something that the State Department would not wish to see happen. Only grudgingly did he concede that an independent federation might be the only viable alternative to further fragmentation.[91]

Interestingly, as soon as Thomas broached, albeit superficially, the possibility of US aid Burdett stated that in his view the prospects of American assistance were 'quite slim' and referred to the unfavourable attitude towards foreign aid in Congress. Before adjourning their meeting, nonetheless, Burdett declared that the Johnson Administration would be watching the unfolding of events in the Seven very closely. Hence, as he put it, the State Department was intending to exchange more specific notes with the Foreign Office and the Colonial Office at a later date. The following observations by Sutherland illustrated very clearly the mood in the State Department after this conference had taken place. More importantly, his comments were highly accurate and well documented because unlike Thomas, who had gone back to London, Sutherland was on the ground in Washington receiving constant feedback from his American contacts.

> He [William Burdett] was clearly very concerned when you [Ambler Thomas] said it was HMG policy to try to hasten the time-table for the grant of independence to a Little Seven Federation despite the lack of any great enthusiasm for the idea in the territories concerned. It came as a shock to him to hear that if the federal plan broke down, we would probably not object to Barbados 'going it alone' or [to] a Federation of what was left.
>
> I do not think that the Americans had hitherto focused much attention on the political future of [these territories]. They have rested contented in the belief that the status quo was likely to remain unchanged for some time. However, the introduction of new constitutions in the Bahamas[92] and in British Honduras[93] this month have also given them cause to consider more closely what the future US relationship should be to those territories. I gather from a remark made to me this week by Tepper, that the State Department is now engaged in one of its periodic appraisals of US policy in the area. What the

conclusion will be I do not know. There are probably divided counsels within the Administration and within the State Department itself.

But I am inclined to think that we shall come under increasing pressure from the Americans to go slowly on constitutional changes in the Caribbean. Certainly, this is the way in which the Bureau of European Affairs in the State Department appears to be thinking and they are likely to be supported by the Department of Defence.

They are also most anxious to preserve and protect the security of the bases and other military facilities that they have in the British islands. They have, of course, the general interest of maintaining and improving political stability in an area close to the US, that is already disturbed not only by the presence of Cuba, but by unstable governments in Haiti and the Dominican Republic and difficulties in Venezuela. They have also their own worries over Puerto Rico.[94]

The scenario was ripe for further Anglo-American exchanges. Not surprisingly, just a few weeks before Sandys and Martin met in Ottawa, Sutherland sent the following note to Patricia Hutchinson at the Foreign Office:

I have received more than one suggestion in recent weeks that the State Department would like to have further exchange of views on the future of the Little Seven and Grenada. Bob Tepper [Officer in Charge of Caribbean Dependencies Affairs at the State Department] asked me particularly about Grenada and the present intentions of Dr. Williams. He also asked in general terms about the proposed London Conference on constitutional developments .... Gordon Knox [Assistant Director of the Office of British Commonwealth Affairs] told me that he intended to discuss the future political prospects with the US Consul in Bridgetown .... I would be most grateful for any information that you and the Colonial Office can let us have for passing on to the State Department.[95]

Without a doubt, the period from late March until mid-December 1964 was becoming of critical importance. The intelligence reports then reaching the State Department and the White House led to a conspicuous change in attitude. By the end of 1964, Burdett's unyielding position would not count for much and the US Government's intention of aiding, albeit partially, these territories would become somewhat clearer. But why the metamorphosis? Of what, for instance, did the advice streaming from the US Consulate General in Bridgetown consist?

Close to a fortnight after Sutherland's note had reached the Foreign Office, Benjamin Read, executive secretary of the Bureau of European Affairs at the US State Department, produced one of the most detailed papers on the Seven so far.[96] In his secret memorandum, addressed to McGeorge Bundy, President Johnson's national security adviser, Read argued that American interests in the archipelago were twofold: firstly, to ensure that the Seven remained in 'friendly hands' and, secondly, to assure that the US maintained unlimited access to its defence installations in the archipelago. Read made special reference to the US's military facilities in Barbados and Antigua.[97] By this stage the US Navy had a base in Barbados consisting of about 100 men, including enlisted men, officers and their families, which was soon to be expanded by a $US800,000 building programme and an increase in personnel. In addition to this, the Pentagon was conducting its own High Altitude Research Project (HARP) in Bajan airspace. In Antigua, where American military presence was more prevalent than in any of the Seven, the US Air Force had a Missile Track Station as well as preferential access to Coolidge Field. In Antigua, the US Navy also operated an Oceanographic Research Station similar to the one existing in Barbados. Regardless of the area's constitutional future, the mighty branches of the US Armed Forces intended to preserve their strategic positioning in these territories.

Read also confided in Bundy that the 'geographic propinquity' of the area in relation to the US placed the islands 'in a category warranting special consideration'. Like Sandys, he was also convinced that a politically unstable federation would present an opportunity for 'Communist, Castroite and Jagan inroads', adversely affecting US policy in the outer Caribbean as well as in Latin America. However, unlike Burdett, Read seemed convinced that only if the Seven achieved a position of greater economic strength could that ominous pitfall be averted. More interestingly, his paper hinted at the serious consequences which any major Soviet infiltration of the Seven could have had on the US's internal political stage.[98] This particular contention had powerful implications. Above all else, the Seven's capacity for posing an excruciatingly complex domestic dilemma for the Johnson Administration could not be overlooked.

In the interests of contingency planning, Read and his American consular sources identified seven potential scenarios, no matter how remote, available to the Seven.

1. Maintenance of the status quo;
2. Formation of an Independent Federation;
3. Independence for Barbados and Dependency Status for Others;
4. Separate Independence for Each of the Seven Islands;
5. Incorporation of Grenada and St. Vincent to Trinidad and Tobago;
6. Revival of the West Indies Federation; and
7. Permanent Constitutional Relationship with the United Kingdom.[99]

Both the executive secretary of the Bureau of European Affairs and the US consul general in Bridgetown agreed that the State Department should start thinking in terms of either the second or the third option. In light of this, Read finally recommended to President Johnson's national security adviser that should an independent entity emerge in the area the US Government's political and military policy should aim at

- Welcoming the emergence in the Caribbean of an independent federation (or an independent Barbados) as an expression of self-determination of the people of the area;
- Welcoming the Commonwealth connection;
- Encouraging early membership in the OAS and participation in the Alliance for Progress, while maintaining the Commonwealth connection;
- Taking legislative steps to afford non-quota status under US immigration law;
- Raising the Consulate General at Barbados to the status of an adequately staffed Embassy. Should the other islands retain their dependent status, efforts should be made to grant Consular Offices at the Embassy with dual exequaturs so that a Consul General assigned to Barbados could render Consular services to the other islands which elected to remain out of the federation;
- Encouraging the establishment of a small Federation Security Force with missions of internal security and civic action, without separate military service identities. This force could receive tripartite assistance, but most advisors and most equipment would be

Commonwealth in origin. The latter would consist of minimal communications, light weapons, small patrol boats, wheeled vehicles and a few light aircraft;

- [Facilitating the] accession of the Federation to the Rio Pact;[100]
- Extending the US Military Alerting System to the Federation.[101]

On the question of economic assistance, the Johnson Administration was being urged to

- Encourage [the British] to recognise the importance of maintaining augmented economic assistance for a ten year period so that the area may succeed economically;
- [Push the British] to obtain Canadian assistance to the maximum extent possible for the economic development of the area;
- If pressed ... be prepared to co-operate with the UK and Canada in providing moderate economic assistance under the Alliance for Progress.[102]

The Americans were now beginning to realize that even though the maintenance of the status quo best served their interests, British withdrawal from the area was unavoidable. The day of a political vacuum was fast approaching. They had to be prepared to assume whatever minimum responsibility appeared necessary to ensure that a lack of economic viability did not disturb the archipelago's political stability. And although no 'subversive group' had yet appeared to make an intelligent concerted effort to create chaos or to present tempting offers of economic assistance, such manoeuvrings could not be discounted at all.[103] Not surprisingly, early in October 1964, Harold Shullaw, director of the US State Department's Office of British Commonwealth Affairs, told Sutherland that the State Department was considering changes to its policies with regard to aid to the British dependent territories in the Caribbean.[104] This informal exchange was followed by more serious Anglo-American talks. On December 18, 1964, Shullaw and his assistants arrived in London for consultations with Sir Alan Dudley, minister of Overseas Development. His primary intention was discussing the possibility of tripartite aid to the Seven.[105] Shullaw confided in Dudley that, following conversations with the British Embassy as well as with the Canadians, it had been agreed that the key to these islands' political progress was on the economic side.[106] Against this background, he unabashedly conceded that it would be helpful if the US Government got back into the field. In addition, Shullaw also admitted that in order to justify the renewal of aid his superiors needed a positive response from both the British and the Canadians on the prospects of coordinating this assistance, the level of aid envisioned and, equally important, its intended duration.

While encouraging, this transatlantic understanding was still considerably fragile. There was little consensus on crucial matters such as the machinery to be used for administering the joint arrangement or even the type of aid to be disbursed. More interestingly, the Americans were actively suggesting that the British Government should agree to a scheme of aid over a longer period. Like O'Loughlin before them, Shullaw and Tepper were also interested in a ten-year plan, even though this openly contravened the British Treasury's stern policy with respect to overseas aid. In the meantime, they were also arguing that it would be much easier to garner congressional support if Britain provided additional assistance, which they would then match.[107] The British, for their part, were insisting that it would not be fair to ask them to match US aid by increasing their own on a dollar for dollar basis.[108] After all, as some in London still saw it, the British Government had to settle the question of its aid to any particular area in the light of its total commitments and not those of any other power. And while the transatlantic triumvirate attempted to settle these critical differences, commissioning the production of yet another economic survey of the area, the federal negotiations were nearing breaking-point.

11

A Federal Project in Cold Storage

> The Federation of the Seven is dead. Whether or not there will be a
> federation of six, time alone will tell ... . Let, therefore, the Colonial
> Office plot and plan ... . Let them walk their last tortuous federal mile
> how they like and with whom they please, but certainly not with
> Antigua.
>
> *The Workers' Voice, Organ of the Antigua Trades and Labour Union, 1965*

The colonial leadership, particularly in Barbados and Antigua, was
becoming increasingly impatient. Not long before Sandys sent his first
substantial submission to the Treasury's chief secretary, Barrow had warned
Stow that the feeling in the island in favour of 'going it alone' was hardening.[1]
He was intending, nonetheless, to see what financial contribution London
would make, before committing himself one way or the other. While the
premier waited for an answer, internal pressures in Barbados as well as in
the remaining territories kept swaying his views and those of the chief
ministers. The constraining forces influencing both Barrow and his
colleagues during this critical period, just before Sandys's vague reply of
February 1964, cannot go unheeded.

In Stow's own words, the premier was certainly going 'through some
rough water'.[2] Since October 1963 he had been increasingly losing political
capital. On the one hand, his alliance with the conservative mayor of
Bridgetown, Ernest D. Mottley, had been totally shattered. While, on the
other, the so-called Windfall Affair had put considerable strain on his
relations with the island's powerful labour movement. The auditor general's
revelation that properly audited accounts of the City Council had not
been received for the past three years, together with the widespread
perception that in Bridgetown assistance to the poor was synonymous
with political patronage prompted Barrow's intervention. However, by

appointing an ad hoc commission to investigate,[3] which shortly afterwards recommended the elimination of the City Council as it stood, the premier dealt a severe blow to the mayor's power base. Ironically, Mottley's fall from grace meant that Barrow's position with respect to the opposition parties in the local House of Assembly became considerably weaker. Mottley's support had been instrumental, not only in guaranteeing the DLP's narrow victory over the BLP in 1961, but in keeping Barrow's government afloat.[4]

In the meantime the Windfall Affair was also brewing. By the end of 1963 the international price of sugar was unusually high, close to £102 per ton and this had resulted in an extra profit of over BWI $6 million to the sugar industry in Barbados. The BWU, in conjunction with the DLP majority in the Assembly, had decided to retain two-thirds of the workers' share in order to set up a rehabilitation and welfare fund. The unilateral nature of their action, nonetheless, gave rise to a vociferous uproar from the sugar workers. Aided by the BLP as well as by the newly founded Barbados Progressive Union of Workers,[5] they were now demanding their total share of the surplus. The pressure became so strong that by late January 1964 the Sugar Producers' Federation revealed its intention of breaching its previous agreement with the BWU and Barrow's Government and thus paying the workers in full. Barrow, who had remained resolute throughout the crisis, in what amounted to a vote of no confidence on the BWU, also made a last minute about-face. In the end, Walcott and his BWU suffered an embarrassing defeat 'involving a loss of confidence, prestige and authority'.[6] And whereas the personal relations between Barrow and the formidable Walcott suffered immensely, the BLP, much to the premier's chagrin, received a much-needed boost at a time when the conflict with Mottley was at its height. It was becoming quite obvious that in future Barrow would have to face the remaining federal hurdles with even less political cover than before. He would have to tread more lightly.

Whereas events at home reminded him of the need to act with more caution, both on the local and regional stages, his numerous trips abroad were swaying him in the opposite direction. On November 26, 1963 a few days after the House of Assembly passed a premature resolution supporting the BWU's position on the Windfall Affair, the premier left for a visit to Israel, at the invitation of Levi Eshkol, and Kenya, for the former

British colony's independence celebrations.[7] Along with his wife Carolyn, Barrow also visited *en route* Lisbon, Rome, Athens, Addis Ababa, Accra, Dakar, Las Palmas and Puerto Rico. Several voices have suggested that on returning to Barbados, four weeks later, he showed tremendous confidence that if territories such as Zanzibar had recently achieved independence,[8] there was no reason Barbados should fall short of that. In his intelligence report for December (1963) Stow warned the Colonial Office that, in particular, the premier's sojourn in Israel, 'a young and progressive nation', seemed to 'forcefully impress him with the view that Barbados must get independence quickly'.[9] The available evidence tends to corroborate the governor's preliminary observation. Speaking in neighbouring Puerto Rico Barrow had gone as far as declaring,

> My Government has been given a mandate to secure independence before the next election. If it is not granted, it will be declared, because I do not feel that we should have to ask for it.[10]

Beyond encouraging his burgeoning interest in 'going it alone' this tour had, to a large extent, a negative impact on Barrow's overall attitude towards the British Government. The disheartening squalor he saw in British Africa but, most importantly, the fruitless private talks he held with Sandys, while in Kenya, gave him a relatively accurate insight into what not to expect from the British Treasury. While there seem to be no written records of what was said at this impromptu *tête-à-tête*, the available documents do show an astounding contradiction in the way both Sandys and Barrow later characterized their brief meeting. On December 18, 1963, three days before the premier's return to Barbados, Sandys had already confided in his junior ministers and senior civil servants at the Colonial Office that he had had 'a useful talk' with Barrow in Nairobi. More importantly, that he had 'gained the impression' that the premier 'might not be so averse to a new federation'.[11] Yet, as soon as he arrived in the island, Barrow saw Stow and referring to his brief discussion with Sandys suggested that, 'it does not appear that the British Government is prepared to face up to its commitments in the Eastern Caribbean.'[12] The British, as he put it, were 'humbugging' the colonial leadership.[13]

Notwithstanding the fact that the minutes of that rather obscure meeting in Nairobi are missing, a few useful inferences might, in all fairness, be suggested. By all accounts the financial question must have taken considerable prominence throughout their conversation. Even though Sandys was still waiting to hear from Boyd-Carpenter, he may have run past Barrow a discreet version of his own ideas on aid. The colonial secretary could have hinted at anything ranging from a vague assurance that aid would not be less than what they were at present receiving or even that his inclination was to allocate £5 million per annum in development capital for each of the first three years of federation. Either way, as Stow later informed the Colonial Office, Barrow's reaction was far from favourable. And even if Sandys misread the premier or the latter kept his misgivings to himself, it was becoming clear that London's preliminary aid proposal would not receive an enthusiastic reception in Bridgetown.

Meanwhile, the chief ministers were also facing trying challenges of their own. In Antigua, where the scattered political opposition was beginning to prepare for the next local elections, Bird and his colleagues seemed anxious to end the uncertainty and reach a final decision on the federal question. However, Bird, less of a firebrand than most surrounding him, was caught up in a very delicate bind. With an obvious split in the ranks of his Trades and Labour Union, on whether to go forward with federation or sever all political ties with the other six units, the casting vote lay squarely with him. He had now become, for all practical purposes, the arbiter between these contending parties. A particularly stormy meeting of the local Executive Council, held in January 1964, must have reminded Bird that being in the saddle could, more often than not, prove very irritating indeed. The archival record shows how on that occasion *l'enfant terrible* of the Trades Union, McChesney George, had demanded Antigua's withdrawal from the federal negotiations. More interestingly, as Sir David Rose reported to the Colonial Office, the minister without portfolio went as far as suggesting that Antigua should follow Western Samoa's pattern of independence.[14] But the minister of social services, E.H. Lake, became 'extremely voluble' and said it was pointless to throw out all the work that had been done without first seeing if it was going to function. In the end, after much wrangling, the members of Antigua's Executive Council decided to 'wait and see' and if their constitutional and financial expectations were not met, they would then demand full internal self-government.

One of the most important elements to bear in mind is that, far from abating, pressure on Bird was mounting. He knew very well that most of the influential members of his Labour and Trades Union would not be satisfied unless a more advanced local constitution was set up in the near future. Besides, as suggested earlier, a feeling of optimism at the prospect of important progress on the capital development front stood behind most of this anti-federal posturing. For instance, the construction of the oil refinery, which would also expedite the electrification of the whole island, was only a month away. A preliminary understanding between the local authorities and the West Indies Oil Company was guaranteeing 10,000,000 kW of power for the island over the first few years from the commencement of production.[15] This explains why some in positions of influence, still bustling after a particularly good tourist season, were beginning to question the wisdom of continuing their involvement in the negotiations. Why wait around for federation, if Antigua's lot was improving without help from its neighbours? This attitude was coupled with a concealed feeling of distrust towards Barbados, for many in Antigua believed that Barrow's recent visits to Israel and Kenya did not bode well. Sooner or later Barbados would move to independence alone, while Antigua, in all probability, would be saddled with the remaining units. The archival record seems to suggest this impression was transcending party lines. The following anonymous verse, which was to become the mantra of the Antigua Democratic Front, echoes this perception with respect to Barbados.

Lovely islands all in a line,
One sought independence, then there were Nine;
Lovely islands trying to federate;
One goes independent, thus leaving Eight;
Lovely islands hoping for a Heaven,
One joins Trinidad, then there were Seven;
Lovely islands now in a fix,
Wondering if Barbados will drop them to Six;
Lovely islands could hardly survive,
If another pulled, leaving only Five;
Lovely islands — small and very poor —
Better stick to BRITAIN, LADS, and be
COLONIES ONCE MORE.[16]

The situation in Montserrat was not much different. Bramble, with the economic wind at his back, was far more interested in his agro-industry and real-estate ventures than in the federal negotiations. By this stage, both Donald Wiles and Dennis Gibbs, colonial administrators from 1960–64 and 1964–68 respectively, were speaking of a 'breakthrough' or 'turning point' in the economic life of the island.[17] For instance, the Esso Standard Oil Company had just built a bulk storage terminal and the Leeward Islands Company, Canadian-owned, had recently set up a tomato-paste factory. Yet, in spite of these minor industrial developments, the export of clean-seed cotton, peppers and bananas still represented the bulk of the territory's economic base. Moreover, the opening of new markets for Montserrat's tomatoes as well as the development of resident tourism, mainly for retirees, were expected to solidify the island's gains. By March 1964, for example, a cable had been received in Plymouth from dealers in Montreal asking to be supplied with 31 tons of tomatoes every year.[18] At the same time, substantial stretches of land were being cleared in Old Road, Woodlands, Richmond and Spanish Point, for tourists, mainly Canadian and American, to buy plots of land and build their own winter villas. This explains, for the most part, why local revenue increased more than 25 per cent in 1965 over the 1964 figures and the total value of imports was BWI $868,000 higher than in the previous year.[19]

In the political arena, Bramble's Trades and Labour Union faced no credible external challenges. The United Workers Movement (UWM), the political wing of its main rival, namely the Montserrat Seamen and Waterfront Workers' Union (MSWWU), had been defunct since its crushing defeat at the hands of Bramble in the 1961 local polls. Much like Bird in Antigua, the chief minister's ascendancy was unparalleled. However, unlike the scenario enveloping the neighbouring territory, the political leadership in Plymouth was not as anxious to elucidate the federal question. This was unsurprising, since Montserratian society had always been traditionally averse to the idea of constitutional advance.

Conversely, the scenario facing the remaining chief ministers was not as encouraging. The situation in St. Kitts, on the one hand, had remained unaltered since Fisher's visit, with business almost at a standstill. In his intelligence report for February 1964, Howard had gone as far as suggesting that there was a 'dead atmosphere'[20] in St. Kitts. On the other, the deepening crisis in the arrowroot industry was severely hampering St. Vincent's economic prospects.[21]

In Dominica and St. Lucia, an environment fraught with economic uncertainty, following a particularly active hurricane season, had plunged both islands into a period of unusual political unrest. Interestingly, the challenge to Le Blanc and Charles did not stem from within their respective political and labour movements, but rather from without that intimate nucleus. For instance, by the end of 1963, Phyllis Allfrey, a former member of the original Federal House of Representatives, founded the Social, Tolerance, Action and Reform Party (STAR).[22] Although it would not last long, Allfrey's political opposition would nonetheless keep Le Blanc's Labour Party under considerable scrutiny during the crucial months ahead.

Yet in St. Lucia, which the Colonial Office had always considered 'the most mendicant of these territories',[23] the partisan effervescence was far more strident than in Dominica. By the beginning of 1964, the island's 'green gold' industry was still recovering from the passing of Hurricane Edith. The total production of bananas for that year was to reflect severe losses. This hindrance, coupled with the impossibility of restoring the island's sugar industry to its previous splendour, was forcing hundreds of St. Lucians to leave for Antigua and even St. Croix in search of work. More specifically, by February, the temporary debacle in the banana industry had led the Charles Government to press for changes in the way the local Banana Growers Association (BGA) discharged its responsibilities. This intervention, however, prompted not only a sharp rebuttal from Swithin Schouten, Chairman and CEO of the BGA, but also incited the opposition to table a motion of no confidence in the Government.[24] And although the motion was defeated, the ruling St. Lucia Labour Party came out from battle fatally wounded. Only a few weeks later, the leadership of the National Labour Movement (NLM) and the People's Progressive Party (PPP) decided to merge into a new political party,[25] the United Workers Party (UWP).[26] In a matter of days the Charles Government imploded. With the resignation of Joseph Bousquet, until then one of Charles's most trusted lieutenants, the St. Lucian Government fell and, thus, the Legislative Council was finally dissolved.

While all these political and economic developments kept unfolding, Sandys's despatch finally reached the premier and the chief ministers. Along with the colonial secretary's dim assurance on aid, came an invitation to hold an RCM meeting with him in London, on April 21, 1964 to discuss the next steps towards federation.[27] Not surprisingly, the colonial leadership declined the invitation from the Colonial Office. The premier and the chief ministers agreed that, with London's assurance on aid falling far short of the O'Loughlin benchmark and with the absence of local unanimity on how the federal constitution should look, there was no point in going to London. They chose instead to hold a meeting in Barbados, under the auspices of Barrow, to discuss, amongst other things, a revised version of the Areas of Agreement paper, prepared by Barbados and soon to be known as the Draft Federal Scheme (DFS).[28]

The eighth meeting of the RCM was convened in Bridgetown and began on Wednesday, April 15, 1964, under the chairmanship of Sir John Stow. Seventeen conference papers were presented for discussion, including three pertaining to the fiscal and constitutional elements of the federal plan.[29] Ironically, the most salient aspect of this local gathering was that no in-depth discussion of the document put forward by Barbados took place. Owing to the dissolution of the St. Lucian Legislative Council, Castries sent no ministerial representation to this meeting. Hence, in the absence of St. Lucia, Dominica, St. Kitts and Montserrat declined to evaluate the more substantive constitutional details contained in the DFS. Notwithstanding this, St. Vincent, Antigua and Barbados immediately contended that those were the only items on the agenda worthy of discussion. In the end, of the four days of the conference, only two-and-a-half hours on the last day were allocated to discussing the constitutional proposals. Whereas the Council unanimously agreed on establishing an Eastern Caribbean Currency Authority, maintaining the regional shipping service and applying for group associate membership to UNESCO,[30] no tangible progress was made towards resolving the pending matters. It is no wonder that Bird remained silent and looked grim throughout the proceedings.[31] Sandys's demeanour could not have been much different when in the middle of his official trip to Ottawa he received the following message from Stow:

> The RCM meeting finished on the 18th April. Since all Ministers were not ready to discuss the Draft Federal Scheme, prepared by Barbados, it was agreed that Ministers would inform the Chairman when they were ready to discuss it and the Chairman would then convene another meeting for that purpose. The RCM will be in no position to suggest a date for the London Conference until after that meeting has taken place.[32]

While, as suggested earlier, the Treasury's 'refusal to play' constituted a major blow to the process, sharp disagreements over the substantive aspects of the federal project were the last straw. Hence, before evaluating in detail the finale of the federal negotiations, it is essential to analyze the constitutional provisions contained in the DFS. Was the Colonial Office satisfied with this arrangement? Were Nigel Fisher's recommendations included in the DFS or was it merely a regurgitation of the Areas of Agreement paper?

Many in London saw the DFS as lacking the fundamentals of a viable federal scheme.[33] More importantly, others, such as Stow, believed that inasmuch as it incorporated decisions to 'whittle down' the executive authority of the federal centre, the DFS would in effect lead to a very weak federation with the real powers firmly resting in the units.[34] The fact that the DFS contained no provision guaranteeing that the executive authority of the federal centre was to extend to all matters contained in the exclusive and concurrent legislative lists was seen as highly problematic. For instance, the Colonial Office, ever since the days of Maudling, an ardent supporter of federal centralization, considered the organic growth of the federal government as vital. Without any such constitutional provision the federal centre could hardly do more than legislate at the behest of the units.[35] Although no reference was made in the Marlborough House Conference Report to the need for such a measure, Fisher had already stressed that the federation 'should not be precluded from having executive powers over matters in the legislative lists'.[36] This requirement was by no means unprecedented. For instance, the federal constitutions of Rhodesia and Nyasaland, Malaya, Nigeria, and even that of the original West Indies Federation, explicitly granted the centre executive authority over all matters for which the legislature could make laws.[37] But, as became evident, Antigua's unyielding pressure to dilute the centre's executive power had not gone unheeded. This, however, was not the only area on which the DFS openly contravened the spirit of the agreements reached at the Marlborough House Conference. The Colonial Office, for instance, had specific problems with those sections detailing the number of ministers, the functioning of the commissions of enquiry and the selection of the attorney general.

Table 11.1
Comparison of the Marlborough House Conference Report and the Draft Federal Scheme

Marlborough House Conference[38]	Draft Federal Scheme[39]
On the number of Federal Ministers: The Federal Cabinet would consist of a Prime Minister and such number of other Ministers as the Prime Minister might decide: by convention this number would not exceed five. The Governor General would assign portfolios to Ministers on the advice of the Prime Minister.[40]	**On the number of Federal Ministers:** The Federal Cabinet would consist of a Prime Minister and such number of other Ministers as the Prime Minister might decide. The Governor General would assign portfolios to Ministers on the advice of the Prime Minister.[41]
On the appointment of the Federal Attorney General: There would be a Federal Attorney General. When the Federal constitution was drafted it would be decided, in consultation with the Governments concerned, whether the post of Attorney General would be a political appointment.[42]	**On the appointment of the Federal Attorney General:** There would be a Federal Attorney General appointed by the Governor General on the advice of the Prime Minister.[43]
On the number of Unit Ministers: The number of members of the Legislatures to be appointed Ministers would remain unchanged until after the first general elections following the establishment of the new Federation. Thereafter, ... the number of members of the Legislatures to be appointed Ministers would not exceed one quarter of the number of members entitled to vote in the elected representative chamber.[44]	**On the number of Unit Ministers:** The Unit Government would each decide the form of legislature suitable for its territory. The legislative authority would be vested in Her Majesty and the House or Houses of the Legislature and the executive authority would be vested in Her Majesty who would act on the advice of the Cabinet.[45]
On Federal Commissions of Enquiry: The Federal Government would have power to appoint a commission of enquiry to investigate any matter tending to undermine financial stability and	**On Federal Commissions of Enquiry:** The Federal Government would have power to appoint a commission of enquiry to investigate any matter tending to undermine financial stability and good government in any part of the Federation.[46]

good government in any part of the Federation. If such a commission submitted a report reflecting adversely upon the conduct of a Unit Government ... the Unit Government concerned would be given sixty days in which to take steps to rectify the position. If at the end of that period the Governor General was not satisfied that any such steps were adequate, he would have power, after consultation with the Federal Prime Minister ... to dissolve the Unit Legislature and set dates for a general election in the Unit.[47] Cmnd. 1746, par.28.	The DFS did not establish sanctions to secure that any steps were taken by the Unit Government under scrutiny following an adverse report.

Nevertheless, in opposing the DFS's provisions on the number of unit and federal ministers, and on the federal attorney general becoming a political appointee, London was departing from convention. First, neither the constitution of the defunct West Indies Federation nor the report of the June 1961 West Indies Constitutional Conference (held in Lancaster House three months prior to Jamaica's secession from the old Federation) made any specific reference to the size of either the local or the federal cabinets.[48] And second, the reason why in the old Federation a civil servant had acted as attorney general stemmed from that entity's colonial nature. Not surprisingly, by 1961, in preparation for independence, the Lancaster House Conference had agreed that the federal attorney general would 'cease to be an office in the public service' and in future would be appointed by the governor general on the advice of the federal prime minister.[49] Even further, the 1962 independence constitutions of Jamaica and Trinidad and Tobago had already set a precedent by granting ministerial status to the office of attorney general.[50] Thus, the fact that the DFS made it clear that the appointment of that position was to fall within the purview of the federal executive should not have been at all surprising or a matter of concern to the Colonial Office. The archival record reveals that London was acutely preoccupied with the DFS's silence on whether there should, in consequence, be a non-political public prosecutor. Once again, if compared to the existing precedent, these misgivings were out of bounds. On the one hand, the British Government and the leadership of the erstwhile West Indies Federation had agreed, over three years ago, that with independence the 'political' attorney general would exercise all powers with respect to prosecutions without being 'subject to the discretion or control of any other person or authority'.[51] In Trinidad and Tobago, on the other hand, the attorney general was performing both his normal duties as chief legal adviser to the government and those of director of public prosecutions.[52]

In addition, the DFS's lack of specificity — if compared to the Marlborough House Conference Report — on how federal commissions of enquiry should operate was also troubling London. Although in this case the Colonial Office's concern was highly justified, especially after the widely publicized cases of misappropriation of public funds in Grenada and St. Vincent,[53] metropolitan expectations were once again departing from established precedent. There had been no mention either in the constitution of the West Indies Federation or at the proceedings of the Marlborough House Conference of the substantive norms that should regulate the proceedings of this type of federal commission. It had been generally understood that the federal centre, in exercising its jurisdictional competence, would be entitled to articulate such rules or norms as it saw fit. Hence, if looked at in its entirety, London's position with respect to all these elements openly begs the following question: was a higher standard being applied now to these islands? And, in view of the available evidence, the answer must be yes. After all, there had always been a feeling, since Maudling's initial visit to Port-of-Spain in January 1962, that in order to succeed, this federal project had to be far stronger than the last one.

Before moving any further, there are three seminal aspects of the DFS, namely the sections pertaining to the public service, the procedural steps for setting up the federation, and the sources of federal revenue, which still warrant a fuller consideration. In terms of the public service, consistent with the Marlborough House Conference Report and with the subsequent Manktelow Report,[54] the DFS embraced the concept of unification, although with a caveat. The following proviso had now been included:

> The [RCM] has approved a unified service for administrative, professional and technical officers. [It] has agreed that the details of such a scheme should be worked out by a committee of Establishment Officers and Financial Secretaries in the light of the proposals put forward in the Report of the Civil Service.... This Committee should be appointed without delay.[55]

The Colonial Office had always attached great importance to this subject, which explains why the previous May 1963, Fisher had included it as part of his litmus test on the viability of the federal project.[56] Even though on this matter the DFS reflected a considerable improvement from the Areas of Agreement paper,[57] appointing yet another commission to evaluate what others had already studied ad nauseam could not have gone down very well in London.

Agreeing on the procedural steps for establishing the federation was also becoming increasingly difficult. The DFS was still adhering to the fast-track version contained in the Areas of Agreement paper. In spite of Fisher's urging, Barrow and Bird were, nevertheless, clinging on to the position they had already espoused at the preparatory conference.[58] The difficulty, as seen by the Colonial Office, was twofold. On the one hand, the DFS, as opposed to the Marlborough House Conference Report,[59] envisaged that 'the inauguration, proclamation of independence and appointment of prime minister and other ministers' should form a single stage.[60] On the other, it was also asking the British Government to grant full internal self-government to the Leeward and Windward units before the inauguration of the federation.[61] All this was highly problematic. First, as Poynton and others saw it, speeding up the process along those lines meant that the federation would move to independence without an expression of the will of either the federal government or the people brought within its borders. Having the existing unit legislatures alone agreeing on independence was a far cry from allowing newly elected governments, both at the local and federal levels, to stand up for it. And second, London's position had consistently been that internal self-government should not be introduced in the units until it was clear 'beyond doubt' that a federation would be established.

The reason behind that was pretty obvious. The concession of internal self-government, as the following chapter further suggests, had typically been conferred on territories on the verge of independence.[62] This intermediate stage, as several constitutional scholars have characterized it,[63] fell short of independence insofar as it implied the absence of full international personality. Yet, in all other areas the territory would enjoy 'full internal independence'.[64] In this particular case, if the federal project did not materialize the British Government would be saddled with seven fully self-governing territories, all of which would most likely welcome this as a transitory station to individual independence. As London saw it, the possibility of fostering the emergence of a group of non-viable mini-states had to be avoided at all costs.

Finally, it becomes essential to dissect the DFS's economic, financial and fiscal provisions, since the failure of the West Indies Federation had been attributed, for the most part, to the absence of an autonomous source of federal revenue. The fundamental principle behind the Marlborough House Conference Report, as Ursula Hicks subsequently suggested, was that the federation should be financially independent right from its inception. Fisher himself had reminded the premier and the chief ministers that the centre would need to have its own 'source of finance' and that 'nothing in the constitution [should] prevent the provision of funds adequate for the federal government's responsibilities'.[65] This explained why the report produced at Marlborough House had made it abundantly clear that the centre 'would have available to it revenues from import duties, postal services, court fees and currency profits'.[66] The Fiscal Report had gone even further, specifying that all revenue accruing from import duties would now go to the federal coffers.[67]

The DFS's position represented a significant turnaround. First, out of the revenue stemming from import duties, by far the most substantial, the federal government would now only retain 35 per cent, paying out to the units the remaining 65 per cent.[68] Interestingly, the DFS recommended that this measure should be made an entrenched provision of the federal constitution. Undermining the federation's financial independence was grave enough, but granting constitutional legitimacy to the demise of the centre's ability to manoeuvre would be, from the Colonial Office's perspective, non-negotiable. Second, the DFS made no mention of the complementary sources of revenue that had already been identified in the Marlborough House Conference Report and in the Fiscal Report. It was not clear whether that silence resulted from an oversight or if it implied that the centre should not be entitled to that revenue. The picture was further complicated, since the DFS, different from the Marlborough House Conference Report, asked for the transference of the postal services to the concurrent legislative list and drew a distinction between the federal and the local judiciaries,[69] effectively blurring the boundary separating federal from unit revenue.

The arrangements concerning external loans to which Fisher had also referred to in his closing remarks remained,[70] for the most part, unaltered. The DFS, nevertheless, contained an addendum to the effects that 'all charges on account of loans would only be levied on a particular unit by the [centre] in respect of loans raised for projects in that unit'.[71] In addition, the provisions relating to the federation's industrial development showed a similar imprint. While the original structure had been left untouched, the position of the units *vis-à-vis* the centre was strengthened as well — since under the DFS the units would be allowed to promote and encourage the development of local industries unilaterally.[72]

On the fiscal side of the equation the DFS represented a clear improvement from the Areas of Agreement paper. Whereas the latter had asked for the administration of income tax to revert to the units, the DFS switched back to the initial position, namely that it should remain a federal responsibility.[73] Equally important, it ratified the decision already reached at the Marlborough House Conference that the inauguration of the federation would coincide with the launching of a customs union. Although, as happened with the unification of the public service, the DFS was also calling for the appointment of yet another commission to evaluate the setting-up of the external tariff.[74]

If compared to the financial provisions contained in the original federal constitution, the ones espoused in the DFS were by far superior. Gone were the days of the sad 'mandatory levy'[75] or of hopelessly wishing for an integrated trade policy and customs union to take form.[76] However, as opposed to the Marlborough Report and the Fiscal Report, the DFS severely curtailed the centre's financial autonomy and, consequently, would hamper its capacity to execute its constitutional responsibilities.

However, the Colonial Office was not the only entity harbouring deep-seated misgivings with regard to the DFS. As would become obvious at the ninth RCM meeting, several units, most notably Antigua and St. Lucia, were also entertaining major reservations of their own. St. Lucia's political leadership was extremely determined to prevent such a drastic curtailment of the sources of federal revenue.[77] The mood in Castries, since the last RCM meeting, had undergone a profound transformation. The landslide election of John Compton and his United Workers Party (UWP), in June 1964, had led to a significant realignment in the island's political scene.[78]

The new chief minister, as far as federal matters were concerned, soon distanced himself and his government from the positions George Charles had previously adopted. Since his election as a junior member of the Legislative Council in 1954, Compton had consistently argued that St. Lucia should only agree to a federation if the centre were granted adequate powers. He had repeatedly suggested that St. Lucia should not compromise on anything less than what had already been stipulated at Marlborough House. Not surprisingly the British authorities had taken an early interest in Compton's political trajectory. For instance, on the eve of the Marlborough House Conference, two full years before his rise to the leadership, the senior civil servants at the Colonial Office had already commissioned and, in turn, received the following profile on this 'Young Turk',

> He is in his late 30's, is single and holds anti-clerical views. He is one of the most intellectually able of the small island politicians. He is a strong supporter of a highly centralised federal structure, on the Eric Williams pattern. He has argued that the need in the Leeward and Windward Islands lies on economic development rather than political independence. However, an unstable temperament spoils his positive qualities. It seems he has a chip on his shoulder, a grudge against society. In addition, it has been suggested he can be unstable, untrustworthy and unpredictable. These qualities, combined with his intelligence, make him dangerous while in opposition. He might well become more balanced and reasonable if he were to attain power.[79]

Whereas Charles and his St. Lucia Labour Party had largely 'strung along' after Barrow and Bird merely for the sake of preserving an obviously fragile consensus, Compton was soon to steer away from that course. The new chief minister would prove unwilling to compromise. Unlike Southwell and Le Blanc, who had also expressed similar reservations with respect to the DFS's federal revenue provision only to back-pedal a few weeks later,[80] Compton would remain resolute. Less than a month before the ninth RCM meeting, the new St. Lucian chief minister fired his initial salvo at the DFS. At the first post-election convention of the UWP a two-third majority of the 300 delegates present endorsed the following ultimatum:

> Be it resolved that this first convention of the UWP declares itself in favour of St. Lucia's participation in a federation of the Eastern Caribbean territories provided that

The [federal centre] is given adequate power to discharge its duties effectively;

The powers and constitution of the federation are such as will ensure economic benefits to the people of St. Lucia; and

The proposed federation achieves independence in 1965;

Be it further resolved that if the three conditions herein stipulated are not met, the Government of St. Lucia should initiate discussions with HMG with a view to achieving [internal self-government] as soon as possible and, in any case, not later than 1966.[81]

While St. Lucia lobbied with all its strength for a more robust federation, Antigua kept pulling in the opposite direction, albeit with the same gusto. Not content with seeing the postal services in the concurrent legislative list,[82] the politicians in St. John's were putting forward additional reservations with the intention of curbing the centre's radius of action even further:

Par. 18 of the DFS – Income Tax

Antigua considers that both the Federal and Unit Governments should have the right to fix rates on both personal and company taxes;

Item No. 3 of the Concurrent Legislative List – Agriculture

Antigua agrees that 'Agriculture' should be on the concurrent legislative list, but wishes the Federal Government's legislative powers ... to be limited to research, financial and technical assistance and the control of pests and diseases;

Item No. 28 of the Concurrent Legislative List — Police

Antigua agrees that 'Police' should be placed on the concurrent legislative list, but wishes the Federal Government's executive powers to be limited to emergencies;

General

Antigua considers that the Federal Government should not have the power to take over the executive control of departments other than those contained in [DFS, par. 17], except by a majority vote of the Legislature in each Unit of the Federation.[83]

The last reservation was, by far, the most problematic. Departing from all existing precedent,[84] Antigua was effectively demanding the power to veto *in perpetuum* any move to expand the centre's executive responsibilities. Under the terms of this proviso the federal government would only mature if and when Antigua so desired. As Sir Arthur Lewis would outspokenly suggest a few months later, this was too 'large a hammer with which to crack such a small nut'.[85]

The available evidence shows that, since the previous April 1964, Bird himself had grown more restless. The intelligence reports for May and August 1964 throw some light on two developments which might have accounted for Antigua's heightened defiance. On the one hand, the visit of a delegation of designate ministers from the Cook Islands sparked in Bird, Lake and the more moderate members of the territory's Trades and Labour Union, a desire to speed-up the conferment upon Antigua of further constitutional authority.[86] The political evolution of these islands must have deeply impressed the chief minister, since soon after bidding farewell to his guests he confided in the colonial administrator that 'by any Cook Islands yardstick surely Antigua was more than qualified for internal self-government'.[87] On the other, Bird's visit to the UN, in particular to the Committee of the Twenty-Four, allowed him to interact with prominent members of the so-called Afro-Asian bloc. The chief minister felt so reassured at this setting that he went as far as openly declaring that if agreement on federation was not forthcoming Antigua would then seek independence on the Western Samoa model, namely in association with a larger member of the Commonwealth.[88] Clearly, the constitutional experiments in the Pacific had left a deep imprint on Antigua's political leadership. While the moderate wing of the Trades and Labour Union began to see in this type of quasi-independent arrangement a suitable alternative to federation, McChesney George and his zealots at the *Workers' Voice* began to galvanize further support for their 'big stick policy' with regard to the ongoing negotiations. The end was nigh.

Against this background the chief ministers and the premier finally met to discuss the DFS and their respective reservations. The ninth RCM meeting, which saw Compton's first appearance as leader of St. Lucia's Legislative Council,[89] began on Wednesday October 28, 1964. The archival record shows how at that gathering, while ratifying previous decisions,[90] the RCM went over the DFS 'paragraph by paragraph'.[91] However, in the light of the unresolved stalemate between Antigua and St. Lucia, the RCM decided to halt the proceedings and reconvene itself yet again in the hope that the rugged terrain could be smoothed in just a matter of weeks.

Interestingly, during this brief interlude the Colonial Office began to receive an assortment of over-optimistic forecasts from its men in the archipelago, in particular from the governor of Barbados, and the colonial administrator of Antigua. Their observations, however, would not stand the scrutiny of time. Governor Stow, for example, confided in his superiors that the environment at this latest sitting of the RCM had been 'better than at any previous [one]' and that there was a clearer realization that 'only in federation lay any real hope of progress'.[92] Moreover, the word from St. John's was that 'just at a time when the alternatives to the [federal project] were being explored with increasing determination the pendulum was swung back to federation'.[93] After a hasty conversation with Bird, who had gone off to Jamaica for a conference of the Commonwealth Parliamentary Association (CPA), Sir David Rose felt 'reasonably confident' that Antigua was going to withdraw its reservations. As he saw it, Bird and his acolytes would end up giving in since 'in their hearts they all believe in federation and ... fear the unfavourable reaction of their supporters to the consequence of isolation'.[94] In a passage reminiscent of the literary technique of magic realism, Sir David went as far as predicting that,

> [T]here seems little doubt that the sudden apparent determination to federate may have been brought by a combination of Bird's pushing for a decision / threatening to opt out and the positive attitude of St. Lucia. All these influences with their varying motives and objectives have tended to produce a common result, namely a sense of urgency in the need to end the period of drift once and for all. Add to this the traditional capriciousness of West Indian politicians and the public mockery of the Seven from Dr. Williams, and one has the answer to this sudden determination to prove him wrong and do what could have been done nearly two years ago.[95]

Whether the local politicians were actively misleading the new colonial administrator or whether he was deluding himself remains an open question. Either way, as became quite obvious soon thereafter, he was on the wrong trail. On arriving from Kingston, on November 14, 1964, Bird and his colleagues publicly announced their intention of maintaining their initial reservations regarding the DFS. They would remain unyielding. And as if to demonstrate their steadfastness the members of Antigua's Executive

Council attacked, for the first time, the principle of freedom of movement.[96] Any serious observer would have characterized this latest misgiving as *déjà vu*, since the previous federation had floundered due, in no small measure, to a devastating feud over that precise subject.[97] The fact that the year 1964 was ending under the cloud of a severe drought did not make matters easier. Owing to the dry season the local sugar factory was closed briefly, sending numerous Antiguan workers in search of temporary employment. Unsurprisingly, the public mood was not particularly welcoming towards expatriate job-hunters.

There is, however, an even more interesting angle to Antigua's about-face with respect to freedom of movement and to the stiffening of its position on the federal project per se. The intelligence report for October 1964 openly suggests that while in Jamaica, for the conference of the CPA, Bird also intended to seek 'advice and counsel from his old friend Norman Manley'.[98] It is highly probable that Manley, now leader of the opposition in Jamaica, held discussions with Bird at that gathering. But in the absence of their respective private papers, it is difficult to assess the nature of their exchange. Yet Manley's input, coming from one of the chief architects of the previous federal hecatomb, may have very well tipped the balance. While this episode is still in need of serious archival research, the decisions Bird soon made spoke for themselves.

Beyond merely staying put, Bird also declared forcefully that he would not attend the second part of the ninth RCM meeting, due to start in Bridgetown on Monday December 7, 1964, or any other meeting on federation. Instead, he was sending the minister of social services off to the gathering with strict and clear instructions. Lake would inform the RCM first, that Antigua was declining representation in the four working committees created under the DFS;[99] and second, that Antigua's reservations would stand even after the January 15, 1965 date, which the RCM had chosen as the deadline for settling all outstanding matters. As Stow scribbled in his notes, the 'waiting game'[100] had begun. Yet it would not take too long, for in a matter of weeks the whole plot would unravel.

Meanwhile, events in London were moving at a tremendous speed. The Labour Party, under the leadership of Harold Wilson, had narrowly defeated the Conservatives at the October 1964 general election. Consequently, Anthony Greenwood, who had just stepped down as chairman of Labour's executive national committee, replaced Duncan Sandys in the Colonial Office. By all accounts the defeat of the Tories was welcomed in the Caribbean press. The overwhelming expectation was that Wilson's Government would be far more flexible and, more importantly, generous in allocating external aid.[101] But after an initial exchange of good wishes, which saw Greenwood visiting the islands in early February 1965,[102] the political leadership of the Seven began to realize that there was little difference between the new Labour Government and the *ancien régime*.[103] In his first despatch to the RCM, stating the Wilson Government's official position with respect to the DFS, Greenwood followed without hesitation the path his predecessors had already trodden.

> During my recent visit I undertook to let your Governments have my views on the Draft Federal Scheme as soon as possible.... HMG shares the view of its predecessors that federation, if it can be brought about on satisfactory terms, offers the best prospect for a solution to the constitutional problems of this area and can make a substantial contribution to [its] economic wellbeing. At the same time, however, before I should be prepared to sponsor the legislation necessary to implement any particular scheme of federation, I should require to be satisfied that it was suited to the needs of the area and likely to endure;

> The Eastern Caribbean will remain dependent for some years to come on external aid for its economic development and the Federal Government must be strong enough not only to ensure that this aid is used to the best advantage but also to inspire the donors of such aid;

> It would, however, in my view be essential to provide that in general the executive authority of the Federation should extend to those matters in respect of which the Federal Legislature has for the time being power to make laws. I should find it very difficult to agree to the Federal Government's executive powers being limited in the way which appears to be envisaged;

> I turn next to the question of Federal finances.... It would be essential in my view that the Federal Government should have its own sources of finance and that these should be adequate to permit it, when it so decides, to carry out all the functions which under the constitution it is empowered to undertake ... I should like some further consideration to be given to the possibility that from the outset the Federal Government might derive some of its revenues from income tax;

> [The DFS] gives the Federal Government the power to set up Commissions of Enquiry in [certain] circumstances but does not provide the Federal Government with any powers to deal with the situation after the Commission of Enquiry has reported. This in my view is a serious defect in the proposals, and I should wish to consider with you ... how this might be remedied.[104]

While Greenwood's submission was hailed in Castries, where the previous day Bousquet had publicly torn a copy of the DFS to shreds,[105] the reaction in St. John's was both 'violent and swift'.[106] After meeting his colleagues, Bird informed Sir David Rose that the Legislative Council would immediately approve a resolution withdrawing Antigua from the federal negotiations. The hard-liners had won the day. The following extract from a leader published in the *Workers' Voice*, a week later, illustrated that,

> What we had hoped, however, was that Mr. Anthony Greenwood, as a Socialist and an educated man would have discerned the dishonest motives of the Colonial Office officials and be strong enough to resist it. Alas, he has proved to be just another Englishman and a rubber stamp for the use of the Imperialist oppressors of the Colonial Office.[107]

In spite of Antigua's defection, the colonial secretary sent a note to Sir John Stow suggesting that the latter's decision did not preclude the formation of a federation of the six. This, in turn, prompted the chairman to convene yet another RCM meeting, on Monday April 26, 1965. This would be the last conference of this feeble regional body. All the remaining delegations attended, including the St. Lucian ministers, together with Sir Stephen Luke as Greenwood's personal representative. Stow immediately sought the delegates' views with regard to the new scenario. While St. Kitts, Dominica and St. Vincent promptly gave assurances of their willingness to go ahead with the project, St. Lucia, Barbados and Montserrat hesitated. At this point Bramble unabashedly admitted that without Antigua his territory would be very reluctant to enter into any federation. This confession allowed Barrow, who had remained silent throughout, to argue that in the light of Montserrat's imminent defection he could not carry on without consulting first with his Cabinet. The meeting was then adjourned until the following day, when the premier finally submitted to the RCM Barbados's official position:

That on the general principle of the desirability of an Eastern Caribbean Federation there was no change in Barbados' position, as expressed some years ago;

That one of the contributing factors to the present state of disagreement and indecision, among the Seven territories, was the continued failure of the UK to state in unequivocal terms the quantum of capital finance it is to make available to the Federation;

That any further discussions on proposals for the establishment of Federation would depend on the willingness of [HMG] to state its intentions as regards the above.[108]

The archival record reveals that various delegations, most notably the Kittitians, Dominicans and Vincentians, tried to persuade Barrow to stay onboard. However, the premier vowed to abide by his ultimatum. According to the minutes, this tense lull exasperated the eager delegates from St. Lucia. It did not take long for the vociferous Bousquet to aim at Barrow's reticence, describing it rather derisively as 'smart alec stuff'. In typical fashion the premier lost his temper and stormed out of the conference room.[109] On the following day, Wednesday April 28, with Compton and Le Blanc absent and Joshua and Southwell withdrawing from the proceedings, Stow had no other option but to adjourn *sine die*. As Greenwood reported to British Prime Minister Wilson a few weeks later, 'we have no alternative but to leave it at this for present'.[110] It was all over. The federal ideal of Marryshow and Cipriani had been finally put to rest.

Part Three: Conclusion

The failure of the federal negotiations was not a one-way affair. On the Seven's part, mutual fears arising from insularity in outlook and discrepancies in standards of living had become serious obstacles in the way of a federation based on equal partnership. As Sir Stephen Luke put it, the 'unplumbed, salt estranging sea' remained a powerful dividing factor. As far as the colonial leadership was concerned, the intense struggle between the Colonial Office, the Treasury and the newly founded Ministry of Overseas Development on the future of British aid to the archipelago had complicated the scenario even further. After three years of waiting for the

British to specify the level of their financial commitment, the local politicians were naturally exhausted. And in the light of the absence of any grassroots enthusiasm for federation there was no alternative but to put the whole project in cold storage. The message reverberated loud and clear. The region was in desperate need of a genuinely fresh initiative.

PART FOUR

NEW ROADS TOWARDS OLD AIMS[1]

At this stage in our colonial history our main task must be to liquidate colonialism, either by granting independence to a number of territories or by evolving forms of government that secure basic democratic rights for the people but which involve a certain type of association with the United Kingdom, without any stigma of colonialism.

Anthony Greenwood, 1965

Introduction

The last part of the book focuses on the constitutional package emerging from the process of decolonization in the Eastern Caribbean during this period: namely, associated statehood for the Leeward and Windward Islands (except for Montserrat) and independence for Barbados. The next chapter contends that free association, as was implemented in these territories, was not consistent with the standards set by the General Assembly of the UN.[2] This *sui generis* constitutional status, as discussed below, was a hybrid political and legal construct of dubious non-colonial standing. Notwithstanding this, associated statehood as applied to the Leeward and Windward Islands fulfilled, albeit momentarily, the expectations of the metropolitan and colonial interlocutors. It had become obvious that no other option, following the collapse of the federal negotiations, could accommodate the special set of circumstances enveloping the Caribbean scenario. These last two chapters reveal the intricate policy-making process leading to the articulation of this modality of political association.

These concluding chapters do not remain oblivious to the American angle. The launching of this fresh initiative came about after close consultation with the Johnson Administration and in particular with US Secretary of State Dean Rusk. The challenge facing the British Government was twofold. First, it had to avoid any solution that might prove totally indefensible before the UN. Second, it needed to reassure the US that British withdrawal would not trigger the emergence of 'seven potential little Haiti's or Cuba's on the American doorstep'.[3] As far as the British were concerned the transfer of political authority in this area of the world was not a matter which justified causing friction between them and the Americans.[4]

The last chapter concentrates on Barbados and its decisive move to independence. It attempts to provide a solid explanation of why, unlike the remaining units, this island moved smoothly to constitutional independence. It also goes in depth into Barbados's domestic political landscape, tracing the immediate catalysts leading Barbados to go it alone. This last chapter evaluates the transition to independence not only from the point of view of the island itself, but also from the perspective of the transatlantic allies.

12

Free Association *Modo Britannico*[1]

> The two ends of the scale of dependent territories somewhere along which we have to place associated states are, at one end, colonies and, at the other, protected states. The prior status of these associated states is that of colonies … to elevate them to the level of protected states requires some positive action to confer upon them a degree of international personality … and I do not see any such positive action here.
>
> *A. Watts, Legal Adviser to the Foreign Office, 1966*

The collapse of the federal negotiations came at a time when the British Government was attempting to redefine its relationship with the remaining outposts of empire.[2] For instance, on the same day that Greenwood recommended to Harold Wilson to 'leave it at this for present',[3] in regard to the Seven, he also sent the British prime minister a comprehensive report on the future of the existing colonial dependencies.[4] In much the same way as the Caribbean islands, all the territories included in that submission presented, in the words of the colonial secretary, 'special difficulties'. The available evidence reveals that by this stage the British Government was bent on liquidating colonialism. In fact, many in the Colonial Office were gearing up for the upcoming acceleration or 'crisis of decolonisation'.[5] Yet the entire process turned out to be more complex than originally envisioned. As the coming months demonstrated, there was no one answer that could accommodate the widely varying set of circumstances enveloping the remaining British dependent territories. Consequently, it proved impossible for the British to articulate a coherent or uniform policy for disengaging from all those units. This latter period of British colonial demobilization demonstrates, perhaps more accurately than any previous stage, how asymmetrical the decolonizing experience really was. Within this context, the drive towards free association in the

Eastern Caribbean scenario stands as a prominent illustration of the arbitrary nature of that process and, hence, deserves closer scholarly attention. Most students of the process of British withdrawal from the archipelago, so far, have tended to circumscribe their analytical focus to evaluating the provisions contained in the 1967 West Indies Act.[6] In so doing, they have refrained from discussing how, during this period, the process of devolution in the Eastern Caribbean called into question the meaning itself of decolonization. It is not enough, for instance, to compare the 1967 West Indies Act to the 1964 Cook Islands Constitution Act.[7] The analytical radius of any such discussion, without a doubt, must be far more encompassing. In the light of the failure of the federal negotiations, the seminal questions that arise are the following: What were the options before the British Government immediately after the breakdown of the tenth RCM meeting in regard to the Seven? What considerations swayed the British Government to select free association as the constitutional status for these Caribbean islands? Why did the colonial leadership settle for that formula instead of demanding independence thenceforth? And, more importantly, to what extent, if at all, does the implementation of this status challenge conventional definitions of decolonization?

Before addressing the substantive aspects of the discussion, it is essential to note that, on the one hand, Montserrat and Barbados (albeit for obviously different reasons) were not to move on towards free association. And that, on the other, the ongoing discussions on annexation between Grenada and Trinidad and Tobago had finally been shelved.[8] While the British Government agreed with Bramble and his associates that Montserrat should remain a dependency of the Crown[9] and acknowledged that Barbados could very well seek independence on its own,[10] it was not at all clear what relationship would evolve with the remaining units. As far as the British were concerned, the constitutional future of Antigua, St. Kitts–Nevis–Anguilla, Dominica, St. Lucia, St. Vincent and Grenada was becoming an increasingly complex conundrum.

In theory, the alternatives available to the British Government were granting independence to each of these islands, maintaining some type of association with them, or facilitating their integration with Britain itself. Although by that time the international community was already recognizing integration with another country as a legitimate decolonizing route,[11] it has since remained the less travelled road.[12] The available evidence demonstrates that integration, although referred to *en passant* at various meetings of the Cabinet's Defence and Overseas Policy Committee,[13] was never considered within the context of the Caribbean archipelago. This is not surprising, since influential voices very close to the British prime minister wished to avoid at all costs a revival of the controversy that had raged over Malta a few years earlier, with its enormous potential for embarrassment in relation to Britain's immigration policy.[14] The archival record shows that the possibility of exploring whether to superimpose on the Caribbean the constitutional model of the Channel Islands was briefly discussed as well. Yet, the fact that the Bailiwicks of Jersey and Guernsey stood in a unique historical and geographical position with Britain meant that such a link could not be exported anywhere else.[15] Hence, that idea was swiftly put aside and no such study was ever commissioned with respect to the Caribbean territories.

The possibility of declaring the immediate independence of each of these units was also a non-starter. As seen from London, granting independence to these islands now, while enticing from a financial point of view,[16] would in all possibility turn out to be totally counterproductive. There was a solid consensus that because of their economic weaknesses, allegedly poor administrative records, marked tendency to boss rule, and location in an internationally sensitive area, anything that went beyond 'some form of continuing association' with Britain was, for the time being, out of the question. The overwhelming impression was that granting premature independence to any of these units, against such a background, would in all probability lead to severe complications, which in the words of Duncan Sandys 'would not constitute good advertisements for past British rule'.[17] Hence, with the elimination of integration and immediate independence as desirable alternatives, the British authorities were saddled at once with the complicated task of defining the type of link to be maintained. The British Cabinet now had to decide whether 'continuing association' meant offering these islands full internal self-government, protectorate status, free association along UN standards, or none of the above.

Full internal self-government, as contended in the previous chapter, was not considered as a reasonable alternative for these territories. Although during this same period the British Government had just conferred it upon, for instance, Basutoland and Mauritius,[18] the Caribbean dependencies would not be allowed to climb on that bandwagon. The prevailing view in the Colonial Office was that to follow what had so far been the conventional pattern of constitutional decolonization in colonial possessions such as these islands, where independence was not forthcoming, hardly made any sense.[19] More importantly, if these units were granted full internal self-government London would not be able to maintain that such status was a permanent one. Thus, as many in the Colonial Office soon concluded, full internal self-government would inevitably lead to the untimely independence of these islands.[20] By the same token, protectorate status, as had been used in the cases of Tonga and the Maldives, was not an option worth pursuing.[21] This leads us to the crux of the matter: what other constitutional formula would allow London to confer upon these dependencies a higher level of self-government without giving away total de facto authority over them?

In attempting to answer this question, the British authorities began to look at free association with special interest. Only five years earlier the UN had defined that novel formula in the following terms,

> Free Association should be the result of a free and voluntary choice by the people of the territory concerned, expressed through informed and democratic processes. It should be one that respects the individuality and the cultural characteristics of the territory and its people.

> It retains, for the people of the territory which is associated with an independent state, the freedom to modify the status of that territory through the expression of their will by democratic means and through constitutional processes.

> The associated territory should have the right to determine its internal constitution without outside interference, in accordance with due constitutional processes and the freely expressed wishes of the people. This does not preclude consultations as appropriate or necessary under the terms of the free association agreed upon.[22]

In principle this constitutional model, which has attracted the attention of numerous legal scholars, was garnering favour in the British Cabinet for three basic reasons. First, the UN General Assembly and the international community regarded it as being non-colonial. This meant that following its implementation the metropolitan power could cease to transmit information on those territories pursuant to article 73(e) of the UN Charter. Consequently, they would not be caught up anymore in the debates of the Twenty-Four. At a time when the Afro-Asian bloc in the UN was being particularly critical of British policy in Aden and the South Arabian Protectorate it made a lot of sense to neutralize its potential for further interference.[23] Second, free association was not regarded as a transitory status. Unlike full internal self-government, which was merely perceived as a rite of passage to independence, free association was seen as a permanent constitutional formula. And while either contracting party could terminate it at any time, unlike full internal self-government, under free association there would be no built-in expectations of immediate independence. Third, there was no precedent of free association per se in the British Commonwealth. Although, as shown further along, the philosophical tenets behind free association sprang from the 1931 Statute of Westminster, the adoption of the term itself and, more importantly, the intention of applying it to British dependencies had no parallel. Hence, these were uncharted waters for the Crown. Notwithstanding the challenge that an absence of precedent certainly entailed, this state of affairs would grant the British enough flexibility to deal with the 'special difficulties' surrounding the Caribbean archipelago. Against that background, free association stood as the only reasonable solution. Yet, it is precisely at this stage of the analysis that most students of this process have tended to be misled. Many have failed to draw a sharp distinction between free association, as the UN had defined it, and the constitutional model that was finally implemented in these territories. The available evidence suggests that even though in the end the British Government would use the term 'free association' to describe its future link to these islands, in fact, that new relationship would not amount to such. The 1967 West Indies Act, as argued below in greater detail, effectively fell well below the UN benchmark. This then begs the following question: if free association as a concept had seemed desirable, what set of forces prevented the British Government from going along with it completely?

From the outset Greenwood had acknowledged that 'in the case of some territories … it may be necessary to adopt a solution which, although endorsed by a general election or a referendum, would strictly fall short of what would satisfy the UN'.[24] The archival record, in particular recently declassified documents pertaining to the Foreign Office and the Ministry of Defence, demonstrates that these Caribbean territories clearly belonged to that group. The available evidence suggests, rather overwhelmingly, that the international and strategic dimensions of the Caribbean question were producing considerable anxiety. By August 1965 the Foreign Office had raised serious objections against the application of 'some form of free association as defined by the UN in a number of Atlantic, Pacific and Indian Ocean islands in which we have strategic interests of our own and those of our friends and allies'.[25] The position of the Ministry of Defence was that if Britain adopted the UN's model it would, in all probability, lose total control over places 'where British and American defence interests made this essential, in, for example, small oceanic islands'.[26] It had become quite obvious that it would not be on Britain's or its allies' best interest to superimpose on the Caribbean scenario the type of relationship that, for instance, New Zealand and the Cook Islands had just inaugurated.[27] Under that compact of free association, which was the first one to emulate the UN's model and as such was able to set the precedent,[28] Wellington had given away all its overriding powers to coerce the legislature of the Cook Islands into complying with its international responsibilities. New Zealand was now acting as the diplomatic agent of the Cook Islands. As far as matters of foreign affairs and defence were concerned, the ministers in Wellington had no other alternative but to rely on the legislature of the Cook Islands to use its self-governing powers to give effect to its obligations.[29] Not surprisingly, the Foreign Office and the Ministry of Defence were extremely concerned over the wider implications such constitutional laxity could have on the strategic interests of Britain's allies. Lord Taylor, parliamentary under-secretary of state for the colonies, summed up the challenge now confronting the British Government in the remaining dependent territories:

> Most have no strategic value to us, but could be a source of anxiety to others, e.g., the US, if they 'went wrong.' But you cannot avoid the risk of people 'going wrong' if you decolonise them.[30]

The British authorities knew that they would be taking a chance in conferring upon these islands a meaningful instalment of further political authority. Nevertheless, there was also a clear understanding that the risky components of that equation had to be kept at a minimum. After all, as the Foreign Office would finally conclude early in October 1965, it was 'vital to carry the Americans with us'.[31] It was self-evident that establishing a new constitutional model in the Caribbean could have a direct impact on the US's national security. Consequently, before going any further, this study must incorporate and evaluate the influence which the Johnson Administration exerted on the British Government, as the latter attempted to articulate a *sui generis* constitutional package for Antigua, St. Kitts–Nevis–Anguilla, Dominica, St. Lucia, St. Vincent and Grenada.

By this stage, as illustrated in the previous chapter, the US State Department was already thinking in terms of independence for Barbados and 'dependency status' for each of the remaining units of the Eastern Caribbean archipelago.[32] Moreover, the participation of the Americans in the Tripartite Survey had served to reassure many in London that gone were the days when the Kennedy and Johnson Administrations had chosen 'to overlook their anti-colonial beliefs'.[33] In some quarters these were seen as encouraging signs. A wide array of voices within the Colonial Office, for example, believed that the US's renewed involvement meant that it would not attempt to exert undue pressure against further British withdrawal from the region. Yet that still remained to be seen. As the historical record suggests, Britain's intention of establishing a watered-down version of free association in these territories and, equally importantly, the spectre of additional Cold War conflicts in the area would soon test the Americans' patience to its limit. It is essential to note that the discussions between Britain and the US, following the last round of federal negotiations, with respect to the decolonization of these islands, took place during a period of acute geopolitical tension in the hemisphere. At a time when the British Guiana crisis had finally been resolved,[34] a new conflict of unforeseen ferocity had just erupted on the Americans' doorstep. The explosion in the Dominican Republic of a massive civil strife, which in a matter of four days led to the landing of over 30,000 US Marines in Santo Domingo, served as the background against which that Anglo-American dialogue developed.

Although the catalysts leading to a crisis of such proportions had been brewing since the assassination of *el generalísimo* Rafael L. Trujillo, in May

1961, the sheer scale of the violence had caught the Johnson Administration almost off balance. Since the ousting of the constitutionally-elected president Juan Bosch, in September 1963, things in Santo Domingo had remained ominously quiet, reminiscent of the calm before a storm. Almost 18 months later, on April 24, 1965, a group of young army officers, supported by close to two-thirds of the country, finally revolted against the 'old Trujillo gang' which had deposed Bosch and annulled the 1963 Constitution. Although most Dominicans sympathized with the constitutionalist cause, the entrenched right-wing elements in the Air Force, Navy and most of the Army quickly overwhelmed Bosch's supporters. Mostly disorganized and ill equipped, the more moderate elements of the constitutionalist forces soon surrendered. Yet, the intelligence reaching the US Embassy in Santo Domingo suggested that the leadership of the crumbling rebel movement was now falling into the hands of extreme left-wing elements or so-called 'communist tommy-gun commandos'. The Johnson Administration observed in dismay how chaotic the situation in the centre of the capital remained, with street fighting, attacks on embassies and widespread looting. As far as the Americans were concerned the 'communist commando boys' seemed to have gained the initiative in Santo Domingo's urban areas. In the light of this, several voices within the president's innermost circle went as far as characterizing this crisis as an 'early skirmish in the projected Cold War attack on the Caribbean Basin, possibly timed to help the upcoming North Vietnam operation'.[35] As Johnson's more hawkish advisors saw it, only a US invasion could 'block off [the explosion] of immediate "wars of liberation" in Haiti, Guatemala, Venezuela and Colombia and others planned elsewhere'.[36] This was the rationale which, in the final analysis, led the president to order military action, coincidentally on the same day when the tenth RCM meeting finally collapsed.

While the US troops would remain stationed in the Dominican Republic, under the belated auspices of the OAS, for over a year, the lessons from this crisis were already out in the open for all to see. The fact that the Americans had just moved a large contingent of forces into Santo Domingo without prior consultation with their allies, and even before having any mandate to do so either from the UN or the OAS, constituted a stark reminder that the often celebrated Anglo-American 'special relationship' did not exist with respect to the Caribbean and Latin America.[37] In addition, this episode led the Johnson White House into a period of acute reappraisals. The available evidence tends to indicate that those closest to the president saw this latest crisis as the spring-board from which to launch a powerful intellectual, psychological and diplomatic offensive against the Sino-Soviet threat. For instance, Adolf Berle, former assistant secretary of state, confided in President Johnson that,

> There is reason to hope, though we cannot count on it, that the American landing in Santo Domingo has prevented [the] activation of Soviet-Castro-inspired movements elsewhere in the Caribbean. [Although] the Soviet Union would not fight the United States, or supply a civil war on the scale needed in [the American Hemisphere], they will [nonetheless] supply money to Communist commandos (one installment designed for the guerrillas in Venezuela was intercepted. It came from the Soviet Union via the Italian Communist Party). Probably they have made money available to commandos in Guatemala and Colombia. They are all too well entrenched in Haiti.
>
> Since the United States is in a mood to act ... Communist commando operations to seize weak governments are unlikely to succeed and, therefore, less likely to be attempted. But if a serious attempt is made, the United States has to be prepared to act immediately. Some attempt is being made in Europe to prove that the United States is a divided country, unable to act again. That impression has to be quickly dispelled.[38]

The minutes of a conversation between President Johnson and the Chancellor of the Exchequer James Callaghan, barely two months after the first platoons of US marines arrived in Santo Domingo, suggests that Johnson agreed with the substance of Berle's argument. While apparently extremely friendly and quite relaxed, the president vehemently defended his actions in the Dominican Republic. Johnson stunned Callaghan when he added that with hindsight he would have sent in the marines even earlier. Johnson's grim suspicion that 'there were potential Santo Domingos in 12 other Latin American countries' was, without a doubt, the most important observation raised during the course of this brief meeting.[39] Ironically, at a time when the British were most determined to withdraw from the area, the US Government was in a state of high alert. The available evidence suggests that the Americans were quite alarmed by the inroads which vigorous social reform movements such as, for example, *el Apra*[40] in

Peru and *Acción Democrática* in Venezuela, were making throughout Latin America.[41] Now, the challenge before the British was obvious; they had to convince the Johnson Administration that their version of free association would not add to the latter's geopolitical worries. More specifically, the British Government had to cast off the suspicion that it was going to 'run out' on its responsibilities in the Caribbean. Several voices in the administration already entertained the view that 'in Whitehall there are many who would like to hand over to the US these territories and this idea is making Washington unhappy'.[42] Along these lines, and in the light of their unilateral invasion of the Dominican Republic, there could be no doubt that should Britain be seen as defaulting on its responsibility for these territories' defence and foreign affairs the Americans would not hesitate to intervene militarily if the need were to arise. This hypothetical scenario was far too plausible for London's comfort. It could very well shatter Anglo-American relations for the unforeseen future and, at the same time, considerably weaken Britain's position in the international community. As Sir Patrick Dean concluded,

> [T]he lesson for the United Kingdom is surely that we should not go too far out of our way to argue with them or to seek to influence them in this hemisphere simply for the sake of principle when our own direct interests, which are few, are not involved. By so doing we shall, without achieving anything, only irritate, and thus lessen our influence on United States policy in other parts of the world where we have more to offer and where our interests are greater.[43]

In other words, since the basis for the Johnson Administration's interest in the Eastern Caribbean archipelago was the national defence of the US, the future constitutional model of those territories should be tailored to safeguard American security. The exchanges that took place thereafter between Anthony Greenwood, Michael Stewart and Dean Rusk stood as a prominent illustration of Britain's intention to abide by Sir Patrick's dictum.

Greenwood's visit to Washington, between October 17 and 21, 1965, set the pace of these conversations. His meeting with Rusk deserves particular attention. After a brief exchange of pleasantries, the US Secretary of State initiated the substantive discussion saying that it would be very useful for him to have some indication of Britain's plans for the future of its Caribbean dependencies. Greenwood replied that 'certain proposals' were about to be made to the colonial leadership regarding the islands' future. Acknowledging that federation had just become a 'non-starter' and relieved to find out that Britain was not proposing to grant independence to these islands, Rusk felt compelled to ask the British colonial secretary, 'How far would it be possible to follow the model of Puerto Rico?'[44] He went on describing how Puerto Ricans enjoyed 'the best of both worlds', with free entry to the American market but no liability to pay US taxes and with authority to amend their own constitution. At this point Greenwood finally revealed that the Colonial Office was about to send an official notice to Antigua, St. Kitts–Nevis–Anguilla, Dominica, St. Lucia, St. Vincent and Grenada proposing 'a form of associated status'.[45] This arrangement, as he preliminarily described it, would give these territories complete responsibility over their internal affairs. Yet, the colonial secretary eagerly pointed out that Britain 'should remain responsible for their defence and foreign policy' and, equally important, would retain power to intervene in their internal affairs 'to the extent necessary to discharge these responsibilities'.[46] While confiding in Greenwood that he was concerned at the large number of new states becoming members of the UN, Rusk welcomed Britain's initiative as being 'an interesting way of proceeding'.[47]

In addition, just prior to the adjournment of their conversation, Rusk made a passing reference to the fact that the State Department had received reports of 'some communist efforts' in the French West Indies. Although openly satisfied to hear that, so far, there was no sign of communist penetration in the British islands, the fact that the topic had surfaced served as a stark reminder of how the red threat kept shaping the Anglo-American agenda.

Besides the obvious international dimension of this question, there was also, as far as the US Government was concerned, a delicate domestic consideration. As the British policy-makers were soon to find out, their proposals for the constitutional future of these six islands would, in all probability, raise very sensitive questions about the political relationship between the United States and Puerto Rico. Although often overlooked, this angle gained special prominence during this period since the US Congress had recently passed an act to establish a joint US–Puerto Rican Status Commission for straightening out 'some of the confusion which exists as a result of previous legislation giving Puerto Rico a special political status'.[48] In one of the most absorbing exchanges between the Johnson Administration and the British Government, prior to the implementation of Britain's version of free association in the area, the Puerto Rican conundrum did play a central role. In a letter to Dean Rusk, intended as a follow-up to Greenwood's visit, the British foreign secretary informed his opposite number in Washington that these islands 'will also be empowered to join international organisations (excluding the UN itself) of which we are ourselves members'.[49] In his reply to Michael Stewart, Rusk sent the clearest signal yet that major concessions on matters of foreign relations could become a source of future difficulty in the already tense relationship with Puerto Rico. Rusk pointed out that

> The plan for each of the six territories "to become a state in voluntary association with Great Britain" does seem a clear step in the direction of preventing a fragmentation of small entities in the area. In light of the reluctance of these islands to form a federation, the new association offers a practical alternative to continued colonial dependence on the one hand and independence on the other.

> You should, however, be aware that the proposal to permit Antigua to join international organisations, other than the UN, may pose some problems to this Government since the US Government is solely responsible for the foreign relations of the Commonwealth of Puerto Rico.[50]

In the 14 years since Puerto Rico had attained its current political status,[51] the US Government had never delegated any authority to it in regard to foreign affairs. In spite of being able to form part of US delegations to international conferences, Puerto Ricans were not allowed to apply for separate membership in international organizations. And although some voices in the Bureau of International Organizations Affairs of the US State Department argued, *sotto voce*, that it would not be completely impossible for Puerto Rico to become a member of an international entity, existing policy in Washington had always ruled that out. From the Americans' point of view, as the Foreign Office eventually concluded, it was possible to conceive of a situation in which the 'associated state', under its delegated authority, wished to enter into an agreement with UN members to promote, for instance, the full independence of Puerto Rico.[52] Unless Britain held overriding responsibilities for the defence and external affairs of these territories any delegation of authority in political matters, as the legal unit of the Foreign Office put it, could prove 'dangerous'.[53] This explains why throughout the course of this process London's mantra became, 'we should try to embarrass them [the Americans] as little as possible'.[54] But what was finally proposed to these six islands? Most importantly, what constituted free association *modo britannico*?

On December 17, 1965, two months after Greenwood's conversation with Dean Rusk, the Colonial Office finally sent a despatch to the colonial administrators of Antigua, St. Kitts–Nevis–Anguilla, Dominica, St. Lucia, St. Vincent and Grenada, outlining a proposal 'to move to self-government in a new relationship of association with Britain'.[55] In that same document the colonial secretary expressed his intention of discussing 'these new arrangements as early as possible'.[56] He went as far as suggesting dates for these conferences, which in the end spanned from late February to late May 1966.[57] The talks that thereafter ensued between London and the colonial leadership, unlike the federal discussions, did not amount to full-scale negotiations. These proved to be a less contentious affair in view of the fact that, for the first time since the collapse of the West Indies Federation, the colonial leadership and London seemed to be on a similar wavelength.

Since the differences between the Colonial Office's initial proposals and what the British Parliament and the colonial legislatures eventually ratified were minor, this discussion pays special attention to the final version. If compared with their current dependent status, this was, in the words of Sir Stephen Luke, a 'bold and hopeful constitutional experiment'[58] as the level of authority devolved to these territories was substantial indeed. For instance, Britain's powers with regard to their internal affairs were considerably curtailed. The 1967 West Indies Act specified from the outset that the British Government:

Shall have no responsibility for the government of any associated state except in respect of:

Any matter which in the opinion of HMG is a matter relating to defence (whether of an associated state or of the United Kingdom or of any other territory for whose government HMG [is] wholly or partly responsible) or to external affairs;

Any matter relating to nationality and citizenship;

Any matter relating to the Succession to the Throne or the Royal Style and Titles.[59]

In all matters, save the ones described above,

no Act of Parliament passed on or after the appointed day shall extend, or be deemed to extend, to an associated state as part of its law, unless it is expressly declared in that Act that the state has requested and consented to its being enacted.[60]

This provision, namely the inapplicability of British laws without the consent of the local legislatures, put these six islands on a par with Canada, Australia, New Zealand, South Africa, the Irish Free State and Newfoundland following the enactment of the Statute of Westminster.[61] Moreover, the fact that this Act explicitly stated that 'notwithstanding anything in the Interpretation Act 1889,[62] the expression 'colony' in any Act of the Parliament ... shall not include an associated state'[63] drew these territories even nearer to the old dominions.[64] The conferment upon the local legislatures of 'full power to make laws having extra-territorial operation',[65] together with their removal from the 1865 Colonial Laws Validity Act, the 1890 Colonial Courts of Admiralty Act[66] and the 1894 Merchant Shipping Act[67] made their proximity to the dominion model self-evident.[68] One of the most salient illustrations of this was their newly acquired capacity to amend or alter any part of their constitutions.[69] If compared with most fully self-governing territories, where the Crown usually retained constituent and even unrestricted legislative powers exercisable by Order in Council,[70] their degree of authority was considerably superior.

Yet, the trappings of local government would now resemble those of territories enjoying full internal self-government. First, the administrator of each island would now be called 'governor' and, more importantly, would no longer summon or preside over the executive committee.[71] In addition, his overarching powers, such as unilaterally reserving or disallowing bills, disposing of land and offering pardons were thenceforth eliminated; while his direct responsibility over the civil service and the police was also discontinued.[72] The intention of the British Government as well as of the colonial leadership was for the governor of an associated state to act, not as the agent of the Crown, but as a constitutional monarch; in the mould of a governor general in an independent country, acting on the counsel of his ministers. And although the advice tendered to the Crown on the appointment of the governor would still be tendered by a British secretary of state, the wishes of the local politicians would now become the deciding factor and the aim would be to appoint a 'local man'.[73] Second, the executive committee, now termed the 'cabinet' would not have any ex officio members: all appointments to the cabinet would be made from among the members of the local legislature. Its proceedings, furthermore, were to fall under the control of the chief minister, now the 'premier', and all ministers would be individually and collectively responsible to the legislature for their respective departments.

Table 12.1
The 1967 West Indies Act

Before Free Association[74]	Under Free Association[75]
On the Queen's Representative:	**On the Queen's Representative:**
The Administrator under the new arrangement should be appointed ... by Her Majesty on the advice of [British] Ministers.[76] Administrator to hold office during Her Majesty's pleasure.[77]	The Queen's Representative will be appointed by the Her Majesty. In relation to such appointments ... the Secretary of State will be guided by the advice of the [premier] of the territory when submitting advice to Her Majesty.[78]
On the Legislative Powers of each Jurisdiction:	**On the Legislative Powers of each Jurisdiction:**
[The legislature] will have power to make laws for the peace, order and good government of the territory. [Nevertheless] the Administrator [will] be required to reserve for Her Majesty's pleasure Bills that fall into any of the following categories: Bills which are inconsistent with the Constitutional Instruments; Bills which appear to him to prejudice the maintenance of law and order; Bills which appear to him to prejudice the efficiency of the Public Service, the Police, the Judiciary or the Audit Service. ... in deciding whether a Bill falls into one of these categories the Administrator should act in his discretion.[80]	The legislature of the territory will have powers of legislation in respect of all matters; the present powers to reserve bills or disallow laws passed by the territorial legislature will be discontinued. [The legislature] will have power to alter the Constitution; Section 2 of the Colonial Laws Validity Act 1865[79] will not apply to laws enacted by the legislature of the territory; Acts of the British Parliament passed after the commencement of the new Constitution (other than those relating to foreign affairs, defence and citizenship) will not extend to the territory except at the request and with the consent of the territory [...][81]

On the Public Service:	On the Public Service:
[T]he power to appoint, promote, transfer, dismiss and exercise disciplinary control over public officers should be vested in the Administrator acting after consultation with the advisory Public Service Commission.[82] [T]he Public Service Commission [will] consist of a Chairman and such number of members (not less than 2 nor more than 4) as the Administrator acting in his discretion shall decide.[83]	The appointment, promotion, discipline and removal of public servants will be the responsibility of a Service Commission. [It] will be independent of the Executive in carrying out its functions […] There will be provision for each department of Government to be placed under a Minister [and] supervised by a Permanent Secretary who will be a public officer. The [Premier] will have a voice in any appointments to the office of Permanent Secretary.[84]
On the Police:	**On the Police:**
Power of appointment and dismissal of and disciplinary control over the Head of the Police Force should be vested in the Administrator acting in his discretion.[85]	The arrangements for the appointment, promotion, discipline and removal from office of members of the Police Force will be in accordance with the principles outlined in [the section on the Service Commission].[86]

Third, the local legislatures would no longer be called legislative councils. In Antigua and Grenada, for example, the legislature would now be divided in two separate chambers, namely, a fully elected house of representatives and an appointed senate.[87] Conversely, in St. Kitts–Nevis–Anguilla, Dominica, St. Lucia and St. Vincent, a unicameral house of assembly, with a minimum of two appointed members, would now replace the legislative council. These constitutional modifications placed these territories on equal footing with Barbados, where since 1964 the executive committee had been abolished and both its powers and functions transferred to a cabinet, while the legislative council, in existence since 1627, was replaced by a local senate.

Parallel to this evolution, the role of the judiciary, as an institution, would undergo an even more meaningful transformation. In future the high court of each territory was going to have jurisdiction 'to declare whether any law, or anything done in purported exercise of authority conferred by the Constitution or any other law, contravenes or alters any of the provisions of the Constitution'.[88] With the introduction of judicial review the local bench would soon become an ever more influential actor in the socio-political life of these territories. More importantly, the recognition of this legal doctrine would inevitably lead to the development of a corpus of local jurisprudence, which would add strength and credibility to these territories' autonomy with respect to Britain. The fact that the new constitutions of these islands would all include a provision 'for safeguarding the fundamental right and freedoms of the individual'[89] meant that the judiciary, in exercising its prerogative of judicial review and, thus, enforcing those basic rights, would also become the guarantor of the civil liberties.[90]

But this relative freedom was offset by London's significant reserve powers in relation to the defence and foreign relations of these territories. This, without a doubt, was the most problematic aspect of this new constitutional model. Since the boundary separating internal from external affairs usually tends to be blurred, the non-colonial nature of this so-called partnership was, as a result, highly compromised. Section 7 of the West Indies Act, in outlining Britain's reserve powers, epitomized the fragility of this covenant.

> Her Majesty may by Order in Council made at the request and with the consent of any associated state make, as part of the law of that state, any provision which appears to Her Majesty to be necessary or expedient for the peace, order or good government of that state.
>
> Where it appears to Her Majesty that in the interests of the responsibilities of Her Majesty's Government in the United Kingdom relating to defence and external affairs a change should be made in the law of an associated state, Her Majesty may by Order in Council expressly stating that fact make, as part of the law of that state, such provision as appears to Her Majesty to be appropriate, including (if by reason of war or other emergency it appears to be necessary and that fact is expressly stated in the Order) provision derogating from the provisions of the constitution of the state relating to fundamental rights and freedoms.[91]

The British Government's initial communication to the colonial leadership had suggested that 'responsibility for external affairs and defence will lie with the British Government'[92] and that, as a result, the latter should have 'the necessary executive authority in the territory'.[93] Yet it was not until the beginning of Antigua's Constitutional Conference, late in February 1966, that the complex task of defining Britain's powers in the fields of defence and external affairs finally got underway. A procedural solution was finally adopted and carved out in a document entitled 'Heads of Agreement', which delineated Britain's reserve powers in matters of defence and foreign affairs.[94] The first part of this agreement with Britain, which was entered into by each territory, dealt with matters of defence. The following three provisions throw additional light on the inflexibility of this new arrangement in respect of London's overriding reserve powers.

> [The associated states] will take all steps, (including, where necessary, steps to secure legislation),

> [T]o provide such facilities *as may be required* by [Britain] for the fulfilment of its responsibilities or obligations with respect to the defence of [the territory] or of the United Kingdom and its associated states and territories or the safety of any other part of the Commonwealth *or of any of the allies of the United Kingdom;*

> [W]ill not, *without the consent of* [Britain], *grant access to any part* of its territory or territorial waters to, or *allow the use of any* of its airfields, communications or harbour facilities by, *the forces or agents* of any government.[95]

From a British point of view, it made a lot of sense to maintain a firm hold over this aspect of the equation since, above all else, it went a long way in easing the concerns of Rusk and his colleagues in Washington. It is particularly helpful to note that there was a strong correlation between the drafting of these clauses and NASA's recent request, under the auspices of the State Department and pursuant to the 1961 Defence Areas Agreement,[96] for a site in Antigua.[97] While the primary intention behind this petition was to install a ground station to track and control the Apollo lunar landing vehicles, the military dimension of this request did not go unheeded. And as the defence provisions in the Heads of Agreement illustrated, the British position was that nothing, including this new constitutional relationship, would be allowed to hamper the access of the US to these territories. Britain's reserve powers in the conduct of the external affairs of these six islands were similarly broad and deserve special attention as well. Although the British Government would in future consult the local authorities before entering into extra-territorial obligations on their behalf, the scope of action of the associated state in the international arena was to be limited indeed.

> [The associated states] will take all steps (including, where necessary, steps to secure the passage of legislation) required by [Britain]

[T]o secure the fulfilment of the Commonwealth or international obligations or responsibilities of [Britain], in the interests of good relations between [them] or [Britain] and another country;

The Antigua Government will not introduce or support legislation which might affect the discharge of [Britain's] Commonwealth or international obligations or responsibilities or the maintenance of good relations between [the associated states] or [Britain] and another country without prior reference to and consultation with [Britain]. The [associated states] will not proceed with or support legislation if [Britain] informs them that its passage would be detrimental to the discharge of those obligations or responsibilities or the maintenance of such relations;

Where in the opinion of [Britain] the enactment of legislation for the [associated states] is required in the interests of the responsibility of [Britain] for [their] external affairs or defence, or of [Britain] and its other territories, [Britain] shall invite the [associated state] either to signify its consent to the enactment of the legislation by the [British] Parliament or by Her Majesty in Council, or; to take steps to secure the enactment of the legislation by the Parliament of the [associated state] or other appropriate authority.[98]

Notwithstanding this, some voices may still want to challenge the notion that these six islands, under their new status, were to remain pawns in Britain's defence strategy and foreign policy. First, they might argue that the British Government intended to delegate enough executive authority for them to apply for full or associate membership of UN specialised agencies or similar international organisations.[99] Second, that these territories would now be able to arrange by themselves visits by representatives of such supranational syndicates, as well as negotiate and conclude trade agreements with independent countries, whether bilateral or multilateral.[100] Along these lines, they might add that the associated states were granted power to sign agreements of purely local concern with any of the remaining British colonies in the area.[101] And, thirdly, they may point out that these islands would also have authority to enter into agreements of a financial, technical, cultural or scientific nature with any member of the Commonwealth and, more importantly, with the US Government.[102]

Yet, as the chief legal counsel to the British foreign secretary scribbled in a note to his colleagues, all these minor responsibilities were just 'tittle tattle'.[103] The British had no intention of endowing these islands with anything more than a cosmetic role in the conduct of their foreign relations. And the evidence sustaining this observation is fairly substantial. While the associated states were allowed to enter into commercial agreements with other parties, this would only apply if and when such arrangements dealt with the treatment of goods. Any other trade agreement dealing with, for example, so-called 'establishment matters', namely those affecting the rights of persons and companies of the contracting party, as well as to civil aviation would still be negotiated by the British Government. In addition, their authority to invite foreign dignitaries was also severely curtailed. Only the British Government could authorize the permanent or even temporary representation of other countries in an associated state, as well as the latter's missions abroad.[104] But, more importantly, if London believed that a conflict might arise between the actions of an associated state in this field and its own international commitments, responsibilities or policies, in all such cases, the said territory was to defer to Britain's judgement.[105]

That was where the resemblance between the associated states and the old dominions ended. The existence of an insurmountable gulf separating these politico-constitutional entities, in terms of their overall legal personality, was all too apparent. Even prior to the enactment of the Statute of Westminster, the old dominions had been enjoying a far more advanced position, in relation to matters of defence and foreign affairs, than had the associated states.[106] Not only could the dominions negotiate freely with foreign countries, but they could also dispatch their own diplomats without British interference and were fully represented in major international bodies such as the League of Nations. Yet the attribute that best depicted this unhindered degree of sovereignty was their capacity to declare neutrality in the face of war. Even in times of crisis, the old dominions were in no legal obligation to aid the so-called mother country.[107]

Against this background, the new status of these six islands seemed a consensual affair in which Britain retained enormous overriding powers. And while this was certainly encouraging for the Americans, the absence of a truly bilateral relationship was to cause widespread concern at the UN. More specifically, the mechanism for terminating the association would encounter strong disapproval in the Twenty-Four. Whereas the British Government could at any time terminate this relationship by an Order in

Council,[108] the onus placed on the associated states was far heavier. After three readings any bill for termination introduced in the legislature of an associated state needed the support of not less than two-thirds of *all* the elected members of that legislature. And, if approved, before submission to the governor, it had to garner not less than two-thirds of all votes cast in a referendum.[109] The fact that the ability of these territories to terminate the relationship unilaterally — which according to international law represents the sine qua non of free association — was severely constrained would in future allow many to question the non-colonial nature of the new constitutional model. This explains why the British Government, unlike New Zealand with regard to the Cook Islands,[110] sought to prevent the UN from playing any role in this process. There is overwhelming evidence to demonstrate that, as far as London was concerned, UN presence on the ground was seen as wholly undesirable. The possibility of being blackmailed by these territories was one of its chief concerns; since many believed UN observers might impress on the colonial leadership that the new arrangements did not go far enough.[111] The following note confirms London's uneasiness,

> If UN observers were invited they would, on the Cook Island precedent, wish to arrive in the territory well before the election to observe the election campaign as well as the poll. We should not ourselves be able to control the selection of the observers who might very well include persons drawn from the Afro-Asian and Communist countries.
>
> The activities of the UN representatives in the territories and later in New York might be embarrassing … . Even the ministers in the island governments might be suborned in this way, particularly about points in the agreed arrangements which they had already accepted as part of the negotiated agreement but which they themselves [might not be] enthusiastic about.[112]

This brings us back to the colonial leadership. First, what was the mood of the so-called small-island politicians prior to the publication of Britain's proposals? And secondly, in the light of the obvious limitations of the new status, why did they sign up for it?

In the case of Antigua, after their withdrawal from the federal negotiations, Bird and his lieutenants had immediately asked for full internal self-government.[113] Yet, consistent with their interest in the Cook Islands and Western Samoa models, they had also confided in the Colonial Office that an arrangement whereby a large Commonwealth country handled their defence and foreign affairs might be suitable. As the political leadership in St. John's put it, any future relationship with Britain had to recognize Antigua's inalienable right to declare its independence unilaterally.[114] In Basseterre, Southwell informed Colonel Howard that he was about to ask his colleagues in the executive committee to send a despatch to the colonial secretary requesting total internal authority. By August 20, 1965, the Kittitian legislative council followed suit and passed a resolution asking Britain 'for the immediate grant of full internal self-government'.[115] In much the same way, Joshua and the members of his PPP had already approved a motion asking for the conferment on St. Vincent of 'full and complete internal self-government in the near future'.[116] In the meantime, a momentous debate took place in Castries, at which the members of the legislative council unanimously called for St. Lucia's attainment of internal self-government by January 1, 1966.[117] The position of Dominica would be no different. A few months later, while canvassing across the island, Le Blanc and the ruling DLP made the grant of a new constitution an essential element of their electoral platform.[118] Even in Grenada, which had not been directly involved in the latest federal miscarriage, there was a consensus amongst the political class that maintaining the status quo was unacceptable. While both Blaize and Gairy, whose past sins were growing dimmer in the public's memory, saw a looser form of association with Britain as a viable alternative; others, particularly in the GULP, were discussing association with Canada and even citing the Isle of Man model.[119] But by July 1965, the politicians in St. George's agreed that their priority was to achieve 'full internal autonomy'.[120]

With the collapse of the federal negotiations and the independence of Barbados a foregone conclusion, the small island politicians faced some difficult challenges. While bent on securing more advanced constitutions, as that avalanche of motions and resolutions showed, they still had to contend with the uncertainty of not knowing where the future of the regional services and of British aid would lie. Thus, the explanation of why they signed up for Britain's proposal of free association must be seen within this context.

On the one hand, Greenwood's overture did entail conferring upon these islands something very close to full internal independence.[121] On the other, his proposal called for a regional organization to take over from the RCM and administer those common services,[122] without precluding the flow of British aid. This made all the difference. Sir David Rose's report to the Colonial Office that these proposals 'came as a surprise to most Grenadians who had not expected that much'[123] summed up the reaction throughout the area. Many were pleasantly surprised to realize that the new arrangements did not constitute a radical departure from all they were familiar with. The fact that the islands would retain a common currency, university and courts system and, equally important, that the West Indies Act promoted further regional cooperation was considerably reassuring.[124]

All those elements, but in particular the provisions outlining how British aid would now be disbursed, constituted an unequivocal reminder of the evolutionary nature of this process. For instance, development aid would continue to take the form of either grants or loans, since the CD&W Acts also applied to any territory 'for the international relations of which [Britain] is responsible'.[125] Thus, the British Government was to carry out in full the undertakings already given in connection with the 1965 Overseas and Service Act,[126] under which CD&W allocations to each of these territories had been made to cover the succeeding triennium. At the same time, the six associated states would remain eligible to receive technical assistance under the programme of the Ministry of Overseas Development.[127] In terms of budgetary aid, while its mechanics were slightly modified, the grant-in-aid system was not eliminated either. Attempting to bolster the non-colonial nature of the new relationship, London devolved considerable control over budgetary matters. The associated states would no longer need clearance from the colonial secretary for raising loans, transferring funds between the recurrent and capital budgets or increasing expenditure from revenue on the capital budget. Yet, in all other respects, the system remained relatively unaltered. Any grant-in-aided associated state would still be expected to submit the audited annual accounts of revenue and expenditure to London for certification. And although this would no longer involve approval from London, the British Government would still retain the prerogative of commenting or advising on the associated state's budgetary policy.

Notwithstanding that, in yet another illustration of this blend of old and new practices, so emblematic of this whole process, two fresh elements were incorporated into this equation. On the one hand, a British

Development Division would now be set up to advise these territories, along with all other dependencies in the archipelago, on all aspects of their development as well as to ensure the effective deployment of assistance to them. On the other, following the publication of the much-awaited Tripartite Economic Survey, early in 1966, the Johnson Administration finally made clear its intentions in respect of aid to these six islands. As Lincoln Gordon, assistant secretary of state for Inter-American affairs and coordinator of the Alliance for Progress, soon confided in the colonial leadership, the US Government would now:

> Assign a full-time officer to its about-to-be-established Embassy in Bridgetown to be available to work on development problems in the entire area;
>
> Provide requested technical assistance for, and be associated with, a commission for regional development in these six islands;
>
> Consider the possibility of providing financial support for a Caribbean Development Bank when established;
>
> Encourage efforts under way for the formation of a private Caribbean investment company;
>
> Negotiate investment guarantee agreements with the islands;
>
> Expand the assistance of the Peace Corps in the field of education;
>
> Assist US firms conducting investment surveys of the area; and
>
> Encourage positive interest in the area by international financial and technical assistance agencies, particularly the World Bank family and the UN Development Programme.[128]

The most salient aspect of Washington's commitment was that, similar to London's, in no way did it make a fundamental departure from previous aid programmes. However, if seen in a more holistic sense, this was but a symptom of a wider phenomenon. The establishment of the new constitutional relationship between Britain and these six territories, while unprecedented, left the colonial superstructure mostly untouched. This was no revolution. Here lies the significance of free association *modo britannico* within the wider Commonwealth historical narrative. It stood as a challenge to conventional definitions of decolonization. The experience of these six islands suggests rather vividly that decolonization, more often than not, tends to be multi-layered and asymmetrical. As colonizer and colonized realized, there was no orthodox or standard pattern of decolonization. While Britain's ultimate aspiration was to disengage totally from the area, the geo-political and economic peculiarities of the colonial landscape made it impossible for it to reproduce the timetables used in other places. Conversely, these six territories, acknowledging their limitations, showed no interest in brusque turnarounds. This might explain why they chose not to petition for immediate independence. They were in it for the long haul. Thus, for many in Antigua, St. Kitts–Nevis–Anguilla, Dominica, St. Lucia, St. Vincent and Grenada, achieving free association seemed like having passed yet another hurdle. It was mostly welcomed as another step along the way of decolonization. The following recollection from Antigua's 'State Day',[129] echoes with unparalleled accuracy this anti-climactic feeling:

> Apart from the display of State symbols … there was no evidence of the grand celebrations promised by [the] government — no street jump-up, no music; no assemblage of school children in their respective schools where patriotic addresses could be delivered… . The children of the nation were told nothing; all they knew was that their schools were closed on that day.[130]

13

Barbados Going it Alone[1]

> The road to destiny is the road to independence.
>
> *Errol Barrow, 1966*

Barbados's decision not to join its neighbours in a federation of Eastern Caribbean territories, late in April 1965, opened up a period of intense political activity in the island. By August 1965 Premier Errol Barrow finally published a white paper asking for the island's immediate independence from Britain. The impassioned debate that soon ensued in Bridgetown and elsewhere across Barbados must be evaluated within a wider context. If seen exclusively in the light of Britain's most recent disengagement commitments, Barrow's decision of going it alone should not have triggered such a high level of public scrutiny. After all, as British Prime Minister Harold Wilson had just included in the Queen's forthcoming speech from the throne,[2] the British Government had already pledged to introduce, early in the following session of parliament, legislation providing for the independence of British Guiana, Bechuanaland, Basutoland and Mauritius.[3] Against such an influx of future Commonwealth mini-states, the advisability of enabling Barbados to achieve independence on its own could hardly have looked surprising. Thus, several questions immediately arise. First, why did the submission of the white paper lead to such a level of public effervescence? Second, what were the seminal elements surrounding the local debate on whether or not to go it alone? Third, if the British Government preserved its overriding authority over Antigua–Barbuda, St. Kitts–Nevis–Anguilla, Montserrat, Dominica, St. Lucia, St. Vincent and Grenada, why did it treat Barbados differently? And, fourth, why did the Johnson Administration in Washington go along with this policy?

The answer to these questions resides, in part, in the set of catalysts propelling Barrow and most of the insular cabinet to press for full sovereignty. While the collapse of the federal negotiations with the neighbouring islands played an obvious role in paving the way for the premier's request, the demand for Barbados's independence also responded to wider imperatives, namely the island's constitutional trajectory and the state of its economy by the turn of 1966. These two variables, which were to resurface constantly throughout the local debate on independence, set Barbados apart from its neighbours and, to some extent, explain why Britain itself saw Barbados in a different light.

Of all British dependencies in the Eastern Caribbean archipelago, Barbados had enjoyed the longest history of constitutional development. Unlike places such as Jamaica and Trinidad and Tobago, originally claimed by the Spanish Kingdom, and others such as Dominica, St. Lucia, St. Vincent and Grenada, initially settled by the French, Barbados had always been British. And, differently from most of these other islands, Barbados was one of the few colonies that fell into European hands without bloodshed and the decimation of the indigenous population.[4] Moreover, the island's House of Assembly, the third oldest legislative body in the Western Hemisphere, had been in continuous session since 1639.[5] Most students of Barbados's colonial history have identified the early presence of British settlers, with their robust commitment to parliamentary democracy, as a defining influence on the island's subsequent constitutional experience. Without a doubt, episodes such as the early 1651 uprising against Cromwell's authority and the so-called Confederation Riots of 1876 left a profound imprint.[6] At a time when most British dependencies in the area were but crown colonies, these events had considerably solidified the hold which representative governance had on the Bajan scenario.[7]

Most casual observers have failed to draw a connection between those distant events and Barrow's determination to go it alone. Yet, at a deeper level, the future prime minister viewed independence as the only route that could facilitate the consolidation of what he saw as the island's glorious patrimony. During the following months he would constantly return to this point, alluding that 'the road to destiny is the road to independence'.[8] This is perhaps one of the most fascinating aspects of the independence debate in Barbados. While the island's 300 years of parliamentary trajectory had, for all practical purposes, perpetuated the power and vested interests of the white plantocracy, a significant segment of the black political leadership, far from disassociating itself from the island's constitutional past, welcomed it. The members of Barbados's political elite, unlike their colleagues in most neighbouring islands, saw themselves as heirs of Captain John Powell and that first wave of British settlers. As members of what some scholars in Barbados have called 'old black middle classes',[9] they seemed more in tune with the events of the seventeenth century than with the emancipation of slavery, almost two centuries later. For the most part propertied, highly educated and freed before 1834, this class had produced prominent figures, such as Samuel Prescod and Conrad Reeves, who during most of the nineteenth century had been able to wield considerable influence along the white corridors of local parliamentary power.[10] Barrow, the scion of a black planter family, represented the epitome of that class.[11] While the tense relationship between the white plantocracy and the black middle classes is still in need of serious scholarly attention, there can be no doubt that Barrow's resolve to press for independence was not divorced from what he had been socialized to perceive as the island's legitimate heritage. In the light of Barbados's apparent impeccable constitutional credentials, which included the attainment of full internal self-government in May 1961, nothing less than immediate independence could please the premier and most members of his cabinet.

In addition, the state of the local economy fuelled their aims even further. By 1965 the financial picture looked very healthy indeed. For instance, the gross domestic product had increased from US$63.9 million in 1961 and $74.6 million in 1963 to almost $90 million by the time independence was finally proclaimed. Although sugar was still the mainstay of the island's economy, accounting for about two-thirds of its exports and contributing close to 80 per cent of foreign exchange earnings, the government's efforts to diversify the economy were beginning to yield handsome dividends. Since 1963, mostly through local statutory instruments, such as the Industrial Development Act and the Export Industries Act, the insular authorities had been actively attracting foreign investment. By January 1966 more than 40 new factories, employing some 2000 workers had been established. These manufacturing units, primarily producing for the local and regional markets, as well as processing imported

211

components for re-export, gave rise to an important light industrial sector. But by far the most important industry, after sugar, was tourism. The period spanning from 1960 to 1965 saw a substantial transformation in the way this industry affected the local economy. While in 1960 Barbados had close to 1,808 beds available for tourists and welcomed 35,535 visitors, the figures for 1965 rose to 3,250 and 64,418, respectively.[12] By 1967, for instance, the number of tourists visiting the island would increase to 91,000, of whom 29,000 were to come from the US alone, and their expenditure once in Barbados would reach $17 million.[13] This boom in the tourist industry not only served as a major foreign exchange earner but also had a positive collateral effect in stimulating the construction and service industries.

The expansion of trade as well as the dramatic increase in the government's revenue constituted eloquent reminders of the strong performance of the local economy. The level of public revenue increased from $13.1 million in 1960–61 to $19.25 million in 1964–65 and $20.05 million in 1965–66. More specifically, the government's earnings from income tax rose from $4.65 million in 1961–62 to $6 million in 1965–66.[14] Import duties and internal consumption taxes, moreover, went from $5.75 million in 1961–62 to $9.25 million in 1965–66, an increase of more than 60 per cent.[15] In terms of trade, imports had also escalated from close to $41.5 million in 1960 to $58.15 in 1965.[16] In 1966 alone Barbados's imports rose to $78 million, while its exports were valued at $41 million.[17] This apparent negative balance of trade was more than offset by a surplus in the so-called invisible export sector, namely tourist expenditures, emigrant remittances and foreign investment.

This rate of economic growth also had an important social impact. For instance, by 1966 the GDP per capita of $327, albeit not spectacular if compared to the Dutch and French Antilles, was higher than in most Latin American countries. More importantly, the introduction of a social security scheme,[18] the decision to provide free secondary education and the establishment of a campus of the University of the West Indies at Cave Hill responded, in part, to the expansion of the local economy. In the light of these social measures the local government could safely boast of having a highly sophisticated labour force, since the literacy rate in Barbados was 98 per cent, one of the highest in the hemisphere. Although the island did face some trying challenges, such as a 14 per cent unemployment rate, dependence on a high-cost subsidized single crop for foreign exchange and a high population density, it was economically viable. The prospects for further development were favourable. Barbados had a well established infrastructure of good roads, an international airport, a deep-water harbour, reliable electricity, gas and water supplies, good postal, telephone and telegraph services and total immunity from Britain's grants-in-aid system. There could hardly be any doubt of its capacity to sustain independence. It was no coincidence that whenever Barbados floated its bonds in London, these were sold, more often than not, almost instantaneously.[19] All available evidence tends to suggest that the island, even before constitutional independence, had earned the confidence of the international capital markets. Both the island's sound economy and its unparalleled tradition of parliamentary government bring us back to the initial question: why was there no internal political consensus on the question of going it alone?

The split between the ruling Democratic Labour Party (DLP) and the opposition parties, namely, the Barbados Labour Party (BLP) and the Barbados National Party (BNP), regarding that momentous decision, had to do with both style and substance. In principle, the concept of independence enjoyed considerable support across the island's political spectrum. However, the controversy arose because a significant portion of the local political elite was still clinging on to the federal ideal. As this group saw it, the attainment of independence could not be unilateral or in isolation but had to come through a federation of the Eastern Caribbean territories. Sir Grantley Adams[20] and most of his BLP followers, for instance, were still in communion with the ideas of the founding fathers of the federal ideal during the interwar period: Arthur Cipriani and T. Albert Marryshow.[21] The leaders of the BLP and BNP still remained openly committed to the federal principle. Their allegiance to that ideal, moreover, also responded to other more pragmatic considerations. The leadership of these two parties, especially the BNP directorate, still held the view that only a well designed regional federation could guarantee the island's future economic stability. As Frederick Goddard, a member of the BNP who happened to be the only white Barbadian sitting in the House of Assembly, put it,

In our case we have only 240,000 consumers in Barbados but in the Eastern Caribbean we can boast of 600,000. We need the larger market. It is better for such purposes and that is why, although we want independence, we see that the better form would be in a Federation with the Eastern Caribbean.[22]

The available evidence suggests that the planter-merchant interest, which for the most part had lent its financial support to the so-called progressive conservative movement, or BNP, did not instantly warm up to the idea of independence for Barbados on its own. There was a strong feeling in those quarters that the government should avoid going it alone, at least in the immediate future, in order to safeguard the industrial development of the island. The following observation from the local chamber of commerce illustrates the lukewarm reception Premier Barrow's initiative met:

From remarks made to the press it appears that the political leaders are now committed on the path to independence ... the present mood could perhaps be said to be one of resignation rather than exultation: Barbados is confronted with Hobson's choice. In the case of independence this certainly seems to be the case. There are external pressures at work to see these islands independent. Local politicians, partly because of a natural sense of national pride, partly because of the bait of greater economic aid when independence is achieved, are now determined to bring it about.[23]

Barrow, however, was not oblivious to these considerations. Although during the 1961 electoral campaign he had denounced the former BLP government for allegedly succumbing to the planter-merchant lobby, while in office he had done nothing to rock the boat. Similar to Sir Grantley Adams and H.G.H. Cummins, who succeeded Adams as premier in 1958, he had pursued a policy of accommodating those powerful interests within the island's incipient mixed economy. Barrow and his colleagues in the local cabinet, like the members of the chamber of commerce, also saw the advantages of a wider market. Therefore their decision, early in July 1965, to join in a free trade area with British Guiana and Antigua–Barbuda was hardly surprising.[24]

While to some the timing of the announcement suggested political expediency,[25] merely a month before the publication of the white paper, Barbados's entry into the free trade area showed that the DLP government and the planter-merchant lobby did share some common ground. And, although in the coming months several voices within the BNP would continue to attack unilateral independence using the same economic argument, the government had literally cut the ground from under their feet. The premier had sent the clearest signal yet that the absence of regional political union did not mean, as far as Barbados was concerned, lack of access to the Eastern Caribbean market. While his government opposed the former, it would certainly embrace the latter.

The sheer number of challenges confronting Barrow increased considerably with the release of the white paper.[26] Now the more ideologically driven supporters of the federal principle came out ready for combat. The intense debate that ensued between federationists and the separatists must be divided into two phases, the first between August and December 1965, the second from January to July 1966. By the time Colonial Secretary Anthony Greenwood made the announcement, in December 1965, that the British Government was putting the federal project in cold storage, effectively eliminating the possibility of decolonizing on the basis of a regional federation, going it alone became a foregone conclusion.[27] From then on, until the adjournment of the Independence Conference in London, the debate would revolve almost exclusively around the need for fresh elections before independence and the type of constitution to be established.

The first of these two stages, namely, the one preceding the colonial secretary's announcement, must be looked at in some detail. This is the period that best illustrates the fragility of the local party structures. As Barrow soon discovered, the political scene in Barbados was considerably fluid; there were hardly any substantive differences between, for instance, the DLP and the BLP. This meant that the major political parties in the island, albeit to varying degrees, had among their members both federationists and separatists. And, not surprisingly, the ruling party was no exception. Close to a fortnight after the release of the white paper it was becoming obvious — as Sir John Stow, the island's colonial governor, soon confided in the new American consul general George Dolgin[28] — that the cabinet was not fully behind the premier.[29]

The resignations from the government of Deputy Premier Wynter Crawford,[30] and Senator Erskine Ward, minister without portfolio, constituted the most eloquent illustrations of that ideological fluidity. On the one hand, Crawford, who simultaneously served as minister of trade, industry, labour and development, had always been a staunch federationist.[31] This is why, as soon as Barrow's official position became known, he made no attempt to advocate going it alone and instead urged further consultations with the chief ministers of the neighbouring islands. Ward, on the other hand, had adopted a similar stand. As former speaker of the legislature of the late West Indies Federation, he felt an even greater ideological attachment to the federal ideal than Crawford himself did. With the deputy prime minister openly speaking and writing against the government's policy, and Ward touring the neighbouring islands in a desperate attempt to defrost the federal project, their position within the cabinet soon became untenable. Although Edwy Talma, minister of agriculture and fisheries, had adopted a somewhat ambivalent stand towards the independence question, it was clear that the remaining ministers,[32] including the premier, continued unremittingly committed to going it alone. As far as Crawford and Ward were concerned, it was a choice between being dismissed and resigning. In the end, by picking the latter they merely pre-empted the former. While some local observers have contended that, to a large extent, personal ambition and political manoeuvrings triggered these resignations,[33] the available evidence disproves that hypothesis. Ideological allegiance, in this particular case, superseded party discipline. It is essential to note, moreover, that the departures of the deputy premier and the minister without portfolio served as ammunition for the federationist camp. Ward's letter of resignation, for instance, was not only an indictment of Barrow's constitutional policy but, albeit subtly, of his leadership style as well.

> You will remember that the discussion in the Cabinet on the White Paper lasted not more than five minutes ... I would point out that the Cabinet was never asked to agree to the contents of the White Paper. On this vital issue I cannot give my support to any proposal for independence alone.
>
> I consider that the Government is pledged to resume the negotiations interrupted at the Tenth Meeting of the Regional Council of Ministers ... it would be dishonourable and a breach of faith to take an action so inimical to West Indian unity. I have no desire to break the party, but in these circumstances I have no alternative but to place my resignation unreservedly at your hands.[34]

In the light of Ward's comments the political opposition began to denounce Barrow's alleged autocracy. There was a strong feeling within the federationist camp that the premier's authoritarianism had wrecked the federal negotiations with the neighbouring islands.[35]

The archival record shows that by this stage the BLP and the BNP, including the leaders of other pro-federal movements such as the so-called 'Under Forties', a grassroots movement founded with the sole purpose of defending the federal ideal, were already campaigning upon the basis that the question of the island's constitutional future would be put to the public either in an election or a referendum.[36] This explains why the island's political environment, especially during the critical months of September and October 1965, was so tense. As Sir John Stow soon reported to the Colonial Office,

> All the parties … have been holding well-attended meetings, which so far have been reasonably orderly. However, the speeches have, since the resignations, gone down to a very low level and the mudslinging as violent as in any election campaign, is now prevalent on both sides. There may be some broken heads at these meetings in the atmosphere of tension in which they take place. Before the resignations, the issues were clear-cut, independence alone or through a federation. Both opposition parties appear, however, in the light of Barrow's abuse at recent meetings, to have come to the conclusion that he must be removed from the scene, that elections must be held before independence [may be] granted to Barbados.[37]

All this intensity was diffused by the announcement the colonial secretary made in December 1965; outlining an offer of full self-government within the framework of an association with Britain to the neighbouring islands. In the sombre words of the island's federal patriarch, Sir Grantley Adams, those who opposed going it alone were now left shocked and utterly dismayed. With federation no longer in the equation and the maintenance of the status quo deemed unsuitable for Barbados,[38] their crusade had reached a dead end. The wind had been taken out of the federationists' sails. Conversely, Barrow and his DLP gained momentum. In a matter of days the leader in the House of Assembly, Cameron Tudor, also minister of education, requested that the speaker, Theodore Brancker, summon the members for a special session to debate the white paper. After four months of ardent public discussion, the House of Assembly finally voted on the following resolution,

Whereas the pre-election Manifesto of this Government, issued in November 1961, stated *inter alia*: the road to destiny is the road to independence. Towards this goal the country must press on.... As the island has never been a grant-in-aided territory there is no reason why, within or without a Federation, Barbados should not attain the full stature of independence now, within the British Commonwealth;

…

And Whereas paragraph 124 of the White Paper states: The House of Assembly will be asked to agree to a resolution requesting the Secretary of State to fix an early date for a Conference on Independence; and if agreed to, the Senate will be invited to concur therein;

Be It Therefore Resolved that this House requests Her Majesty's Principal Secretary of State for the Colonies to convene, at the earliest opportunity, a Conference to arrange the constitutional, financial, defence and other details incidental to, and arising from, the assumption, by the People of Barbados, of Sovereign Nationhood within the Commonwealth in 1966.[39]

The position of the British Government regarding these latest developments cannot go unheeded. The archival record reveals that, for the British Cabinet, maintaining the island as a self-governing colony was seen as highly problematic, particularly from a foreign policy perspective. Moreover, forging a relationship along the lines of what had been recently agreed for the neighbouring territories made little sense for Barbados since it already enjoyed complete internal autonomy.[40] There is enough evidence suggesting that by this stage the British Government, albeit privately, preferred independence; as Sir Burke Trend, then secretary to the Cabinet, conveyed to Prime Minister Harold Wilson, of all the available options it was the 'more clear-cut and more easily defensible internationally'.[41] Yet London's official position remained unchanged. It decided not to concern itself with the matter of Barbados's future until after the local House of Assembly had voted favourably on a resolution asking the Colonial Office to fix a date for an independence conference in London. Once that occurred, as Sir John Stow confessed to the US consul general in Bridgetown, Britain 'could not and would not resist a call for constitutional talks'.[42] With the passing of the independence resolution and the scheduling of the debate, the road to Lancaster House would become wide open.

While there is no need to regurgitate every single word uttered at the debate,[43] it is essential to pay special attention to the underlying ideological subtext. The themes of identity and nationhood were at the heart of it. There was a solid understanding that sociologically and culturally the people of Barbados, although part of the West Indian conglomerate, constituted a nation. As the premier put it,

> You cannot be a West Indian unless you are a Barbadian first, and a Barbadian cannot be a West Indian otherwise because you cannot be a West Indian in a vacuum.[44]

The archival record demonstrates, moreover, that most members of the House of Assembly acknowledged the distinctiveness of Barbados, *vis-à-vis* its neighbours, both historically and culturally. Barrow's lengthy intervention was very revealing; for him the island's uninterrupted constitutional experience was an unequivocal expression of nationhood.

> In the year 1651 the Lords in Council and the General Assembly of this island in protest against the Navigation Laws, the same type of Navigation Laws the thirteen American colonies rebelled against 125 years later, they were a bit slower than the people of Barbados, issued their famous Declaration of Independence.... The significant thing about this is that I have not been able to discover anywhere in the records of this House that the unilateral declaration of independence which was made in 1651 has ever been repealed by this House or any other person.... Shortly [afterwards], General George Ayscue bombarded the township of Oistin and after two days of fighting a long boat was launched with a white flag and the Treaty was signed between the people of Barbados and the United Kingdom Government.... Our relationship with Great Britain, therefore, has never been one of the status, from the very early days, which existed in places more properly described as Crown Colonies and which achieved internal self-government only in the 1950s — territories like Trinidad and Tobago, the Lesser Antilles, Mauritius and all other island territories over which Britain held sway. That is what has probably distinguished Barbados from any other West Indian island. Its approach has always been a contractual approach and not an approach of status. We continued to make laws.... We have a long history of constitutional government that antedates the constitutional history of the United States, which antedates the constitutional history of any of the West Indian territories, which antedates the constitutional history of the South American countries.[45]

Philip Greaves, who had just replaced Ward in the Senate, echoed more eloquently than most the premier's line of reasoning:

> The questions [that] arise are, why do we want Independence? Why do we want freedom? What were our founding fathers striving for? What were the architects of our representative institutions striving for? What are we striving for? Not to dominate other countries, not to reduce the people of Barbados to a state of tyrannical subjugation. We are merely asking to be accorded our freedom. The next question is — are we ready for this freedom? If the criterion is character then I can do no better than to quote the words of Dr Bruce Hamilton in his book "Barbados and the Confederation Question" ... he wrote: In trying to assess the characteristics of the people it must be realized that they do constitute a nation. In the first place they feel themselves to be one.[46]

But as Frank Walcott, on behalf of the mighty Barbados Workers' Union (BWU), forcefully argued, going it alone was also a matter of nation building and of consolidating a collective sociocultural identity.

> Our first loyalty is to Barbados and not to St Lucia, Grenada or Dominica.... Federation cannot be the first loyalty to the Barbadian ... I am not projecting independence as a panacea for all our ills, that we need not work anymore, that the day after independence the Sun will not rise anymore in the East, but will come up in the West and bring gold with it and we will not have to work. I know and I believe that the mere fact that we are going to run our country independently means that we have to work harder, and we have to introduce new dimensions in our thinking to grapple with the problems that independence brings.[47]

After three long days of continued debate the white paper was finally adopted both by the House of Assembly and the insular Senate.[48] This finally brings us to the Barbados Independence Conference in London, by far the most fascinating episode of this drama.[49] It is precisely here that the Barbadian experience begins to test the very meaning of decolonization, raising a corpus of relevant questions that go to the essence of that concept. First, did Barrow's Government have a legitimate popular mandate for leading Barbados to independence? If, as the premier was fond of arguing, only the people of Barbados could decide what was in their best interest, would they be allowed to express their collective will? In other words, would the people of Barbados be granted the opportunity to exercise their indivisible right to self-determination? And, second, was independence intended to constitute a real departure from the existing order? Would there be a decisive breakaway from the colonial establishment, not only constitutionally but also socially, economically and geopolitically?

Once the Barbados Independence Conference got under way, the British Government was confronted with a very delicate situation. It had to decide whether to insist on fresh elections before Barbados could move on to independence. The archival record reveals that the timing of independence in relation to the next local elections soon became, in the words of Sir Hilton Poynton, then permanent under-secretary of state for the colonies, the 'real bone of controversy'.[50] On the one hand, Barrow was contending that his party had secured a mandate for independence at the last elections because the status question had already been addressed in the DLP's 1961 manifesto.[51] The fact that the DLP had more seats in the House of Assembly than the BLP and BNP combined meant, according to the premier, that the people of Barbados were wholeheartedly behind his government's policy. On the other hand, he emphasized that only his government could decide when to hold the elections and that such a decision could only be made pursuant to local legislation. As he saw it the British Government should fix the date of independence irrespective of the electoral question. To do otherwise would be 'playing straight into the hands of the opposition'.[52] The opposition contended rather unrelentingly that the DLP's parliamentary majority was entirely artificial; that it was an outgrowth of the archaic system of two member constituencies that had been abolished a year earlier.[53] The BLP and BNP delegates were convinced that fresh elections, held on the basis of the new single member constituencies, would eliminate the DLP's majority altogether.[54]

While the opposition delegates could not deny that the DLP's 1961 manifesto had touched upon the issue of independence, they had not forgotten Barrow's pledge to go to the country in three years; having broken that pledge, they firmly believed his moral mandate had expired in November 1964.[55] Their overall position was that the official proclamation of independence could not precede the local elections. The BLP and BNP delegates felt that, since the constitutional instrument to be drafted at the conference would be binding on all future governments; it should be put directly to the colonial electorate. Besides, only a government with a clear popular mandate could settle, on behalf of the people of Barbados, all outstanding constitutional disagreements such as, for instance, the composition of the Senate or of the insular electoral commission. This is why the opposition held the view that Barbados should not proceed to independence before the first meeting of a newly elected House of Assembly. But what was the position of the British Government? Sir Harold St. John, one of only two BLP delegates at the Independence Conference, has suggested that,

> The general consensus was that an election should take place first, as happened in Mauritius. But the British Government, during the course of the Conference, changed its position. And although in principle the British were in favour of an election, they refused to state it publicly.[56]

Sir Harold's recollection brings to the fore the most crucial question, namely, did the British believe, as he claims, that the opposition's case for new elections rested on legitimate grounds? Interestingly, the archival record demonstrates that the British Government did share the view of the BLP and BNP delegates. Only three days before inaugurating the conference, Frederick Lee, Britain's last colonial secretary, had advised Prime Minister Wilson to 'insist upon fresh elections before Barbados moves to independence'.[57] More importantly, Lee adhered to the opposition's case, arguing that,

> If new elections are to provide a more accurate reflection of the popular will, they ought to be held on the basis of the revised constituencies. Unless therefore all parties agree that Barbados should proceed to independence without further reference to the electorate, I propose to make it a condition of independence that a resolution requesting us to grant it should be passed by the new Legislature, after a general election has been held. Further, I should have to insist that the elections were held after the report of our Conference had been published so that the electors knew what they were voting about, and on the basis of the new constituencies.[58]

If the colonial secretary felt so strongly about pressing for new elections 'on the basis of the revised constituencies', why then did he fix the date of Barbados's independence for November 30, 1966? With the statutory life of the DLP government extending until December 19, 1966, it would now be possible for the ruling party to lead the island to independence without any popular mandate to do so. This is why most BLP and BNP delegates had been expecting the British Government to superimpose the same solution it had recently applied, for instance, in Mauritius. There independence would come after a general election, under a new method for allocating seats in the local legislature, and only if the newly elected government passed a resolution in favour of it.[59] For the Barbadian opposition this was the most obvious road because the British Government, particularly during the post-war era, had never moved a country to independence when its legislative body was so near the end of its natural term.[60] The available evidence shows that the British Government was not oblivious to the complications that might arise from this scenario. The record reveals, moreover, that a few hours before announcing the date of independence, Colonial Secretary Lee, along with Sir John Stow, met Prime Minister Wilson to discuss at length the Barbadian question.[61] And, by the end of their conversation, the colonial secretary had modified his initial stand. This turnaround deserves particular attention. What accounted for it?

The colonial secretary's decision to grant independence without regard to the date of elections was not taken unilaterally or in isolation. It was the collective policy of the British Cabinet. While minor arguments such as the desirability of maintaining good relations with the island's ruling party had been broached during the course of the meeting with Wilson, what stood behind this new position went beyond such a narrow context. The British, as US Consul George Dolgin put it, 'wanted out'. It was as simple as that. Waiting for the election of a new government, under the revised constituencies, meant that the conference would be put on hold at least until the spring of 1967. As far as the British were concerned there was no need to prolong these discussions any further. The fact that Barbados had always been politically stable and financially self-sufficient and, even more importantly, that the US had already accepted its independence as a foregone conclusion, had solidified their determination to withdraw at once. This explains why they were so willing and anxious to facilitate Barrow's request for independence in 1966. It was no coincidence, as shown below, that on all major areas of constitutional disagreement between Barrow and the opposition parties, the British delegation sided with Barrow. While engaging, this explanation is still incomplete. It fails to address a glaring inconsistency: if the US had all along opposed further fragmentation in the area, why did it support Britain's withdrawal from Barbados?

Table 13.1
Areas of Disagreement between the DLP Government and the BLP Opposition, 1966

Point of Contention	BLP's Position	DLP's Position	British Position
The Senate	The [Senate] should be so composed that the government would be unable to secure amendment of an entrenched provision of the Constitution without the support of at least part of the Opposition.	This was unacceptable this proposal [meant] that Opposition Senators might exert an influence on important issues out of proportion to the representation of the Opposition in the Assembly.	Sided with DLP
The House of Assembly	The provisions for qualification and disqualification for membership the Assembly [as well as for electors] should be included in the Constitution and entrenched.	These were matters which by long tradition had been regulated by the laws of the Barbados Legislature […] and this position should be retained.	Sided with DLP
Election Commission	The Constitution should provide for an independent and impartial commission charged with the duty of supervising the registration and the conduct of elections.	The existing method of conducting elections in Barbados was satisfactory and, in the circumstances, there was no need to include in the Constitution provision for an elections commission.	Sided with DLP
Constituencies	The Constitution should provide that each constituency should return one member [and] establish a permanent boundaries commission to keep the constituency boundaries under review.	Constituency arrangements were essentially a matter for the House of Assembly and should therefore not be dealt with in the Constitution.	Sided with DLP

Source: *Report of the Barbados Constitutional Conference 1966*, Cmnd. 3058 (London: HMSO), 4–6.

The archival record shows that the transatlantic allies, although for different reasons, saw eye to eye on the issue of Barbados's future status. For the British, granting independence to Barbados ran parallel to a wider project of colonial disengagement. It was no secret, as the Americans themselves acknowledged, that Britain was bent on liquidating the last remnants of the old Empire.[62] Under pressure from the UN to move along at an even faster pace, it had already withdrawn from other colonies, such as Zambia and The Gambia, and was about to do so from others like British Guiana, Basutoland, Bechuanaland and Mauritius. In the light of this progression the idea of leaving Barbados at this particular time could hardly have seemed shocking. For the Americans, however, the scene was far more complex. The devolution of political authority, in any of the Caribbean islands, was usually met with scepticism in Washington. Their strategic location, so close to Cuba and the Dominican Republic, as well as to British Guiana and other sensitive areas of northern Latin America, placed them squarely within the US's national security radar screen.

The available evidence reveals that by 1965–66 the US's policy towards the Eastern Caribbean archipelago rested on three fundamental principles: first, ensuring that the islands remained in friendly hands; second, maintaining its military installations in the area; and third, retaining access to additional base rights and missile tracking stations.[63] By the time Barbados decided to go it alone, the US Navy, which ran a naval base on the island, was expanding its operations there. At the turn of 1965 Barbados was also the site of a joint US—Canadian Government High Altitude Research Program (HARP) and, more importantly, the NASA was examining the area with the possibility of constructing another missile tracking station.[64] The level of US activity in the island suggests that at this particular stage of the Cold War the Americans were in a state of high alert. Perhaps no other statement expressed the US's acute concern as clearly as President Johnson's televised declaration on May 2, 1965: 'the American nations cannot, must not and will not permit the establishment of another Communist government in the Western Hemisphere'.[65]

Despite this degree of anxiety, the US's aversion to regional fragmentation proved not to be absolute. A few seminal elements led the US to adopt a more functional, less dogmatic, approach to the question of Barbados's independence. The archival record shows that, following the

1965 transfer of responsibility within the US State Department for Britain's Caribbean dependencies, from the Office of British Commonwealth and Northern European Affairs (BNA) to the Bureau of Inter-American Affairs (ARA), the US's policies took a slightly different turn.[66] Those now in charge of US policy towards the British islands were particularly interested in strengthening the Inter-American system. The Anglophone Caribbean was now seen, not as an isolated unit, but as a cardinal component of a wide hemispheric alliance. And in Barrow the Inter-American Bureau found a useful ally. The available evidence reveals that the Johnson Administration considered the future Bajan prime minister as being pro-US.[67] As far as US security interests were concerned, the position in Washington was that 'the US had nothing to fear as long as he remained in power'.[68] Barrow's pledge to apply, once independence was granted, for membership of the OAS and to fully cooperate in the US-led Caribbean Development Bank, Regional Development Agency and the Alliance for Progress, was warmly received in Washington. Thus, supporting Barbados's independence soon became part and parcel of the US's overall Inter-American strategy. Many in the Johnson Administration believed that Barbados's entry, as a sovereign state, into the US's camp would go a long way in dragging in Jamaica, Trinidad and Tobago, and British Guiana, all of which had yet to join the OAS and other American-led regional organizations. The fundamental idea behind the US's position was that an independent Barbados, firmly grounded in the American orbit, would encourage its neighbours to follow suit.

The other fundamental element swaying the US position was that Britain's withdrawal from Barbados did not amount to its complete disengagement from the region. Sovereignty was not going to spread to the smaller islands, namely Antigua–Barbuda, St. Kitts–Nevis–Anguilla, Montserrat, Dominica, St. Lucia, St. Vincent and Grenada. The fact that the British Government and the colonial leadership of these islands had already agreed on non-independent associated status meant that, Barbados's independence aside, the possibility of immediate further fragmentation in the archipelago was firmly kept under wraps.

There can be little doubt that the coalescence of these elements, along with the fact that the proposed independence constitution left the colonial superstructure virtually unchanged, formed the basis of the US's approach to the Barbadian question. If taken together, they seem to show that the US Government stood to gain more from Britain's formal withdrawal from Barbados than from the indefinite prolongation of the status quo. Garnering the goodwill of an independent and, more importantly, friendly Barbados ran parallel to the US's most basic security interests.

The timetables and wider expectations of the transatlantic allies took precedence over the right of the people of Barbados to fully determine their future. And, although Barrow would call for elections three weeks before the date of independence, his mandate would remain unclear since the poll would be held on the basis of the old apportionment system.

In the case of Barbados, independence did not constitute a clear breakaway from the existing order. Not only did the colonial apparatus remain for the most part in place, but also the framers of the independence project had never intended to spearhead a radical departure from the colonial past. The retention of Sir John Stow as governor even after independence, the maintenance of the monarchical system and of the appeal as of right to the Judicial Committee of the Queen's Privy Council,[69] among other elements, conveyed in no uncertain terms a robust desire to maintain close ties with the former colonial master. Here the devolution of constitutional authority, as in the neighbouring territories, signalled the beginning of yet another journey. The legal, cultural and even spiritual dimensions of decolonization were yet to unfold. But for the thousands of Barbadians gathered at the Garrison on November 29, 1966, a few minutes before midnight, a new era was unfolding before their own eyes. After flying for 341 years over the island, the Union Jack was not there any more. It had finally given way to the newly born Barbadian trident, now braving the warm tropical breeze.

Part Four: Conclusion

The dual outcome in these latitudes, namely, the independence of Barbados and the associated status of the neighbouring islands, stands as a prominent illustration of the arbitrariness and unpredictability of the decolonizing process. The British Government found it impossible to superimpose on the Eastern Caribbean landscape the same solutions and timetables it was applying elsewhere. Even at a time when Britain was bent on liquidating colonialism within the confines of the Commonwealth system, it became virtually impossible to articulate a one-size-fits-all policy. The process leading to the independence of Barbados and to the articulation of a *sui generis* model of political association in the remaining dependencies illustrates that the decolonizing experience, more often than not, reflects the peculiarities of the scenario in question. The absence of fresh elections in Barbados, for instance, could hardly have been exported anywhere else. In this specific case the manner in which independence was negotiated precluded, for all practical purposes, the people of Barbados from exercising their right to self-determination. It amounted, quite clearly, to an intimate dialogue between the metropolis and a fragmented colonial leadership. Yet the particular characteristics of the Barbadian landscape, without forgetting the US's subtle acquiescence, enabled the British Government to behave differently than it did in Mauritius, for example. It was the interaction between these complex and sometimes contending variables that made it very difficult for the British to extrapolate blithely from one case to another and, therefore, impossible to predict any given outcome.

There can be little doubt that the process and the outcome from the Anglo-Barbadian dialogue under scrutiny here revealed both the discontinuities and complexities of a phenomenon that was both profound and far-reaching. Barbados's decolonizing experience during this period prepared the ground for future transformations. The stage had been set for Barbadians to reinvent the island's institutional repertoire.

In the past few years fundamental questions, such as the future of the monarchical system, whether or not to maintain an appeal as of right to the Queen's Privy Council and, moreover, the desirability of repatriating the Barbadian Constitution, have besieged not only the island's political leadership but, more importantly, Bajan civil society at large. By the end of the millennium the findings of the Forde Constitution Review Commission openly indicated that there was a national consensus for Barbados's transformation into a republic. Clearly, more than 40 years later, the decolonizing process in Barbados has yet to reach its completion. The search for a truly postcolonial order still goes on, which is why the legacy of the 1965–66 negotiations endures.

Conclusion:
Towards New Postcolonial Societies?

The experience of the Eastern Caribbean, during the period under scrutiny, constitutes an eloquent case study on the complexity and evolutionary nature of decolonization. Decolonization is more than the vessel transporting a given community from the colonial to the postcolonial station. This in itself is an incomplete definition that cannot possibly grapple with a process that is neither absolute nor static but both relative and dynamic. The absence of formal colonial rule at the politico-constitutional level does not necessarily lead to the eradication of other forms of colonial domination in the economic, socio-cultural, legal, religious and inter-ethnic contexts.[1] This is precisely why constitutional decolonization or the actual transfer of political authority cannot be characterized as the sole decisive rite of passage from the colonial to the postcolonial order. Not surprisingly, the boundary separating these intertwined spheres has become increasingly blurred and inexact. Drawing on the Eastern Caribbean's example, one can conclude that decolonization is not about brusque strokes. On the contrary, gradual transition and evolution are its defining characteristics. While the designing and drafting of new statutory instruments and constitutional orders are seminal components of any decolonizing exercise, they symbolize but the beginning of a protracted and even boundless journey. Nkrumah's old proverb to the effects that once the political kingdom is achieved everything will be 'added unto it'[2] has not stood the test of time.

The achievement of associated statehood by Antigua-Barbuda, St. Kitts-Nevis-Anguilla, Dominica, St. Lucia, St. Vincent and Grenada and even the independence of Barbados did not put an end to the discussions on the advisability of maintaining close political, legal and economic ties to the former colonial master. More importantly, public debate thereafter revolved around attempting to define identity while fully exercising the attributes of nationhood. The coming years, especially after the independence of the associated states between the mid 1970s and the early 1980s,[3] brought along a renewed impetus for replacing the remaining trappings of an enduring colonial superstructure.

The coming of age of an aware Eastern Caribbean citizenry, eager to determine its own fate and conditions of life, willing to preserve its cultural identity and determined to infuse into these communities a strong sense of self-confidence, maintained the decolonizing dialogue alive. The intense debate that soon sprang up in the archipelago on the desirability of repatriating the existing constitutions and seeking republican status, together with the abolition of the jurisdiction of the Judicial Committee of the Queen's Privy Council (which was finally crystallised on April 16, 2005 with the inauguration of the Caribbean Court of Justice), demonstrated how these matters, even after formal devolution, struck an overwhelmingly emotional chord. The search for the second instalment of decolonization began in earnest.

Yet the tragic demise of the Eastern Caribbean's federal project made it extremely difficult for future generations of local politicians to embrace further modalities of regional unification as viable alternatives for the archipelago. The ever-widening influence of the insular electorates and the localization of cultural identity along insular not regional lines figured prominently behind the aversion to integration. The lessons learned from the 1962-67 decolonizing dialogue did not go unheeded. By the end of the federal negotiations the small island politicians left with the impression that these eight territories, while sharing a common colonial past and similar sociological inheritance, were irretrievably driven apart by sharp differences in their respective constitutional and economic developments and, hence, in their expectations.

Not surprisingly, the possibility of forging a strong political and economic union similar to the federal design envisioned in the 1960s remained for the most part in cold storage. The establishment of the Caribbean Community (CARICOM)[4] in 1973, together with the founding in 1981 of the Organization of Eastern Caribbean States (OECS),[5] effectively powerless and structurally weak organizations, epitomized the enduring legacy of the failed federal negotiations of the 1960s. Not even the prominent role played by regional institutions such as the University of the West Indies, the Caribbean Meteorological Organization, the Caribbean News Agency (CANA), the Caribbean Development Bank (CDB) and the widely acclaimed West Indies cricket team tipped the balance in favour of a strong economic and political union. In spite of the existence of regional labour and credit unions as well as a wide array of regional associations of bankers, physicians, lawyers, accountants, architects, engineers, preachers, civil servants, hoteliers, insurance brokers and media workers, plodding along a unitary road yet again did not become part of the Eastern Caribbean's agenda, at least during the final decades of the 20th century. Change, however, is in the air. A decade into the 21st century the countries of the Eastern Caribbean are moving in a new direction.

The rise of an increasingly interdependent world order, together with the emergence of transnational regimes of investment, tourism, migration and even culture, with their profound impact on identity, has once more propelled the decolonizing dialogue to the forefront of public debate in the Eastern Caribbean archipelago. Today's challenges have compelled these islands to revisit the imperative of mounting a common front to common challenges, on the basis of meaningful integration.

This first decade of the 21st century has so far witnessed the birth of the CARICOM Single Market and Economy (CSME) — a strong union in the mould of the federal design premised on the free movement of goods, skilled nationals, services and capital. The CSME offers the archipelago endless possibilities for further integration on other equally sensitive fronts; most saliently on the articulation of a coherent, robust and independent Caribbean foreign policy. The Eastern Caribbean today seems to have arrived at the realization that emerging global trends, both in terms of trade and geopolitics, must be faced from a perspective of a robust union. The quest for economic sustainability, post-industrial growth and overall stability means that unified action has now become a matter of compulsion. The onslaught of common adversaries such as the volatility of the economic variables, the energy crisis, the pervasive smuggling of arms, narco-trafficking, global terrorism and environmental spoliation, among others, must be met from a platform of deepened integration. For these islands the decolonizing journey is far from finished. The road ahead is without limits.

Figure 14.1
The Evolution of Decolonization in the Eastern Caribbean

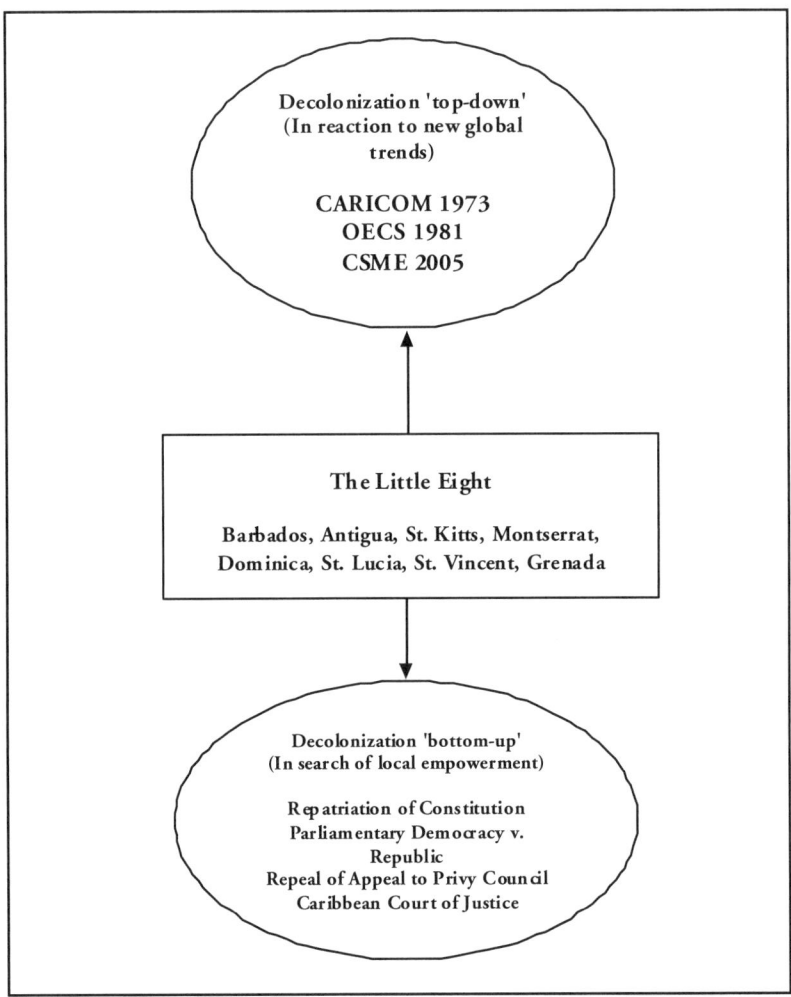

This is precisely why, more than forty years after the independence of Barbados and the attainment of associated statehood by the British Leeward and Windward Islands, the process leading to that dual outcome is still highly relevant for understanding the region's future possibilities. Without any doubt, that decolonizing dialogue set forth the stage upon which the Eastern Caribbean is attempting to face the challenges confronting it today.

There can be no doubt that the decolonizing process that took place in the 1960s prepared the ground for further debate in the area. Both the process and the outcome from that dialogue revealed the discontinuities and complexities of a phenomenon that was both profound and far-reaching. Four decades later the decolonizing experience of the Eastern Caribbean has not reached its completion; the search for a truly postcolonial order still goes on. The legacy from this foundational period endures. As these islands navigate up and down the uncharted waters of the 21st century, the relevance of this period, all too often relegated to oblivion, will become even more apparent. Rediscovering, reassessing and reinterpreting that legacy, many aspects of which have remained obscure for so long, constitutes the essential first step of any effort to truly procure the social, economic, cultural and psychological decolonization of the people of the Eastern Caribbean.

Notes

Introduction: Britain's Colonial Disengagement from the Eastern Caribbean

1. The term Eastern Caribbean, as used in this work, encompasses Barbados along with the so-called British Leeward and Windward Islands. The British Leeward Islands include Antigua-Barbuda, St. Kitts–Nevis–Anguilla and Montserrat. The British Windward Islands comprise Dominica, St. Lucia, St. Vincent and Grenada. For purposes of orthographical consistency and ease of reference this work uses the abbreviated form of these islands' official names; hence, the 'Saint' formulation has been discarded and the 'St.' abbreviation adopted.

2. Montserrat did not move on to free association. Instead, it remained a British dependency.

3. D. Balogh to Anthony Greenwood, July 13, 1965, CO 967/426, National Archives (Kew Gardens).

4. This study concurs with Roger Louis's definition of Commonwealth or Imperial historiography, namely 'the evolving or changing interpretations of the British Empire.' Refer to Robin Winks, ed. *History of the British Empire* vol. 5 (Oxford: Oxford University Press, 1999), 1. For a relevant analysis of the concept of historiography see the interviews with E.P. Thompson and C.L.R. James contained in Henry Abelove, et al., *Visions of History* (Manchester: Manchester University Press, 1983), 5–23 and 265–77.

5. Sir Hilton Poynton to Sir Burk Trend, September 28, 1965, CO 967/433.

6. President Eisenhower to Harold Macmillan, July 21, 1957, PREM 11/2880, National Archives (Kew Gardens).

7. Harold Macmillan to Sir Norman Brooke, February 21, 1963, PREM 11/3666.

8. Iain Sutherland to O. Armstrong, January 14, 1964, DO 200/280, National Archives (Kew Gardens).

9. Anthony Greenwood to Harold Wilson, August 10, 1965, CO 967/430.

10. *Report of the Barbados Constitutional Conference 1966*, Cmnd. 3058 (London: HMSO), 1.

11. Arthur Lewis, *The Agony of the Eight* (Bridgetown: The Advocate Printery, 1965), 38.

12. See, for example, John Mordecai, *The West Indies: Federal Negotiations* (London: George Allen, 1968), 461, and Eric Williams, *From Columbus to Castro*, 2nd ed. (New York: Vintage, 1984), 508.

13. Reginald Maudling to interviewer, April 25, 1968, MSS Brit Emp s. 484 at 15, Bodleian Library (Oxford).

14. The term has been borrowed from Harold Laski, 'The Obsolescence of Federalism,' *The New Republic* 98, (1939): 367.

15. B.W. Higman, 'The British West Indies', *History of the British Empire* vol. 5 ed. Robin Winks (Oxford: Oxford University Press, 1999) 135–45.

16. Note that the corpus of scholarly literature produced in the Caribbean focusing on the federal experiment in the post-war period is abundant. For an early work on the subject see Louis Miekle, *Confederation of the British West Indies v. Annexation to the U.S.* (London: S. Low & Marston, 1912). From the publication of that work until the late 1950s most studies tended to advocate federation or confederation, an indubitable sign of the support of the post-war intelligentsia for that ideal. See, for example, Jesse Proctor, 'The Development of the Idea of Federation in the British Caribbean Territories', *Caribbean Quarterly* 5, no. 1 (June 1957): 3–55; also see S. S. Ramphal, 'Federalism in the West Indies,' *Caribbean Quarterly* 6, nos. 2–3 (May 1960): 210–229. Once the future of the old federation seemed uncertain, as early as 1959, the historical literature on federation undergoes a slow but apparent evolution, it becomes more critical and far less optimistic. See C.L.R. James, *Federation: We Failed Miserably How and Why?* (St. Juan, Trinidad: Verdic, 1962); Hugh Springer, *Reflections on the Failure of the First West Indian Federation*, Occasional Papers in International Affairs, 4 (Harvard University, July 1962). Other students of the political evolution of the region, such as Trevor Munroe and Ann Spackman, took the discussion to a new dimension by questioning some of the assumptions previous studies had espoused. See Trevor Munroe, *The Politics of Constitutional Decolonization in Jamaica 1944–1962* (Kingston: University of the West Indies, 1972); also refer to Ann Spackman, *Constitutional Development of the West Indies* (Bridgetown: Caribbean University Press, 1975).

17. Arcadio Díaz Quiñones ed. 'El Caribe entre imperios' in *Revista del Centro de Investigaciones Históricas de la Universidad de Puerto Rico* (Río Piedras: Universidad de Puerto Rico, 1997), xv.

Part One: Introduction

1. The Interpretation Act of 1889 defined crown colonies as those territories in which 'the Crown retains complete control of the public officers carrying on the government'. In these territories 'the legislative power is either delegated to the officer administering the government, or is exercised by a Legislative Council which is nominated by the Crown either entirely or partly, the other part being elected. In these colonies the Crown has also reserved to itself the power of legislating by Order in Council, which is the original method for legislating for the colonies'. See Interpretation Act of 1889, sec. 18(2), 52 & 58 Vict. c 63. Also refer to the 'Colonial Laws Validity Act,' 1865, 28 & 29 Vict. c 63.

2. The chronology speaks for itself: riots in Antigua (1858); disturbances in St. Vincent (1862); the Morant Bay Rebellion in Jamaica (1865); the Confederation Riots in Barbados (1876); popular uprising in Dominica (1884); riots in the British Virgin Islands (1890); labour disputes in British Guiana (1896). From a constitutional standpoint the timetable went as follows: crown colony rule was established in the British Virgin Islands (1854); Dominica (1865); St. Vincent, Montserrat and Jamaica (1866); British Honduras (1870); Tobago (1874; which became a unit of Trinidad in 1889); and Grenada (1875). For a relevant analysis on the impact these

developments had in the region's constitutional history see, for instance, Frederick Madden, and John G. Darwin eds. *The Dependent Empire 1900–1948: Colonies, Protectorates and Mandates* vol. 7 (London: Greenwood Press, 1994), 56–58. See Gordon Lewis, *The Growth of the Modern West Indies* (London: Macgibbon, 1968), 95–117. Also refer to Fred Phillips, *Freedom in the Caribbean: A Study in Constitutional Change* (New York: Oceana, 1977) 7–10.

Chapter 1: The Federal Concept

1. For an illuminating discussion on the striking parallelisms between the different Caribbean communities see C.L.R. James, 'From Toussaint. L'Overture to Fidel Castro' in *The Black Jacobins*, 4th edition (London: Alison & Busby, 1994) 391–418.

2. Antonio Benítez Rojo, *The Repeating Island: The Caribbean and the Post-Modern Perspective* (Durham: Duke University Press, 1996), 1.

3. The first British settlements in the Eastern Caribbean were administered from Barbados, which until 1671 was the seat of the Leeward Islands. Robert H. Schomburgk, *The History of Barbados*, 4th ed. (London: Cass, 1998), 201. Also refer to Jesse Proctor, "The Development of the Idea of Federation in the British Caribbean Territories," *Caribbean Quarterly* 5, no. 1 (June 1957): 5–6.

4. For further reading on the political life of Ramón E. Betances (1827–98) see, for instance, Ada Suárez Díaz, *El Antillano: Biografía del Dr. Ramón Emeterio Betances* (San Juan: Centro de Estudios Avanzados de Puerto Rico y el Caribe, 1988). Also refer to Paul Estrade and Félix Reyes Ojeda, *Ramón Emeterio Betances: El anciano maravilloso* (San Juan: Centro de Estudios Avanzados de Puerto Rico y el Caribe, 1995); and Andrés Ramos Mattei, *Betances en el ciclo revolucionario antillano: 1867–1875* (San Juan: Instituto de Cultura Puertorriqueña, 1987).

5. Paul Estrade, 'La nación antillana: sueño y afán del Antillano' in *La nación soñada: Cuba, Puerto Rico y Las Filipinas ante el 1898*, ed. Consuelo Naranjo (Madrid: Doce Calles, 1995) 34. Also refer to Carlos M. Rama, *La idea de la Federación Antillana en los independentistas puertorriqueños del siglo XIX* (Río Piedras: Librería Internacional, 1971), 26–27.

6. Luis Bonafoux, ed. *Betances*, 3rd edition (San Juan: Instituto de Cultura Puertorriqueña, 1987), lxxi.

7. Thomas Matthews, 'The Project for a Confederation of the Greater Antilles', in *Caribbean Historical Review* nos. 3–4 (December 1954): 77. For an illuminating analysis on Hostos (1839–1903) and his ideas of Caribbean union see, for instance, María Dolores González Ripoll, 'Independencia y Antillanismo en la obra de Hostos' in *La nación soñada: Cuba, Puerto Rico y Las Filipinas ante el 1898*, ed. Consuelo Naranjo (Madrid: Doce Calles, 1995) 37–47.

8. These figures are considered the forefathers of the idea of a postcolonial Caribbean union. Martí, the ideologue of the Cuban Revolution, died in the battle of Dos Ríos in 1895. Months later Maceo, the military leader of Cuba's two wars of independence, also perished in combat (1896). Less than a year later Luperón, the father of the Dominican Republic's second independence, passed away (1897). Betances died in September of the following year in Paris. Hostos and Anténor

Firmin, the most outspoken Haitian defender of the federal project, died early in the twentieth century — in 1903 and 1911, respectively.

9. R.L. Watts, *New Federations: Experiments in the Commonwealth* (Oxford: Clarendon Press, 1966), 10. For a particularly relevant analysis on the theoretical aspects of federalism see, for instance, K.C. Wheare, *Federal Government*, 4th edition (Oxford: Oxford University Press, 1963), 1–52. For a penetrating analysis on the sociology of federalism see, for example, William S. Livingston, *Federalism and Constitutional Change* (Oxford: Clarendon Press, 1956), 1–5.

10. Munroe suggests that 'between the wars, however, desire for Federation grew autonomously in the Southern Caribbean but Jamaica remained outside these developments; primarily because of the absence of communications with the rest'. See Trevor Munroe, *The Politics of Constitutional Decolonization: Jamaica 1944–1962*, 117.

11. For a relevant, albeit brief, comment on the impact the war had on these colonial soldiers see Howard Johnson, 'The British Caribbean from Demobilization to Constitutional Decolonization' in *The Oxford History of the British Empire* vol. 4, eds. J. Brown and Roger W. Louis (Oxford: Oxford University Press, 1999), 597–600.

12. See 'Hasan' in Clennel Wickham, *Pen and Ink Sketches of Barbadian Politicians and Other Essays* (Bridgetown: The Herald Printery, 1921).

13. Clennell Wilsden Wickham (1895–1938) received his early education at St. Giles Boys' School in Barbados. Unlike the most prominent pedagogues and politicians of his times, he did not attend university. Wickham's vast knowledge and culture, for the most part, had been self-taught. His intellectual curiosity and impressive analytical powers were thus the product of his wide reading and constant travels. By 1928 he became the editor-in-chief of the *Barbados Herald*, a progressive newspaper from which he openly denounced the terrible living conditions endured by the masses and the oligarchy's corruption. Refer to John Wickham, *A Man with a Fountain Pen* (Bridgetown: Nation Publishing Co., 1995), vii. Senator John Wickham (son of Clennell Wickham), in discussion with the author, February 20, 1999, Bridgetown, Barbados.

14. F.A. Hoyos, *Grantley Adams and the Social Revolution* (London: Macmillan, 1974), 24.

15. The term has been borrowed from Trevor Munroe. Refer to *The Politics of Constitutional Decolonization: Jamaica 1944–1962*, 116–122.

16. Arthur Cipriani (1875–1945) of clear Corsican background had been born in Port-of-Spain. A member of the island's upper middle-class, he served in the British West Indies Regiment during the Great War. Back in the island, Cipriani joined the Trinidad Workingmen Association. Although it never functioned as a trade union per se, this organization pressed for universal adult suffrage as well as for legislative and economic reform.

17. Theophilus Albert Marryshow (1887–1958), who in 1958 would be appointed to the West Indies Federal Senate, had been born in Grenada. Unlike Cipriani, he came from a humble family and eventually got involved in journalism. Marryshow also created the Representative Government Association of Grenada. From the outset of his public career he advocated for a federation of the Eastern Caribbean,

earning the title of 'father of federation'. Springer, for instance, has argued that Marryshow 'was the most outspoken defendant of the federal principle, although that influence was almost exclusively confined to the eastern territories'. See Hugh Springer, *Reflections on the Failure of the First West Indian Federation*, Occasional Papers in International Affairs, 4 (Harvard University, July 1962), 3.

18.   Ibid. 38–39.

19.   Please note that, according to several voices,

> West Indian nationalism was born and developed in the UK, Canada and the US, primarily in response to the experience of West Indian students.... Transported to the West Indies, it remained largely an affair of the elite groups in the society. Thus, it was not surprising to find a large number of professional institutions organised on a West Indian-wide basis. The commitment to federation was, however, never shared by the great masses of the West Indian people.

See Richard Cheltenham, 'Constitutional and Political Development in Barbados, 1946–1966' (PhD dissertation, University of Manchester, 1970), 224, and Lloyd Braithwaite, 'Federal Association and Institutions in the West Indies', *Social and Economic Studies* 6, no. 2 (June 1957): 311–21.

20.   R.L. Watts, *New Federations: Experiments in the Commonwealth* (Oxford: Clarendon Press, 1966), 42:

> Thus there developed clashes between two conflicting sets of historical forces: between the narrow nationalism based on the traditional political, linguistic, racial and religious loyalties and the wider nationalism of the Westernised elite, which has grown within and wishes to inherit the larger cohesive units created by British colonial rule.

21.   For a relevant analysis of the behaviour of the middle classes during this period see Arthur Lewis, *Labour in the West Indies* (London: Fabian Research Bureau, 1939), 32. According to Lewis,

> historically the educated coloured elements had either identified themselves with the ruling oligarchy or sought to secure a higher status for the negro. This had always been true of West Indian politics; even before the emancipation of slavery the free coloured were in constant conflict with the plantocracy, and throughout the nineteenth century that conflict continued. It came to head after the Great War with the formation of the Representative Government Associations throughout the Lesser Antilles. These associations, however, were narrowly middle class in their aims. They advocated for more middle class representation in the legislative councils and for an increase in the number of civil service posts for educated blacks. But there was hardly anything of direct working class interest.

22.   Keith Hunte clearly illustrates what effectively became a dilemma for middle class leaders, in the inter-war period, using the example of Dr. Charles Duncan O'Neale (1879–1936) of Barbados. Hunte suggests:

> O'Neale called for the disendowment of the Church on the grounds that no man should be asked to support financially another man's religion. He also called for a universal pension scheme. But even as O'Neale was addressing the crowd that had gathered in front of the Bridgetown City Council in March 1927, he was painfully aware of the fact that the vast majority of his hearers did not have the vote.

See Keith Hunte, 'Duncan O'Neale: Apostle of Freedom', *The New World Quarterly*, 3 no.1 (1966): 84.

23. Cipriani made this assertion at The West Indian Conference held in Roseau, Dominica between October and November 1932. The Dominica's Tax Payers Reform Association convened this conference with the objective of drafting a federal constitution for the region.

24. *Report on Visit to West Indies and British Guiana 1922*, Cmnd. 1679 (London: HMSO).

25. This class felt threatened by any possibility of self-government for the colonies; federation, as espoused by the black middle classes, was part of a wider design for self-government. The close connection between these two complimentary objectives was not lost on the oligarchy. This aspect on its own should explain their reluctance to even consider any federal project, at least at this time. The oligarchy's main fears were that self-government could disrupt their access to preferential treatment by the Empire, which enabled them to sell sugar and rum in Canada and Britain cheaper than their competitors, and that self-government could also undermine their access to British military power in the event of major labour disturbances. See Richard Hart, *From Occupation to Independence: A Short History of the Peoples of the English-Speaking Caribbean Region* (London: Pluto Press, 1998), 92.

26. Wood contended the following, as regards the possibility of a federal union:

    The establishment of West Indian political unity is likely to be a plant of slow and tender growth. If any advance in this direction is to be achieved, it can only be as the result of a deliberate demand of local opinion, springing from the realisation of the advantages of co-operation under modern world conditions. I am satisfied that, so long as public opinion stands where it does today, it is both inopportune and impracticable to attempt amalgamation of existing units of Government into anything approaching a general federal system.

    Report on Visit to West Indies and British Guiana 1922, Cmnd. 1679 (London: HMSO), 32.

27. John Mordecai, *The West Indies: The Federal Negotiations* (London: George Allen, 1968), 20.

28. The Wood Report recommended the elective principle for the Legislatures of Trinidad, Grenada, St. Vincent, St. Lucia and Dominica. By 1924 the British Government would implement these recommendations. However, the elected officials would only represent a fourth of the Legislative Councils.

29. Please note that even by the beginning of the 1930s the drive for federation came from the black middle classes in the eastern territories of the Anglophone Caribbean. For example, during the proceedings of the 1932 Dominica Conference, the most informed sections of Jamaican society did not send any representation. However, the delegations from Trinidad, Barbados, the Windward, the Leeward, and the British Virgin Islands made a firm federal commitment.

30. Hansard Parliamentary Debates, Commons, 5th ser., (1938) col. 181 contained in Arthur Creech Jones Papers, container ACJ 25/3, Rhodes House Library (Oxford).

31. Ibid.

Chapter 2: Slums of Empire

1. Nigel Bolland, *On the March*: *Labour Rebellions in the British Caribbean, 1934–1939* (Kingston: Ian Randle Publishers, 1995), 111.

2. *Report on Visit to West Indies and British Guiana 1922*, Cmd. 1679 (London: HMSO).

3. For an illuminating analysis of this particular migratory wave see, for instance, Velma Newton, *The Silver Men*: *West Indian Labour Migration to Panama, 1850–1914* (Bridgetown: University of the West Indies Press, 1984).

4. F.A. Hoyos, *Grantley Adams*, 55; Arthur Lewis, *Labour in the West Indies*, 33 and Eric Williams, *From Columbus to Castro*, 474.

5. C.L.R. James, *Black Jacobins*, 404.

6. Eric Williams, *From Columbus to Castro*, 474.

7. Ibid.

8. Note that by the time of the Restoration, Barbados had become the most precious jewel of the British Crown. In 1661, for example, Charles II marked its importance by creating 13 baronets in Barbados on the same day, none of them earning less than £1,000 and some of them £10,000 per annum. See, for instance, Robert Schomburgk, *The History of Barbados*, 286–87 and Eric Williams, *From Columbus to Castro*, 114.

9. In an open letter published in The *Manchester Guardian*, in the summer of 1938, W. Garthwaite suggested that

   > We are for good or evil a protectionist nation; we have protected our home beet sugar producers so that they make a handsome profit. Yet we give our colonies an inadequate preference, which fails to shield them from the competition of Cuban sugar.

   Refer to W. Garthwaite, 'Poverty and Unrest in the British Colonies', The *Manchester Guardian*, August 18, 1938 — contained in MSS Brit Emp s. 332 Box 25/7, Bodleian Library (Oxford).

10. Arthur Lewis, *Labour in the West Indies*, 5 — contained in MSS Brit Emp s. 332 Box 25/6.

11. W.H. Macmillan, *Warning from the West Indies* (Harmondsworth: Penguin Books, 1936), 44.

12. Michael Havinden and David Meredith, *Colonialism and Development: Britain and its Tropical Colonies 1850-1960* (London: Routledge, 1996), 202.

13. The Norman Commission had suggested that 'the black population of these colonies was originally placed in them by force as slaves; the race was kept up and increased under artificial conditions, which were maintained by the British Government'. In other words, these were the 'children' of the slaves brought by force during the seventeenth and eighteenth centuries, which by 1838 had been, at least theoretically, emancipated. Refer to *Report of the West Indian Royal Commission*, C. 8655 (London: HMSO) 1897.

14. In a moving editorial, *Reynolds News* compared the then appalling state of affairs in the archipelago with slavery.

   > Slavery in the West Indies ended, officially, one hundred years ago. Today mass strikes and military terrorism expose emancipation as a myth and reveal

the grim truth. Thousands of British citizens are exploited with the same ruthless cunning and barbarity as were their forebears who came under the lash of the slave-traders — and they are exploited in the same interest, the interest of private property.

See 'Spotlight on Empire', May 29, 1938 in MSS Brit Emp s. 332 Box 25, Bodleian Library (Oxford).

15. In 1937 Barbados exported over 100,000 tons of sugar and more than 10 million gallons of molasses. See Francis Mark, *The History of the Barbados Workers Union* (Bridgetown: Advocate Commercial Printing, 1966), 32; also refer to Havinden and Meredith, *Colonialism and Development*, 185.

16. Note that between 1934 and 1938, oil represented 57.3 per cent of Trinidad's exports. 'These oil companies paid dividends ranging from 43 per cent to 30 per cent; while earning in profits for their English shareholders a sum equivalent to three times their wages bill.' See H.N. Brailsford, 'The Slavery that is Jamaica', The *Times*, June 5, 1938. The correspondent of The *Manchester Guardian* in Port-of-Spain reported that 'it is often said that the real rulers of Trinidad are not the Governor or his Legislative Council but the representatives of the oil industry'. See 'Unrest in the Oilfields', The *Manchester Guardian*, August 10, 1937, 21 — contained in Arthur Creech Jones Papers, container ACJ 25/5 3, Rhodes House Library (Oxford). It was not unfamiliar for top ranking civil servants, even colonial governors, to retire from active duty in order to join the boards of these oil companies. That would be the case of Governor Rance (1951–55), who by 1957 would accept a highly paid job as an executive for one of these companies.

17. Rexford Tugwell, *The Stricken Land: The Story of Puerto Rico* (New York: Doubleday, 1947), 65.

18. Arthur Lewis, *Labour in the West Indies*, 6.

19. Lewis, *The Growth of the Modern West Indies*, 226.

20. M.G. Smith, *Culture, Race and Class in the Commonwealth Caribbean* (Mona: University of West Indies Press, 1990), 115.

21. Francis Mark, *The History of the Barbados Workers Union*, 32.

22. George Lamming, for example, has argued that referring to the existence of a colonial middle class during this period is wholly inappropriate. In an interview a few years ago Lamming suggested,

> In the Caribbean we do not have that class. We do not have a native class of West Indians who have in fact been the owners and controllers of the process of production, beginning from plantation society to the entrepreneurial open society that we have today. What we have is an educated minority that can be called a "salariat class". These are the people who by virtue of training, by virtue of something called education are in fact paid to be the caretakers for people who actually own or control the Caribbean economy. Therefore what I mean is that you may have a class that may play a middle class role, but they are not the middle class because they do not have, nor are they supported by the economic base that makes the term 'middle classes' meaningful.

See Richard Drayton ed. *Conversations: George Lamming – Essays, Addresses and Interviews, 1953-1990* (London: White Castle, 1992), 268–69.

23. Sir Henry G. Bushe to Viscount Cranborne June 23, 1942, CO 28/327/13.

24. Ibid. Adams was then the leader of the progressive movement in Barbados. His significance and trajectory is discussed in detail below.

25. *Economic Survey of the Colonial Empire 1938*, Colonial no. 149 (London: HMSO).

26. Ibid.

27. H.N. Brailsford, 'The Slavery that is Jamaica', The *Times*, June 5, 1938.

28. Clennel Wickham, *Pen and Ink Sketches of Barbadian Politicians*, 1–2.

29. W.J. Makin, 'Jamaica: Trouble Looms Again', The *Daily Herald*, May 16, 1938.

30. Arthur Lewis, *Labour in the West Indies*, 3–4.

31. Lord Olivier, Speech to the House of Lords, February 23, 1938, *Parliamentary Debates*, Lords columns 830–50; contained in ACJ25/2.

32. John La Guerra, 'The Moyne Commission and the West Indian Intelligentsia 1938–1939', *Journal of Commonwealth and Political Studies* 9, (1971), 134.

33. *Report of the West Indian Royal Commission 1945*, Cmnd. 6607 (London: HMSO). For an interesting and brief analysis on the impact of that observation see F.A. Hoyos, *Grantley Adams*, 88–89.

34. Ibid.

35. P.J. Cain and A.G. Hopkins, *British Imperialism: Crisis and Deconstruction, 1914–1990* (London: Longman, 1993), 230.

Chapter 3: The Anglo-American Caribbean Commission

1. An earlier version of this chapter appeared in *Diplomacy & Statecraft*. See Rafael Cox Alomar, 'Revisiting the Transatlantic Triangle: The Decolonisation of the British Caribbean in Light of the Anglo-American Special Relationship', *Diplomacy & Statecraft* 15, no. 2 (June 2004): 353–73.

2. The 1901 Hay-Pauncefote Treaty nullified the 1850 Clayton-Bulwer Treaty, stipulating that neither the US nor Britain would in future build and unilaterally control any isthmian canal in Central America. For the treaty's text see *Treaties, Conventions, International Acts, Protocols and Agreements between the United States and Other Powers* (Washington DC: Government Printing Office, 1910), 659–63. For a penetrating analysis on the impact of these diplomatic negotiations see Donald Yerxa, *Admirals and Empire: The USA Navy and the Caribbean 1898-1945* (South Carolina: University of South Carolina Press, 1991), 5–15.

3. Yerxa, *Admirals and Empire*, 9. For a brief analysis of the strategic considerations of the British in anticipation of the Great War see Darwin, *Britain and Decolonisation*, 34.

4. Rexford Tugwell, *The Sticken Land: The Story of Puerto Rico* (New York: Doubleday, 1947), 65.

5. Rexford Tugwell (1891–1979) joined the Roosevelt Administration in March 1933. By August 1941 President Roosevelt appointed him Governor of Puerto Rico, a position he held until 1946. This appointment allowed him to travel the Caribbean on a constant basis and to appreciate the peculiar challenges confronting the area.

6. Charles Taussig (1896–1948) played a crucial role in the process of reassessing the strategic value of the Caribbean. Since the early days of the Roosevelt Administration Taussig chose to devote a good part of his time to Caribbean affairs, frequently

representing President Roosevelt at official Caribbean-related meetings.

7. Rexford Tugwell, *The Stricken Land: The Story of Puerto Rico*, 64.

8. Guianese bauxite was no small concern for the US. During this period approximately 60 per cent of its aluminium needs were supplied by this colony. Aviation requirements, in turn, made aluminium an indispensable strategic material for the war effort.

9. Long staple cotton was essential for the war effort since parachutes were made from it.

10. Trinidad and Tobago, Aruba and Curaçao possessed important oil refineries upon which both Britain and France depended.

11. The US also possessed overseas territories in the Caribbean: Puerto Rico, ceded by Spain following the 1898 Spanish American War, and the Virgin Islands, bought from Denmark in 1917 for $US25 million.

12. For details on the negotiations leading to the Destroyers Agreement refer to *Foreign Relations of the US* (Washington: Government Printing Office, 1941), vol. 3, 1–84. Under its terms the US transferred 50 WWI vintage destroyers to Britain in exchange for base rights for 99 years in Antigua–Barbuda, The Bahamas, Bermuda, British Guiana, Jamaica, St. Lucia and Trinidad and Tobago.

13. William L. Langer and Everett S. Gleason, *Challenge to Isolation 1937–1940* (New York: Harper, 1952), 760.

14. FDR to Secretary of State Cordell Hull, January 1941, FRUS vol.3, 3. Also refer to Wm Roger Louis, *Imperialism at Bay* (Oxford: Oxford University Press, 1978), 182.

15. *Report of the West Indian Royal Commission* 1945 Cmnd. 6607 (London: HMSO). The Moyne Commission Report was presented to the British Government on December 21, 1939 and published six years later.

16. Ibid.

17. This phrase has been attributed to De Gaulle; see D. Balogh to Anthony Greenwood, July 13, 1965, CO 967/426.

18. Cain and Hopkins, *British Imperialism*, 230.

19. Lord Moyne to Major Sir Hubert Young, April 23, 1941, CO 1042/5213.

20. Note on the Future of Anglo-American Relations, March 27, 1941, CO 1042/52127.

21. On this note Whitehead argued,

    > It is very easy to assume, whenever a divergence of outlook develops between America and ourselves, that it is our task to try and persuade America of the error of her ways. This partly results from the fact that when two collaborators are of unequal age, the older of the two usually appears to possess the more balanced judgment. However, there is merit in the cautious judgment of maturity and another equally important merit in the bold imagination of youth. Americans may not always be wise, they will try anything once, but the rise of their nation to wealth and power and their success in maintaining peace within an entire continent suggests that we have something to learn from them. If Anglo-American collaboration is to be a success we shall have to bear this very carefully in mind. CO 1042/52127.

22. After the fall of Holland and France, the US occupied all Dutch and French

possessions in the area.

23. See recollection of US Cabinet meeting, chaired by President Roosevelt and Secretary of State Cordell Hull in August, 1940 in Harold L. Ickes, *The Secret Diary of Harold L. Ickes: The Lowering of the Clouds 1939–1941* (New York: Simon and Schuster, 1954), vol. 3, 288–89.

24. Yerxa, *Admirals and Empire*, 118. By December 1944, US military officers in the Pentagon, including General Marshall, suggested, that the 'continuation of the British Empire, in some reasonable strength, is in the strategic interest of the US'. See *FRUS* vol.5, 486.

25. The historical record contains enough evidence suggesting that the morale of the people in the Caribbean region was a favoured target of the Axis propagandists. See, for instance, CO 28/327/14. Also refer to Ickes, *The Lowering of the Clouds*, 368–69.

26. Tugwell, *The Stricken Land*, 100.

27. Note that following the exchange of destroyers for bases, President Roosevelt, on January 7, 1941, appointed an official commission to survey the area's social and economic problems. The commission, consisting of Charles Taussig and two military officers, visited Puerto Rico, the US Virgin Islands and the British territories (with the exception of British Guiana and British Honduras). It identified the advantages that the Caribbean dependencies would derive from working as a unit, both in meeting the emergency and in carrying out broad-scale research activities in agriculture, labour and social services. See Tugwell, *The Stricken Land*, 95–96.

28. By 1942–43 regional cooperation was under way in other parts of the Empire. For example, Ghana, Nigeria and Sierra Leone were sharing a regional town planner and a development adviser.

29. Cmnd. 6607, 327.

30. Coert du Bois (1881-1960) was appointed head of the US State Department's Caribbean Division.

31. During this period the US State Department inaugurated (and in some cases re-inaugurated) various consular offices across the Caribbean. In Georgetown (British Guiana) and St John's (Antigua), where US consulates had existed from 1904–32 and 1878–1908 respectively, these were re-opened. In other islands such as St. Lucia, the American consular agency which since 1870 had existed was finally awarded full consular status in January 1942.

32. The German campaign, headed by Admiral Dönitz, extended for most of the spring and summer of 1942. Although there is a discrepancy between the sources on an exact tally, the German U-boats sank over 250 merchant ships in Caribbean waters, totalling approximately 1.3 million tons.

33. The official press release, published simultaneously in Washington and London, announced 'the creation of an Anglo-North American Caribbean Commission which will seek to encourage and strengthen social and economic co-operation between North American and British outposts in the Caribbean'. See, for instance, 'Joint Commission Appointed', The *Barbados Advocate*, March 10, 1942.

34. The Commission was composed of three American and three British members, with Charles Taussig as the American co-chairman and Sir Frank Stockdale (1883–

1949, also comptroller of the development and welfare organization for the region) as his British counterpart. Rexford Tugwell and Coert du Bois were the remaining American members of the commission. See Memorandum on the Organization of the Anglo-American Caribbean Commission, June 15, 1942, CO 1042/53.

35. Ibid. The terms of reference establishing the Anglo-American Caribbean Commission described it as an advisory body not an executive one.

36. For an illuminating analysis on how constitutional issues gained prominence during and immediately after the Second World War see David Goldsworthy, *Colonial Issues in British Politics 1945–1961* (Oxford: Clarendon Press, I 97 I), 10–13.

37. Governor Bushe to Sir George Gater, December 22, 1942, CO 28/327/14.

38. Ibid.

39. *The Caribbean and the War: A Record of Progress in Facing Stem Realities* (Washington: US Government Printing Office, 1943), 57.

40. For a relevant analysis of the Atlantic Charter, particularly its treatment of the concept of self-determination, see Louis, *Imperialism at Bay*, 121–33. A considerable number of legal scholars have suggested that during the Great War there was a widespread belief in the existence of a right to national independence, which the Central Powers had breached, and that the primary objective of the Allies was then to reinvindicate such right. Thus, by 1918 that right to national sovereignty came to be known as the principle of self-determination. For a classical study on the historical origins of this principle and its impact on the postwar world see, for instance, Alfred Cobban, *National Self-Determination* (Oxford: Oxford University Press, 1944). Also see Dov Ronen, *The Quest for Self-Determination* (New Haven: Yale University Press, 1979).

41. For a relevant analysis on the impact the Anglo-American Caribbean Commission had, for instance, on Puerto Rico's constitutional development, see Mayra Rosario Urrutia, 'Detrás de la vitrina: Las expectativas del Partido Popular Democrático y la política exterior norteamericana 1942-1954' in eds. Alvarez Curbelo y Rodriguez Castro *Del Nacionalismo al Populismo: Cultura y Política en Puerto Rico* (Río Piedras: Ediciones Huracán, 1993).

42. Oliver Stanley to Governor of Jamaica, January 5, 1942 in Spackman, *Constitutional Development of the West Indies*, 129.

43. The executive committee had been established in 1881 immediately after the constitutional crisis that led to the 1876 Confederation Riots. The governor-sitting-in executive committee shared with the governor most executive responsibilities. It was composed of the governor and the attorney general, together with one member from the legislative council and four from the house of assembly (all nominated by the governor). For all practical purposes the executive committee was the real executive, being responsible for introducing the annual budget, for the initiation of money bills, for overseeing public works as well as for controlling and managing public property. For the history of this institution see Cheltenham, *Constitutional and Political Development in Barbados,* 1–6. For the correspondence between the Colonial Office and the governor of Barbados on the appointment of Grantley Adams see CO 28/327/13.

44. In Barbados, women exercised for the first time their right to vote in 1944. For the

manifesto of C.N. Weekes, one of the first women to participate in the island's political process, see 'A Daughter of the City Speaks Out: To the Electors of the City of Bridgetown', in The *Barbados Advocate*, October 4, 1944, in CO 28/332/4.

45. Governor Bushe to Sir George Gater December 22, 1942, CO 28/327/14.

46. Ibid.

47. Letter from Governor Bushe to Colonial Secretary March 27, 1942, CO 28/327/13.

48. *The Caribbean and the War*, 57.

49. Ibid.

50. Ibid.

51. Immediately after the war, on March 19, 1946, the French Assembly approved the Assimilation Law (Law No. 46-451), pursuant to which Guadeloupe, Martinique and French Guiana were elevated to the status of Departments of the French Republic.

52. Olive Holmes, 'Anglo-American Caribbean Commission: Pattern of Colonial Cooperation', *Foreign Policy Reports* 20, no. 19 (December 15, 1944): 238–47. Also see 'The Colonial Issue' in The *Economist* 148, no. 5301 (March 31, 1945): 401–02.

53. Oliver Stanley, 'Looking Ahead: The Benefits of Regional International Cooperation', *The Imperial Review* (January 15, 1943): 128. Also see Lord Hailey's papers. Mss. 600 18s. 20 (Rhodes House Library, Oxford.)

54. *Conference on the Closer Association of the British West Indian Colonies 1947*, Cmnd. 7120 (London: HMSO) Appendix 1.

55. Ibid.

Chapter 4: From the Montego Bay Conference to the Jamaican Referendum

1. Oliver Stanley to Governor of Jamaica, in *Constitutional Development of the West Indies* ed. Ann Spackman, 131 (Bridgetown: Caribbean University Press, 1975). In the same speech, the colonial secretary also expressed that there was a moral imperative for maintaining a close relationship with these territories,

> there is, of course, a moral responsibility. You have got these people. You have got to realise that if you withdraw your help, your advice and your guidance vast areas of the world might well relapse into barbarism and chaos.

Others, such as Home Secretary Herbert Morrison, sustained starker views. Morrison was quoted as suggesting,

> it would be ignorant, dangerous nonsense to talk about grants of full self-government to many of the dependent territories for some time to come. In those instances it would be like giving a child of ten a latch key, a bank account and a shotgun.

See The *Manchester Guardian*, January 11, 1943.

2. Sydney Caine, 'General Political Development of Colonial Territories' in *Parliamentary Papers, 1947–48*, vol. 11. Caine explicitly weighed the encouragement of local self-government against claims for sovereignty. The period 1945–48 witnessed the articulation of a policy, which saw 'gradual devolution' of political

authority as the desideratum. By June 1948 an official publication of the British Government defined the goal of its policy as 'to guide the territories to *responsible self-government within the Commonwealth*'. Note that there was no mention of independence. See Cmd. 7433 (London: HMSO, 1948).

3. See Richard Drayton ed. *Conversations: George Lamming*, 269. Also refer to Arthur Lewis, *Labour in the West Indies*, 31–32.

4. For an illuminating study on the post-war leadership see A.W. Singham, *The Hero and the Crowd in a Colonial Polity* (New Haven: Yale University Press, 1968), 152. For instance, in this seminal study Singham suggests that by then there were two types of political leaders in the Anglophone Caribbean. There is 'the middle class hero, claiming that he has sacrificed his career for the sake of helping the people; he often argues that he might have been an international lawyer or scholar of some repute'. Additionally, there is the hero who 'comes from humble origins and bases his claims to political leadership on his role as a trade union leader'.

5. John Mordecai, *The West Indies: The Federal Negotiations*, 32.

6. Mr. Richard Hart kindly donated this copy of Mr Bird's unpublished letter, dated July 17, 1947, to the author.

7. VC Bird (1910–99) was by then an executive member of the Antigua Trades and Labour Union.

8. For the official definition of dominion status, refer to the Statute of Westminster of 1931, 22 & 23 Geo 5 c.4.

9. The British Guiana and West Indies Labour Congress had been renamed the Caribbean Labour Congress at its fourth conference, which was held in Barbados from September 17 to 27, 1945. According to Hoyos,

> for the first time in the history of the Congress, representatives came not only from British Guiana and Trinidad but also from Jamaica, Bermuda, the Leeward and Windward Islands. Since delegates also came from Dutch Guiana (later Surinam), the name of the organisation was changed to the more comprehensive title of the Caribbean Labour Congress.

See F.A. Hoyos, *Grantley Adams*, 111. For the official position of the Caribbean Labour Congress, as adopted in the 1945 conference, on self-government and federation, see *Caribbean Labour Congress: Official Report of Conference* (Bridgetown: Advocate Printers, 1945), 50–57.

10. Ibid., 56–57. Also refer to Mordecai, *The West Indies: Federal Negotiations*, 33–35.

11. 'Colonial Office Memoranda on Federation' in *Caribbean Labour Congress: Special Bulletin*, ed. Richard Hart (Kingston: Secretary's Office, 117 Tower Street) *c.* 1947. Mr Hart kindly donated a copy of this document to the author.

12. Norman Manley (1893–1969), as becomes apparent below, played an enormous role throughout the drama of federation. Of mixed ancestry, partly Irish and Afro-Caribbean, Manley belonged by birth and education to the Jamaican middle classes. Initially educated at Jamaica College, Manley went on to win a Rhodes scholarship for entrance to Oxford in 1914. After a bruising interregnum as a sergeant in the Royal Horse Artillery during the Great War, Manley returned to Jesus College, Oxford, where he received a First Class Honours BA Degree in Law. Called to the Bar in 1921, Manley returned to Jamaica late in the 1920s. Soon thereafter he

became the most respected wig in the Jamaican bar, earning by 1931 a most coveted appointment as King's Counsel (KC). Confronted with the plight of the Jamaican masses, while being a strong supporter of self-government for the island, Manley founded in 1938 the People's National Party. Elected for the first time to the House of Representatives in 1953, less than two years later Manley became the colony's chief minister. He held this position until 1962. After his party's defeat in April 1962 just before the attainment of independence, Manley became leader of the opposition, a position he held until 1969. The former premier has been declared by the island's governmental authorities a Jamaican National Hero.

13.   See 'A Cause Vital to our Progress' in *Norman Washington Manley and the New Jamaica: Selected Speeches and Writings, 1938–1968*, ed. Rex Nettleford (London: Longman, 1971), 162–68. For the positions of other leaders, while at the Labour Congress in Kingston, on the question of dominion status see, for instance, F.A Hoyos, *Grantley Adams*, 126–27; and Mordecai, *West Indies: Federal Negotiations*, 35–36.

14.   Alexander Bustamante (1884–1977), together with his cousin and political rival Norman Manley, dominated Jamaica's political life from the late 1930s until the time of his death. Of mixed Irish and Afro-Caribbean ancestry as well, Bustamante had left Jamaica in his youth and had travelled, lived and worked in Cuba, Spain, the US and Canada until 1934 when he decided to return to the island. By May 1938 Bustamante assumed the de facto leadership of the 'masses'. After his release from prison, in 1942, Bustamante established what became Jamaica's most powerful labour union, the 'Bustamante Industrial Trade Union', which complemented the efforts of the People's National Party. Although an associate of Manley's, Bustamante broke off relations with his cousin and a year later founded the Jamaica Labour Party. Jamaica's first chief minister, Bustamante led his party to victory in the first two elections under adult universal suffrage in 1944 and 1949, respectively. An unambiguous anti-federalist, Bustamante assumed the leadership of the movement to withdraw Jamaica from the West Indies Federation; leading Jamaica to independence on its own. Considered by many as the architect of Jamaica's independence, Bustamante became the island's first prime minister under independence. By 1967, at the age of 83, Sir Alexander retired from public life having been declared by the island's government a Jamaican National Hero.

15.   For the proceedings of the 1947 Montego Bay Conference (held from September 11 to 19) see *Conference on the Closer Association of the British West Indian Colonies 1948*, Cmnd. 7120 (London: HMSO). It would take almost eleven years, after the Montego Bay Conference, to finally establish the Federation. This conference led to the establishment of the Standing Closer Association Committee under the chairmanship of Sir Hubert Rance (1898–1974), then governor of Trinidad and Tobago. The report of this committee published in 1950 provided a detailed examination of the political and economic implications of federation. See *Report of the Standing Closer Association Committee 1950*, Cmd. 255 (London: HMSO). Its recommendations, which were ratified by the Legislatures of Jamaica, Trinidad and Tobago, Barbados, Antigua–Barbuda, St. Kitts–Nevis–Anguilla, Montserrat, Dominica, St. Lucia, St. Vincent and Grenada, formed the basis of the Plan for a

British Caribbean Federation drawn up by the London Conference of 1953 and subsequently adopted by all the aforementioned Legislatures. See *Plan for a British Caribbean Federation 1953*, Cmd. 8895 (London: HMSO). In February 1955 the Colonial Office announced that the British Government would proceed with the 'next steps towards a Federation' and accordingly set up three commissions to examine the fiscal, civil service and judicial aspects of federation. The reports of these commissions were published early in January 1956 and paved the way for the enactment of the British Caribbean Federation Act of 1956 (4 & 5 Eliz 2 c63) and thus for the formal inauguration of Federation on January 3, 1958. See *Report of Fiscal Commission 1956*, Cmd. 9618 (London: HMSO) and *Report of Civil Service Commission 1956*, Cmd. 9619 (London: HMSO). For one of the most complete accounts of this process see John Mordecai, *West Indies: The Federal Negotiations*, 39–75.

16. Cmnd. 7120, 5.
17. Ibid.
18. Ibid., 6–7.
19. The term constitutional 'evolution' for describing the developments unfolding in the archipelago would gain ever more prominence. In one of Sir Anthony Eden's (later Lord Avon) multiple letters to Lord Hailes (governor general of the West Indies Federation) this point is clearly illustrated. Lord Avon wrote, 'everything I hear about your part of the world is encouraging … if, as it seems, *the constitutional evolution* still goes forward, you ought to feel proud of your part in this'. Lord Avon to Lord Hailes, October 14, 1960, Lord Hailes Papers, container HAIS 4/11, Churchill Archive Centre (Cambridge). (Emphasis added.)
20. Cmnd. 7120, 7.
21. Ibid., 9
22. Ibid., 63.
23. The following units were represented at Montego Bay: Antigua-Barbuda, St. Kitts-Nevis-Anguilla, Montserrat, Dominica, St. Lucia, St. Vincent, Grenada, Barbados, Trinidad and Tobago, Jamaica, British Guiana and British Honduras. The remaining British territories in the Caribbean, namely, the Bahamas, Bermuda, the British Virgin Islands and the Turks and Caicos Islands had not been included in the federal project from the outset. Thus the federation would be composed of ten territories (Jamaica, Trinidad and Tobago, Barbados, St. Vincent, Grenada, Dominica, St. Lucia, Antigua, St. Kitts–Nevis–Anguilla and Montserrat).
24. Note that it was at the Montego Bay Conference that for the first time Jamaica was represented in a conference to discuss federal proposals; as suggested above, the federal ideal had not been as popular in Jamaica as in the eastern colonies. For a penetrating analysis on how Jamaica's volte-face came about see, for instance, Richard Hart, 'Federation: An Ill-fated Design', *The Jamaica Journal* 25, no. 1 (October 1993): 10–16. Hart himself had been Jamaica's first official delegate to any regional conference, when in September 1945 he led the Jamaican delegation to the Caribbean Labour Congress' Conference held in Barbados. Richard Hart, in discussion with the author, April 1, 1999, London.
25. Bustamante's oratory was legendary. Many described him as a 'flamboyantly-speaking

figure'. William Makin, a British news correspondent in Kingston between 1938 and 1940 wrote: 'nightly his voice declaims through the streets of Kingston and carries like a high wind into the remote countryside of Jamaica. There is something Epstein-like in his poses before the crowd, and there is no doubt that the crowd believes in him'. See *News Chronicle* March 19, 1938, 12.

26. Cmnd. 7120, 21.

27. Ibid., 22.

28. Ibid., 23.

29. Ibid.

30. Wynter Crawford, leader of Barbados's Congress Party, was the editor-proprietor of *The Observer*.

31. Cmnd. 7120, 75. Others, such as Grantley Adams, disagreed with Crawford's view. In a subsequent intervention Adams contended,

> over and over again we have deplored the suggestion of a transfer to the US and I once more emphasise this. Over and over again since the bases were leased the Caribbean Labour Congress has deplored the transfer of the areas. I think the last general election results in Barbados allow me to claim to speak for more people in Barbados than Mr. Crawford. In my opinion if a plebiscite were taken 99.9 per cent of the people would vote against the view expressed.

Adams's strong reaction shows the issue of relations with the US did stir strong passions amongst the leadership and presumably the people.

32. The British Government's aim underwent an evolution; while Clement Atlee and Ernest Bevin between 1947–51 looked for 'equality', Macmillan by 1957–58 (around the time the Federation was inaugurated) would speak of 'interdependence' and 'junior partnership' with the US. See, for instance, Roger W. Louis and Ronald Robinson, 'The Imperialism of Decolonization', *Journal of Imperial and Commonwealth History* 22, no. 3 (September 1994): 481.

33. President Eisenhower to Harold Macmillan, July 20, 1957 and Harold Macmillan to President Eisenhower July 21, 1957, PREM 11/2880.

34. Confidential Despatch No. 158, November 29, 1966, FO 371/185004, National Archives (Kew Gardens).

35. Harold Macmillan to Sir Norman Brooke, February 21, 1963, PREM 11/2880.

36. Lord Perth to Harold Macmillan, February 23, 1957, PREM 11/3239.

37. Duncan Sandys to John Boyd-Carpenter, November 26, 1963, DSND 15/5, Lord Sandys's Papers, Churchill Archive Centre (Cambridge)

38. Harold Macmillan to Duncan Sandys, August 1, 1960, DSND 15/5, Lord Sandys's Papers, Churchill Archive Centre (Cambridge).

39. Alan Lennox-Boyd to Harold Macmillan, November 5, 1958, PREM 11/2880.

40. The historical record shows that the colonial secretary and his colleagues in the Cabinet were expecting an imminent Communist take-over of the West Indian labour movement. For instance, in August 1952 the governor of Jamaica reassured his superiors in the Colonial Office: 'Adams [then President of the CLC] is said to have taken an anti-communist stand and expelled those unions which have maintained World Federation of Trade Union affiliations'. A few months later, the governor warned, 'it may be that the Caribbean Labour Congress will be captured

by Communists'. For the next two decades this ideological onslaught would undoubtedly impinge on the region's constitutional evolution, not the least by fragmenting its labour movement. See Report to the Colonial Office from the governor of Jamaica for the months of August and October 1952, CO 1031/132. As an illustration of the divisions this produced in the labour movement, refer to 'Adams's speech denounced', in *Caribbean Labour Congress: Monthly Bulletin* (September–October 1948):1. The US missile range project, on the other hand, almost coincided with Montego Bay — as the earliest records on its existence are from 1949. Under the aegis of the US Air Missile Test Centre (Patrick Air Force Base, Cape Canaveral) this project represented the spinal cord of the missile testing programme. Under the terms of the Long Proving Ground Agreement (between the US and the British Government) the US would have the right to 'establish, maintain and use submarine cables' within those British Caribbean territories included in the Federation of the West Indies. Consequently, since the 1950s the coast off of the Leeward Islands (particularly Antigua) would function as an impact area, more often than not in connection to the testing of Inter-Continental Ballistic Missiles (ICBMs). See, for instance, FO 371/148606.

41. The literature on the federal demise is remarkably abundant. See, for example A. Etzioni, 'A Union that Failed: The Federation of the West Indies 1958–1962' in *Political Unification* (New York: Holt, 1965); C.L.R. James, *Federation 'We failed miserably' How and Why* (Port-of-Spain: PNM Publishing, 1962); Lewis, Gordon, *The Growth of the Modern West Indies*, 368-86; John Mordecai, *The West Indies: The Federal Negotiations*, 457–62; Trevor Munroe, *The Politics of Constitutional Decolonization*, 122-46; Norman Manley, 'Reflections on the former Federation' in *Norman Manley and the New Jamaica*, ed. Rex Nettleford 178–84; Jesse Proctor, 'Constitutional Defects and the Collapse of the West Indian Federation', *Public Law* (Summer, 1964); Hugh Springer, *Reflections on the Failure of the First West Indies Federation*, Occasional Papers in International Affairs, 4 (Harvard University, July 1962).

42. Present Position and Prospects for the Federation, April 1961, CAB 133/287.

43. Ibid.

44. Please note that until 1960 two governors had full executive responsibility over the Leeward and the Windward groups: one governor for each set of islands. In 1956 new constitutions incorporating the ministerial system came into effect in all the territories of the Windward and Leeward groups. Further constitutional advances led in January 1960 to new local constitutions for each territory and the abolition of the posts of governor for the two groupings. See, for instance, 'Leeward and Windward Islands: Comparative Study of the Existing Constitutional Provisions' (Port of Spain: Federal Attorney General's Chambers, 1961) as well as 'Questionnaire with Commentary on the Independence Constitutions' (Port of Spain: Federal Attorney General's Chambers, 1961).

45. Unlike what most regional studies suggest, it was London, not the political leadership in Kingston that in the end enabled the holding of the Jamaican referendum. The files pertaining to the Colonial Office, particularly CO 1031/3264 'Discussions with Jamaica on Federation 1960–61, portray a clearer picture. In January 1960

Norman Manley (premier of Jamaica) held lengthy discussions with the newly appointed Colonial Secretary Iain Macleod and among other things 'asked how Jamaica would stand for separate Commonwealth membership were she to go it alone'. Although sustaining the view that 'international conditions made it necessary for sovereign states to be of and have a reasonable size, population and resources', Macleod did not discourage the possibility wholeheartedly. The transcript of the last meeting between them records that 'it was accepted that no threat, undue pressure or punitive action was contemplated' [in the case of Jamaica seceding]. Thus the suggestion that the British Government did not put enough pressure on Jamaica to prevent its secession is, to a large extent, accurate. After the referendum, and in reply to mounting criticism for not preventing the secession, the Colonial Office suggested

> HMG was not consulted before Manley gave the undertaking to submit the matter to a referendum; indeed we were as much surprised as anybody. The undertaking having been given, however, it is difficult to see how [we] could have ordered Manley not to hold a referendum. Constitutionally, by that time, we had no power to do so. What we could have done, of course, was to announce that we would take no notice of the referendum whatever the result. But again politically it would have been extremely difficult for [us] to do this in the teeth of a decision by the premier of the largest and perhaps the most affluent unit of the Federation.

D. Williams to Lord Hailes, June 17, 1965, HAIS 5/79.

46. As suggested below, Trinidad and Tobago would soon achieve full independence.

47. US Embassy in London to Dean Rusk, 741f.00/9-1461, September 14, 1961, RG 59, (National Archives and Records Administration at College Park, Maryland).

48. CO 1031/4274, quoted for instance in *The West Indies: British Documents on the End of Empire* eds. S.R. Ashton and David Killingray (London: HMSO, 1999), lxxi.

49. Captain B. Ryan to R.H. Foster, November 15, 1961, 741f.5/11-1561, RG 59, (National Archives and Records Administration at College Park, Maryland).

50. Norman Manley to Arthur Creech Jones, September 27, 1961, ACJ 25/6.

Chapter 5: The Colonial Office and the Eastern Caribbean Crisis

1. US Embassy in London to Dean Rusk, 741f.00/9-1461, September 14, 1961, RG 59, (National Archives and Records Administration at College Park, Maryland).

2. Iain Macleod to Harold Macmillan, September 22, 1961, PREM 11/ 4074. Also see Douglas Williams to Lord Hailes, June 17, 1965, Lord Hailes Papers, container HAIS 5/79, Churchill Archive Centre (Cambridge). In retrospect and in reference to the outcome of the Jamaican referendum Douglas Williams contended 'indeed we were as much surprised as anybody'.

3. Harold Macmillan to Lord Avon, February 21, 1962, CAB 134/1561.

4. PREM 11/4074. Note that Macleod's specific contention on this regard went as follows: 'In view of the size, population (1.6 million) and economic viability of Jamaica this will be a demand which, with the precedents of Sierra Leone and Cyprus before us, we could not resist.'

5. Note that the People's National Movement was founded by Dr Eric Williams in 1956 and wielded power from its inception until 1981.

6. On the financial aspect please note that by 1961 the national income per capita per annum under the Federation was £104, compared with Portugal's £71, the Congo's £24.50 or India's £22. Nonetheless, at least then, the Little Eight (plus Jamaica) lagged behind Puerto Rico's £174. See Brief for Harold Macmillan's Visit to the West Indies, April 1961, CAB 133/ 287.

7. Dr Eric E. Williams (1911-1981) pertains to the pantheon of Caribbean leaders, who like Alexander Bustamante and Norman Manley, brought the Anglophone Caribbean to its current postcolonial status. The closest to the archetype of a 'philosopher-king' in the Caribbean, Williams had been born and educated, up to secondary school, in Trinidad. After receiving an islandwide scholarship, he enrolled in 1929 in St. Catherine's Society in Oxford, where three years later he was awarded a First Class Honours BA degree in modern history. By 1938 Williams attained the degree of Doctor of Philosophy from Oxford, after his submission of the widely acclaimed *The Economic Aspect of the West Indian Slave Trade and Slavery*, which was first published in 1944 as *Capitalism and Slavery*. In 1939 he migrated to the US to teach at Howard University. While at Howard, Williams began working as a consultant to the Anglo-American Caribbean Commission. By 1948 he left Howard to head the research branch of the Caribbean Commission. After eight years Williams retired from this position while publicly denouncing what he saw as the Commission's 'crypto-colonialist' policies. Simultaneously, Williams returned to his native Trinidad and Tobago and became heavily involved in politics. A year later, in 1956, Williams founded the People's National Movement, of which he immediately became the leader. In September of the same year his newly formed party won the local elections and Williams rose to the position of chief minister of the Trinidadian archipelago. By August 1962, as Trinidad and Tobago achieved independence within the Commonwealth, Williams became her first prime minister, remaining as such until his death in March 1981.

8. *Report of the West Indies Constitutional Conference 1961*, Cmnd. 1417 (London: HMSO).

9. Iain Macleod to Harold Macmillan, PREM 11/ 4074.

10. Ibid.

11. Vere Bird dominated the politics of Antigua for more than four decades. He held on to power from 1951 to 1994, with a five-year interregnum in the early 1970s. Born late in 1910, Bird grew up in a crowded slum in St. John's, the capital. His schooling was irregular and brief, but he was able to amplify his education with the help of the Salvation Army. Bird's first step on the political ladder came with his election to the executive of the Antigua Trades and Labour Union in 1939. As in the neighbouring territories, the Union found an influential political arm in the Antigua Labour Party — which Bird dominated and through which he became the island's first chief minister in 1951 and eventually its first prime minister in 1981. Although his tenure in public office is usually intertwined with the introduction of free secondary education, domestic electricity, an airport, a deep-water harbour, new roads and an aggressive promotion of tourism, all in all it was not a completely

rosy picture. Bird's legacy has been forever stained with the proven charge, as he himself admitted in 1992, that during his years in office he had succumbed to corruption in order to make things rather comfortable for his family. The historical figure of this complex Caribbean leader needs in-depth examination and those who embark upon a serious study of his public life and persona will have to juggle these competing elements in assessing the true meaning and value of his legacy. See, for instance, 'Antiguan Leader Bird's Funeral Set for July 11', The *Weekly Gleaner* (July 7– 13, 1999): 13.

12. Please note that at least until 1962, St. Kitts–Nevis–Anguilla was the only island of the Little Eight, besides Barbados, not receiving grant aid from the British Treasury.

13. For a detailed analysis of Eric Williams's policy and general philosophy towards federation and how it should be implemented see, for instance, *The Economics of Nationhood* (Port of Spain: Office of the Premier and Ministry of Finance, September 11, 1959). For Norman Manley's position see, *The Federation of the West Indies*, Ministry Paper no. 18 (Kingston: Office of the Premier, May 1959).

14. Prime Minister Macmillan on the Future of Jamaica, September 27, 1961, PREM 11/ 4074.

15. Ibid. Please note that the then ruling party in British Guiana, the Indian People's Progressive Party, was almost exclusively made up of members of East Indian ancestry. The argument described above on the demographics of the region, regarding Jamaica *vis-à-vis* British Guiana, does make some sense. If the population of Jamaica by 1961 was approximately 1.642 million, and that of British Guiana almost 450,000 (of which almost half were of African descent) then it was understandable that the East Indian establishment did not advocate joining a predominantly black federation. However, the removal of Jamaica would still leave (including Trinidad and Tobago) almost 1.493 million souls mostly of African descent to contend with. In other words, the Colonial Policy Committee's reasoning was at least on this count somewhat faulty.

16. See, for instance, Robert Shepherd, *Iain Macleod* (London: Hutchinson, 1994). In this biography of Iain Macleod the author suggests that during the latter part of September 1961, Macmillan had discussed with Macleod his plan for removing him from the Colonial Office. As the Uganda Constitutional Conference was fast approaching, no official announcement was produced until Monday, October 9, 1961.

17. See, for example, Harold Macmillan, *At the End of the Day* (London: Macmillan, 1973). In his political memoirs Macmillan comments, 'had I thought there would be some relief from the Colonial Office, I was doomed to disappointment. I soon found that Maudling was quite as "progressive" as Macleod. Indeed in some respects he seemed *plus royaliste que le roi*.'

18. See, for instance, Richard Lamb, *The Macmillan Years 1957–1963: The Emerging Truth* (London: Murray Publishers, 1995), 309. The agenda for this summit, as Lamb suggests, dealt almost exclusively with the issue of whether or not to resume atmospheric nuclear testing. By the end both men had agreed to make preparations for renewed atmospheric tests at Christmas Island and to 'hold their hand to see whether progress could be made on Berlin and disarmament'.

19. Brief from West Indian Department A to Foreign Office, December 12, 1961, FO 371/ 155731.

20. Ibid. Please note that, as suggested below, what really disturbed the British Government was not the increase of population in the Caribbean per se, but rather the impact that surge could most definitely have on the number of black immigrants streaming to the British Isles. On that account, and echoing what had been Churchill's position in the early 1950s, in this same paper then Colonial Secretary Reginald Maudling suggested that the British Government

> cannot allow the flow [of immigrants] into the UK to continue at its present rate. Otherwise we would run the risk of precipitating a sharp increase in racial feeling in the UK. Our experience has been that even a few such incidents produce an entirely disproportionate adverse reaction in world opinion, which is most harmful to our posture as an enlightened colonial power.

21. Ibid.

22. Iain Macleod to Lord Hailes, January 29, 1960, HAIS 4/31. Churchill Archive Centre (Cambridge).

23. FO 371/ 155731.

24. Harold Macmillan to Duncan Sandys, August 1, 1960, DSND 15/5. As contended below, the issue of whether or not to join the European Common Market did exercise a moderate influence in the British Government's attitude throughout this process. In August 1960, Prime Minister Harold Macmillan conveyed the significance of this in a letter to the newly appointed Minister for Commonwealth Relations Duncan Sandys:

> The second great question which I want you to study is the problem of the Commonwealth in relation to Europe. If we went into the Common Market we should give up the preferences and all that that implies. Finally there is the question that we would really be discriminating against the Commonwealth. This is perhaps the most urgent problem in the free world today.

25. For further reference to the rise of racial tension in Jamaica between 1959 and 1961 refer for instance to Lord Hailes to Iain Macleod, August 19, 1960, HAIS 4/31. Also see John Mordecai to Lord Hailes, March 1, 1961, HAIS 4/28. It is important to note that most of the references to racial tension in Jamaica, during this period, referred mostly to the Rastafarian Movement and not surprisingly to its alleged relationship with the Communist world. For instance, in his letter to Lord Hailes Mordecai suggests that he [Manley] was worried by reliable accounts of small Communist cells developing in the distant parishes, with an illogical opposition to Federation as one of their fixations.'

26. Brief from Reginald Maulding to Harold Macmillan, December 15, 1961, CO 967/ 400.

27. Ibid.

28. Please note the actions taken by the US Government, immediately after the Jamaican referendum, signalled a strong degree of reticence at the prospect of being further involved in the affairs of the British Government in the Caribbean. The Americans expressed their reluctance to implement their part of the Leeward and Windward Joint Economic Mission until the disentangling of the political future of the area.

29. Ambler Thomas became the liaison between the Colonial Office and the Government of the Federation of the West Indies in February 1960. Thomas was the civil servant who had more direct contact with the issues pertaining to the Federation. For more details on Thomas's acquaintance with West Indian affairs refer to his first letter to Lord Hailes, written just a few days after his appointment. Ambler Thomas to Lord Hailes, February 17, 1960, HAIS 4/ 35.

30. John Mordecai to Ambler Thomas, October 11, 1961, HAIS 4/ 28.

31. Ibid.

32. For a detailed analysis of the Federation's legal structure see the British Caribbean Federation Act of 1956, 4 & 5 Eliz 2 c63.

33. Ibid.

34. Sir Grantley Adams's (1898–71) life is closely intertwined with the modern history of Barbados. The son of the prominent headmaster of St. Giles Boys' School, Adams came from a respected and well-established black middle-class family. By 1910, young Grantley was granted a scholarship to study at Harrison College, the most prestigious secondary school in Barbados. Like other talented students before him, such as for example Charles Duncan O'Neale in 1899, he sat for the Barbados Scholarship in 1918. After winning that prize, Adams departed for Oxford where, during the first week of Michaelmas Term 1919, he matriculated as a member of the then St. Catherine's Society. The archives in St. Catherine's show that in 1921, young Grantley successfully sat the Classical Moderations. However, for the next two years he would study Theology and Law. After obtaining his BA in Law, in 1923, Adams moved to London where he read law for two more years at the Gray's Inn. Unlike Clennel Wickham some years before him, Adams returned to Barbados a liberal in the Asquith mould. His ideas, however, underwent a transformation and by the 1930s he began to identify himself with the colony's more progressive forces. After two unsuccessful attempts, in 1934 Adams won a seat in the House of Assembly representing the parish of St. Joseph. The riots and their aftermath, however, marked his real political birth. During this episode Adams became the de facto spokesman of the working masses. This period became a defining moment in his public life, for Adams had now crossed the Rubicon. In 1940, under his leadership, the Barbados Labour Party won its first general election and from then on he would become chief minister from 1946 until 1954, premier from 1954 until 1958, and first and only prime minister of the West Indies Federation from 1958 until 1962. After the demise of the Federation Adams returned to Barbados and after independence in 1966, became leader of the opposition, a position he held until his final retirement in 1970. Less than a year later, on November 28, 1971, Sir Grantley Adams passed away in his native Barbados.

35. Transcript of meeting between Harold Macmillan and Grantley Adams, December 4, 1961, PREM 11/ 3623.

36. Ibid.

37. Note that there seems to be an inconsistency, or at least it appears so, between what Grantley Adams suggested in his meeting with Macmillan and what the intelligence stemming from the West Indies reveals. On the one hand, the transcript of that meeting has Adams contending that 'a Federation of the Leeward, Windward and

Barbados would be lamentable.' See PREM 11/ 3623. However the briefing sent to Macmillan a few days before the meeting with Adams suggested that

> Sir Grantley Adams should be given no encouragement to think the British Government would give much financial aid to a rump Federation which excluded Trinidad and Tobago. Since he and certain other Federal Ministers are believed to be hoping for a Federation limited to Barbados, the Leeward and Windward Islands.

See Ibid. Minutes from colonial secretary to Prime Minister, December 1, 1961.

38. Ibid. Citing Macleod's commitment in that same minute, Maudling reminds Macmillan, 'he [Macleod] had agreed [before leaving the Colonial Office] that early in the present parliamentary session legislation would be introduced to enable Jamaica to secede ... if possible this legislation will be enacted by March 1962.'

39. Reginald Maudling to the Lord Chancellor, January 9, 1962, PREM 11/ 4074. It is important to note that precisely in January 1962 the British Cabinet confronted a very difficult and sensitive issue in regard to the future of the Federation of Central Africa. The African leadership had by then demanded majority rule against the wishes of the white settler community, and it should be added against the wishes of some influential members of the British Cabinet, and thus the spectre of dissolution was quite ominous.

40. Brief from West Indian Department A to Foreign Office, December 12, 1961, FO 371/ 155731.

41. Federation in the Caribbean: Predictions and Possibilities, October 31, 1961, CO 1031/ 3374.

42. Ibid.

43. Interview to Reginald Maudling, April 25, 1968, MSS Brit Emp s. 484 at 14, Bodleian Library (Oxford).

44. Reginald Maudling to Lord Chancellor, January 9, 1962, PREM 11/ 4074.

45. Ibid.

46. See the West Indian Act of 1962, 10 & 11 Eliz 2 c19. This Act of Parliament granted the Colonial Office

> (i) the power to provide for the secession of colonies from, and dissolution of, the West Indies Federation; (ii) the power to provide for the interim performance of functions heretofore performed by the Federal authorities for the benefit of the federated colonies; (iii) the power to establish common courts for the West Indian colonies; (iv) the power to provide for the government of certain West Indian colonies and (v) the power to establish new forms of government in place of the West Indies Federation.

This legislation received Royal Assent on April 18, and consequently an Order in Council was made on May 23, providing for the dissolution of the Federation on May 31, 1962.

47. Reginald Maudling to Lord Chancellor, January 9, 1962, PREM 11/ 4074.

48. Ibid.

Chapter 6: The Little Eight Scenario

1. Interview with Reginald Maudling, April 25, 1968, MSS Brit Emp s. 484, Bodleian Library (Oxford).

2. In a 1961 confidential brief the Colonial Office described Sir Arthur Lewis (1915-1991) as a '47 year old St. Lucian, educated at the London School of Economics and Principal of the University College of the West Indies. He is an eminent man. He has been Professor of Economics at Manchester. Later he was Dr. Nkrumah's economic adviser. He was for a time Deputy Director of the United Nations Special Fund...He is universally respected, is known to have no political bias, and, above all, is liked by Dr. Williams and can get access to him which is not easy except for the favoured few.' For this confidential brief on Lewis see, for instance, 'Attitudes of Units to formation of a Federation of the Eight' CO 1031/ 3374. Also note that Professor Lewis was the same one who many years earlier in 1939 had published 'Labour in the West Indies'. By 1979 Lewis was awarded the Nobel Prize for Economics.

3. Arthur Lewis to Hugh Fraser, January 2, 1962, CO 1031/ 3374.

4. See, for instance, Arthur Lewis, *The Agony of the Eight*, 10. Please note that Lewis knew Williams very well, and as Lewis years later claimed, 'Dr. Williams and I are old friends, who have known each other since we were both students 30 years ago. We admire and respect each other, and each of us knows that he can call on the other's talents in support of national causes.'

5. CO 1031/ 3374.

6. Please note that that senior civil servants in the Colonial Office and in the Commonwealth Relations Office produced a very detailed briefing on the personality of this man Maudling was about to meet. The contents of this file are so interesting that they deserve special mention:

    > Dr. Williams has a very involved personality. It is always useful to remember that he is somewhat deaf and wears a hearing aid. He is very intelligent and can exercise great charm in discussion, if in the mood. He has, however, been seriously overworking for some time. He has made himself something of a recluse, socially. He is inclined to brood and is also apt to take seriously remarks that may be passed rather casually. In consequence, he sometimes imagines slights where none are intended. Some of these difficulties of personality are caused by an unsuccessful married life. Legal complications arising from the divorce of his first wife in the US make it impossible for him to visit that country. This point has increased his sensibility of dealing with the US authorities.

    See DO 200/ 27. The American archives confirm his 'alimony problems' in the US; see, for instance, despatch from US Consul General [in Port-of-Spain, Trinidad] to the US State Department, March 1961; contained in 741f.13/2-460 RG 59.

7. Mordecai, *The West Indies: The Federal Negotiations*, 441. Please note that some time later, in a conversation with Governor Solomon Hochoy, Eric Williams would offer a very candid post mortem on the PNM's decision. In this interview Eric Williams would suggest that the decision had been entertained for quite some time.

    > We made it clear two years ago [in 1960] that we never intended to go in, with Manley out of the Federation; one from ten did not amount to nine, it amounted to zero. Britain gave in to Manley on every account giving him everything. Macleod asked me not to attack Manley on his proposal to hold a referendum but it became silly... . When Macleod came to the Colonial

Office it was immediately clear that Britain had abandoned the Lennox-Boyd policy. In my opinion — and I acted on this assumption — Britain was tired of the West Indies and wanted to get rid of them as quickly and as cheaply as possible. This was clear to Manley and he took advantage of it ... when Macleod came he made it plain that he was in as much of a hurry as we were to get West Indian independence. His mistake, in my view, was that he would accept any compromise, after him the deluge. But he was going to get a settlement and so it went on until I could not accept the Lancaster House constitution [proposed by the Colonial Office in June 1961] and you could not have sent a gunboat to make me.

Transcript of conversation between Solomon Hochoy and Eric Williams, HAIS 4/32.

8. Iain Macleod to Lord Hailes, November 15, 1960, HAIS 4/31.
9. John Stow to Lord Hailes, December 20, 1961, HAIS 4/27.
10. Please Note that Eric Williams and his PNM had scored a landslide victory at the last local general elections on December 4, 1961. With an electoral participation of 88.4 per cent, the PNM took 58 per cent of the poll, against 41 per cent for the main opposition party – the Democratic Labour Party (DLP). This meant Eric Williams' effectively controlled 20 out of the 30 seats in the territory's General Legislature. See, for instance, the *Trinidad Guardian*, December 5, 1961.
11. Minutes of meeting between Reginald Maudling and Eric Williams, January 16, 1962, CO 1031/ 3374.
12. Ibid.
13. Ibid.
14. Ibid.
15. Ibid.
16. Interview to Reginald Maudling, April 25, 1968, MSS Brit Emp s. 484, Bodleian Library (Oxford), 15.
17. Errol Barrow (1920–87), the son of an Episcopal Minister (Reginald Barrow), was born in the northern parish of St. Lucy in Barbados. Barrow was a direct descendant of Charles Duncan O'Neale, as his mother was the sister of the late founder of the Democratic League. In December 1939 Barrow won a scholarship in classics to Codrington College but chose instead to join the Royal Air Force. For the next few years Barrow served as personal navigation officer to the commander in chief of the British army at the Rhine (1940–42), Air Chief Marshall Sir Sholto Douglas. Once the war in Europe finished, Barrow enrolled as a student of economics and law at the London School of Economics (LSE) in 1947. Perhaps one of the most fundamental intellectual influences on Barrow and his contemporaries was Professor Harold Laski (1893–1950), who since 1926 had been teaching at the LSE and was best known for his strong socialist persuasion. Amongst Barrow's contemporaries at the LSE were Michael Manley and Forbes Burnham. Barrow took his final exams at the Inns of Court in 1949 and graduated from the LSE in 1950 with a BSc in economics. On completion of his studies Barrow was recalled by the Royal Air Force for release and repatriation, and his application to resign his commission was approved. Having retained his rank as flying officer and already married with a child, Barrow returned to Barbados in 1950. Like others before him, Barrow did

not hesitate in joining the Barbados Labour Party (BLP) under the leadership of Grantley Adams. His immersion in the island's political process crystallized in 1951. By 1955, together with other disaffected colleagues from the BLP, Barrow founded the Democratic Labour Party and in December 1961 became Barbados's third chief minister. By 1966 he led his country to independence, thus becoming Barbados's first prime minister, a position he held, albeit with an interregnum between 1976 and 1986, until his death on June 1, 1987.

18. Minutes of meeting between Reginald Maudling and Federal Cabinet, January 15, 1962, CO 1031/ 3374.

19. Arthur Lewis to Hugh Fraser, January 2, 1962, CO 1031/ 3374.

20. Sir John Stow (1911–98), as becomes apparent in the following chapters, played a key role throughout this process. The son of the late Sir Alexander Stow, young Stow attended the Harrow School and Pembroke College, Cambridge. Upon completing his formal education, he joined the Colonial Office as an administrative officer in Lagos, Nigeria, in 1934. The next twenty years would see him as an officer of the Secretariat in Gambia (1938), chief secretary of the Windward Islands (1944), colonial administrator of St. Lucia (1947), director of establishments in Kenya (1952–55) and chief secretary of Jamaica (1955–59). In 1959 the colonial secretary appointed him governor and commander in chief of Barbados; he remained in this position until independence in 1966. Stow's strong rapport with the colonial leadership led to his appointment as Barbados's first governor general after independence.

21. Interview to Reginald Maudling, April 25, 1968, MSS Brit Emp s. 484, Bodleian Library (Oxford), 14–15. The historical record shows that by the time of this visit the colonial secretary and his colleagues saw the sheer presence of the federal ministers as an impingement on the British Government's capacity to unravel the crisis. The criticisms levelled at Sir Grantley Adams and his colleagues were very sharp, 'they [the federal ministers] were not and never had been a strong Government and had no prospect of ever producing one'. Additionally Maudling was convinced that these ministers were 'in no position to co-operate as they had no influence'. Note that documents pertaining to the Colonial Office as well as to the Hailes private collection reveal constant references to the federal prime minister's 'decrepitude', 'sleepy exterior' and 'general laziness'. Philip Rogers to Lord Hailes, January 18, 1960, HAIS 4/20; Ambler Thomas to Lord Hailes, February 17, 1960, HAIS 4/ 20, Note on Adams, April 22, 1959, PREM 11/3623.

22. Antigua's Speech from the Throne, January 3, 1962, CO 1031/ 3283.

23. Ibid.

24. See Richard Cheltenham, 'Constitutional and Political Development in Barbados, 1946–1966' (PhD dissertation, University of Manchester, 1970), 196–97.

25. Note that the DLP had won 14 out of the 24 seats in the House of Assembly. However the total number of votes it accumulated, of 39,533 (36.3 per cent of the poll), was less than the Barbados Labour Party's (BLP) 40,150 which amounted to 36.8 per cent of the poll. It seems that the DLP's victory was largely aided by the constituency disposition of 14,017 votes (22 per cent supporting a third party — the Barbados National Party (BNP), led by influential local conservatives). See, for

instance, *The Barbados Advocate*, December 5, 1961. Additionally, refer to John Mordecai, *The West Indies: The Federal Negotiations*, 435–36.

26. See Arthur Lewis, *The Agony of the Eight*, 21.

27. Statement on West Indies Federation by the Barbados Democratic Labour Party 1960, CO 1031/ 4272. On that occasion the DLP had gone as far as to conclude [in reference to the Jamaica Labour Party's insistence on withdrawing], 'the solution is not secession; it is to remain and lead'.

28. Minutes of meeting between Reginald Maudling, Hilton Poynton, Ambler Thomas and Saville Garner at the House of Commons, January 30, 1962, CO 1031/ 3374.

29. Minutes from third meeting of Colonial Policy Committee, February 2, 1962, CAB 134/ 1561.

30. Memorandum by Reginald Maudling to the Colonial Policy Committee, January 31, 1962, CAB 134/ 1561. Note that this Order in Council would also establish an interim organization to oversee the regional common services; as one of the constitutional duties of the outgoing federal government was looking after the University College of the West Indies, the Federal Supreme Court, the Eastern Caribbean Currency Board and various other advisory and technical services from which all the territories benefited. Acknowledging that none of the smaller territories could support any of these services on its own, the establishment of an interim organization would ensure, at least in theory, that pending the definition of the area's political future, nothing would prejudice their continuation on a regional basis. In essence the political side of the original federation would be dissolved, while this new apolitical organization took over the federal assets, liabilities and responsibilities.

31. Ibid., 4–5.

32. Ibid. Minutes of third meeting of Colonial Policy Committee, February 2, 1962.

33. Ibid.

34. Ibid.

35. Ibid.

36. See Arthur Lewis, *The Agony of the Eight*, 11–12. Note that the British West Indian dollar, which by 1966 would become the Eastern Caribbean dollar, was by then worth approximately 58.24 US cents or 4/2d sterling. Carleen O'Loughlin, *Economic and Political Change in the Leeward and Windward Islands* (New Haven: Yale University Press, 1967), vi.

37. Memorandum by Reginald Maudling to the Colonial Policy Committee, January 31, 1962, CAB 134/1561.

38. Transcript of conversation between Mr. Christensen (US Consul General in Trinidad and Tobago) and Eric Williams, March 1962, CO 1031/ 3375.

39. Refer to the Trinidad Independence Act of 1962, 10 & 11 Eliz 2 c54. For newly declassified evidence demonstrating that indeed a feud ensued between the British Government and the Trinidadian Government over the financial settlement on independence see, for instance, Letter from Duncan Sandys (by then colonial secretary) to Harold Macmillan, November 13, 1962, DSND 8/12. An extract from that letter as follows:

> Dr. Williams has written to you in discourteous terms complaining of the financial settlement which, after long negotiation with the Treasury, I was able to offer him. We must expect Dr. Williams sooner or later to attack the British Government publicly for what he will no doubt call "niggardliness". To give him anything like he wants would be out of line with the settlements, which we have recently made with Jamaica and Uganda, and would therefore create further problems with those other countries. The Treasury, in any case, is not prepared to find any more money and I see no reason to press them to do so.

40. Lewis, *The Growth of the Modern West Indies*, 330–42. Also refer to O'Loughlin, *Economic and Political Change in the Leeward and Windward Islands*, 16-17, 23-25, 30-32, 54-56.

41. Interview with Reginald Maudling, April 25, 1968, MSS Brit Emp s. 484, Bodleian Library (Oxford), 15.

42. Minutes of Meeting of the Colonial Policy Committee, December 20, 1961, CAB 134/ 1561. See also Briefs from West Indian Department A to Foreign Office, December 12, 1961, FO 371/ 15571.

43. PREM 11/ 3666.

44. Minutes of Colonial Policy Committee Meeting, May 18, 1962, CAB 134/ 1561.

45. See Richard Lamb, *The Macmillan Years*, 342.

46. See, for instance, Theodore C. Sorensen, *Kennedy* (New York: Harper & Row, 1965), 326–46. Also refer to John F. Kennedy 'Inaugural Address' in *Great Speeches* (London: Harper Collins Audio Books, 1996), sound cassette. Note that at his first State of the Union Address (on January 30, 1961) President Kennedy issued the following warning to the members of Congress:

    > Each day the crises multiply. Each day their solution grows more difficult. *Each day we draw nearer to the hour of maximum danger.* I feel I must inform the Congress that in each of the principal areas of crisis, the tide of events has been running out and time has not been our friend. (Emphasis added.)

47. Minutes of Meeting of the Colonial Policy Committee, December 19, 1962, CAB 134/ 2153.

48. Memorandum from Harold Macmillan to Norman Brooke, February 21, 1962, PREM 11/ 3666.

49. John Stow to Ambler Thomas, February 8, 1962, CO 1031/ 3374.

50. Telegram from Ebenezer Joshua to the Colonial Office, February 10, 1962, CO 1031/ 3375.

51. Telegram from Charles Southwell to other Chief Ministers, February 3, 1962, CO 1031/ 3375.

52. Hansard Parliamentary Debates, Commons (February 6, 1962) cols 231-36, CO 1031/ 3377.

53. Ibid.

Chapter 7: The Marlborough House Conference

1. Richard Cheltenham, 'Constitutional and Political Development in Barbados, 1946–1966 (PhD dissertation, University of Manchester, 1970), 198.

2. Frank L. Walcott (1916–99) as the next chapters illustrate, played a key role in the

political process of Barbados during this period. Walcott, a contemporary of Errol Barrow and Cameron Tudor, had nonetheless a completely different social, educational and political background. The son of a policeman from the parish of St. Peter, Walcott lost his father at a very early stage. Unlike, for instance, Grantley Adams and Hugh Springer, he did not attend university and unlike Wickham and Barrow he had not served in the military. Walcott represents another type of colonial leader and as such he deserves special attention, as the people of Barbados nowadays revere him as a national hero. Walcott epitomizes the colonial hero who comes from humble origins and bases his claim to leadership on his role as a trade union leader. He rose from the status of an unpretentious clerk at an obscure shop in downtown Bridgetown to assistant to the general secretary of the Barbados Workers Union (BWU, founded in 1941). Walcott inherited the Union's leadership from Springer in 1947, when the latter became the first Registrar of the University College of the University of the West Indies. By 1951 his responsibilities in Barbados's Executive Committee were quite diverse as he oversaw all matters pertaining to trade, commerce, customs and the post office. Walcott, then only 35, had earned in his own right the respect and trust of Adams and his lieutenants in the Barbados Labour Party (BLP). Yet the subsequent introduction of the ministerial system in Barbados, on February 1954, would alter that relationship. Walcott, who had anxiously cherished the prospect of a ministerial appointment, was not promoted. It is not clear how the decision was made, although it is quite obvious that Adams was behind it. There is no evidence on whether or not Walcott was consulted regarding his immediate political future. There is, however, a consensus amongst West Indian academics and commentators that Walcott felt very hurt as a result of this. This incident, which may well have served as a catalyst, marked the end of an intense professional and personal relationship between Walcott and the parliamentary leaders of the BLP. More importantly, this break-up meant that the close link between the BWU and the BLP would also be dissolved. Perhaps the dissolution of these ties would have eventually happened anyway, but certainly this personal fall out accelerated things. From then on, Walcott would play a very critical and independent role in Barbados's political life. Walcott effectively became a symbol of strength and inspiration for the BWU and as such also became an influential power broker. See Trevor Marshall, 'Give Sir Frank his proper dues', The *Barbados Advocate* (March 5, 1999): 9.

3. Richard Cheltenham, 'Constitutional and Political Development in Barbados, 1946–1966' (PhD dissertation, University of Manchester, 1970), 199–200. Arthur Lewis, *The Agony of the Eight*, 23. Also refer to the *Daily News* February 27–March 3, 1962.

4. Conference of Chief Ministers of Leeward and Windward Islands and Premier of Barbados: Comprehensive Summary of Decisions, March 3, 1962, CAB 134/1561.

5. Ibid. No federal income tax was to be levied during the first five years of the proposed federation.

6. Ibid.

7. Ibid; also refer to despatch no. 130, Barbados Government (1962).

8. Ibid.

9. Milton Cato to H. Burrowes, March 23, 1962, CO 1031/ 3375.

10. Ibid. Memorandum from Charles Southwell to other Chief Ministers, March 31, 1962.

11. Telegram from John Stow to Reginald Maudling, March 15, 1962.

12. Lord Hailes to Ambler Thomas, March 17, 1962, CO 1031/ 3375.

13. Lord Hailes and Lord Avon, HAIS 4/ 11. Correspondence between Lord Hailes and R.A. Butler, HAIS 4/12. Correspondence between Lord Hailes and Harold Macmillan, HAIS 4/16. Note that Lord Hailes's strong connection to the Tory establishment had led influential voices in the West Indian press of the time to oppose and strongly criticize his appointment to lead the West Indies. In a peculiarly poignant editorial, published in Jamaica in 1958, these feelings were sharply conveyed:

> In Lord Hailes, Lennox-Boyd found his man. An 'uninspiring' choice booed the British press — notably the conservative London Times. Professional politician for 25 years, Hailes never emerged from second-rater. His sojourn in the West Indies as human symbol of the British Throne and personal representative of the Queen raises his official stature far beyond the wildest dreams of the boy from Prestwick, Scotland. But, as the British press implied, it is doubtful if he will be able to rise above the personal mediocrity — for all his dashing good looks and the fine figure he cuts in his uniforms of state as well as his own clothes.

See Evon Blake, 'Press: Hour of Small Talk', *Newday* (March 1958): 33.

14. Note that Bequia, together with the islands of Canouan, Mustique, Mayero and Union Island, is part of the so-called St. Vincent Grenadines. Additionally, *c.* 1962–63, the population of this tiny territory barely reached 3,750 inhabitants. For a detailed analysis of the economic realities of this small archipelago during this period see, for instance, Carleen O'Loughlin, *Economic and Political Change in the Leeward and Windward Islands,* 50–51.

15. Lord Avon to Harold Macmillan, February 11, 1962, CO 1031/ 3377. A copy of the original letter was sent to the Colonial Office and, accordingly, the quotation above comes from that version. Further research still needs to be conducted using both the Eden and Macmillan private papers to uncover whether or not there was further correspondence between them on this particular topic.

16. Ibid. Lord Avon to Reginald Maudling, April 13, 1962; for Maudling's reply, refer to his letter dated April 16, 1962, CO 1031/ 3377.

17. Minutes of the Colonial Office Meeting, CO 1031/ 3375.

18. Ibid. Sir John Stow to Errol Barrow, March 1, 1962, CO 1031/ 3375. Note that while the Bridgetown gathering was still in progress the colonial secretary had authorized Sir John Stow to transmit to the chief ministers the preliminary views of the Colonial Office on the conditions it expected a federation of the eight to satisfy. The conditions or criteria were the following:

> (i) the proposed [federal] constitution must have the approval of all the units' legislatures; (ii) the federal government must have an effective administration capable of carrying out all the duties entrusted to it; (iii) adequate arrangements should be made to preserve the law and order within the federation, providing

at least a deterrent for external aggression; (iv) there must be a diplomatic organisation capable of handling the federation's external relations with other countries and the United Nations; (v) the federation should be expected to have adequate financial resources based on independent taxing and loan-raising powers, enough to finance its own recurrent expenditure and obligations as it develops; (vi) a start must be made on a customs union; (vii) the federation must have central control of the currency; (viii) freedom of movement should be provided for its citizens; (ix) the federation should have the power to negotiate treaties that sovereign nations are entitled to forge.

19. Federation of the Eight: Background Paper, April 6, 1962, CAB 134/ 1561 (CPC 62/14).

20. Ibid. Minutes of Colonial Policy Committee Meeting, April 11, 1962, CAB 134/ 1561.

21. CO 1031/3377.

22. Federation of the Eight: Background Paper, 4-5, CAB 134/ 1561.

23. Ibid., 5, par. 7.

24. Ibid. Conference of Chief Ministers of Leeward and Windward Islands and Premier of Barbados: Comprehensive Summary of Decisions; for the politico-constitutional recommendations see, for instance, 1–7. For the economic aspects of their proposals see pp. 8–11.

25. Ibid. Federation of the Eight: Background Paper, 6.

26. Note that, for instance, during 1961 the Colonial Development and Welfare payments had been suspended in Montserrat. In addition, the Colonial Office commissioned the principal auditor for the Leeward Islands to investigate these matters. In the case of Antigua–Barbuda, irregularities had also come to light in the summer of 1961. Consequently, the colonial administrator was charged with the special responsibility of reporting to the colonial secretary on the veracity of these allegations.

27. Federation of the Eight: Background Paper, 7, CAB 134/ 1561.

28. Arthur Lewis, *The Agony of the Eight*, 22-23.

29. Professor Lewis summed up the basic underpinnings of these arguments as follows: The chief reason why the Windward and Leeward Islands are grant-in-aided is that their governments cost too much. On a strictly comparable national income basis it is normal for governments to use, for civilian purposes, around 9 to 10 per cent of the GDP. The Trinidadian proportion in 1959 was 9.5 per cent and the Barbados proportion in 1958 was 10.9 per cent. By contrast, in 1959, the proportion in the Windward Islands was 16.6 per cent and in the Leeward 22.6 per cent. This abnormal situation is due, not to the excessive use of real resources in administration, but to the abnormally high level of civil service wages and salaries in relation to national income... The cause of these islands' financial crisis is typified by the Windward Islands, where the average citizen has an income only 33 per cent of that of the average citizen of Trinidad, out of which he must pay taxes to give his civil servants an average income of 60 per cent of that of a Trinidad civil servant. The fiscal situation in the Leeward and Windward Islands will not come right until this situation is corrected.
See Working Parties Discuss Dissolution of Federation, CO 1031/ 3286.

30. During this period (*c.* 1961–62) the British Government, for instance, had agreed on a so-called taper block grant to Aden for a period of years 'immutable except under exceptional circumstances'.

31. CAB 134/ 1561.

32. Federation of the Eight: Background Paper, 7, CAB 134/ 1561.

33. Ibid., 6.

34. Ibid.

35. Ibid., 8.

36. Ibid., 10 and CO 1031/ 3375, Minutes of Colonial Office Meeting, March 21, 1962. Note that the colonial secretary was willing to make an exception with Barbados.

37. Ibid.

38. Ibid.

39. Douglas Williams to F.G. Burrett, May 21, 1962, CO 1031/ 3365.

40. CAB 134/ 1561.

41. Ibid.

42. The main features of the counter-proposals which the Cabinet put forward were the following:

    (i) add to the concurrent powers of the Federation a provision whereby the Federal Legislature could by simple majority declare any subject to be concurrent, and add by way of explanation that in our view all services should be run on a federal basis unless there was strong reasons why this should not be the case (as in education because of religious differences); (ii) federal powers should be so constructed as to ensure a flow of funds to the centre. For this purpose income tax should become an exclusive Federal subject from the beginning, but there should be a fiscal inquiry into the way in which the Federation would be financed and the division of revenues between the Federal Government and the units. One of the reasons for making this proposal is that, if political and financial power is concentrated at the centre in this way, the political leaders from the islands will go to the Federal Government, and unit politics (with all the corruption and chicanery that goes with them) will have much less importance; (iii) the Conference has itself proposed that the Federal Government shall have the power to set 'Commissions of Enquiry in respect of any matter tending to undermine good government or financial stability in any part of the Federation. [We should further propose] that there be a further provision (on the lines of that in the Nigerian Constitution) whereby the Federal Government could take over the administration of any island in the event of the collapse of the administration in an individual unit; (iv) as for unit constitutions, [we should] propose that if the Federation still wished to preserve a Senate, we might provide that the elected commissioners should in addition sit as an Upper House, with certain revisionary functions. Otherwise, the Federal Senate should be abolished; (v) it will probably be necessary that grants-in-aid should be given to the Federal and not the Unit Governments. Subject to this and to discussions of this proposal with the Treasury, we would be prepared to settle for a tapering block grant over a fixed period of years with no detailed financial control by HMG, on the understanding (as in Aden) that it is immutable except under exceptional circumstances. (Emphasis added.)

See Ibid., 9–10.

43. CO 1031/3264.

44. CAB 134/ 1561.

45. Despatch from Governor Stow to Ambler Thomas, April 13, 1962, CO 1031/ 3378.

46. Ibid. Telegram no. 53 from I.G. Turbott to Colonial Secretary, April 17, 1962.

47. Lewis, *The Agony of the Eight*, 24 and Richard Cheltenham, 'Constitutional and Political Development in Barbados, 1946–1966'" (PhD dissertation, University of Manchester, 1970), 201.

48. Lewis, *The Agony of the Eight*, 23.

49. See, for instance, Raymond Cohen, 'Meaning, Interpretation and International Negotiation', *Global Society*, 14 no. 3 (2000): 317.

50. See note 11, chapter 5.

51. CO 1031/4982.

52. This openly derogatory characterization, with its obvious racist undertones, unavoidably raises the issue of whether prejudice played a role in the interactions British ministers and senior civil servants had with the Eastern Caribbean's political and labour leadership. This angle deserves closer attention and as such further scrutiny.

53. See note 17, chapter 6.

54. Colonial Secretary to Colonial Policy Committee, June 18, 1962, CAB 134/ 1561.

55. Ibid., 2. Also refer to the *Report of the East Caribbean Federation Conference 1962*, Cmnd. 1746 (London: HMSO), 8.

56. Cmnd. 1746, 11.

57. Colonial Secretary to Premier of Barbados, March 12, 1962, CAB 134/ 1561.

58. Cmnd. 1746, 10.

59. CAB 134/ 1561.

60. In an open reference to this theme, years later, the former Colonial Secretary Maudling argued that 'when you get a man who calls himself Premier of a country with 10,000 people in it, it does become a little unusual'. See Interview with Reginald Maudling, April 25, 1968, MSS Brit Emp s. 484, Bodleian Library (Oxford).

61. CAB 134/ 1561.

62. The Fiscal Commission was under the supervision of Ursula Hicks, then lecturer in public finance at Oxford. Additionally, the civil service commissioners were Sir Richard Manktelow, former deputy undersecretary of agriculture, and T. M. Skinner, former director of establishments in Kenya. Dr Carleen O'Loughlin, then a research fellow at the University of the West Indies (Mona Campus), would undertake the preparation of the economic survey of the region.

63. CAB 134/ 1561.

64. Cmnd. 1746, 18.

    The Conference agreed that an advisory Regional Council of Ministers should be set up which would consist of the premier and chief ministers of each unit government (or their nominees). It would consider any problems of common interest to the eight territories concerned in connection with setting up the Federation.

In a brief to Duncan Sandys, some months later, the senior civil servants at the Colonial Office indicated that

> it was recognised to be extremely important during the interval that must necessarily elapse between the Conference and the possible establishment of the new Federation that the Governments concerned should have some machinery capable of representing their collective interests. For this purpose the Conference agreed that an advisory regional council of ministers should be set up.

The Establishment of the Regional Council of Ministers, CO 1031/ 3366.

65. Douglas Williams to F.G. Burrett, May 21, 1962, CO 1031/ 3365.

66. Record of the 12th Plenary Session, May 17, 1962, CAB 133/ 202.

67. Lewis, *The Agony of the Eight*, 24.

Chapter 8: The Suspension of the Grenada Constitution

1. Douglas Williams to F.G. Burrett, May 21, 1962, CO 1031/ 3365.

2. Note that the first three meetings of the Regional Council of Ministers (held in May, June and October 1962) mostly addressed financial and technical matters. Questions such as where to house the Council's secretariat, and so on, were considered. (Eventually it was housed in Sherbourne House, two miles away from the centre of Bridgetown). See CO 1031/ 3365 which for the most part contains all the discussions on the setting up of the Regional Council of Ministers, primarily exchanges between senior civil servants in the Colonial Office and the Treasury.

3. F.G. Burret to Douglas Williams, May 25, 1962, CO 1031/3365.

4. John Stow to Douglas Williams, May 29, 1962, CO 1031/3365.

5. Douglas Williams to F.G. Burrett, June 19, 1962, CO 1031/3365.

6. F.G. Burrett to Douglas Williams, June 28, 1962, CO 1031/3365.

7. Colin Thain and Maurice Wright, *The Treasury and Whitehall* (Oxford: Clarendon Press, 1995), 3.

8. Cmnd. 1746, 18.

9. Hugh Fraser to Edward Boyle, July 2, 1962, CO 1031/3365.

10. Edward Boyle to Hugh Fraser, July 4, 1962, CO 1031/3365.

11. See *Report of the Commission of Enquiry into the Control of Public Expenditure in Grenada During 1961 and Subsequently 1962*, Cmnd. 1735 (London: HMSO), 18–21.

12. Ibid., 3.

13. Reginald Maudling to Harold Macmillan, June 15, 1962, PREM 11/ 3664.

14. T. Bligh to J.T.A. Howard-Drake, June 18, 1962, PREM 11/ 3664.

15. Reginald Maudling reported on his action before the Commons on June 26, 1962.

16. Lord Hailes to Ambler Thomas, March 17, 1962, CO 1031/ 3375. During these meetings, held late in February 1962, the Grenada delegation advanced the following points:

> (i) the link between Grenada and Trinidad and Tobago is a natural one because of the flow of population and trade between the territories; (ii) an association on the lines of that between the British Government and Northern Ireland might be a suitable one; (iii) any decision as to the future must be put

before the GULP's Executive, the Legislature and the people of Grenada; and (iv) Grenada would need financial assistance.

17. Note that during the period 1961–63, in spite of immigration restrictions, the usual drift of predominantly male workers continued to flow from Grenada to Trinidad and Tobago. Already, by this time, some 40,000 people of Grenadian origin had established themselves in Trinidad. See, for instance, DO 200/27. Also see O'Loughlin, *Economic and Political Change in the Leeward and Windward Islands*, 53.

18. Lord Hailes to Ambler Thomas, March 17, 1962, CO 1031/3375.

19. Ibid.

20. Refer to DO 200/28 for the Colonial Office's intelligence brief on Herbert Blaize. Therein Grenada's new chief minister is described as follows:

> Mr. Blaize is aged 44. He was the first Chief Minister of Grenada and Minister of Finance, when these offices were created in 1960. His party lost the elections in March 1961, but retained his seat in the Council. His party won the recent elections, [having a six to four majority in the Executive Council]. It has the backing of the business community, planters and middle classes. He is moderate and intelligent and has sound, balanced judgment. One of the most constructive and sensible politicians in the Leeward and Windward Islands.

21. Note that since July 12, 1962 Reginald Maudling had become chancellor of the Exchequer and, consequently, Macmillan appointed Duncan Sandys (later Lord Sandys) as colonial secretary.

22. Telegram from J.M. Lloyd to Duncan Sandys, September 29, 1962, CO 1031/3375.

23. British High Commission in Port-of-Spain to the Colonial Office, September 25, 1962.

24. Colonial Secretary to British High Commissioner in Port-of-Spain, September 25, 1962.

25. Trinidad and Tobago Order-in-Council S.I. 1962 no. 1875.

26. *Trinidad Guardian*, December 5, 1961. Note that for amending an entrenched clause of the post-independence Trinidadian Constitution at least 23 out of the 30 members of the local House of Representatives had to vote in favour of it.

27. N.E. Costar to Walsh Atkins, September 25, 1962, CO1031/3365.

28. Colonial Secretary to Administrator of Grenada, October 17, 1962, CO 1031/3365.

29. Telegram no. 53 from Antigua–Barbuda's Administrator to the Colonial Secretary, April 17, 1962, CO 1031/ 3378.

30. John Stow to Stephen Luke, July 7, 1962, CO 1031/ 3368.

31. Cmnd. 1746, 18.

32. C.A. Paul Southwell to H.A.C. Howard, August 14, 1962, CO 1031/3377. Also refer to letter from H.A.C. Howard to Duncan Sandys, August 21, 1962, CO 1031/3377.

33. By 1962 the St. Lucia Labour Party held six of ten seats in the local Legislative Council.

34. D.J.G. Rose to the Colonial Office, September 20, 1962, CO 1031/3377.
35. The *Vincentian*, September 22 and 29, 1962.
36. D.A. Wiles to the Colonial Office, September 15, 1962, CO 1031/3377.
37. One of these meetings held on October 11, 1962, was sponsored by the Montserrat Teachers Union. The summary of the proceedings was summed up as follows:

    [N]o reasonable solution was arrived at in the meeting, since Bramble nor the teachers knew whether Trinidad would be willing to accept Montserrat into unitary statehood and, if so, under what conditions. The teachers went on to discuss with Bramble the possibilities of the Federation of the Little Eight, Crown Colony, *and unitary statehood with Canada*. The Chief Minister expressed his entire ignorance of the last. Concerning the first he said the teachers probably knew more about them than he could tell them. (Emphasis added)

    Montserrat Mirror, October 20, 1962.
38. Note that by 1884 the Barbadian Agricultural Society had openly enquired of John Macdonald (then Canada's Prime Minister) whether his Government could 'favourably entertain an application from Barbados to be admitted as a member of that Confederation'. The urge was simultaneously voiced in Jamaica and the Leeward Islands. See, for instance, H.O.B. Wooding, 'The West Indies Economy: A West Indian View' in *Canada and The West Indies*, ed. P.A. Lockwood, 38–39 (New Brunswick: Mount Allison University, 1957). Also refer to Eric Williams, *From Columbus to Castro*, 404–05. For Sir John Macdonald's position on the issue of annexation see his speech before the Board of Trade of the City of Toronto on January 18, 1889, entitled 'Canada, the West Indies and British Guiana' in *An Imperial Federation*, James R. Boosé, (London: Imperial Federation League, 1889), 2–17. For an illuminating study on trade relations and migration between Canada and the area, with a special emphasis on the post-war period, see the compilation of papers prepared by the Institute of Social and Economic Research in connection with the Canada–Commonwealth Caribbean Conference of July 1966: refer to the *West Indies–Canada Economic Relations* (Kingston: University of the West Indies, Mona Campus, 1967.)
39. E.L. Sykes to Douglas Williams, November 5, 1962, CO 1031/ 3365.
40. Refer to British North America Act of 1867, 30–31 Vict., c.3 (UK).
41. Ibid.
42. Alec Lovelace to Douglas Williams, November 16, 1962, CO 1031/ 3365.
43. I.G. Turbott to Ambler Thomas, April 24, 1962, CO 1031/3375.
44. Hugh Fraser to Reginald Maudling, March 20, 1962, CO 1031/3374.
45. Ibid.
46. John Stow to the Colonial Office, April 17, 1962, CO 1031/3378.
47. Ibid.
48. John Stow to Douglas Williams, October 9, 1962, CO 1031/3368.
49. John Stow to Douglas Williams, October 15, 1962, CO 1031/3376.
50. Ibid.
51. Richard Cheltenham, 'Constitutional and Political Development in Barbados, 1946–1966' (PhD dissertation, University of Manchester, 1970), 224. Lewis, *The Agony of the Eight*, 23. *Daily News*, February 27–March 3, 1962.

52. Douglas Williams to Ambler Thomas, September 13, 1962, CO 1031/3376.

53. Errol Barrow, 'Federation and the Democratic Way of Life' in *Speeches by Errol Barrow* ed. Yussuff Haniff (Georgetown: Hansib Publishing Limited, 1987), 49.

54. Ibid.

55. Note the aforementioned debate lasted on and off from late June 1962 until January 1963.

56. Richard Cheltenham, 'Constitutional and Political Development in Barbados, 1946–1966' (PhD dissertation, University of Manchester, 1970), 202. Also contained in the *The House of Assembly Debates, Official Report*, 2d. sess. 1961–66 (July 31, 1962), 663.

57. Ibid.

58. *Daily News*, July 6, 1962.

59. *Voice of St. Lucia* October 20, 1962.

60. Carleen O'Loughlin, *A Survey of the Economic Potential and Capital Needs of The Leeward Islands, Windward Islands and Barbados* (London: HMSO, 1963), 120.

61. Note that since April 1961 Bird had been engaged in conversations with the agents of Natomas, a US oil industry holding company with interests in the Caribbean. By then Natomas, the parent company of the West Indies Oil Company, was already planning to diversify into the region for oil trans-shipment, refuelling and refining purposes.

62. The Commonwealth Sugar Agreement, signed in 1951, had been originally established between the British Government and sugar exporters from Australia, South Africa, the West Indies and British Guiana, British Honduras, Mauritius and Fiji.

63. Cmnd. 1746, 11-12.

64. John Stow to Douglas Williams, July 23, 1962, CO 1031/3376.

65. *Daily News* December 7, 1962.

66. Duncan Sandys to Harold Macmillan, October 26 1962, DSND 8/12.

67. Answer in Commons, December 11, 1962, CO 1031/3378.

68. Duncan Sandys to Harold Macmillan, October 26 1962, DSND 8/12.

69. CO 1031/4519. Refer to the minutes of the private meeting between the political leadership in Montserrat and Duncan Sandys, as well as to the transcripts of the exchange between the political leadership of Dominica and Sandys on December 22 and 27, 1962 respectively. For an unambiguous illustration of this dynamic refer to the Policy Statement of the People's Action Movement, which sprang up between 1962 and 1963 to oppose the ruling St. Kitts Labour Party. Together with the Barbuda Democratic Front and the Nevis National Movement its agenda centred on socioeconomic matters. Its platform was based on:
    (i) the establishment of a higher standard of living and adequate housing; (ii) more schools and expansion of secondary school education to the entire population; (iii) the expansion of public health; (iv) the improvement of water supplies; (v) the provision of an efficient plan for electricity distribution; (vi) the extension and building of roads in Nevis and Anguilla; (vii) the organisation of a proper ferry service between Nevis and St. Kitts and the linking up of Anguilla with the other two islands; (viii) the building of a

         deep-water harbour; (ix) the development of an international airport; (x) the introduction of new industries for local consumption and export; (xi) the setting up of industrial areas and (xii) the encouragement of foreign capital investment and overseas loans.

Intelligence Reports from St. Kitts-Nevis-Anguilla 1963, CO 1031/4772.

70.   Ibid. Also refer to the transcript of the meeting between Duncan Sandys and H. Burrowes (St. Vincent's Administrator) December 28, 1962.

71.   Ibid. Refer to the record of the confidential meeting between Duncan Sandys and H.A.C. Howard (St. Kitts–Nevis–Anguilla's Administrator) December 23, 1962. Note that Western Samoa's association to New Zealand is referred to in more detail in the following chapters.

72.   Refer to the confidential minutes from meeting of the Regional Council of Ministers, CO 1031/4772.

73.   Ibid.

74.   Note that, while this meeting was in progress, the Fiscal Commissioner Ursula Hicks was also in the Caribbean on the second of two visits. While assistants from each unit were collaborating with her, the date of her final submission depended on the progress made by the Civil Service Commission. This commission had already left for Barbados on November 18, 1962 and was not expected to report before the middle of March 1963. Additionally, the Economic Survey was not due before mid March 1963.

75.   CO 1031/3378. Note that the Legislatures of Montserrat and St. Kitts–Nevis–Anguilla were the only ones which so far had in principle approved the proposals. The position in the remaining territories was as follows: in Antigua–Barbuda the debate was tabled for the next session; in Barbados they had been debated on June 20, July 14, July 31, August 10, October 9 and adjourned on November 27, 1962; in Dominica, St. Lucia and St. Vincent no debate had been scheduled so far.

76.   CO 1031/4519.

77.   Ibid.

78.   Ibid. Refer to the first meeting between Duncan Sandys and the Antiguan leadership held on December 22, 1962. Note that by the time of this meeting Antigua–Barbuda had achieved, particularly since the last semester of 1961, a considerable degree of development. Unlike its neighbours, Antigua–Barbuda was no longer a grant-in-aided territory. It was in the midst of a tourism boom (the only island, except Barbados, with an international airport) and a cycle sustained industrial growth (refer to the oil refinery project).

79.   Ibid. Refer to meeting between Sandys and the Barbadian leadership held on December 27, 1962.

80.   Ibid.

81.   Ibid.

82.   Duncan Sandys to John Stow, January 9, 1963, DSND 8/13.

Part Three: Introduction

1.   Stephen Luke to Anthony Greenwood, May 28, 1965, CO 1031/ 4517.

2.   *Barbados Advocate*, April 1, 1965.

Chapter 9: Dissension within the Ranks

1. Note that previous commissions had already produced reports on these matters. In 1955 Sir Sydney Caine and Sir Hilary Blood (former colonial governor of Barbados) had been asked by the Colonial Office to report on the fiscal and civil service arrangements, respectively. See Cmnd. 9618 and Cmnd. 9619. Also refer to the findings of the McLagan and Croft Committees commissioned by Grantley Adams on these issues. See *Report on Trade and Tariffs* (1957–1958); WI 1/58 – 2 vols.

2. John Stow to Ambler Thomas, March 5, 1963, CO 1031/4519.

3. *Report of the Fiscal Commissioner 1963*, Cmnd. 1991 (London: HMSO). *Report of the Civil Service Commission 1963*, Cmnd. 1992 (London: HMSO).

4. I.G. Turbott to Douglas Williams, April 19, 1963, CO 1031/4532.

5. *Barbados Advocate*, May 13, 1963.

6. Intelligence Report from Antigua–Barbuda, April 5, 1963, CO 1031/4776.

7. Intelligence Report from Antigua–Barbuda, May 4, 1963, CO 1031/4776.

8. Carleen O'Loughlin, *Economic and Political Change in the Leeward and Windward Islands* (New Haven: Yale University Press, 1968), 25.

9. Carleen O'Loughlin, *A Survey of the Economic Potential and Capital Needs of the Leeward Islands, Windward Islands and Barbados* (London: HMSO, 1963), 38.

10. Ibid., 46, table A2. Please note that the rate of growth of the Barbadian economy during the fiscal year 1962–63 was of 1.7 per cent. See 124, table B2.

11. Cmnd. 1991, 27. In US dollars their GDP per capita was $215 and $270, respectively.

12. Note for instance, that Antigua–Barbuda's sugar crop for 1963 was lower than expected. It ended in mid July with approximately 27,958 tons of sugar produced, short from the initial estimate of 30,000 tons. It seems as if the local authorities were experiencing difficulties with peasants as, in the words of Turbott, 'they [were] no longer prepared to work as they did previously'. Refer to Intelligence Report from Antigua–Barbuda, August 8, 1963, CO 1031/4776.

13. During this period Antigua's customs revenue had increased from BWI $2,745,000 to $3,225,000, accounting for 49.6 per cent of the island's total revenue. Although (in real terms) St. Lucia's and Barbados's customs revenue surpassed that figure, if seen within the per capita context the average Antiguan enjoyed a greater proportion of that revenue than any of his extraterritorial neighbours. Carleen O'Loughlin, *A Survey of the Economic Potential and Capital Needs of the Leeward Islands, Windward Islands and Barbados* (London: HMSO, 1963).

14. Refer to O'Loughlin, *Financial and Economic Survey of the Hotel Industry in Antigua* (Eastern Caribbean: Institute of Social and Economic Research, November 1964), 3. The White Sands, Admirals Inn, Curtain Bluff, Hawksbill and the developments in Mamora Bay stood as the most salient exponents of the construction boom. Note that Bird and his colleagues had addressed the issue of property taxation at the last Speech from the Throne in December 1962. And eventually by October 1963 in preparation for the upcoming elections, the Antigua Labour Party's programme relied heavily on what Turbott called the property tax issue. The expectation was that the revenue from that would substitute the grants-in-aid coming from the British Exchequer. Also see Intelligence Report from Antigua, November 1, 1963,

CO 1031/4776. Also note that during the period 1962–63, the construction of hotels contributed between BWI $1.5 and $2 million to Antigua's local payroll. In fact, according to O'Loughlin, in 1962 the contribution made to the payroll by building hotels or their extensions was greater than the contribution made by hotel employment itself. See O'Loughlin, *Financial and Economic Survey of the Hotel Industry in Antigua*, 7.

15. Cmnd. 1746, 8–9.

16. Cmnd. 1991, 9. Also refer to Cmnd. 1746, 12. These fiscal departments were Customs and Excise, Inland Revenue and Audit.

17. Cmnd. 1991, 8.

18. Ibid., 9.

19. Ibid., 27–29.

20. Note that for fiscal year 1963, 58.93 per cent of St. Lucia's total revenue came from customs duties, as did 50.04 per cent of St. Vincent's. Refer to O'Loughlin, *A Survey of the Economic Potential and Capital Needs of the Leeward Islands, Windward Islands and Barbados*, 94, table L2 and 109 table V2. For the exact amount of appropriation in general grant for each island see Cmnd. 1991, 28.

21. Note that while the population of Antigua–Barbuda between 1962 and 1963 was (approximately) 60,000 (of whom 1,000 lived in Barbuda), in St. Lucia and St. Vincent it was 86,000 and 80,000, respectively.

22. Although grants-in-aid were only meant to supplement the structural accounts or budgets of the territories, the practice in Antigua had been to use these grants for development purposes. For an accurate description of this practice refer to Cmnd. 1991, 26. For an in-depth look at the state of Antigua–Barbuda's public utilities refer to O'Loughlin, *Economic and Political Change in the Leeward and Windward Islands*, 29. Also note that the Economic Survey, commissioned to Dr. O'Loughlin, was circulated shortly after the publication of the Fiscal and Civil Service Reports; although advanced copies of the Survey had already been sent out in April 1963 to all units.

23. Intelligence Report from Antigua, May 4, 1963, CO 1031/4776.

24. Ibid.

25. Ibid.

26. Ibid. For more on McChesney George refer to the following brief, which the Colonial Office compiled by the turn of 1964:

> [E]lected member of the Legislative Council for the island of Barbuda, barrister at law and a former civil servant and member of the Antigua Labour Party, [George is] Mr. Bird's *éminence grise*. He is a vain, arrogant mischief-maker [and] quick to take offence at any imagined slight. He seems to have some mysterious hold over Mr. Bird. Regards himself, on account of his legal training, as a considerable cut above his colleagues.

CO 1031/4982.

27. Minutes of meeting in the Colonial Office, May 20, 1963, DSND 8/13.

28. I. Turbott to Douglas Williams, April 19, 1963, CO 1031/4532.

29. Arthur Lewis, *The Agony of the Eight*, 26.

30. Note that although Nigel Fisher (1913–96) had become a member of Parliament in 1950, his ministerial career was somewhat limited. During the last Churchill

Government he had served as parliamentary private secretary to the minister of food (1951–54), soon thereafter he served in the same capacity in the Home Office (1954–57). After a ministerial interregnum of almost five years, Fisher became (as late as July 1962) parliamentary under-secretary at the Colonial Office.

31. Late in January 1963, almost a month after Sandys's visit, Barrow flew to New York for discussions with UN agencies and the Ford Foundation for the purpose of expediting aid programmes. However, as is apparent below, the crux of the matter for the DLP leadership would be Barbados's colonial status. In most places and particularly in the US, the whole archipelago (at least until late in 1964) was seen as an area of British primary concern and as such ineligible for foreign aid. For this particular trip, refer to Intelligence Report from Barbados, February 4, 1963, CO 1031/4764.

32. Joint Statement following meetings between President John F. Kennedy and Prime Minister Lester B. Pearson, at Hyannis Port, Massachusetts on May 10–11, 1963, contained in National Security File Box 1, Lyndon B. Johnson Presidential Library (Austin, Texas.)

33. Kennedy M. Crockett to Gordon Chase, July 13, 1964, National Security File Box 1, Lyndon B. Johnson Presidential Library (Austin, Texas.)

34. CO 1031/4513 contains the most complete records of these proceedings. Most of the briefs produced by the Colonial Office in preparation for Nigel Fisher's visit are preserved in CO 1031/4547.

35. Ibid.

36. Refer to *Conference on the Closer Association of the British West Indian Colonies 1948*, Cmnd. 7120 (London: HMSO).

37. CO 1031/4513.

38. Ibid.

39. Between May 20 and 23, 1963 the chief ministers had held informal discussions at Government House (Bridgetown), leading to the articulation of the 'Areas of Agreement'. Whether the Colonial Office and Fisher in particular knew about this, of so short notice, is not clear.

40. Minutes of sixth meeting of the Regional Council of Ministers (first session), May 24, 1963, CO 1031/4513.

41. Douglas Williams to Ambler Thomas, September 13, 1962, CO 1031/3376.

42. CAB 134/1561.

43. Statement by Nigel Fisher, May 30, 1963, CO 1031/4513.

44. Sources: Cmnd.1746, 1991, 1992, 1962.

45. Source: CO 1031/4513.

46. 10 & 11 Eliz 2 C19, secs. 6, 7.

47. Cmnd. 1746, par. 24 (iii).

48. Ibid., par., 26.

49. Cmnd. 1746, par. 24 (iv).

50. Cmnd. 1746, par. 24 (v). Also refer to Cmnd. 1992, 83–84, table L, Police Department.

51. Cmnd. 1746, par. 24 (vi). Also refer to Cmnd. 1992, 88, table P, Postal Department.

52. Cmnd. 1746, par. 48 et. seq.

53. Cmnd. 1992.
54. CO 1031/4513.
55. Ibid.
56. Refer to Table 9.1 detailing the proposals contained in the Areas of Agreement.
57. CO 1031/4513.
58. Ibid.
59. Ibid.
60. Ibid.
61. Ibid.
62. Ibid.
63. Ibid.
64. CO 1031/3365.
65. CO 1031/4513.
66. Ibid.
67. Nigel Fisher left for British Guiana on Saturday May 25, remaining in that territory all through the weekend plus Monday, Tuesday and Wednesday. He would return to Bridgetown late on Wednesday, which meant the meeting of the Regional Council of Ministers remained adjourned until the early hours of Thursday May 30, 1963.
68. Nigel Fisher to Duncan Sandys, May 24, 1963, DSND 8/13.
69. Intelligence Report from Barbados, April 2, 1963, CO 1031/4764.
70. Ibid.
71. Ibid.
72. The BNP and the BLP as well as the local Chamber of Commerce had already expressed a few reservations with the federal project as it stood.
73. Note that while the combined national income of Dominica, St. Lucia and St. Vincent by 1963 was approximately $US35,200,000, that of Barbados alone was $US59,600,000. The average per capita income for these three Windward territories was $US162, while the figure for Barbados was $270. And, while the combined population of Dominica, St. Lucia and St. Vincent was 225,972, Barbados on its own had approximately 232,085 inhabitants. Refer, for instance, to Airgram A-12, US Consul in Bridgetown to the US State Department, August 2, 1963, Eastern Caribbean Federation Country File, National Security File, Box 1, Lyndon B. Johnson Presidential Library (Austin, Texas.)
74. Intelligence Report from Barbados, March 3, 1963, CO 1031/4764.
75. *Daily News*, December 7, 1962.
76. Intelligence Report from Barbados, February 4, 1963, CO 1031/4764.
77. Intelligence Report from Barbados, April 2, 1963, CO 1031/4764.
78. Intelligence Report from Barbados, May 3, 1963, CO 1031/4764.
79. H.A.C. Howard, colonial administrator of St. Kitts, had noticed early in March 1963 that 'political opposition to the [St. Kitts] Labour Party has been somewhat dormant since the elections last year [1962]'. Refer to Intelligence Report from St. Kitts–Nevis–Anguilla, March 4, 1963, CO 1031/4772.
80. Intelligence Report from St. Kitts–Nevis–Anguilla, April 9, 1963, CO 1031/4772.
81. Ibid.
82. St. Kitts–Nevis–Anguilla did not become a grant-in-aided territory until 1962.

However, since late 1958 the British Exchequer had been disbursing a periodic grant for financing recurring expenditure in this unit. O'Loughlin, *Economic and Political Change in the Leeward and Windward Islands*, 19.

83. The Jamaican economy, from the time of the 1947 Montego Bay Conference to the inauguration of the West Indies Federation in 1958, had gone through important transformations. From 1953 to 1958, the production of bauxite had risen from 1 million to 6 million tons. By then, the island had re-negotiated the terms of agreements with several foreign mining companies. Sir Hugh Springer contended that

> whereas before, in 1947, her economic position had been such that *it was natural to believe that union with the Eastern Caribbean islands was the best*, if not the only avenue to economic improvement, by 1958 the position changed. Now it was possible to hope that Jamaica would achieve *on her own self-sustaining economic growth* that would lead her eventually to the ranks of the developed countries. (Emphasis added.)

Refer to Hugh Springer, *Reflections on the Failure of the First West Indian Federation*, 18–19.

84. Intelligence Report from St. Kitts–Nevis–Anguilla, March 4, 1963, CO 1031/4772.

85. Note that early in May 1963 Sir John Stow had confided in Ambler Thomas,

> it is however *disappointing* that the Premier *intends to leave* for Canada from the 8th to the 18th May... . just *at a time in which his Cabinet should be devoting thought to the recommendations of the* [*Fiscal and Civil Service*] *reports*. The reports have been turned over to a working party under the chairmanship of H.A. Vaughan (Minister without Portfolio)... . It seems *unlikely that the Cabinet can properly consider the reports* before Barrow meets his fellow Ministers on the 20th May and Mr. Fisher three days later. (Emphasis added.)

Intelligence Report from Barbados, May 3, 1963, CO 1031/4764. Also note that between May 20 and 23 Barrow and his colleagues had been producing the Areas of Agreement. Whether they studied the official reports with any rigour is still open to question. Nonetheless, this seems highly unlikely. Meanwhile, Bird ignored these command papers in a more direct way. Ian Turbott had forwarded a similar despatch to the Colonial Office. In it he narrated that

> Bird himself rang me on the morning of the 26th April [the day after the reports were circulated]... . He said that *he had read the first few pages* of Mrs. Hicks' report and *was not going to bother to read anything more* of any reports. (Emphasis added.)

Refer to Intelligence Report from Barbados, May 4, 1963, CO 1031/4776.

86. Intelligence Report from St. Kitts–Nevis–Anguilla, May 10, 1963, CO 1031/4772.

87. For details on Bradshaw's appointment to the Executive Council see Intelligence Report from St. Kitts–Nevis–Anguilla, February 6, 1963, CO 1031/4772.

88. John Stow to Douglas Williams, October 15, 1962, CO 1031/3376.

89. Intelligence Report from St. Kitts–Nevis–Anguilla, May 10, 1963, CO 1031/4772.

90. See note 40.

91. See notes 16 and 17 in chapter 1.
92. O'Loughlin, *Economic and Political Change in the Leeward and Windward Islands*, 19.
93. Ibid., 39.
94. The agenda of Dominica's chief minister prior to Fisher's visit had been focused on refurbishing the capital's major roads. Intelligence Report from Dominica, April 8, 1963, CO 1031/4767.
95. Fred Phillips, *Freedom in the Caribbean: A Study in Constitutional Change* (New York: Oceana, 1977), 75.
96. Sources: CO 1031/4513 and Cmnd. 1746.
97. Source: CO 1031/4513.
98. Since the last London Conference the British Government had been consistent in its intention of establishing a dependent or colonial federation. In a letter to the Cabinet, late in May 1962, Sir Hilton Poynton had made this point clear: 'as the Federation would in the first place be dependent, or colonial, the appointment of the Governor General would be made by the Queen, on the advice of Her Ministers'. Sir Hilton Poynton to Tim Bligh, May 29, 1962, CO 1031/3366. Interestingly, a reply came from Buckingham Palace. Early in June 1962. Sir Michael Adeane wrote:

    > HM is glad to learn of the provisional arrangement for the establishment of a Federation of Barbados, the Leeward and Windward Islands. She notes that should the Federation be established it would call for the appointment of a Governor General. The Queen notes, furthermore, that in these circumstances the Colonial Secretary would probably wish to submit the name of Sir John Stow for this appointment.

    Sir Michael Adeane to Sir Hilton Poynton, June 5, 1962, CO 1031/3366.
99. Cmnd. 1746, 19.
100. Statement by Nigel Fisher, May 30, 1963, CO 1031/4513.
101. Nigel Fisher to Duncan Sandys, May 24, 1963, DSND 8/13.
102. For a novel analysis of the changes in Whitehall's policy regarding British Guiana, particularly since early September 1962, refer to Carey Fraser, 'The "New Frontier" of Empire in the Caribbean: The Transfer of Power in British Guiana, 1961–1964', *The International History Review* 22, no. 3 (September 2000): 602.
103. Statement by Nigel Fisher, May 30, 1963, CO 1031/4513.
104. Note that during this discussion Fisher contended that 'the application of a new Commonwealth country for membership of the Commonwealth must be made formally to all the other members of the Club'. Consistent with the position Reginald Maudling had espoused before the Colonial Policy Committee, as early as April 1962, Fisher subtly emphasized how Commonwealth membership was not automatic. See CAB 134/1561.
105. Refer to the British Nationality Acts 1948–64, *Halsbury's Statutes* vol. 31, 4th ed. (London: Butterworth, 1994), 12–52.
106. CO 1031/4513.
107. Ibid.
108. The 1961 Manifesto of the Democratic Labour Party concluded with the following paragraph:

[t]he road to destiny is the road to Independence. Towards this goal our country must press on. As the island has never been a grant-in-aided territory there is no reason why *within or without a Federation* Barbados should not attain the full stature of *independence now* within the British Commonwealth. (Emphasis added.)

Operation Take-over published by the DLP on November 19, 1961.

109. CO 1031/4513.

110. Ibid.

111. Ibid.

112. Duncan Sandys to Sir Anthony Eden (then Lord Avon), June 18, 1963, DSND 8/13.

113. Intelligence Report from Dominica, July 11, 1963, CO 1031/4767.

114. Broadcast by chief minister, June 20, 1963 contained in Intelligence Report from Montserrat, July 8, 1963, CO 1031/4774.

115. Press Release by chief minister, June 24, 1963 contained in Intelligence Report from St. Kitts-Nevis-Anguilla, July 1, 1963, CO 1031/4772.

116. Ibid.

117. Intelligence Report from Dominica, July 11, 1963, CO 1031/4767.

118. Intelligence Report from St. Lucia, October 4, 1963, CO 1031/4763.

119. *Antigua and Federation*, September 5, 1963, contained in Intelligence Report from Antigua-Barbuda (Appendix A), September 30, 1963, CO 1031/4776.

120. Note that following the November 1966 elections, Sir Grantley's BLP became the official opposition to the Government. As a result he became the leader of the Opposition until his retirement from active politics in 1970, a year prior to his death.

121. This meeting took place at the Barbados Airport, where Duncan Sandys had made a stopover from New York *en route* to Port-of-Spain.

122. Note of talk between Duncan Sandys and John Stow, July 9, 1963, DSND 8/15.

123. Ibid.

124. Ibid.

125. Note of talk between Duncan Sandys and Errol Barrow, July 15, 1963, DSND 8/15.

126. Ibid.

127. Circular 405/63, August 9, 1963, contained in Colonial no. 360 (HMSO: London, 1965), 5–8.

128. O'Loughlin, *A Survey of the Economic Potential and Capital Needs of the Leeward Islands, Windward Islands and Barbados*, 12.

129. *Attitudes of Island Governments to Federation*, CO 1031/4982.

130. Arthur Lewis, *The Agony of the Eight*, 25.

131. Minutes of the seventh meeting of the Regional Council of Ministers (held in St. John's, Antigua) contained in CO 1031/4527.

Chapter 10: Aid within a Transatlantic Triangle

1. Duncan Sandys to John Boyd-Carpenter, November 26, 1963, DSND 8/15.

2. Ibid.

3. Grants-in-aid for the expenses of administration were first made in 1878. These grants were subventions to the ordinary budgets of certain colonies. The finances of the grant-in-aided territories were under the strict control of the Treasury. It should also be noted that until 1950 direct assistance from the British Exchequer to the dependencies was confined to those territories lacking responsible government. Clearly, this excluded the old Dominions, India: Ceylon (after 1931), Burma and Southern Rhodesia. Refer to *Colonial Development: British Aid – 5* (London: Overseas Development Institute, 1964), 8–10. Also see Cmnd. 4677, 6. In the case of the Eastern Caribbean territories, by the time of the federal breakup they were all, with the exception of Barbados and St. Kitts–Nevis–Anguilla, grant-in-aided territories. While Antigua and St. Lucia had emerged from grant-in-aid in 1963 and 1965, respectively, by 1964 St. Kitts–Nevis–Anguilla was submerged into it. Attention should also be paid to the fact that up until 1964, grant-in-aid was settled after a detailed item-by-item examination of draft budgets. In that year, however, the Colonial Office introduced changes designed to increase the degree of local responsibility to the greatest extent compatible with the requirements of the British Public Accounts Committee. Under that new operating principle, the annual block grants were determined on an examination of revenue and expenditure trends over recent years and on the financial implications of agreed new policies. The amount of the block grant represented the difference between the expenditure and the revenue figures. If the expenditure figure determined by the Colonial Office was lower than that proposed by the government concerned, it was left to the local ministers to determine where cuts should be made. Brief no.7, CO 1031/4982.

4. Note that the Colonial Development and Welfare Act of 1945 and the amending Acts of 1949, 1950 and 1955 were consolidated in 1959 and these, together with further amendments in 1963 and 1965, made £390 million available for development and welfare schemes between April 1, 1946 and March 31, 1970. Out of this amount £2.5 million a year was provided from 1950 to 1956 for research, £8 million between 1956 and 1960 and £7.5 million between 1960 and 1964. Cmnd. 4677, 8–9, 15.

5. The Commonwealth Development Corporation (CDC), financed by funds from the British Government, was established by an Act of Parliament in 1948 to facilitate the economic development of the colonial dependencies. It operated on a commercial basis, promoting and investing in projects which could be expected not only to increase the wealth of the country concerned but also able to yield a reasonable return on the money invested. Its undertakings usually consisted of partnerships with private enterprises, territorial governments and public or international corporations. During the period under scrutiny the CDC's impact on these small island economies was not particularly significant. However, from the end of 1966 until 1971 its investments in the area increased by nearly 150 per cent. During this five-year period the Eastern Caribbean territories (excluding Barbados) would get almost £25,661,000 in grants and/or loans, almost 1/3 of the CDC's total investment in the region during this same period. *Britain and the Developing Countries: The Caribbean* (London: HMSO, 1973), 24–26, table 5.

6. See note 62, chapter 8.

7. CO 1031/4982.

8. The Colonial Development Fund was established pursuant to the 1929 Colonial Development Act, 20&21 Geo 5 c5. It represented the British Government's first recognition of its responsibility for the development of the dependent territories. The Fund, which ran until 1940, disbursed approximately £8.8 million across the Empire. The major difference between the 1929 Colonial Development Act and the subsequent CD&W Acts were their terms of reference and their levels of spending. The 1929 Fund, as defined in the enabling Act, was meant to aid and develop agriculture and industry in the colony or territory and *thereby promote commerce with or industry in the United Kingdo*m. The CD&W funds, for their part, were to be applied to any purpose likely to *promote the development of the resources of any colony or the welfare of the people.* Cmnd. 4677, 6–7. For further details on the 1929 Colonial Development Act see *Colonial Development: British Aid – 5* (London: Overseas Development Institute, 1964), 14–30.

9. Out of the total £8.8 million disbursed between 1929 and 1940, by virtue of the Colonial Development Act, the Eastern Caribbean territories received a combined sum of approximately £628,000. Out of the total £324,393,000 disbursed under the various CD&W Acts (from 1946 until the end of these arrangements in 1970) the Eastern Caribbean territories were awarded a combined sum of £23,530,000. See *British Aid –5* (London: Overseas Development Institute Ltd, 1964), 28 and Cmnd. 4677, table 1.

10. Cmnd. 4677, 17.

11. The 16 units in question were the Bahamas, Barbados, British Guiana, British Honduras, the Cayman Islands, Jamaica, Trinidad and Tobago, the Turks and Caicos Islands, Antigua, Montserrat, St. Kitts–Nevis–Anguilla, the British Virgin Islands, Dominica, Grenada, St. Lucia, and St. Vincent. Bermuda was not included in these figures.

12. The McLean Report, PREM 13/1359.

13. Out of the £324,393,000 the Caribbean's total share was £71,366,460 and with a population of 4,569,300 the per capita figure was around £15.62.

14. For the combined population of British Africa see *U.N. Statistical Yearbook 1963*, 15th edition (New York: UN, 1964). In sum, its total share was around £145,976,850 and with a population of almost 69 million the per capita figure was approximately £2.13.

15. Roads were a big concern to most African colonies. The Gold Coast had spent 40 per cent of its allocation on roads while other African countries had spent considerable sums on the same sector: Gambia 30 per cent, Tanganyika 33 per cent, Uganda 26 per cent, Northern Rhodesia and Nyasaland 18 per cent, Basutoland 16 per cent, Bechuanaland 10 per cent and Swaziland 23 per cent. In the case of the Eastern Caribbean territories, Dominica had spent 46 per cent of its funds on roads, St. Lucia 23 per cent, St. Vincent 32 per cent and Montserrat 19 per cent. Also note that while education claimed 21 per cent of total CD&W expenditure, roads came in second place with 17 per cent and health-care in fourth place with 9.2 per cent. Cmnd. 4677, 16–19, table 1.

16. The year in parentheses stands for the year each of these colonies attained independence. Note that the British Government ceased to have any special financial responsibility over its territories after their independence. This is why most newly independent units were usually encouraged to develop their own credit and, hence, raise loans in London, New York or elsewhere. Between 1945–46 and 1962–63 the independent countries of the Commonwealth received £230 million (£172 million in loans and £58 million in grants) both in economic and technical assistance from the British Government. More interestingly, most of this aid was disbursed after 1957. For the specific figures per country see *British Aid – 1* (London: Overseas Development Institute, 1963), 27–28.

17. *U.N. Statistical Yearbook 1963*, 15th edition (New York: UN, 1964).

18. The McLean Report, PREM 13/1359.

19. Mauritius achieved its independence two years after Barbados, in 1968.

20. By the turn of 1963 a scandal of corruption had just erupted in St. Vincent. There were strong allegations to the effect that the minister without portfolio, Ivy Joshua (the chief minister's wife), had misappropriated public funds. Intelligence Reports from St. Vincent, CO 1031/4760. Also see the report prepared by the US Consul in Bridgetown regarding these allegations. Eileen R. Donovan to the US Department of State, February 20, 1964, Pol. 2-3 BWI, (National Archives and Records Administration at College Park, Maryland.)

21. Refer to Malta, Cyprus and Gibraltar. Together they comprised 3,723mi², with a combined population of 921,737. Their total CD&W allocation, according to Cmnd. 4677, amounted to £25,951,440; with close to 80 per cent going to Malta. Their funding per capita was amongst the highest, near to £28.15. Other sources suggest the total aid to Malta, including technical assistance, amounted to £57 million. See *British Aid –1* (London: Overseas Development Institute, 1963), 27.

22. In terms of CD&W grants Nigeria received £40 million, Kenya £23 million, Malta £20 million, Tanganyika £14 million, British Honduras £13 million and British Guiana £12 million. Cmnd. 4677, 16.

23. Malta, British Guiana and British Honduras together had an area of 91,987mi² and a combined population of 1,052,620, although Malta had among the highest population densities in the world, with 1,041 people per km of area. *U.N. Statistical Yearbook 1963*, 15th edition (New York: UN, 1964).

24. Note that Malta, with its Grand Old Harbour and its proximity to Northern Africa, had provided the Royal Navy a phenomenal location from which to defend British interests in Suez and in the Middle East. During World War II, for instance, the Maltese had repelled the Axis powers against severe odds, having been heavily bombed during that conflict. This explains, in part, the high level of British aid flowing into the Maltese archipelago. Refer to the 1947 Malta (Reconstruction) Act as well as to Cmnd. 1261 (1961). Also refer to John Darwin, *Britain and Decolonisation: The Retreat from Empire in the Post-War World* (London: Macmillan, 1988), 279–80.

25. Kenya's strategic importance, however, cannot be forgotten. Bordering the Arabian Peninsula as well as the Indian Sea, Kenya had also proven a vital naval post from

which to defend British interests in the Middle East.

26. Patrick Emmanuel, 'Independence and Viability: Elements of Analysis' in *Size, Self-Determination and International Relations: The Caribbean*, ed. Vaughan Lewis (Kingston: Institute of Social and Economic Research, 1976), 3–4.

27. Douglas Lockhart and David Drakakis-Smith, eds. *Development Process in Small Island States* (London: Routledge, 1993), 1–9.

28. Note that between 1946 and 1970 a total CD&W allocation of £10 million (in grants) was distributed in the Caribbean area for civil aviation alone; nearly a third of that went to the smaller dependencies of the region. In the Eastern Caribbean territories the breakdown was as follows: Barbados £513,000; Antigua–Barbuda, £373,000; St. Kitts–Nevis–Anguilla £329,000; Dominica £364,000; St. Lucia £293,000; St. Vincent £328,000 and Montserrat £166,000. Cmnd. 4677, 22.

29. In most small islands the sea is constantly eroding the coastlines, which might very well comprise most of the total area. In such small units most soil lost becomes irreplaceable.

30. O'Loughlin, *A Survey of the Economic Potential and Capital Needs of the Leeward, Windward Islands and Barbados*, 1–6.

31. The Duke of Edinburgh to Lord Longford (colonial secretary), March 3, 1966, CO 967/ 434.

32. Duncan Sandys to John Boyd-Carpenter, November 26, 1963, DSND 8/15.

33. National Income, as defined by the U.N. is

> the sum of all income accruing within a year to the factors of production supplied by the normal residents of a country, before deduction of direct taxes. It equals the sum of compensation of employees, income from unincorporated enterprises, rents, interests and dividends accruing to households, savings of companies, direct taxes on corporations and general government income from property and entrepreneurship.

U.N. Statistical Yearbook 1963, 15th edition (New York: UN, 1964), 516.

34. For area and population of each island refer to Table 10.3.

35. The status of Martinique and Guadeloupe remained unchanged following the establishment of the 1958 Constitution for the Fifth French Republic.

36. For the specifics of their constitutional position in relation to metropolitan France see A. Blaustein and P. Blaustein, *Constitutions of Dependencies and Special Sovereignties* vol. 4 (New York: Oceana Publications, 1988.)

37. For a comparative analysis of the incentives offered in the French Antilles during the early 1960s, in relation to the remaining units of the Caribbean, refer to G. Peter, *Industrie et surpeuplement aux Antilles* Cahier no. 10 (Fort de France: CERAG, 1966.)

38. Aarón Segal, *The Politics of Caribbean Economic Integration* Special Study no. 6 (Río Piedras: Institute of Caribbean Studies of the University of Puerto Rico, 1968), 78.

39. Franklin Knight, *The Caribbean: The Genesis of a Fragmented Nationalism*, 1st edition (New York: Oxford University Press, 1978), 210.

40. Helen Hintjens, 'France in the Caribbean' in *Europe and the Caribbean*, ed. Paul Sutton (London: Macmillan, 1991), 36–47. By the early 1970s France's aid to its Caribbean departments, including French Guiana, increased dramatically, from

about FF 686 million per annum in 1970 to FF 980 million by 1972. Irene Hawkins, *The Changing Face of the Caribbean* (Bridgetown: Cedar Press, 1976), 164–65.

41. Their associate membership to the EEC was made possible pursuant to Article No. 277 of the Treaty of Rome.

42. The figures provided in the study conducted by Aarón Segal, *The Politics of Caribbean Economic Integration,* are in US dollars. The author reveals that the French Antilles had received two grants of $US30 million each. The figure suggested above is based on the average 1964 exchange rate, which was of US$2.79 dollars per £1. *International Financial Statistics* 28, no.1 (Washington: IMF, January 1965), 21–23.

43. Aarón Segal, *The Politics of Caribbean Economic Integration*, 79. For the specific figures regarding their trade with the EEC during 1963–64 see *Caribbean Plan, Annual Report 1963* (Hato Rey, Puerto Rico: Caribbean Organization, 1964), 7.

44. Refer to the Preamble of the Statuut van het Koninkrijk contained in Blaustein, *Constitutions of Dependencies and Special Sovereignties* vol. 5. For a relevant and updated legal analysis of the Netherlands Antilles's constitutional status see Hurst Hannum, *Autonomy, Sovereignty and Self-Determination: The Accommodation of Conflicting Rights*, revised edition (Philadelphia: University of Pennsylvania Press, 1996), 347–52.

45. Irene Hawkins, *The Changing Face of the Caribbean*, 165.

46. Refer to art. 36 *in toto* and art. 37(d).

47. Aarón Segal, *The Politics of Caribbean Economic Integration,* 81.

48. The Netherlands Antilles became associated overseas territories of the EEC on October 1, 1964 pursuant to part 4 of the Treaty of Rome.

49. *Nationale Rekeningen, 1957–1965* (Willemstad: Bureau Voor De Statistiek, Departement van Social-en Economische Zaken, Nederlandse Antillen, Augustus 1966).

50. In the aftermath of its defeat at the hands of the US in the Cuban Spanish–American War, Spain ceded Puerto Rico to the victors in 1898. Nineteen years later in 1917 the US purchased the Virgin Islands from the Danish Kingdom.

51. Refer to the so-called Insular Cases. These decisions, rendered by the US Supreme Court at the beginning of the twentieth century, established the constitutional basis upon which these newly acquired territories would relate to the Union. Unlike Alaska and Hawaii, these unincorporated territories were not to be groomed for annexation as states. See, among others, De Lima v. Bidwell, 182 US 1 (1901); Goetze v. United States, 182 US 221 (1901); Dooley v. United States, 182 US 222 (1901); and Downes v. Bidwell, 182 US 244 (1901).

52. Under the terms of the 1954 *Statuut* the Netherlands Antilles and Surinam retained their own currency and central bank. The Eastern Caribbean territories, although part of the sterling area, had their own Eastern Caribbean Currency Board based on the British West Indian Dollar.

53. The People of Puerto Rico and the People of the Virgin Islands became US citizens in 1917. For the federal statute granting citizenship to Puerto Ricans refer to 39 Stat. at L. 951, 64th Cong., 2d sess. (March 2, 1917), 145. With respect to the

inhabitants of the Virgin Islands see 'Proclamation of the Convention between the US and Denmark for Cession of the Danish West Indies' in *Treaties, Covenants, Protocols and Agreements between the US and Other Powers*, vol. 3 (Washington, DC: US Government Printing Office, 1923), 2563.

54. Since 1900 Puerto Rico has elected a resident commissioner to represent the island's interests before the US Government who also sits as a non-voting delegate in the US Congress. The Virgin Islands, for their part, would have to wait (along with Guam) until 1972 to send a non-voting delegate to Congress.

55. *Informe Económico al Gobernador* (San Juan: Junta de Planificación del Estado Libre Asociado de Puerto Rico: 1968), table 11.

56. Ibid.

57. *Informe Económico al Gobernador* (San Juan: Junta de Planificación del Estado Libre Asociado de Puerto Rico, 1972), table 15.

58. Guy Lasserre and Albert Mabileau, 'The French Antilles and their Status as Overseas Departments' in *Patterns of Foreign Influence in the Caribbean*, ed. Emanuel De Kadt (London: Oxford University Press, 1972), 88.

59. Irene Hawkins, *The Changing Face of the Caribbean*, 179.

60. Aarón Segal, *The Politics of Caribbean Economic Integration*, 181.

61. Closer scholarly attention should be paid to the issue of migration within the wider narrative of the decolonization of the Caribbean. The following figures reflect the net immigration from the Caribbean for the years 1963 and 1964: 7,928 and 14,848, respectively. Net immigration means the numbers admitted minus numbers embarked. Assessing the actual migratory picture is further complicated by people who entered and left more than once as well as by people who entered for a short period but stayed over the calendar year. During this same period the total number of black immigrants living in the UK were Africans, 40,000; Indians-Pakistanis-Ceylonese, 290,000; West Indians, 278,000, plus 'other' black immigrants: 90,000, for a grand total of almost 700,000. Interestingly, by 1963–64 the figure of immigrants from the white Commonwealth living in the UK amounted to over one million. See Memorandum from Private Secretary to Colonial Secretary, March 17, 1965, CO 967/431. For further figures on the net arrivals from India, Pakistan and the Caribbean from 1955 to 1967, see E.J.B. Rose, *Colour and Citizenship* (London: Oxford University Press, 1969), 83, table 8.1.

62. Following the victory of the British Labour Party, in October 1964, Thomas Balogh joined the Cabinet Office as adviser to Prime Minister Harold Wilson on economic affairs, with special reference to external economic policy. See *Dictionary of National Biography 1980–1990* (Oxford: Oxford University Press, 1995), 25-26.

63. CAB 147/36.

64. Ibid.

65. The Department of Technical Co-operation, which was created in 1961 to take over most of the Colonial Office's non-political functions was transformed in 1964 into the Ministry of Overseas Development. Among other responsibilities, this ministry took over in full the day to day administration of the Colonial Development and Welfare Acts. Together with the Colonial Office and later with the Foreign and Commonwealth Office, it promoted development in the remaining dependencies.

For more on the negotiations leading to the creation of the Ministry of Overseas Development see CO 967/432.

66. Robin L. Marris to Andrew B. Cohen, January 25, 1965, CAB 147/36.

67. On that day Macmillan sent Sandys the following note,

> Dear Duncan, I have today submitted my resignation to the Queen; and as you will know, this carries with it the resignation of the whole of the present Administration. This does not require other Ministers to tender their individual resignations to HM; but they should, of course, regard their offices as at the disposal of my successor. Meanwhile, I ask all Ministers to carry on the necessary administration of their Departments until a new government is formed. Yours ever, Harold Macmillan.

Refer to DSND 15/5. For a well documented analysis of this political transition see, for instance, Richard Lamb, *The Macmillan Years 1957–1963: The Emerging Truth*, 491–501.

68. Memorandum to the Prime Minister, October 29, 1963, DSND 8/15.

69. Prime Minister's Personal Minute, January 3, 1964, DSND 8/15.

70. Prime Minister's Personal Minute, January 13, 1964, DSND 8/15.

71. Note of meeting between Colonial Secretary and the Chief Secretary to the Treasury, February 17, 1964, DSND 8/21.

72. Ibid.

73. Ibid.

74. Ibid.

75. Ibid.

76. CO 1031/4527.

77. Ibid.

78. FO 371/173580.

79. Note that Dr. O'Loughlin had recommended an allocation £9.5 million for each of the first three years, and even if the Treasury disbursed £5 million during that same period, the difference would nonetheless be significant, namely of £4.5 million per annum.

80. O'Loughlin, *A Survey of the Economic Potential and Capital Needs of the Leeward, Windward Islands and Barbados*, 12.

81. According to the Economic Survey, after the first three years and for the succeeding seven years the scale of assistance should be approximately £4.43 million per annum.

82. Note that Dr. O'Loughlin had chosen the 1963–1973 period because, as she saw things, it would not be possible to foresee viability on recurrent account for all territories concerned in a shorter period. O'Loughlin, *A Survey of the Economic Potential and Capital Needs of the Leeward, Windward Islands and Barbados*, 11.

83. CO 1031/4534.

84. UN Special Committee on the Granting of Independence to Colonial Countries and People.

85. The actual speech was delivered on May 7, 1964. See Intelligence Report from Barbados, June 2, 1964, CO 1031/4765. Refer as well to Eileen R. Donovan to the US Department of State, May 27, 1964, p.9, Pol. 2-3 BWI, (National Archives and Records Administration at College Park, Maryland).

86. Note of meeting between Colonial Secretary and Canadian Minister of External

Relations, April 15, 1964, DSND 8/16.

87. Ibid.

88. CO 1031/4706.

89. After the collapse of the West Indies Federation no new US aid was made available to the Eastern Caribbean territories. Even the activities of the American Aid Mission in Trinidad and Tobago, which had been accredited to the Federation, were run down and eventually terminated in 1964. FO 371/185004.

90. Before 1965 all British dependent territories in the Caribbean fell within the jurisdiction of the European Affairs Bureau, which had almost no contact with the Inter-American Bureau, since the latter's responsibility mostly covered Latin America and the Spanish Caribbean. FO 371/185004.

91. The minutes of this meeting are contained in FO 371/173580.

92. See Cmnd. 2048.

93. See Cmnd. 2124.

94. Ibid.

95. IJM Sutherland to Patricia Hutchinson, March 24, 1964, FO 371/173580.

96. Benjamin Read to McGeorge Bundy, April 9, 1964, Pol 19 BWI, (National Archives and Records Administration at College Park, Maryland).

97. St. Lucia was the only other island with US military installations. By this stage the Atlantic Missile Range tracking site in Beane Field was wholly inactive. Nonetheless, while the US Government was contemplating an early release of this station, the Pentagon was bent on retaining certain rights of access.

98. By September 1964 a report published on the front page of the Barbadian *Advocate*, suggested that the Soviet Government had retained a British firm to make a comprehensive complex survey of many key elements in the Eastern Caribbean territories for the purpose of promoting export trade. Although the American Consulate General could not ascertain the reliability of the source, it did send a complete report to the State Department. Refer, for instance, to Airgram A-41, US Consul General in Bridgetown to the US State Department, September 30, 1964, vol. 1, National Security File, Box 1, Lyndon B. Johnson Presidential Library (Austin, Texas.) Also see Intelligence Report from Barbados, October 6, 1964, CO 1031/4765.

99. Benjamin Read to McGeorge Bundy, April 9, 1964, Pol 19 BWI, 4-5 (National Archives and Records Administration at College Park, Maryland).

100. The 1947 Rio Pact, followed by the formation of the Organization of American States at the Bogotá Conference in early 1948, pledged Inter-American solidarity against external aggression.

101. Benjamin Read to McGeorge Bundy, April 9, 1964, Pol 19 BWI, 6-7.

102. Ibid.

103. US Consul to US State Department, May 27, 1964, Pol. 2-3 BWI, 8 (National Archives and Records Administration at College Park, Maryland).

104. CAB 134/155. Note that Sutherland's recollection of his conversation with Shullaw is contained in a memorandum, dated October 13, 1964, sent to the Parliamentary Committee on Latin America and the Caribbean. The members of this Committee discussed the implications of Shullaw's comments eight days later on October 21 of the same.

105. The Americans had already participated in a joint US/UK/Canadian economic mission to the Leeward and Windward Islands in July 1961.
106. CO 1031/4706.
107. CAB 134/155.
108. Ibid.

Chapter 11: A Federal Project in Cold Storage

1. Intelligence Report from Barbados, November 1, 1963, CO 1031/4764.
2. Intelligence Report from Barbados, March 3, 1964, CO 1031/4764.
3. Dr Richard M. Jackson, Fellow of St. Johns College, Cambridge, chaired this commission. The workings of the commission were completed in February 1964 and the final report was produced in July of the same year.
4. Sir Harold St. John, Senator, in discussion with the author, March 4, 1999, Bridgetown, Barbados.
5. Influential elements within the BLP launched the Barbados Progressive Union of Workers at the beginning of 1963.
6. Richard Cheltenham, 'Constitutional and Political Development in Barbados, 1946–1966' (PhD dissertation, University of Manchester, 1970), 246.
7. On December 12, 1963 Kenya became an independent state within the Commonwealth. See the Kenya Independence Act of 1963, 11 & 12 Eliz 2 c54.
8. On December 10, 1963 Zanzibar ceased to be a British protectorate and became an independent state within the Commonwealth. See Zanzibar Act of 1963, 11 & 12 Eliz 2 c55.
9. Intelligence Report from Barbados, January 2, 1964, CO 1031/4764.
10. *Daily News*, December 16, 1963.
11. DSND 8/20.
12. Intelligence Report from Barbados, January 2, 1964, CO 1031/4764.
13. Ibid.
14. Intelligence Report from Antigua, February 12, 1964, CO 1031/4776.
15. Intelligence Report from Antigua, April 6, 1964, CO 1031/4776. The groundbreaking ceremony was held on March 18, 1964. The oil refinery, however, began operations early in 1967. By 1968 it reached its maximum capacity of 10,000 barrels a day, producing gasoline, diesel oil, jet fuels and liquefied petroleum gas. By 1970 its capacity increased to 16,000 barrels per day. Besides supplying Antigua's needs, it also sold to the other islands. The refinery also supplied its profitable bunkering operation on the north entrance of St. John's Harbour. Deep-water harbour facilities were completed in St. John's harbour in 1968. Brian Dyde, *A History of Antigua: The Unsuspected Isle* (London: Macmillan-Caribbean, 2000), 271.
16. Brian Dyde, *A History of Antigua: The Unsuspected Isle*, 250.
17. H.A. Fergus, *Montserrat: History of a Caribbean Colony* (London: Macmillan-Caribbean, 1994), 163.
18. Intelligence Report from Montserrat, March 13, 1964, CO 1031/4774.
19. Ibid.
20. Intelligence Report from St. Kitts–Nevis–Anguilla, March 18, 1964, CO 1031/4772.

21. O'Loughlin, *Economic and Political Change in the Leeward and Windward Islands*, 48.
22. Intelligence Report from Dominica, December 16, 1963, CO 1031/4767.
23. Margaret Z. Terry to Douglas Williams, March 27, 1963, CO 1031/4763.
24. Intelligence Report from St. Lucia, March 6, 1964, CO 1031/4763.
25. Intelligence Report from St. Lucia, April 8, 1964, CO 1031/4763.
26. Ibid.
27. CO 1031/4527.
28. John Stow to Administrators of Leeward and Windward Islands, March 3, 1964, CO 1031/4527.
29. For the minutes of the eight meeting of the Regional Council of Ministers see CO 1031/4514.
30. United Nations Educational, Scientific and Cultural Organization.
31. Incoming Telegram, US Consul General in Bridgetown to the US State Department, April 16, 1964, vol. 1, National Security File, Box 1, Lyndon B. Johnson Presidential Library (Austin, Texas.)
32. CO 1031/4514.
33. Anthony Greenwood to James Johnson, September 30, 1965, CO 967/438.
34. Intelligence Report from Barbados, May 2, 1964, CO 1031/4764.
35. CO 1031/4982.
36. CO 1031/4513.
37. See Federation of Rhodesia and Nyasaland Constitution, S.I. 1953 No. 1199, sec. 36; Malaya Constitution, S.I. 1957 No. 1533, sec. 80; Nigeria Constitution 1960, S.I. 1960 No. 1652, secs. 79, 80; and West Indies Federation Constitution, S.I. 1957 No. 1364, sec. 56(1).
38. Source: Cmnd. 1746.
39. Source: Colonial No. 360. Also refer to 'Draft Federal Scheme' (as amended at the ninth meeting of the Regional Council of Ministers held in October 1964.) The Secretariat of the Regional Council of Ministers did not publish the 'Draft Federal Scheme' until February 10, 1965.
40. Cmnd. 1746, par.16.
41. Colonial No. 360, par. 10.
42. Cmnd. 1746, par. 17.
43. Colonial No. 360, par. 11.
44. Cmnd. 1746, par. 21.
45. Colonial No. 360, pars. 13–14.
46. Ibid., par. 20.
47. Cmnd. 1746, par. 28.
48. See S.I. 1957 No. 1364, sec. 63 (including provisos a & b); and to the *Report of the West Indies Constitutional Conference 1961*, Cmnd. 1417 (London: HMSO), appendix d, item 30.
49. Cmnd. 1417, 12.
50. See Constitutions of Jamaica and Trinidad and Tobago, S.I. 1962 No. 1550, sec. 79 and S.I. 1962 No. 1875, sec. 62, respectively.
51. Cmnd. 1417.

52. S.I. 1962 No. 1875, sec. 62.

53. Cmnd. 1735.

54. Cmnd. 1992.

55. Draft Federal Scheme, 15.

56. CO 1031/4513, item iv.

57. See Colonial No. 360, Table x.

58. See Tables 9.1 and 11.1

59. See Cmnd. 1746, 17-19.

60. Draft Federal Scheme, 18, 24, Appendix 1.

61. Ibid.

62. In the cases of Tanganyika, Uganda and Kenya the transition from internal self-government to independence had merely taken a few months. Other territories such as Malta and Singapore had to wait longer, three and five years, respectively.

63. Stanley A. Smith, *The New Commonwealth and Its Constitutions* (London: Stevens & Son, 1964), 55-76. Also see Fred Phillips, *Freedom in the Caribbean*, 84.

64. Ibid, 85.

65. CO 1031/4513.

66. Cmnd. 1746, 12.

67. Cmnd. 1991, 8.

68. Draft Federal Scheme, 11.

69. In respect to the transfer of postal services compare the Exclusive Legislative List included in Cmnd. 1746, item 22, to the Concurrent Legislative List included in Draft Federal Scheme, item 29. For the distinction regarding the Judiciary see Cmnd. 1746, 9, item 4 versus Draft Federal Scheme, 5–6, item 3. Note that the Areas of Agreement paper had already suggested that the administration of magistrate courts should remain a unit responsibility. Refer to Table 9.1.

70. CO 1031/4513.

71. Draft Federal Scheme, 6–7.

72. Ibid., 9–10.

73. Areas of Agreement, Table III. For the new position refer to the Draft Federal Scheme, 6.

74. Draft Federal Scheme, 10.

75. See S.I. 1957 No. 1364, sec. 93 and the Appendix to Schedule 5.

76. See Preamble of S.I. 1957 No. 1364.

77. For the exact wording of St. Lucia's reservation, refer to Draft Federal Scheme, 24–25, Appendix II.

78. For the British and American points of view regarding the elections held on June 25 1964 in St. Lucia see Intelligence Report from St. Lucia, May 8, June 4 and July 8, 1964, CO 1031/4764. Also see US Consul General to Department of State, August 28, 1964 Pol 14 BWI (National Archives and Records Administration at College Park, Maryland).

79. CAB 133/202. Also M.Z. Terry to D. Williams, March 27, 1963, CO 1031/4763.

80. For St. Kitts and Dominica's reservations with regard to the Draft Federal Scheme refer to Appendix 2, 24-25.

81. Intelligence Report from St. Lucia, November 10, 1964, CO 1031/4764.

82. The main reason behind Antigua's eagerness to have the postal services in the concurrent legislative list was financial. Out of the remaining Eastern Caribbean territories, Antigua was the one with the highest postal income per capita. See O'Loughlin, *Economic and Political Change in the Leeward and Windward Islands*, 225–26. The Draft Federal Scheme entailed transferring the postal services to the concurrent legislative list; this was a departure from recent precedent. While the constitution of the West Indies Federation had the postal services in the concurrent legislative list, the 1961 Constitutional Conference had agreed that such subject should be transferred to the exclusive legislative list. Refer to S.I.1957 No. 1364, 3rd Schedule, Concurrent Legislative List, item 27; see also Cmnd. 1417, 37, appendix E, item 8.

83. Draft Federal Scheme, 25–26, Appendix 2.

84. Cmnd. 1417, Cmnd. 1746 and the Draft Federal Scheme had all coincided that the executive responsibilities of the federation should be entrenched provisions of the federal constitution. These three documents agreed that these provisions should only be amended by a two-thirds majority in the federal legislature and by absolute majorities *in a majority* of the legislatures of the units. The idea was to prevent any unit from unilaterally holding the centre's growth to ransom. Cmnd. 1417, 10–11; Cmnd. 1746, 14; and the Draft Federal Scheme, 13-14.

85. Lewis, *The Agony of the Eight*, 32.

86. The Cook Islands, which between 1888 and 1901 had been British colonies, were about to enter into a compact of free association with New Zealand.

87. Intelligence Report from Antigua, June 8, 1964, CO 1031/4776.

88. Intelligence Report from Antigua, September 9, 1964, CO 1031/4776.

89. Joseph Bousquet, minister of communications and works; Maurice Mason, minister without portfolio, and Noel Venner, financial secretary, were also in attendance on behalf of St. Lucia.

90. On the first day, on October 28, 1964, the Regional Council of Ministers ratified the original draft currency agreement; put names forward for directors of the Eastern Caribbean Currency Board; agreed on establishing an Institute of Tropical Meteorology; and asked Robert Bradshaw to represent the archipelago at the upcoming UNESCO General Conference in Paris.

91. For interesting notes on these sessions refer to Incoming Telegrams, US Consul General in Bridgetown to the US State Department, October 28 and October 31, 1964 10/29 vol. 1, National Security File, Box 1, Lyndon B. Johnson Presidential Library (Austin, Texas).

92. Intelligence Report from Barbados, November 1, 1964, CO 1031/4765.

93. Intelligence Report from Antigua, November 12, 1964, CO 1031/4776.

94. Ibid.

95. Ibid.

96. Freedom of movement, as a major corollary of the federal project, had remained untouched so far. Both the Marlborough House Conference Report as well as the Draft Federal Scheme made reference to it as a cardinal element of the federal project. Refer to Cmnd. 1746, 10 and to the Draft Federal Scheme, 7.

97. In St. Kitts, during this same period, similar reservations were being espoused

against freedom of movement. By December 1963, Bradshaw called for the expulsion of 61 St. Lucians illegally employed in the island's sugar industry. See Intelligence Report from St. Kitts January 13, 1964, CO 1031/4772.

98. CO 1031/4776.

99. The Draft Federal Scheme called for the establishment of Legal, Fiscal, Customs Union and Public Service Committees. Draft Federal Scheme, 10, 12, 15.

100. Intelligence Report from Barbados, January 4, 1965, CO 1031/4765.

101. The archival record demonstrates that the Labour Government, at least at the beginning of its tenure, enjoyed a warm relationship with the governments of many former British colonies. Special attention should be given to the close contact between Dr. Eric Williams and Harold Wilson. Refer, for instance, to Eric Williams to Harold Wilson, October 26,1964 and to Harold Wilson's reply of November 13, 1964, PREM 13/3.

102. For further details on Greenwood's trip to the archipelago refer to MS Eng. C. 6308,ff. 28–32 in Sir Anthony Greenwood's Papers, Bodleian Library (Oxford). Also see CO 1031/4982. For his remarks at a press conference held before his return to London see Incoming Telegram, US Consul General in Bridgetown to the US State Department, February 12, 1965, vol. 1, National Security File, Box 1, Lyndon B. Johnson Presidential Library (Austin, Texas.)

103. For a brief, but accurate, comparison between the Conservative and Labour Parties' positions on colonial and commonwealth matters, as reflected in their respective 1964 Manifestos, see D.E. Butler, and Anthony King, *The British General Election of 1964* (London: Macmillan, 1965), 132.

104. Anthony Greenwood to John Stow, March 22, 1965, contained in Colonial no. 360, 33–35 and in MS Eng. C. 6308, ff. 28-32 Bodleian Library (Oxford.)

105. *Advocate*, March 21, 1965.

106. Intelligence Report from Antigua, April 10, 1965, CO 1031/4777.

107. *The Workers' Voice*, April 2, 1965, 2; contained in CO 1031/4550.

108. Intelligence Report from Barbados, May 3, 1965, CO 1031/4765.

109. For the minutes of the tenth meeting of the Regional Council of Ministers see CO 1031/4516.

110. Colonial Secretary to Prime Minister, May 26, 1965, PREM 13/155.

Part Four: Introduction

1. The phrase "New Roads Towards Old Aims" has been borrowed from the title of a series of articles written by then President of Puerto Rico's Senate Luis Muñoz Marín (1898–1980), which were published in *El Mundo* in June 1946; these essays were entitled in Spanish "*Nuevos caminos hacia viejos objetivos.*"

2. See 'Declaration Guiding the Determination of Self-Government', G.A. Res. 1541 (XV) (Annex) of December 15, 1960, 15 UN GAOR, Supp., (No. 14), UN Doc. A/4684 (1960) at 29.

3. Bernard Burrows to Hilton Poynton, October 7, 1965, FO 371/ 179142.

4. G.E. Hall to R.W. Piper, May 28, 1965, FO 371/179590.

Chapter 12: Free Association *Modo Britannico*

1. An earlier version of this chapter appeared in *The Journal of Imperial and Commonwealth History*. See Rafael Cox Alomar, 'Britain's Withdrawal from the Eastern Caribbean 1965–67: A Reappraisal', *The Journal of Imperial and Commonwealth History* 31, no. 3 (September 2003): 74–106.

2. By 1965 the Colonial Office was administering, besides the Eastern Caribbean archipelago (including Grenada), the following dependent territories: the Bahamas, Bermuda, British Guiana, British Honduras, British Solomon Islands Protectorate, British Virgin Islands, Cayman Islands, Falkland Islands, Fiji, Gibraltar, Gilbert and Ellice Islands, Hong Kong, Mauritius, New Hebrides, Pitcairn, St. Helena (including the island group of Tristan da Cunha and Ascension Island), Seychelles, the South Arabian Federation (including Aden), Basutoland, Bechuanaland, Swaziland, Tonga and the Turks and Caicos Islands.

3. Anthony Greenwood to Harold Wilson, May 26, 1965, PREM 13/155.

4. Report from Anthony Greenwood to Harold Wilson, May 26, 1965, CO 967/430. Also note that preliminary discussions on the future of the remaining colonies, both in the Colonial Office and in the Cabinet, pre-dated the collapse of the federal negotiations. See Ducan Sandys to Harold Macmillan, October 29, 1963, DSND 8/15 and Sir Hilton Poynton to Sir Burke Trend, March 20, 1964, CAB 21/5296.

5. Anthony Greenwood to Harold Wilson, August 10, 1965, CO 967/430.

6. Refer to 11 & 12 Eliz 2 1967 c4, contained in *Halsbury's Statutes of England and Wales* volume 7, 4th edition (London: Butterworths, 1985), 271-85.

7. For the 1964 Cook Islands Constitution Act see Blaustein, *Constitutions of Dependencies and Special Sovereignties* vol. 6, 169–207. For a study along the lines described *supra* refer to Margaret Broderick, 'Associated Statehood – A New Form of Decolonisation', *The International and Comparative Law Quarterly* vol. 17 (1968): 368-403.

8. For the intelligence reports pertaining to this period, written by Grenada's new colonial administrator Sir Ian Turbott, who had also occupied that same position in Antigua-Barbuda from 1958–64, refer to CO 1031/4771. For Greenwood's impression of the situation in the island refer to MS Eng. C. 6308, ff. 82-87 (Bodleian Library, Oxford.)

9. Note that the political leadership of Montserrat, as Bramble was to confide to Dennis Gibbs and to Sir Stephen Luke, did not wish to sever the colonial ties. The leadership believed Montserrat could derive more economic advantages in remaining a colony. For further detail refer to the minutes of the meeting between Bramble and Sir Stephen Luke, held on November 18, 1965, and contained in CO 1031/4555. Also see Intelligence Report from Montserrat for October and November 1965, CO 1031/4774.

10. Note that by this stage, as becomes apparent below, the British and US Governments understood that it would prove extremely difficult to refuse independence to Barbados on its own. See CO 1031/4554.

11. Integration, according to international standards, can only decolonize if it can assure complete equality of rights and status between the people of the dependent territory

and those of the independent country. For the complete definition of integration, according to the UN, refer to Res. 1541 (XV).

12. Note that among the few illustrations of integration were Somaliland in Somalia, Togoland in Ghana, the Northern and Southern Cameroons in Nigeria and Cameroun, respectively, the Borneo territories in Malaysia and Zanzibar in Tanganyika.

13. See, for instance, the minutes relating to the September 1965 meeting of the Defence and Overseas Policy Committee contained in CAB 148/18.

14. Refer, for example to Memorandum from Sir Burke Trend to Prime Minister Harold Wilson, September 15, 1965, CAB 21/5296. On Harold Wilson's interest on the possibility of integrating Gibraltar see Memorandum from Cabinet Office to A.P. Cumming-Bruce, December 7, 1966, CO 967/442.

15. Sir Burke Trend to the Prime Minister Harold Wilson, September 15, 1965, CAB 21/5296. For the constitutional instruments of the Channel Islands see, for instance, Blaustein, *Constitutions of Dependencies and Special Sovereignties*, vol. 8.

16. CAB 148/18.

17. Duncan Sandys to John Boyd-Carpenter, November 26, 1963, DSND 8/15.

18. Note that Basutoland had achieved full internal self-government on April 30, 1965. A conference to work out a constitution for full internal self-government in Mauritius had been scheduled for September 1965.

19. Colonial Office to Administrators, September 28, 1964, CO 1031/4982.

20. Private Secretary Stacpoole to Ian Wallace, August 17, 1965, CO 967/431.

21. Refer to the Treaty of Friendship between Tonga and Britain, which established that Britain was responsible for defence and external affairs. Interestingly, by this stage that treaty was under revision, since Tonga was seeking a greater degree of freedom. By early June 1970 this relationship eventually evolved towards independence. For a brief definition of 'protected independent states' and 'protected dependent states' see, for instance, Hurst Hannum, *Autonomy, Sovereignty and Self-Determination*, 16, 18, respectively.

22. See 'Declaration Guiding the Determination of Self-Government', G.A. Res. 1541 (XV) (Annex) of December 15, 1960, 15 UN GAOR, Supp., (No. 14), UN Doc. A/4684 (1960) at 29.

23. Lord Caradon to Anthony Greenwood, January 29, 1965, CO 967/426.

24. Refer to note 4 *supra*.

25. Nichols to C.G. Eastwood, August 25, 1965, CAB 21/5296.

26. Sir Ronald Melville to C.G. Eastwood, August 25, 1965, CAB 21/5296.

27. Note that the compact of free association between New Zealand and the Cook Islands had just entered into force on August 2, 1965, only three weeks before the Foreign Office and the Ministry of Defence had brought their concerns to the attention of the Colonial Office.

28. Note that following the establishment of this arrangement the UN removed the Cook Islands from the list of non self-governing territories. Refer to G.A. Res. 1064, 20 UN GAOR, Supp. (No.14), UN Doc. A/6014 (1965), 56.

29. Margaret, Broderick, *Associated Statehood – A New Form of Decolonisation*, 391.

30. Note to Colonial Secretary, June 16 1965, CO 1031/4554.

31. Note from F.P.B. Derrick, October 1, 1965, FO 179142.

32. Benjamin Read to McGeorge Bundy, April 19, 1964, Pol. 19 BWI (National Archives and Records Administration at College Park, Maryland.)

33. FO 371/185004.

34. British Guiana was set to initiate independence negotiations with Britain in November 1965.

35. Adolf A. Berle to President Lyndon B. Johnson, June 3, 1965, National Security File, Box 4, Lyndon B. Johnson Presidential Library (Austin, Texas.)

36. Ibid.

37. Michael Stewart to R.H.S. Crossman, May 20, 1965, PREM 13/233.

38. See Note 35 *supra*.

39. Minutes of Meeting between President Johnson and Chancellor of the Exchequer, June 28, 1965, PREM 13/233.

40. Alianza Popular Revolucionaria Americana or American Popular Revolutionary Alliance.

41. FO 371/185004.

42. Michael Stewart to Mr. Hohler, May 10, 1966, FO 371/A 1017/36.

43. FO 371/185004.

44. Meeting between Anthony Greenwood and US Secretary of State, October 18, 1965, CO 1031/4865.

45. Ibid.

46. Ibid.

47. Ibid.

48. Trías Monge, vol. 4, 216. For the act in question see US Public Law 88-271, 78 Stat. 17, February 20, 1964.

49. Michael Stewart to the US Secretary of State, April 29, 1966, FO 371 A 1017/36.

50. US Secretary of State to Michael Stewart, May 28, 1966.

51. US Public Law 81-600, 64 Stat. 319, July 3, 1950 and ditto 82-447, 66 Stat. 327, July 3, 1952.

52. Mayhew to Staacpole, May 17, 1966, FO 371/184566.

53. Ibid.

54. Ibid., Note from R.E.L. Johnstone to Mayhew, June 20, 1966.

55. See Despatch to Antigua No. 429, December 17, 1965, in Cmnd. 2865, appendix 2.

56. Ibid, par. 4.

57. For the sessions of the Antigua Constitutional Conference (February 28 to March 25, 1966) refer to CAB 133/327 and for the workings of the Legal Committee see ditto/ 328, Windward Islands Constitutional Conference (April 18 to May 6, 1966) refer to CAB 133/350, for the Legal Committee ditto/ 351, for Dominica ditto/ 353, for Grenada ditto/ 354, St. Lucia ditto/ 355 and for St. Vincent ditto/ 356. For the St. Kitts–Nevis–Anguilla Conference (May 10 to May 26, 1966) see CAB 133/348.

58. Sir Stephen Luke to Douglas Williams, December 3, 1965, CO 967/428.

59. 1967 c. 4, sec. 2(1).

60. Ibid., sec. 3(1).

61. See 22 Geo. 5 c. 4, sec 4. Note that, in this respect, the wording of the 1931 Statute of Westminster and of the 1967 West Indies Act is almost identical. Section 4 of the Westminster Act explicitly stated that no Act of Parliament passed after the commencement of the Act shall extend or be deemed to extend to a Dominion as part of the law of that Dominion, unless it was expressly declared in that Act that the Dominion had requested, and consented to, the enactment thereof.

62. 1889 c. 63, sec. 18(2).

63. 1967 c. 4, sec. 3(5).

64. The Statute of Westminster contained this provision as well. See 1931 c. 4, sec. 11.

65. 1967 c. 4, Schedule 1, sec. 2.

66. 1890 c. 27.

67. 1894 c. 60.

68. Ibid., secs. 1(a) and 3(a) and 3(b), respectively. Also refer to 1931 c. 4, secs. 2(1), 3, 5 and 6.

69. 1967 c. 4, sec. 5(2).

70. See de Smith, 56–57.

71. See Leeward Islands Letters Patent, arts. 19, 20.

72. See Ibid.

73. A. P. Cumming-Bruce to J.F. Hewitt, October 28, 1966, CO 967/438.

74. Sources: SI 1959 No. 2199, 2200; 2201 & 2202; Cmnd. 804; Leeward Islands Letters Patent (LILP). See Dominica, Grenada, St. Vincent and St. Lucia's (Constitutions) Orders in Council 1959 and *Report of the Leeward and Windward Islands Constitutional Conference* (London: HMSO, 1959).

75. Sources: Cmnd. 2865; 11 & 12 Eliz 2 1967 c. 4. See *Constitutional Proposals for Antigua, St. Kitts-Nevis-Anguilla, Dominica, St. Lucia, St. Vincent and Grenada* (London: HMSO, 1965).

76. Cmnd. 804, 2, par. 8.

77. LILP, sec. 3.

78. Cmnd. 2865, 5, par. 1.

79. Note that Section 2 of the 1865 Colonial Laws Validity Act read as follows,
    Any colonial law which is or shall be in any respect repugnant to the provisions of any Act of Parliament extending to the colony to which such law may relate, or repugnant to any order or regulation made under authority of such Act of Parliament, or having in the colony the force and effect of such Act, shall be read subject to such Act, order or regulation, and shall, to the extent of such repugnancy, but not otherwise, be and remain absolutely void and inoperative.
    28 & 29 Vict. 1865 c. 63 in *Halsbury's,* 211–14.

80. LILP., 2, par. 10.

81. Ibid., 6, pars. 8 & 9.

82. Ibid., 8, par. 35.

83. Refer to the Public Service Ordinances (for the Leeward Islands), sec. 3.

84. Cmnd. 2865, par. 20.

85. Refer to the Leeward and Windward Islands (Police Service Commission) Order 1959.

86. Cmnd. 2865, par. 21.

87. For the composition of the Senate in Antigua and Grenada refer to SI 1967 no. 225 sec. 23 and no. 227 sec. 24, respectively.

88. *Report of the Antigua Constitutional Conference 1966*, Cmnd. 2963 (London: HMSO), 15.

89. Ibid., 11.

90. The rights in question, as outlined in Greenwood's proposal to the colonial leadership, were (i) the right to life; (ii) the right of personal liberty; (iii) protection from slavery and forced labour; (iv) protection from inhuman treatment; (v) protection from deprivation of property; (vi) protection against arbitrary search or entry upon property; (vii) the right to a fair trial in criminal and civil proceedings; (viii) freedom of conscience; (ix) freedom of expression; (x) freedom of assembly; (xi) freedom of association; (xii) freedom of movement and (xiii) protection from discrimination on grounds of race, political opinions, colour or creed. See Cmnd. 2865, 8. For the specific list of rights and freedoms enshrined in each constitution refer to, SI 1967 no. 225, secs. 1-16; no. 226, secs. 1-17; no. 227, secs. 1–18; no. 228, secs. 1–18; no. 229, secs. 1–18; SI 1969 no. 1500, secs. 1-18.

91. 1967 c. 4, sec. 7.

92. Cmnd. 2865, 10.

93. Ibid.

94. For the Heads of Agreement see CAB 148/27, Annex c. Also refer to Cmnd. 2963 (Antigua Constitutional Conference), 19–20, Annex c; Cmnd. 3021 (Windward Islands Constitutional Conference), 18–20, Annex d and Cmnd. 3031 (St. Kitts–Nevis–Anguilla Constitutional Conference), 23–25, Annex c.

95. Heads of Agreement pars. 4–6. (Emphasis added).

96. For details on the 1961 Defence Areas Agreement see FO 371/148606.

97. Captain French, Senior British Representative in US Patrick Air Force Base, to A. Niman, Ministry of Aviation, May 19, 1965 and E.G. Donohoe (CO) to N.H. Young (FO), July 29, 1965, FO 371/179594.

98. CAB 148/27, FO 371/179594.

99. Ibid.

100. Ibid.

101. Ibid.

102. Ibid.

103. Note from FPB Derrick, April 7, 1966, FO 371/ A 1017/55.

104. CAB 148/27.

105. Ibid.

106. Note that even before the 1887 Colonial Conference, which recommended that the self-governing dependencies should be given permission to enter into direct negotiations with foreign governments with respect to commercial matters, Canada had negotiated several different tariff agreements. By 1894 these privileges were also extended to the Australian states and New Zealand. See Broderick, *Associated Statehood – A New Form of Decolonisation*, 369.

107. Robert M. Dawson ed. *The Development of Dominion Status*, 2nd ed. (London: Frank Cass, 1965), 234–51.

108. 1967 c. 4, sec. 10(2).

109. Ibid, schedule 2, sec. 2.

110. Note that in the case of the Cook Islands the local electorate was consulted on the covenant with New Zealand by means of a general local election, not a referendum. Yet a team of UN observers witnessed this election, at which the two major political parties supported the new constitutional proposals.

111. CAB 133/327.

112. Ibid.

113. Intelligence Report from Antigua, June 14, 1965, CO 1031/4777.

114. Intelligence Report from Antigua, September 13, 1965, CO 1031/4777.

115. Intelligence Report from St. Kitts–Nevis–Anguilla, September 16, 1965, CO 1031/4772.

116. Intelligence Report from St. Vincent, February 15, 1965, CO 1031/4761.

117. Intelligence Report from St. Lucia, August 12, 1965, CO 1031/4763.

118. Intelligence Report from Dominica, December 10, 1965, CO 1031/4767.

119. Intelligence Report from Grenada, February 4, 1965, CO 1031/4771.

120. Intelligence Report from Grenada, August 9, 1965, CO 1031/4771.

121. Phillips, *Freedom in the Caribbean*, 84.

122. Note that the West Indies Associated States Council of Ministers (WISA) replaced the RCM. The WISA was founded in St. Lucia in September 1966 and rapidly established itself as a forum for inter-island discussions. It played a role, for instance, in the negotiations between the Associated States and Britain regarding the EEC and trade preferences. The WISA was not formally constituted by statute until May 1972, when it also assumed full juridical personality and its staff full diplomatic privileges.

123. Intelligence Report from Grenada, January 7, 1966, CO 1031/4771.

124. See 1967 c. 4, secs. 6, 9, 12, and schedule 2, sec. 4.

125. Aid to Territories in Association with Britain, May 12, 1966, DO 200/278.

126. See 1965 c. 38.

127. DO 200/278.

128. Tripartite Survey Conference, held in Antigua on November 2, 1966.

129. Note that the constitution orders for the associated states, with the exception of St. Vincent's, were finally approved on February 22, 1967. Each of these territories held separate celebrations. Antigua's was on February 28; St. Kitts-Nevis-Anguilla, February 27; Dominica, March 1; St. Lucia, March 2; Grenada, March 3, 1967. In the case of St. Vincent the constitution order establishing associated statehood came on October 22, 1969 and was formally inaugurated on October 27 of that same year. For the details of St. Vincent's transition to associated statehood, which span from 1968 to 1969 see PREM 13/ 348.

130. *Antigua-Barbuda Democratic Movement Newsletter* 5, no.19 (February 28, 1967).

Chapter 13: Barbados Going it Alone

1. An earlier version of this chapter appeared in *The Round Table*. See Rafael Cox Alomar, 'An Anglo-Barbadian Dialogue: The Negotiations Leading to Barbados' Independence, 1965-66', *The Round Table* 93, no. 377 (October 2004): 671–90.

2. CO 967/437.

3. 1966 c. 14, c. 23 and c. 24.

4. By the time Sir William Courteen and his crew arrived at Holetown, Barbados in 1624, the neighbouring Carib Indians had already decimated the original Arawak Indians and had abandoned the island altogether. Robert Schomburgk, *The History of Barbados* 4th edition (London: Frank Cass, 1998), 258–60.

5. Only the Virginia House of Burgesses (1619) and that of Bermuda (1627) predate the Barbadian House of Assembly.

6. The Lord in Council and the Assembly of Barbados, following the precedent set by colonies such as Virginia, Maryland and Bermuda, repudiated in 1651 the Lord Protector and his Commonwealth. As early as 1646 Barbados had informed the Royal Commission for Plantations that it would govern itself until the Roundheads and Cavaliers settled their differences. See Eric Williams, *From Columbus to Castro*, 177–78. By the 1870s the Colonial Office attempted, albeit unsuccessfully, to diminish Barbados's relative autonomy *vis-à-vis* the Crown. That plan, which met the fierce resistance of the island's white plantocracy and of an incipient black middle class, subsequently failed. See, for instance, Bruce Hamilton, *Barbados and the Confederation Question 18/1-1885* (London: Crown Agents, 1956).

7. Although by 1652 Cromwell's fleet had quelled the aforementioned revolt, the Articles of Capitulation upheld the 'old representative system'. The relationship between the Governor, the Legislative Council and the House of Assembly remained intact. However, from then on the Assembly's consent would be necessary for the imposition of any taxes as well as for the disbursement of public funds. This strengthened the House of Assembly's influence over budgetary matters. See Velma Newton, *The Barbados Constitution: Facts and Questions*, Bridgetown (University of the West Indies Press, 1997), 3.

8. *We Now Have A Country: Manifesto of the Democratic Labour Party* (Bridgetown: Democratic Labour Party's Printery, 1966), 1.

9. Professor George Belle, University of the West Indies, in discussion with the author, February 23, 1999, Cave Hill, Barbados.

10. Samuel Prescod, editor of *The Liberal*, was elected in 1843 to the House of Assembly, becoming the first man of known black ancestry to sit in that body. Conrad Reeves, a prominent black lawyer, played a pivotal role in the crisis of 1876 and became Chief Justice of Barbados in 1882.

11. For Errol Barrow's biographical note see note 17, chapter 6.

12. *Barbados Development Plan 1967–1972* (Bridgetown: Government Printing Office, 1972), table 10.

13. National Security File, Box 4, Lyndon B. Johnson Presidential Library (Austin, Texas.)

14. Ibid.

15. *Barbados Development Plan 1967–1972* (Bridgetown: Government Printing Office, 1972), table 13.

16. *Barbados Government, Annual Overseas Trade Report* (Bridgetown: Barbados Statistical Service, 1966).

17. National Security File, Box 4, Lyndon B. Johnson Presidential Library (Austin, Texas).

18. This social insurance scheme, introduced in June 1965, had its origins in a report the UN commissioned to H.W. Stockman. It envisaged a contributory system to

provide benefits for illness, maternity, invalidity, funeral grants, social security grants, survivors' benefits and employment injury benefits.

19. National Security File, Box 4, Lyndon B. Johnson Presidential Library (Austin, Texas).

20. For Grantley Adams's biographical note see note 34, chapter 5.

21. For Arthur Cipriani's and Albert Marryshow's biographical notes see notes 16 and 17, respectively, chapter 1.

22. Frederick Goddard, Speech to the House of Assembly, January 4, 1966, Debates, 2d sess. (1961–66).

23. *The Journal* (Bridgetown: Chamber of Commerce Printery, 1965).

24. This free trade agreement, which was finally signed on December 15, 1965, in Dickenson Bay (Antigua), was the precursor to the Caribbean Free Trade Association commonly known as CARIFTA. Although trade barriers, mostly tariffs and quantitative restrictions, were removed, the agreement did not provide for the free movement of labour and capital or the coordination of agricultural and industrial policies. By July 1, 1968, under the terms of the St. John's Treaty, this area was widened to include St. Kitts–Nevis–Anguilla, Dominica, St. Lucia, St. Vincent and Grenada. Jamaica and Montserrat joined on August 1, 1968.

25. The announcement was made on July 5, 1965. See CO 1031/4765.

26. *Constitutional Proposals for Antigua, St. Kitts-Nevis-Anguilla, Dominica, St. Lucia, St. Vincent and Grenada 1965*, Cmnd 2865 (London: HMSO), Appendix d.

27. *The Federal Negotiations 1962–65 and Constitutional Proposals for Barbados, Bridgetown* (The Barbados Government Printing Office, 1965).

28. Eileen Donovan, the first US Consul General for Barbados, the Windward and Leeward Islands, had left her post on July 6, 1965. George Dolgin, an economist with diplomatic experience in Nigeria, replaced her on July 28, 1965.

29. Pol. 19 BWI, (National Archives and Records Administration at College Park, Maryland).

30. Wynter Crawford was a founding member of Barbados's first progressive labour movement in the 1930s. After the local elections held in 1940, Crawford left the Progressive League and founded a more radical movement known as the West Indian National Congress Party. Crawford, also the editor-proprietor of the *Observer*, became affiliated to the DLP in 1956.

31. Intelligence Report from Barbados, September 1, 1965, CO 1031/4765.

32. Besides Barrow, the ministers referred to above were George Ferguson (Minister of Communications, Works and Housing), Da Costa Edwards (Minister of Social Services) and J. Cameron Tudor (Minister of Education).

33. Senator Philip Greaves, in discussion with the author, March 5, 1999, Bridgetown, Barbados.

34. 'Why I resigned from the DLP', The *Sunday Advocate*, October 3, 1965, l.

35. Harold St. John, in discussion with the author, March 4, 1999, Bridgetown, Barbados.

36. The BLP's resolution of August 22, 1965, as well as the BNP's of August 27 of the same year, demanded that the issue 'be put to the people to decide by way of a general election'. See, for instance, *Report on 27th Annual Conference of the Barbados*

Labour Party (Bridgetown: Barbados Labour Party's Printery, 1965).

37. Intelligence Report from Barbados, October 16, 1965, CO 1031/4765.
38. The reaction of Barbados's federationists to associated statehood, as the Colonial Secretary had defined it in his despatch to the Leeward and Windward Islands, was not welcoming. See, for instance, 'Proposals by the UK under Fire', The *Advocate*, January 1, 1966, l.
39. CO 1031/4765.
40. Secretary to the Cabinet to the Prime Minister, June 16, 1966, PREM 13/1326.
41. Ibid.
42. Pol. 19 BWI, (National Archives and Records Administration at College Park, Maryland).
43. The 24 members of the House of Assembly debated the White Paper, with the accompanying resolution asking for sovereign nationhood within the Commonwealth, between January 4 and 6, 1966. For the complete transcript of the debate see House of Assembly Debates, 2d sess. (1961–66). For local press coverage of the debate in the Assembly see 'Big Day in Island's History' the *Advocate*, January 4, 1966, 1; 'Premier Raps Vested Class,' 'Angry Premier Is Restrained,' the *Advocate*, January 5, 1966, l, 5; and 'Miller: My Country Needs Me,' 'Clashes in the House' and 'Federation is of Greater Advantage Mottley', the *Advocate*, January 6, 1966, 1, 5.
44. The House of Assembly Debates, Official Report, 2d sess. 1961–66.
45. Ibid. For the unabridged version of Errol Barrow's speech, see 'This is the Parting of the Ways,' in *Speeches by Errol Barrow* ed. Haniff Yussuff (Georgetown: Hansib Publishing Limited, 1987), 65–83.
46. Ibid.
47. Ibid.
48. When the question was put to the House of Assembly the ayes garnered 14 votes and the noes eight. In the Senate the tally was 17 in favour with only three against.
49. The Conference opened on June 20, 1966, and was adjourned on July 4, 1966. For the transcripts of all 17 plenary sessions, see Barbados Constitutional Conference 1966, DO 200/274-78.
50. Sir Hilton Poynton to Sir Michael Adeane, July 8, 1966, CO 967/433.
51. See note 8 *supra*. In December 1961 the DLP won 14 out of the 24 seats in the House of Assembly. However, its total count of 39, 533 (36.3 per cent of the poll) was less than that of the Barbados Labour Party's (BLP) 40,150 which amounted to 36.8 per cent of the poll. *The Advocate*, December 5, 1961. Also see John Mordecai, *The West Indies: The Federal Negotiations*, 435–36.
52. Frederick Lee to Harold Wilson, June 29, 1966, PREM 13/1326.
53. The Letters Patent and the Royal Instructions stipulated that Barbados's House of Assembly would have two representatives from each of the 11 parishes. In 1843 the number of seats was increased to 24 with the introduction of two seats for Bridgetown. Before 1961 the DLP and the BNP had consistently argued that there should be single member constituencies which would give more votes to the heavily populated parishes and Bridgetown than to the remote, lightly populated, rural parishes. The DLP adopted this recommendation in its 1961 manifesto. See

Memorandum from US Consul General to US State Department on Barbados Voter Registration, April 18, 1966, Pol. 14, BWI (National Archives and Records Administration at College Park, Maryland.)

54. Note that the Order defining the new single-member constituencies was adopted in June 1965. See Intelligence Report from Barbados July 2, 1965, CO 1031/4765.

55. Pol. 12, BWI (National Archives and Records Administration at College Park, Maryland).

56. Harold St. John, in discussion with the author, March 4, 1999.

57. Frederick Lee to Harold Wilson, PREM 13/1326.

58. Overseas Policy Committee Meeting, June 17, 1966, CAB 148/25. Present at this meeting were Prime Minister Harold Wilson, Chancellor of the Exchequer James Callaghan, Foreign Secretary Michael Stewart, Arthur Bottomley, Anthony Greenwood, Lord Longford and Roy Jenkins.

59. Anthony Greenwood to Professor Mackenzie, November 10, 1965, CO967/428. Also see Frederick Lee to Harold Wilson, PREM 13/1326.

60. See M.H. Reid, Prime Minister's Private Secretary to Cumming-Bruce, July 1, 1966, CO 967/439.

61. Frederick Lee to Harold Wilson, PREM 13/1326.

62. Annual Politico-Economic Assessment, Barbados Consular District, May 26, 1965, Pol. 2-3 BWI (National Archives and Records Administration at College Park, Maryland.)

63. Ibid., 8.

64. Ibid., 7.

65. FO 371/185004

66. For a relevant discussion on the impact of these changes, see, for instance, FO 371/185004. In particular refer to Sir Patrick Dean's position paper entitled: 'United States Policy in the Caribbean', December 20, 1965.

67. Local Assessment, Barbados Constitutional Conference, August 5, 1965, Pol. 16, BWI (National Archives and Records Administration at College Park, Maryland).

68. Ibid.

69. See SI 1966 No. 1455, sec. 11.

Conclusion: Towards New Postcolonial Societies?

1. Nicholas Thomas, *Colonialism's Culture* (Cambridge: Polity Press, 1999), 1.

2. Olisanwuche P. Esedebe, *Pan Africanism* (Washington DC: Howard University Press, 1982), 199.

3. Note that all six associated states achieved independence within the Commonwealth between the late 1970's and the early 1980's: Grenada, 1974; Dominica, 1978; St. Lucia and St. Vincent 1979; Antigua, 1981 and St. Kitts-Nevis-Anguilla in 1983.

4. The Caribbean Community and Common Market, established in virtue of the Treaty of Chaguaramas, focuses on economic integration and the operation of some common services.

5. The Organization of Eastern Caribbean States, established pursuant to the Treaty

of Basseterre, is made up of Antigua-Barbuda, St. Kitts-Nevis, Montserrat, Dominica, St. Lucia, St. Vincent and the Grenadines and Grenada. Currently, Anguilla and the British Virgin Islands enjoy associate membership.

Bibliography

Archival Sources

National Archives, Kew Gardens, London:
PREM 11/ 2880, 3623, 4074, 3239, 3240.
PREM 13/155, 172, 233, 1326, 1348, 1359.
CAB 21/5296/5, 21/5304, 5296/5.
CAB 128/ 35, 36.
CAB 129 / 106.
CAB 133 / 202, 287, 327, 328, 330, 331, 348, 349, 350, 351, 352, 353, 354, 355, 356, 1560.
CAB 134 / 2370, 2371, 2153, 2154, 2155.
CAB 147/36, 163, 166.
CAB 148 /1, 3, 17, 18, 20, 25, 27, 28, 30.
CO 967/378, 398, 400, 426, 427, 428, 429, 430, 431, 432, 433, 437, 438, 439, 440, 442, 443.
CO 1042 /52, 53, 54.
CO 1031/ 3264, 3283, 3284, 3286, 3365, 3366, 3367, 3368, 3374, 3375, 3376, 3377, 3378, 4225, 4226, 4513, 4514, 4515, 4516, 4517, 4518, 4519, 4527, 4528, 4532, 4533, 4534, 4547, 4548, 4554, 4555, 4706, 4764, 4765, 4776, 4777, 4772, 4773, 4774, 4775, 4760, 4761, 4763, 4767, 4770, 4771, 4865, 4982, 4983, 5003.
DO 200 / 27, 28, 273, 274, 275, 276, 277, 278, 4549, 4550, 4551, 4553.
FO 371/ 148606, 148607, 148608, 155731, 173580, 179142, 179590, 179591, 179594, 184566, 184567, 185004.
Lord Sandys's Papers, Churchill Archive Centre, Cambridge: DSND 8/12, 13, 14, 15, 16, 17, 20, 21.
Lord Hailes's Papers, Churchill Archive Centre, Cambridge: HAIS 4/11, 12, 14, 16, 17, 18, 20, 24, 27, 28, 30, 31, 32, 33, 35; HAIS 5/77.
Sir Anthony Greenwood's Papers, Bodleian Library, Oxford: MS Eng. C. 6308, ff. 28-32, 82-87, 101-110, 111-113.
Arthur Creech Jones's Papers, Rhodes House Library, Oxford: MSS Brit Emp S 332, Box 25 ff. 1, 2, 3, 6, 7, 8, 11, 12,15, 17, 32.
National Archives and Records Administration, at College Park Maryland: Boxes 741G, 741 K and 741 N.

Boxes POL 1963 BWI and POL 1964 BWI.

Lyndon Johnson Presidential Library, Austin, Texas:

National Security File, Caribbean General Vol. 1, Box 1.

Vol. II, Box 1.

Eastern Caribbean Federation, Box 1.

National Security, Country File, West Indies, Vol. I, April 1964 to October 1964.

Barbados, Vol. I, July 1966 – September 1967.

Barbados, Prime Minister's Visit, September 1968.

Official Publications of the British Government:

United Kingdom. Parliament. *Report of the West Indian Royal Commission.* C. 8655. 1897.

United Kingdom. Parliament. *Report on Visit to West Indies and British Guiana.* Cmd. 1679. 1922.

United Kingdom. Parliament. *Report of the West Indian Sugar Commission.* Cmd. 3517. 1930.

United Kingdom. Parliament. *Economic Survey of the Colonial Empire.* Colonial No. 149. 1938.

United Kingdom. Parliament. *Report of the West Indian Royal Commission.* Cmnd. 6607. 1945.

United Kingdom. Parliament. *Conference on the Closer Association of the British West Indian Colonies.* Cmnd. 7120. 1947.

United Kingdom. Parliament. *Parliamentary Papers:* 1947–48 (XI).

United Kingdom. Parliament. *Report of the Standing Closer Association Committee.* Cmd. 255. 1950.

United Kingdom. Parliament. *Plan for a British Caribbean Federation.* Cmd. 8895. 1953.

United Kingdom. Parliament. *Report of Fiscal Commission.* Cmd. 9618. 1956.

United Kingdom. Parliament. *Report of Civil Service Commission.* Cmd. 9619. 1956.

United Kingdom. Parliament. *Report of the Leeward and Windward Islands Constitutional Conference.* Cmnd. 804. 1959.

United Kingdom. Parliament. *Report of the West Indies Constitutional Conference.* Cmnd. 1417. 1961.

United Kingdom. Parliament. *Report of the East Caribbean Federation Conference.* Cmnd. 1746. 1962.

United Kingdom. Parliament. *Report of the Commission of Enquiry into the Control of Public Expenditure in Grenada During 1961 and Subsequently.* Cmnd. 1735. 1962.

A Survey of the Economic Potential and Capital Needs of The Leeward Islands, Windward Islands and Barbados. London: HMSO, 1963.

United Kingdom. Parliament. *Report of the Fiscal Commissioner.* Cmnd. 1991. 1963.

United Kingdom. Parliament. *Report of the Civil Service Commission.* Cmnd. 1992. 1963.

Colonial Development: British Aid-5. London: Overseas Development Institute Ltd, 1964.

United Kingdom. Parliament. *Constitutional Proposals for Antigua, St. Kitts–Nevis–Anguilla, Dominica, St. Lucia, St. Vincent and Grenada.* Cmnd. 2865. 1965.

United Kingdom. Parliament. *Report of the Antigua Constitutional Conference.* Cmnd. 2963. 1966.

United Kingdom. Parliament. *Report of the Windward Islands Constitutional Conference.* Cmnd. 3021. 1966.

United Kingdom. Parliament. *Report of the St. Kitts–Nevis–Anguilla Constitutional Conference.* Cmnd. 3031. 1966.

United Kingdom. Parliament. *Report of the Barbados Constitutional Conference.* Cmnd. 3058. 1966.

The Tripartite Economic Survey of the Eastern Caribbean. London: HMSO, 1966.

United Kingdom. Parliament. *Colonial Development and Welfare Acts 1929–1970,* Cmnd. 4677. 1971.

Britain and the Developing Countries: The Caribbean. London: HMSO, 1973.

Official Publications of West Indian Governments:

Proceedings of the West Indian Conference. Roseau: Voice Printery, Oct. – Nov. 1932.

Report of the Deane Commission. Bridgetown: Advocate Co., Ltd., 1937.

The Economics of Nationhood. Port-of-Spain: Office of the Premier, September 1959.

The Federation of the West Indies. Ministry Paper no. 18. Kingston: Office of the Premier May 1959.

Barbados House of Assembly Debates. Bridgetown: The Barbados Government Printing Office, 1962–66.

Draft Federal Scheme. Bridgetown: Secretariat of the Regional Council of Ministers, November 1964.

The Federal Negotiations, 1962–65 and Constitutional Proposals for Barbados. Bridgetown: The Barbados Government Printing Office, 1965.

Other Printed Primary Sources:

Treaties, Conventions, International Protocols and Agreements Between the United States and Other Powers. Washington D.C.: U.S. Government Printing Office, 1910.

The Caribbean and the War: A Record of Progress in Facing Stern Realities. Washington: U.S. Government Printing Office, 1943.

Caribbean Labour Congress: Official Report of Conference. Bridgetown: Advocate Co., Ltd Printers, 1945.

Foreign Relations of the United States vols. 3 & 4. Washington D.C.: U.S. Government Printing Office, 1947.

Statutory Instruments:

1865 Colonial Laws Validity Act., 28 & 29 Vict. c 63.

1867 British North America Act., 30-31 Vict., c.3.

1889 Interpretation Act., 52 & 58 Vict. c 63.

1931 Statute of Westminster, 22 & 23 Geo 5 c.4.

1956 British Caribbean Federation Act., 4 & 5 Eliz 2 c63.

West Indies Federation Constitution, S.I. 1957, No. 1364.

1962 West Indian Act., 10 & 11 Eliz 2 c19.

1962 Trinidad Independence Act., 10 & 11 Eliz 2 c54.

Trinidad and Tobago Order-in-Council S.I. 1962, No. 1875.
Jamaica Order-in-Council S.I. 1962, No. 1550.
1966 Barbados Independence Act c. 37.
Barbados Independence Order, S.I. 1966 No. 1455.
1967 West Indies Act 11 & 12 Eliz 2 c4.
Antigua Order-in-Council S.I. 1967 No. 225.
Dominica Order-in-Council S.I. 1967 No. 226.
Grenada Order-in-Council S.I. 1967 No. 227.
St. Kitts-Nevis-Anguilla Order-in-Council S.I. 1967 No. 228.
St. Lucia Order-in-Council S.I. 1967 No. 229.
St. Vincent Order-in-Council S.I. 1969 No. 1500.

Newspapers:

The Barbados Advocate: 1942, 1944, 1961, 1962, 1963, 1965 and 1966.
Daily News: 1962 and 1963.
Daily Nation: 1999 and 2001.
Weekly Gleaner (UK): 1993, 1999, 2001.
Montserrat Mirror: 1962.
Observer: 1943.
Sunday Advocate: 1965.
Trinidad Guardian: 1961.
Voice of St. Lucia: 1962.
Workers' Voice: 1965.

Interviews:

Best, Robert
Former Editor of the *Advocate*   February 25, 1999

Bell, George
Professor of Political Science   February 23, 1999
Cave Hill, UWI

Cheltenham, Richard
Member of the House of Assembly   February 26, 1999
of Barbados

Greaves, Philip M.
Delegate to the 1966 London   March 5, 1999
Conference for Independence
Senator (1965–66)
Deputy Prime Minister (1967–76)
(Only DLP delegate to the
London Conference alive)

Hart, Richard
Secretary of Caribbean Labour   April 1, 1999
Congress (1945–48)

Sandiford, Erskine
Prime Minister (1987–94)   February 26, 1999
Minister of Education (1967–76)
Assistant to Errol Barrow (1966–67)

St. John Harold Sir
Prime Minister (1985–86)   March 4, 1999
Leader of Opposition (1986–91)
BLP Delegate to London
Independence Conference
(Only BLP delegate alive)

Wickham, John
Son of Clennell Wickham   February 20, 1999
Member of the Senate of
Barbados

Secondary Sources

Books:

Abelove, Henry, ed. *Visions of History*. Manchester: Manchester University Press, 1983.

Alexis, Francis. *Changing Caribbean Constitutions.* Bridgetown: Antilles Publications, 1984.

Ashton S.R. and David Killingray, eds. *The West Indies: British Documents on the End of Empire.* London: HMSO, 1999.

Bayly, Christopher, ed. *Atlas of the British Empire.* London: Hamlyn, 1989.

Beckles, Hilary. *A History of Barbados*. London: Cambridge University Press, 1990.

Benítez Rojo, Antonio. *The Repeating Island: The Caribbean and the Post-Modern Perspective.* Durham: Duke University Press, 1996.

Bhabha, Homi. *The Location of Culture.* 2nd ed. London: Routledge, 1995.

Blaustein, A. and P. Blaustein, *Constitutions of Dependencies and Special Sovereignties.* vol. 4 New York: Oceana Publications, 1988.

Bolland, Nigel. *On the March: Labour Rebellions in the British Caribbean 1934-1939.* Kingston: Ian Randle Publishers, 1995.

Bonafoux, Luis. *Betances* 3rd ed. San Juan: Instituto de Cultura Puertorriqueña, 1987.

Brady, Alexander. *The West Indies: A New Federation*. Toronto: Canadian Institute of International Affairs, 1958.

Butler, D.E. and Anthony King. *The British General Election of 1964.* London: Macmillan, 1965.

Cain P.J. and A.G. Hopkins. *British Imperialism: Crisis and Deconstruction 1914 – 1990.*

London: Longman, 1993.

Carmichael, Trevor, ed. *Barbados: Thirty Years of Independence*. Kingston: Ian Randle Publishers, 1996.

Chapman, Richard. *The Treasury in Public Policy-Making*. London: Routledge, 1997.

———. *Leadership in the British Public Service*. London: Croom Helm, 1984.

Cobban, Alfred. *National Self-Determination*. Oxford: Oxford University Press, 1944.

Cumper, George E. ed. *The Economy of the West Indies*. Kingston: Institute of Social and Economic Research, UWI, 1960.

Currie, David P. ed. *Federalism and the New Nations of Africa*. Chicago: University of Chicago Press, 1964.

Darwin, John G. *Britain and Decolonisation: The Retreat from Empire in the Post-War World*. London: Macmillan, 1988.

Dawson, Robert, ed. *The Development of Dominion Status* 2nd ed. London: Frank Cass, 1965.

De Smith, Stanley A. *The New Commonwealth and Its Constitutions*. London: Stevens & Son, 1964.

Deosaran, Ramesh. *Eric Williams: The Man, His Ideas and His Politics*. Port-of-Spain: Signum Publishing, 1981.

Derx, Jo, ed. *Netherlands Antilles and Aruba: A Bibliography 1980-1995*. Leiden: KITLV Press, 1996.

Díaz Quiñones, Arcadio, ed. *Op. Cit.: Revista del Centro de Investigaciones Históricas*. Río Piedras: Editorial de la Universidad de Puerto Rico, 1997.

Drayton, Richard, ed. *Conversations: George Lamming – Essays, Addresses and Interviews, 1953–1990*. London: White Castle, 1992.

Dyde, Brian. *A History of Antigua: The Unsuspected Isle*. London: Macmillan Caribbean, 2000.

Emerson, Rupert. *Self-Determination Revisited in the Era of Decolonization*. Cambridge MA: Center for International Affairs, Harvard, 1964.

Esedebe, Olisanwuche P. *Pan Africanism*. Washington D.C: Howard University Press, 1982.

Estrade, Paul and Félix Reyes Ojeda. *Ramón Emeterio Betances: El anciano maravilloso*. San Juan: Centro de Estudios Avanzados de Puerto Rico y el Caribe, 1995.

Fergus, H.A. *Montserrat: History of a Caribbean Colony*. London: Macmillan-Caribbean, 1994.

Ferrer Canales, José. *Antillanismo y Anti-Colonialismo en Betances, Hostos y Martí*. 2nd. ed. Río Piedras: Editorial de la Universidad de Puerto Rico, 1990.

Gautier Mayoral, Carmen, Ángel Rivera Ortiz, et. al. *Puerto Rico en las Relaciones Internacionales del Caribe*. Río Piedras: Ediciones Huracán, 1990.

Goldsworthy, David. *Colonial Issues in British Politics 1945-1961*. Oxford: Clarendon Press, 1971.

Halperín Donghi, Tulio, V. Bulmer-Thomas, and Laurence Whitehead. *The Colonial and Post-Colonial Experience: Five Centuries of Spanish and Portuguese America*. Cambridge: Cambridge University Press, 1992.

Halsbury's Statutes vol. 31. 4th ed. London: Butterworth & Co., 1994.

Hamilton, Bruce. *Barbados and the Confederation Question 1871-1885*. London: Crown

Agents, 1956.

Haniff, Yussuff, ed. *Speeches by Errol Barrow.* Georgetown: Hansib Publishing Limited, 1987.

Hannum, Hurst. *Autonomy, Sovereignty and Self-Determination: The Accommodation of Conflicting Rights.* rev. ed. Philadelphia: University of Pennsylvania Press, 1996.

Hargreaves, John. *Decolonization in Africa.* New York: Addison, Wesley & Longman Limited, 1996.

———. *From Occupation to Independence: A Short History of the Peoples of the English-Speaking Caribbean Region.* London: Pluto Press, 1998.

Havinden, Michael and David Meredith. *Colonialism and Development: Britain and its Tropical Colonies 1850–1960.* London: Routledge, 1996.

Hawkins, Irene. *The Changing Face of the Caribbean.* Bridgetown: Cedar Press, 1976.

Hennessy, Alistair, ed. *Intellectuals in the 20th Century Caribbean.* London: Macmillan Caribbean, 1992.

Hintjens, Helen M. and Malyn Newitt, eds. *The Political Economy of Small Tropical Islands: The Importance of Being Small.* Exeter: University of Exeter Press, 1992.

———. *Alternatives to Independence: Explorations in Post-Colonial Relations.* Aldershot: Dartmouth University Press, 1995.

Honychurch, Lennox. *The Dominica Story: A History of the Island.* 3rd ed. London: Macmillan Caribbean, 1995.

Hoyos, F.A. *The Road to Responsible Government.* Bridgetown: Letchworth Press, 1960.

———. *Grantley Adams and the Social Revolution.* London: Macmillan, 1974.

———. *Tom Adams: A Biography.* Basingstoke: Macmillan Caribbean, 1988.

Ickes, Harold L. *The Secret Diary of Harold L. Ickes: The Lowering of the Clouds 1939 – 1941* vol. 3. New York: Simon and Schuster, 1954.

Ince, Basil A. *Decolonization and Conflict in the United Nations: Guyana's Struggle for Independence.* Cambridge MA: Schenkman, 1974.

International Financial Statistics vol. 28, no.1. Washington: International Monetary Fund, January 1965.

James, C.L.R. *The Case for West Indian Self-Government.* London: Hogarth Press, 1933.

———. *Federation: We Failed Miserably How and Why?* St. Juan, Trinidad: Verdic Ltd., 1962.

Kirkman, Williams, P. *Unscrambling an Empire: A Critique of British Colonial Policy 1956-1966.* London: Chatto & Windus, 1966.

Knight, Franklin. *The Caribbean: The Genesis of a Fragmented Nation* 2nd ed. New York: Oxford University Press, 1990.

Lamb, Richard. *The Macmillan Years 1957–1963: The Emerging Truth.* London: Murray Publishers, 1995.

Langer, William L. and Everett S Gleason. *Challenge to Isolation 1937-1940.* New York: Harper, 1952.

Lewis, Arthur. *Labour in the West Indies.* London: Fabian Research Bureau, 1939.

———. *The Agony of the Eight.* Bridgetown: The Advocate Printery, 1965.

Lewis, Gordon. *The Growth of the Modern West Indies.* London: Macgibbon & Kee, 1968.

Livingston, William S. *Federalism and Constitutional Change.* Oxford: Clarendon Press, 1956.

Lockhart, Douglas and David Drakakis-Smith, eds. et. al. *Development Process in Small Island States.* London: Routledge, 1993.

Louis, Roger Wm. *Imperialism at Bay.* Oxford: Oxford University Press, 1978.

Lynch, Louis. *The Barbados Book.* London: Andre Deutsh, 1964.

Macmillan, Harold. *At the End of the Day.* London: Macmillan, 1973.

Macmillan, W.H. *Warning from the West Indies.* Harmondsworth: Penguin Books, 1936.

Madden, Frederick and John G. Darwin, eds. *The Dependent Empire 1900 –1948: Colonies, Protectorates and Mandates* vol. 7. London: Greenwood Press, 1994.

Mannoni, Octave. *Prospero and Caliban: The Psychology of Colonization* 2nd ed. New York: Praeger, 1964.

Mark, Francis. *The History of the Barbados Workers Union.* Bridgetown: Advocate Commercial Printing, 1966.

Maudling, Reginald. *Memoirs.* London: Sidwick and Jackson, 1978.

Miekle, Louis. *Confederation of the British West Indies v. Annexation to the US.* London: S. Low & Marston, 1912.

Mitchell, Harold P. *Europe in the Caribbean: The Policies of Great Britain, France and the Netherlands towards the West Indian Territories in the Twentieth Century.* Edinburgh: W&R Chambers, 1963.

Mongia, Padmini, ed. *Contemporary Postcolonial Theory: A Reader.* London: Arnold, 1996.

Mordecai, John. *The West Indies: The Federal Negotiations.* London: George Allen Ltd, 1968.

Morgan, Peter. *The Life and Times of Errol Barrow.* Caribbean Communications Inc., Bridgetown, 1995.

Munroe, Trevor. *The Politics of Constitutional Decolonization in Jamaica 1944–1962.* Kingston: Institute of Social and Economic Research, 1972.

———. *Readings in Government and Politics of the West Indies* rev. ed. Kingston: Department of Government (UWI) 1971.

Murphy, Philip. *Alan Lennox-Boyd: A Biography.* London: I.B. Tauris, 1999.

Murray, Gilbert and Francis Hirst. *Liberalism and Empire: Three Essays.* London: R.B. Johnson, 1900.

Naipaul, V.S. *The Suffrage of Elvira.* London: Penguin Books, 1969.

———. *The Middle Passage.* London: Penguin Books, 1969.

Nandy, Ashis. *The Intimate Enemy: Loss and Recovery of Self Under Colonialism.* 12th ed. Delhi: Oxford University Press, 1998.

Nationale Rekeningen 1957–1965. Willemstad: Bureau Voor De Statistiek, Departement van Social-en Economische Zaken, Nederlandse Antillen, Augustus 1966.

Nettleford, Rex, ed. *Norman Washington Manley and the New Jamaica: Selected Speeches and Writings 1938–1968.* London: Longman, 1971.

Newton, Velma. *The Silver Men: West Indian Labour Migration to Panama 1850-1914.* Bridgetown: University of the West Indies Press, 1984.

———. *The Barbados Constitution: Facts and Questions.* Bridgetown: The Cabinet Office, 1997.

Ogot, Bethwell A. and William Ochieng. *Decolonization and Independence in Kenya.* London: Currey, 1995.

O'Loughlin, Carleen. *Economic and Political Change in the Leeward and Windward Islands.* New Haven: Yale University Press, 1967.

Peter, G. *Industrie et Surpeuplement aux Antilles*. Fort de France: CERAG, 1966.

Phillips, Fred. *Freedom in the Caribbean: A Study in Constitutional Change*. New York: Oceana, 1977.

———. *West Indian Constitutions: Post Independence Reform*. New York: Oceana, 1985.

Post, Ken. *Arise Ye Starvelings: The Jamaican Labour Rebellion of 1938 and Its Aftermath*. The Hague: Nijhoff, 1978.

Ramos Mattei, Andrés. *Betances en el ciclo revolucionario antillano: 1867-1875*. San Juan: Instituto de Cultura Puertorriqueña, 1987.

Rama, Carlos M. *La idea de la Federación Antillana en los independistas puertorriqueños del siglo XIX*. Río Piedras: Librería Internacional, 1971.

Rodríguez-Beruff, Jorge and Peter Figueroa et. al. *Conflict, Peace and Development in the Caribbean*. Basingstoke: Macmillan, 1991.

Ronen, Dov. *The Quest for Self-Determination*. New Haven: Yale University Press, 1979.

Rose, E.J.B. *Colour and Citizenship*. London: Oxford University Press, 1969.

Said, Edward. *Culture and Imperialism*. New York: Vintage Books, 1994.

———. *Orientalism* 4th ed. New York: Penguin Books, 1995.

Schomburgk, Robert H. *The History of Barbados* London: Frank Cass, 1998.

Segal, Aarón. *The Politics of Caribbean Economic Integration* special study no. 6. Río Piedras: Institute of Caribbean Studies of the University of Puerto Rico, 1968.

Shepherd, Robert. *Iain Macleod*. London: Hutchinson, 1994.

Sherlock, Philip. *Norman Manley*. London: Macmillan, 1980.

Simms, Peter. *Trouble in Guyana: An Account of People, Personalities and Politics*. London: Allen & Unwin, 1966.

Singham, A.W. *The Hero and the Crowd in a Colonial Polity*. New Haven: Yale University Press, 1968.

Smith, M.G. *Culture, Race and Class in the Commonwealth Caribbean*. Mona: University of West Indies Press, 1990.

Sorensen, Theodore C. *Kennedy*. New York: Harper & Row, 1965.

Spackman, A. *Constitutional Development of the West Indies*. Bridgetown: Caribbean University Press, 1975.

Spencer, Ian R. G. *British Immigration Policy since 1939: The Making of Multi-Racial Britain,* London: Routledge, 1997.

Stern, Fritz, ed. *The Varieties of History* 3rd ed. New York: Vintage Books, 1973.

Suárez Díaz, Ada. *El Antillano: Biografía del Dr. Ramón Emeterio Betances*. San Juan: Centro de Estudios Avanzados de Puerto Rico y el Caribe, 1988.

Theodoropoulos, Christos. *Colonialism and International Law: The Contemporary Theory of National Sovereignty and Self-Determination*. Benin City: New Horizon, 1988.

Thomas, Nicholas. *Colonialism's Culture*. Cambridge: Polity Press, 1999.

Trías Monge, José. *Historia Constitucional de Puerto Rico* vol. 5. Río Piedras: Editorial de la Universidad de Puerto Rico, 1994.

Tugwell, Rexford. *The Stricken Land: The Story of Puerto Rico*. New York: Doubleday, 1947.

UN Statistical Yearbook 1963. New York: United Nations, 1964.

Watts, R.L. *New Federations: Experiments in the Commonwealth*. Oxford: Clarendon Press, 1966.

Wheare, K.C. *Federal Government*. 4th ed. Oxford: Oxford University Press, 1963.

Whitehead, Laurence, ed. *The International Dimensions of Democratization: Europe and The Americas*. Oxford: Oxford University Press, 1996.

Wickham, John. *A Man with a Fountain Pen*. Bridgetown: Nation Publishing Co., 1995.

Williams, Eric. *From Columbus to Castro*. 2nd ed. New York: Vintage, 1984.

Winks, Robin, ed. *The Oxford History of the British Empire* vol. 5. Oxford: Oxford University Press, 1999.

Wright, Maurice and Colin Thain. *The Treasury and Whitehall*. Oxford: Oxford University Press, 1995.

Yerxa, Donald. *Admirals and Empire: The USA Navy and the Caribbean 1898–1945*. South Carolina: University of South Carolina Press, 1991.

Periodicals:

Alexis, Francis. "The Case Against West Indian Appeals to the UK Privy Council." *Bulletin of Eastern Caribbean Affairs* 1, no. 4 (June, 1975):1–3.

Braithwaite, Lloyd. "Federal Association and Institutions in the West Indies." *Social and Economic Studies* 6, no. 2, (June 1957): 311–21.

Broderick, Margaret. "Associated Statehood – A New Form of Decolonisation." *The International and Comparative Law Quarterly* 17 (1968): 368–403.

Cohen, Raymond. "Meaning, Interpretation and International Negotiation." *Global Society* 14, no. 3 (2000): 317–35.

Connell, John. "Britain's Caribbean Colonies: The End of the Era of Decolonization?" *The Journal of Commonwealth and Comparative Politics* 32, no. 1 (March, 1994): pp.87–106.

Cox Alomar, Rafael "An Anglo-Barbadian Dialogue: The Negotiations Leading to Barbados' Independence, 1965-66." *The Round Table* 93, no. 377 (October 2004): 671-90.

———. "Revisiting the Transatlantic Triangle: The Decolonisation of the British Caribbean in Light of the Anglo-American Special Relationship." *Diplomacy & Statecraft* 15, no. 2 (June 2004): 353-73.

———. "Britain's Withdrawal from the Eastern Caribbean 1965-67: A Reappraisal." *The Journal of Imperial and Commonwealth History* 31, no. 3 (September 2003): 74-106.

De V. Phillips, Anthony. "Grantley Herbert Adams, Asquith Liberalism and Socialism. Which way forward for Barbados from the 1920's to the 1940's?" *Journal of the Barbados Museum and Historical Society* 44 (November/ December 1998): 1–20.

Duncan, Neville. "An Analysis of Political Manifestos and Objectives in Barbados 1937-1976." E.E. Mottley, ed. *People, Parties and Politics: A Guide to General Electors*. Bridgetown: 1976, 7–17.

Emmanuel, Patrick. "Independence and Viability: Elements of Analysis." Vaughan Lewis, ed. *Size, Self-Determination and International Relations: The Caribbean*. Kingston: Institute of Social and Economic Research (UWI), 1976, 1–15.

Estrade, Paul. "La nación antillana: sueño y afán del Antillano" C. Naranjo, ed. *La nación soñada: Cuba, Puerto Rico y Las Filipinas ante el 1898*. Madrid: Doce Calles, 1995, 25–36.

Etzioni, A. "A Union that Failed: The Federation of the West Indies 1958–1962" *Political Unification*. New York: Holt, 1965.

Fraser, Carey. "The 'New Frontier' of Empire in the Caribbean: The Transfer of Power in

British Guiana, 1961–1964." *The International History Review* 22, no. 3 (September 2000): 583–607.

González-Ripoll, María Dolores. "Independencia y Antillanismo en la obra de Hostos." Naranjo ed. *La nación soñada: Cuba, Puerto Rico y Las Filipinas ante el 1898*. Madrid: Doce Calles, 1995, 37–47.

Hart, Richard. "Federation: An Ill-fated Design." *Jamaica Journal* 25, no.1 (October 1993): 10–16.

Hearne, John. "What The Barbadian Means to Me." George Lamming, ed. *Barbados Independence Issue: The New World Quarterly* 3, nos.1 & 2, 1966, 6-9.

Hintjens, Helen. "France in the Caribbean." Paul Sutton, ed. *Europe and the Caribbean*. London: Macmillan, 1991, 36–47.

Holmes, Olive. "Anglo-American Caribbean Commission: Pattern of Colonial Co-operation." *Foreign Policy Reports* 20, no.19 (December 15, 1944): 238–47.

Hunte, Keith. "Duncan O'Neale: Apostle of Freedom." George Lamming, ed. *Barbados Independence Issue: The New World Quarterly* 3, nos.1 & 2, 1966, 84–86.

James, CLR. "From Toussaint L'Overture to Fidel Castro." *The Black Jacobins*. 4th ed. London: Alison and Busby, 1994, 391–418.

Johnson, Howard. "The British Caribbean from Demobilization to Constitutional Decolonization." J. Brown and Roger W. Louis, eds. *The Oxford History of the British Empire* vol. 4. Oxford: Oxford University Press, 1999, 597–622.

La Guerra, John. "The Moyne Commission and the West Indian Intelligentsia 1938-1939." *Journal of Commonwealth and Political Studies* 9 (1971): 134–157.

Laski, Harold. "The Obsolescence of Federalism." *The New Republic* 98 (1939).

Lasserre, Guy and Albert Mabileau. "The French Antilles and their Status as Overseas Departments." Emanuel De Kadt. *Patterns of Foreign Influence in the Caribbean*. London: Oxford University Press, 1972.

Layne, Anthony. "Race, Class and Development in Barbados." *Caribbean Quarterly* 25, nos. 1 & 2 (March–June 1979): 40–51.

Louis Roger, W.M. and Ronald Robinson. "The Imperialism of Decolonization." *The Journal of Imperial and Commonwealth History*, 22, no. 3 (September, 1994): 462–511.

Macdonald, John. "Canada, the West Indies and British Guiana." Boosé, James. *An Imperial Federation*. London: Imperial Federation League, 1889, 2–17.

Malmsten, Neal R. "The British Labour Party and the West Indies 1918-39" *The Journal of Imperial and Commonwealth History* 5, no. 2 (January, 1977): 172–205.

Matthews, Thomas. "The Project for a Confederation of the Greater Antilles." *Caribbean Historical Review* nos. 3 & 4 (December 1954): 70–107.

Proctor, Jesse. "Constitutional Defects and the Collapse of the West Indian Federation." *Public Law* (Summer 1964).

———. "The Development of the Idea of Federation in the British Caribbean Territories." *Caribbean Quarterly* 5, no. 1 (June 1957): 3–55.

Ramphal, S. S. "Federalism in the West Indies." *Caribbean Quarterly* 6, nos. 2 & 3 (May 1960): 210– 29.

Reyes y Ruscalleda. "El ideal de la Confederación de las grandes Antillas españolas en Hostos y Martí." *Revista del Instituto de Cultura Puertorriqueña* no. 58 (January-

March1973): 39–55.

Schrijver, Nico. "The Changing Nature of State Sovereignty." *The British Year Book of International Law*. Oxford: Oxford University Press, 1999, 65–98.

Springer, Hugh. *Reflections on the Failure of the First West Indian Federation*, Occasional Papers in International Affairs, no. 4, Harvard, (Cambridge: July 1962).

Stanley, Oliver. "Looking Ahead: The Benefits of Regional International Co-operation." *The Imperial Review* (January 15, 1943): 128.

Wickham, Clennel. "Hasan" in *Pen and Ink Sketches of Barbadian Politicians and Other Essays,* Bridgetown: The Herald Printery, 1921, 48–52.

Wooding, H.O.B. "The West Indies Economy, A West Indian View." P.A. Lockwood, ed. *Canada and The West Indies*. New Brunswick: Mount Allison University, 1957, 38–39.

Dissertations:

Cheltenham, Richard. "Constitutional and Political Development in Barbados, 1946–1966." PhD. diss., University of Manchester, 1970.

Thorndike, A. E. "The Concept of Associated Statehood, With Special Reference to the Eastern Caribbean." PhD. diss., University of London, 1979.

Index

Adams, Sir Grantley, 22, 256n; and Barbados's independence, 126–127, 213; and WI Federation, 47–48

Aid: EC Federation and Canadian, 148; British, 124, 125–155, 206–207, 280n; from the European Development Fund, 141; from the Hague, 141; from the US, 141–142

Allfrey, Phyllis: and the STAR, 162

Anglo-American Caribbean Commission, 21–24, 27

Anglo-American relations: and British Guiana, 59, 121–122; and the Caribbean, 18–24, 45–47, 57–62, 190–195, 201–203; and the Little Seven, 148–155; and WI Federation, 34–36

Anglophone Caribbean: union of the, 4–5

Antigua and Barbuda: and British aid, 126; constitutional conference, 200–203; and the DFS, 173, 174–175, 177; and the EC Federation, 114–116, 159–160, 172–175; economy, 107–108; and the Fiscal Civil Service Commissions, 106–110; and independence, 205; national income of, 139; refinery agreement, 97-98; and self-government, 43, 173; US military presence in, 152, 201–203

Antigua Labour Party: and the Fiscal Commission, 109

Areas of Agreement: comparison between DFS and the, 170; and EC Federation, 111–128, 163; comparison between the Marlborough House Conference and, 112–114, 120–121

Atkins, Walsh: and the Grenada issue, 89

Atlantic Charter (1941), 22, 27

Attorney general: the DFS and the role of the federal, 166–167

Banana Growers' Association (St Lucia): opposition to Charles administration, 162

Banana industry: St Lucian, 162

Barbados: constitutional development, 210–211; electoral franchise in, 22; and EC federation, 54, 94–98, 116–117, 156–159, 177; economy, 211-213; independence, xxv, 124, 126, 209–228; national income in, 139; political structure in colonial, 14; and self-government, 43; sugar industry, 211–212; US military presence in, 152; whites in, 12–13, 14; withdrawal from the EC Federation, 209–228

Barbados Independence Conference, 220–227

Barbados Labour Party (BLP): and independence, 213, 215, 221, 222; and the Windfall Affair, 157,

Barbados National Party (BNP): and the EC Federation, 96; and independence, 213, 214, 221

Barbados Progressive Union of Workers: and the Windfall Affair, 157

Barbados Workers' Union (BWU): and the Windfall Affair, 157

Barrow, Errol, 259n–260n; and the Areas of Agreement, 110–114, 115–116; and Barbados's independence, 123–124, 158, 209–215, 219, 221, 228; and